UNITED NATIONS CONFERENCE ON TRADE AND DEVELOPMENT

UNCTAD

W9-BMZ-460

WORLD INVESTMENT REPORT 2014

INVESTING IN THE SDGs: AN ACTION PLAN

UNITED NATIONS
New York and Geneva, 2014

NOTE

The Division on Investment and Enterprise of UNCTAD is a global centre of excellence, dealing with issues related to investment and enterprise development in the United Nations System. It builds on four decades of experience and international expertise in research and policy analysis, intergovernmental consensus-building, and provides technical assistance to over 150 countries.

The terms country/economy as used in this *Report* also refer, as appropriate, to territories or areas; the designations employed and the presentation of the material do not imply the expression of any opinion whatsoever on the part of the Secretariat of the United Nations concerning the legal status of any country, territory, city or area or of its authorities, or concerning the delimitation of its frontiers or boundaries. In addition, the designations of country groups are intended solely for statistical or analytical convenience and do not necessarily express a judgment about the stage of development reached by a particular country or area in the development process. The major country groupings used in this *Report* follow the classification of the United Nations Statistical Office. These are:

Developed countries: the member countries of the OECD (other than Chile, Mexico, the Republic of Korea and Turkey), plus the new European Union member countries which are not OECD members (Bulgaria, Croatia, Cyprus, Latvia, Lithuania, Malta and Romania), plus Andorra, Bermuda, Liechtenstein, Monaco and San Marino.

Transition economies: South-East Europe, the Commonwealth of Independent States and Georgia.

Developing economies: in general all economies not specified above. For statistical purposes, the data for China do not include those for Hong Kong Special Administrative Region (Hong Kong SAR), Macao Special Administrative Region (Macao SAR) and Taiwan Province of China.

Reference to companies and their activities should not be construed as an endorsement by UNCTAD of those companies or their activities.

The boundaries and names shown and designations used on the maps presented in this publication do not imply official endorsement or acceptance by the United Nations.

The following symbols have been used in the tables:
- Two dots (..) indicate that data are not available or are not separately reported. Rows in tables have been omitted in those cases where no data are available for any of the elements in the row;
- A dash (–) indicates that the item is equal to zero or its value is negligible;
- A blank in a table indicates that the item is not applicable, unless otherwise indicated;
- A slash (/) between dates representing years, e.g., 1994/95, indicates a financial year;
- Use of a dash (–) between dates representing years, e.g., 1994–1995, signifies the full period involved, including the beginning and end years;
- Reference to "dollars" ($) means United States dollars, unless otherwise indicated;
- Annual rates of growth or change, unless otherwise stated, refer to annual compound rates;

Details and percentages in tables do not necessarily add to totals because of rounding.

The material contained in this study may be freely quoted with appropriate acknowledgement.

UNITED NATIONS PUBLICATION
Sales No. E.14.II.D.1
ISBN 978-92-1-112873-4
eISBN 978-92-1-056696-4
Copyright © United Nations, 2014
All rights reserved
Printed in Switzerland

PREFACE

This edition of the World Investment Report provides valuable analysis that can inform global discussions on how to accelerate progress toward the Millennium Development Goals and shape a long-range vision for a more sustainable future beyond 2015.

The Report reveals an encouraging trend: after a decline in 2012, global foreign direct investment flows rose by 9 per cent in 2013, with growth expected to continue in the years to come. This demonstrates the great potential of international investment, along with other financial resources, to help reach the goals of a post-2015 agenda for sustainable development. Transnational corporations can support this effort by creating decent jobs, generating exports, promoting rights, respecting the environment, encouraging local content, paying fair taxes and transferring capital, technology and business contacts to spur development.

This year's World Investment Report offers a global action plan for galvanizing the role of businesses in achieving future sustainable development goals, and enhancing the private sector's positive economic, social and environmental impacts. The Report identifies the financing gap, especially in vulnerable economies, assesses the primary sources of funds for bridging the gap, and proposes policy options for the future.

I commend this Report to all those interested in steering private investment towards a more sustainable future.

BAN Ki-moon
Secretary-General of the United Nations

ACKNOWLEDGEMENTS

The *World Investment Report 2014* (*WIR14*) was prepared by a team led by James X. Zhan. The team members included Richard Bolwijn, Bruno Casella, Joseph Clements, Hamed El Kady, Kumi Endo, Masataka Fujita, Noelia Garcia Nebra, Thomas van Giffen, Axèle Giroud, Joachim Karl, Guoyong Liang, Anthony Miller, Hafiz Mirza, Nicole Moussa, Jason Munyan, Shin Ohinata, Sergey Ripinsky, William Speller, Astrit Sulstarova, Claudia Trentini, Elisabeth Tuerk, Joerg Weber and Kee Hwee Wee.

Jeffrey Sachs acted as the lead adviser.

Research and statistical assistance was provided by Mohamed Chiraz Baly, Bradley Boicourt, Lizanne Martinez and Tadelle Taye. Contributions were also made by Amare Bekele, Kwangouck Byun, Chantal Dupasquier, Fulvia Farinelli, Natalia Guerra, Ventzislav Kotetzov, Kendra Magraw, Massimo Meloni, Abraham Negash, Celia Ortega Sotes, Yongfu Ouyang, Davide Rigo, John Sasuya, Christoph Spennemann, Paul Wessendorp and Teerawat Wongkaew, as well as interns Ana Conover, Haley Michele Knudson and Carmen Sauger.

The manuscript was copy-edited with the assistance of Lise Lingo and typeset by Laurence Duchemin and Teresita Ventura. Sophie Combette and Nadege Hadjemian designed the cover. Production and dissemination of WIR14 was supported by Elisabeth Anodeau-Mareschal, Evelyn Benitez, Nathalie Eulaerts, Natalia Meramo-Bachayani and Katia Vieu.

At various stages of preparation, in particular during the experts meeting organized to discuss drafts of WIR14, the team benefited from comments and inputs received from external experts: Azar Aliyev, Yukiko Arai, Jonathan Bravo, Barbara Buchner, Marc Bungenberg, Richard Dobbs, Michael Hanni, Paul Hohnen, Valerio Micale, Jan Mischke, Lilach Nachum, Karsten Nowrot, Federico Ortino, Lauge Poulsen, Dante Pesce, Anna Peters, Isabelle Ramdoo, Diana Rosert, Josef Schmidhuber, Martin Stadelmann, Ian Strauss, Jeff Sullivan, Chiara Trabacchi, Steve Waygood and Philippe Zaouati. Comments and inputs were also received from many UNCTAD colleagues, including Santiago Fernandez De Cordoba Briz, Ebru Gokce, Richard Kozul-Wright, Michael Lim, Patrick Osakwe, Igor Paunovic, Taffere Tesfachew, Guillermo Valles and Anida Yupari.

UNCTAD also wishes to thank the participants in the Experts Meeting held at the Vale Columbia Center on Sustainable International Investment and the brainstorming meeting organized by New York University School of Law, both in November 2013.

Numerous officials of central banks, government agencies, international organizations and non-governmental organizations also contributed to WIR14. The financial support of the Governments of Finland, Norway, Sweden and Switzerland is gratefully acknowledged.

TABLE OF CONTENTS

KEY MESSAGES

GLOBAL INVESTMENT TRENDS

Cautious optimism returns to global foreign direct investment (FDI). After the 2012 slump, global FDI returned to growth, with inflows rising 9 per cent in 2013, to $1.45 trillion. UNCTAD projects that FDI flows could rise to $1.6 trillion in 2014, $1.7 trillion in 2015 and $1.8 trillion in 2016, with relatively larger increases in developed countries. Fragility in some emerging markets and risks related to policy uncertainty and regional instability may negatively affect the expected upturn in FDI.

Developing economies maintain their lead in 2013. FDI flows to developed countries increased by 9 per cent to $566 billion, leaving them at 39 per cent of global flows, while those to developing economies reached a new high of $778 billion, or 54 per cent of the total. The balance of $108 billion went to transition economies. Developing and transition economies now constitute half of the top 20 ranked by FDI inflows.

FDI outflows from developing countries also reached a record level. Transnational corporations (TNCs) from developing economies are increasingly acquiring foreign affiliates from developed countries located in their regions. Developing and transition economies together invested $553 billion, or 39 per cent of global FDI outflows, compared with only 12 per cent at the beginning of the 2000s.

Megaregional groupings shape global FDI. The three main regional groups currently under negotiation (TPP, TTIP, RCEP) each account for a quarter or more of global FDI flows, with TTIP flows in decline, and the others in ascendance. Asia-Pacific Economic Cooperation (APEC) remains the largest regional economic cooperation grouping, with 54 per cent of global inflows.

The poorest countries are less and less dependent on extractive industry investment. Over the past decade, the share of the extractive industry in the value of greenfield projects was 26 per cent in Africa and 36 per cent in LDCs. These shares are rapidly decreasing; manufacturing and services now make up about 90 per cent of the value of announced projects both in Africa and in LDCs.

Private equity FDI is keeping its powder dry. Outstanding funds of private equity firms increased to a record level of more than $1 trillion. Their cross-border investment was $171 billion, a decline of 11 per cent, and they accounted for 21 per cent of the value of cross-border mergers and acquisitions (M&As), 10 percentage points below their peak. With funds available for investment ("dry powder"), and relatively subdued activity in recent years, the potential for increased private equity FDI is significant.

State-owned TNCs are FDI heavyweights. UNCTAD estimates there are at least 550 State-owned TNCs – from both developed and developing countries – with more than 15,000 foreign affiliates and foreign assets of over $2 trillion. FDI by these TNCs was more than $160 billion in 2013. At that level, although their number constitutes less than 1 per cent of the universe of TNCs, they account for over 11 per cent of global FDI flows.

REGIONAL INVESTMENT TRENDS

FDI flows to all major developing regions increased. Africa saw increased inflows (+4 per cent), sustained by growing intra-African flows. Such flows are in line with leaders' efforts towards deeper regional integration, although the effect of most regional economic cooperation initiatives in Africa on intraregional FDI has been limited. Developing *Asia* (+3 per cent) remains the number one global investment destination. Regional headquarter locations for TNCs, and proactive regional investment cooperation, are factors driving increasing intraregional flows. *Latin America and the Caribbean* (+6 per cent) saw mixed FDI growth, with an overall positive due to an increase in Central America, but with an 6 per cent decline in South America. Prospects are brighter, with new opportunities arising in oil and gas, and TNC investment plans in manufacturing.

Structurally weak economies saw mixed results. Investment in the *least developed countries* (LDCs) increased, with announced greenfield investments signalling significant growth in basic infrastructure and energy projects. *Landlocked developing countries* (LLDCs) saw an overall decline in FDI. Relative to the size of their economies, and relative to capital formation, FDI remains an important source of finance there. Inflows to *small island developing States* (SIDS) declined. Tourism and extractive industries are attracting increasing interest from foreign investors, while manufacturing industries have been negatively affected by erosion of trade preferences.

Inflows to developed countries resume growth but have a long way to go. The recovery of FDI inflows in developed countries to $566 billion, and the unchanged outflows, at $857 billion, leave both at half their peak levels in 2007. Europe, traditionally the largest FDI recipient region, is at less than one third of its 2007 inflows and one fourth of its outflows. The United States and the European Union (EU) saw their combined share of global FDI inflows decline from well over 50 per cent pre-crisis to 30 per cent in 2013.

FDI to transition economies reached record levels, but prospects are uncertain. FDI inflows to transition economies increased by 28 per cent to reach $108 billion in 2013. Outward FDI from the region jumped by 84 per cent, reaching a record $99 billion. Prospects for FDI to transition economies are likely to be affected by uncertainties related to regional instability.

INVESTMENT POLICY TRENDS AND KEY ISSUES

Most investment policy measures remain geared towards investment promotion and liberalization. At the same time, the share of regulatory or restrictive investment policies increased, reaching 27 per cent in 2013. Some host countries have sought to prevent divestments by established foreign investors. Some home countries promote reshoring of their TNCs' overseas investments.

Investment incentives mostly focus on economic performance objectives, less on sustainable development. Incentives are widely used by governments as a policy instrument for attracting investment, despite persistent criticism that they are economically inefficient and lead to misallocations of public funds. To address these concerns, investment incentives schemes could be more closely aligned with the SDGs.

International investment rule making is characterized by diverging trends: on the one hand, disengagement from the system, partly because of developments in investment arbitration; on the other, intensifying and up-scaling negotiations. Negotiations of "megaregional agreements" are a case in point. Once concluded, these may have systemic implications for the regime of international investment agreements (IIAs).

Widespread concerns about the functioning and the impact of the IIA regime are resulting in calls for reform. Four paths are becoming apparent: (i) maintaining the status quo, (ii) disengaging from the system, (iii) introducing selective adjustments, and (iv) undertaking systematic reform. A multilateral approach could effectively contribute to this endeavour.

INVESTING IN THE SDGs: AN ACTION PLAN FOR PROMOTING PRIVATE SECTOR CONTRIBUTIONS

Faced with common global economic, social and environmental challenges, the international community is defining a set of Sustainable Development Goals (SDGs). The SDGs, which are being formulated by the United Nations together with the widest possible range of stakeholders, are intended to galvanize action worldwide through concrete targets for the 2015–2030 period for poverty reduction, food security, human health and education, climate change mitigation, and a range of other objectives across the economic, social and environmental pillars.

The role of the public sector is fundamental and pivotal, while the private sector contribution is indispensable. The latter can take two main forms, good governance in business practices and investment in sustainable development. Policy coherence is essential in promoting the private sector's contribution to the SDGs.

The SDGs will have very significant resource implications across the developed and developing world. Global investment needs are in the order of $5 trillion to $7 trillion per year. Estimates for investment needs in developing countries alone range from $3.3 trillion to $4.5 trillion per year, mainly for basic infrastructure (roads, rail and ports; power stations; water and sanitation), food security (agriculture and rural development), climate change mitigation and adaptation, health, and education.

The SDGs will require a step-change in the levels of both public and private investment in all countries. At current levels of investment in SDG-relevant sectors, developing countries alone face an annual gap of $2.5 trillion. In developing countries, especially in LDCs and other vulnerable economies, public finances are central to investment in SDGs. However, they cannot meet all SDG-implied resource demands. The role of private sector investment will be indispensable.

Today, the participation of the private sector in investment in SDG-related sectors is relatively low. Only a fraction of the worldwide invested assets of banks, pension funds, insurers, foundations and endowments, as well as transnational corporations, is in SDG sectors. Their participation is even lower in developing countries, particularly the poorest ones.

In LDCs, a doubling of the growth rate of private investment would be a desirable target. Developing countries as a group could see the private sector cover approximately the part of SDG investment needs corresponding to its current share in investment in SDG sectors, based on current growth rates. In that scenario, however, they would still face an annual gap of about $1.6 trillion. In LDCs, where investment needs are most acute and where financing capacity is lowest, about twice the current growth rate of private investment is needed to give it a meaningful complementary financing role next to public investment and overseas development assistance (ODA).

Increasing the involvement of private investors in SDG-related sectors, many of which are sensitive or of a public service nature, leads to policy dilemmas. Policymakers need to find the right balance between creating a climate conducive to investment and removing barriers to investment on the one hand, and protecting public interests through regulation on the other. They need to find mechanisms to provide sufficiently attractive returns to private investors while guaranteeing accessibility and affordability of services for all. And the push for more private investment must be complementary to the parallel push for more public investment.

UNCTAD's proposed Strategic Framework for Private Investment in the SDGs addresses key policy challenges and options related to (i) guiding principles and global *leadership* to galvanize action for private investment, (ii) the *mobilization* of funds for investment in sustainable development, (iii) the *channelling* of funds into investments in SDG sectors, and (iv) maximizing the sustainable development *impact* of private investment while minimizing risks or drawbacks involved.

Increasing private investment in SDGs will require leadership at the global level, as well as from national policymakers, to provide guiding principles to deal with policy dilemmas; to set targets, recognizing the need to make a special effort for LDCs; to ensure policy coherence at national and global levels; to galvanize dialogue and action, including through appropriate multi-stakeholder platforms; and to guarantee inclusiveness, providing support to countries that otherwise might continue to be largely ignored by private investors.

Challenges to *mobilizing* funds in financial markets include start-up and scaling problems for innovative financing solutions, market failures, a lack of transparency on environmental, social and corporate governance performance, and misaligned rewards for market participants. Key constraints to *channelling* funds into SDG sectors include entry barriers, inadequate risk-return ratios for SDG investments, a lack of information and effective packaging and promotion of projects, and a lack of investor expertise. Key challenges in managing the *impact* of private investment in SDG sectors include the weak absorptive capacity in some developing countries, social and environmental impact risks, and the need for stakeholder engagement and effective impact monitoring.

UNCTAD's Action Plan for Private Investment in the SDGs presents a range of policy options to respond to the mobilization, channelling and impact challenges. A focused set of action packages can help shape a *Big Push* for private investment in sustainable development:

- *A new generation of investment promotion and facilitation.* Establishing SDG investment development agencies to develop and market pipelines of bankable projects in SDG sectors and to actively facilitate such projects. This requires specialist expertise and should be supported by technical assistance. "Brokers" of SDG investment projects could also be set up at the regional level to share costs and achieve economies of scale. The international investment policy regime should also be reoriented towards proactive promotion of investment in SDGs.

- *SDG-oriented investment incentives.* Restructuring of investment incentive schemes specifically to facilitate sustainable development projects. This calls for a transformation from purely "location-based" incentives, aiming to increase the competitiveness of a location and provided at the time of establishment, towards "SDG-based" incentives, aiming to promote investment in SDG sectors and conditional upon their sustainable development contribution.

- *Regional SDG Investment Compacts.* Launching regional and South-South initiatives towards the promotion of SDG investment, especially for cross-border infrastructure development and regional clusters of firms operating in SDG sectors (e.g. green zones). This could include joint investment promotion mechanisms, joint programmes to build absorptive capacity and joint public-private partnership models.

- *New forms of partnership for SDG investments.* Establish partnerships between outward investment agencies in home countries and investment promotion agencies (IPAs) in host countries for the purpose of marketing SDG investment opportunities in home countries, provision of investment incentives and facilitation services for SDG projects, and joint monitoring and impact assessment. Concrete tools that might support joint SDG investment business development services could include online tools with pipelines of bankable projects, and opportunities for linkages programmes in developing countries. A multi-agency technical assistance consortium could help to support LDCs.

- *Enabling innovative financing mechanisms and a reorientation of financial markets.* Innovative financial instruments to raise funds for investment in SDGs deserve support to achieve scale. Options include innovative tradable financial instruments and dedicated SDG funds, seed funding mechanisms, and new "go-to-market" channels for SDG projects. Reorientation of financial markets also requires integrated reporting. This is a fundamental tool for investors to make informed decisions on responsible allocation of capital, and it is at the heart of Sustainable Stock Exchanges.

- *Changing the business mindset and developing SDG investment expertise.* Developing a curriculum for business schools that generates awareness of investment opportunities in poor countries and that teaches students the skills needed to successfully operate in developing-country environments. This can be extended to inclusion of relevant modules in existing training and certification programmes for financial market actors.

The *Action Plan for Private Investment in the SDGs* is meant to serve as a point of reference for policymakers at national and international levels in their discussions on ways and means to implement the SDGs. It has been designed as a "living document" and incorporates an online version that aims to establish an interactive, open dialogue, inviting the international community to exchange views, suggestions and experiences. It thus constitutes a basis for further stakeholder engagement. UNCTAD aims to provide the platform for such engagement through its biennial *World Investment Forum*, and online through the *Investment Policy Hub*.

OVERVIEW

GLOBAL INVESTMENT TRENDS

Cautious optimism returns to global FDI

In 2013, FDI flows returned to an upward trend. Global FDI inflows rose by 9 per cent to $1.45 trillion in 2013. FDI inflows increased in all major economic groupings – developed, developing, and transition economies. Global FDI stock rose by 9 per cent, reaching $25.5 trillion.

UNCTAD projects that global FDI flows could rise to $1.6 trillion in 2014, $1.75 trillion in 2015 and $1.85 trillion in 2016. The rise will be mainly driven by investments in developed economies as their economic recovery starts to take hold and spread wider. The fragility in some emerging markets and risks related to policy uncertainty and regional conflict could still derail the expected upturn in FDI flows.

As a result of higher expected FDI growth in developed countries, the regional distribution of FDI may tilt back towards the "traditional pattern" of a higher share of developed countries in global inflows (figure 1). Nevertheless, FDI flows to developing economies will remain at a high level in the coming years.

Figure 1. FDI inflows, global and by group of economies, 1995–2013 and projections, 2014-2016
(Billions of dollars)

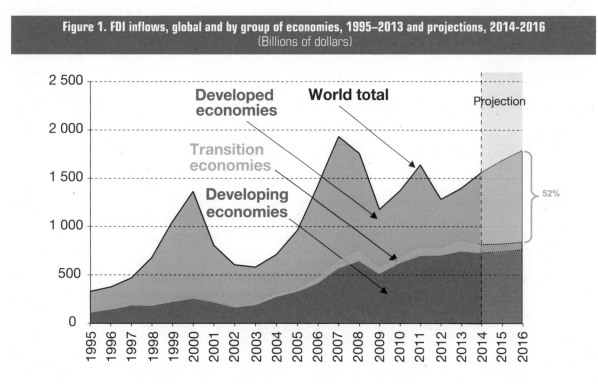

Developing economies maintain their lead

FDI flows to developing economies reached a new high at $778 billion (table 1), accounting for 54 per cent of global inflows, although the growth rate slowed to 7 per cent, compared with an average growth rate over the past 10 years of 17 per cent. Developing Asia continues to be the region with the highest FDI inflows, significantly above the EU, traditionally the region with the highest share of global FDI. FDI inflows were up also in the other major developing regions, Africa (up 4 per cent) and Latin America and the Caribbean (up 6 per cent, excluding offshore financial centres).

Table 1. FDI flows, by region, 2011–2013
(Billions of dollars and per cent)

Region	FDI inflows			FDI outflows		
	2011	2012	2013	2011	2012	2013
World	**1 700**	**1 330**	**1 452**	**1 712**	**1 347**	**1 411**
Developed economies	880	517	566	1 216	853	857
European Union	490	216	246	585	238	250
North America	263	204	250	439	422	381
Developing economies	725	729	778	423	440	454
Africa	48	55	57	7	12	12
Asia	431	415	426	304	302	326
East and South-East Asia	333	334	347	270	274	293
South Asia	44	32	36	13	9	2
West Asia	53	48	44	22	19	31
Latin America and the Caribbean	244	256	292	111	124	115
Oceania	2	3	3	1	2	1
Transition economies	95	84	108	73	54	99
Structurally weak, vulnerable and small economies[a]	**58**	**58**	**57**	**12**	**10**	**9**
LDCs	22	24	28	4	4	5
LLDCs	36	34	30	6	3	4
SIDS	6	7	6	2	2	1
Memorandum: percentage share in world FDI flows						
Developed economies	51.8	38.8	39.0	71.0	63.3	60.8
European Union	28.8	16.2	17.0	34.2	17.7	17.8
North America	15.5	15.3	17.2	25.6	31.4	27.0
Developing economies	42.6	54.8	53.6	24.7	32.7	32.2
Africa	2.8	4.1	3.9	0.4	0.9	0.9
Asia	25.3	31.2	29.4	17.8	22.4	23.1
East and South-East Asia	19.6	25.1	23.9	15.8	20.3	20.7
South Asia	2.6	2.4	2.4	0.8	0.7	0.2
West Asia	3.1	3.6	3.0	1.3	1.4	2.2
Latin America and the Caribbean	14.3	19.2	20.1	6.5	9.2	8.1
Oceania	0.1	0.2	0.2	0.1	0.1	0.1
Transition economies	5.6	6.3	7.4	4.3	4.0	7.0
Structurally weak, vulnerable and small economies[a]	**3.4**	**4.4**	**3.9**	**0.7**	**0.7**	**0.7**
LDCs	1.3	1.8	1.9	0.3	0.3	0.3
LLDCs	2.1	2.5	2.0	0.4	0.2	0.3
SIDS	0.4	0.5	0.4	0.1	0.2	0.1

Source: UNCTAD, FDI-TNC-GVC Information System, FDI/TNC database (www.unctad.org/fdistatistics).
[a]Without double counting.

Although FDI to developed economies resumed its recovery after the sharp fall in 2012, it remained at a historically low share of total global FDI flows (39 per cent), and still 57 per cent below its peak in 2007. Thus, developing countries maintained their lead over developed countries by a margin of more than $200 billion for the second year running.

Developing countries and transition economies now also constitute half of the top 20 economies ranked by FDI inflows (figure 2). Mexico moved into tenth place. China recorded its largest ever inflows and maintained its position as the second largest recipient in the world.

FDI by transnational corporations (TNCs) from developing countries reached $454 billion – another record high. Together with transition economies, they accounted for 39 per cent of global FDI outflows, compared with only 12 per cent at the beginning of the 2000s. Six developing and transition economies ranked among the 20 largest investors in the world in 2013 (figure 3). Increasingly, developing-country TNCs are acquiring foreign affiliates of developed-country TNCs in the developing world.

Megaregional groupings shape global FDI

The share of APEC countries in global inflows increased from 37 per cent before the crisis to 54 per cent in 2013 (figure 4). Although their shares are smaller, FDI inflows to ASEAN and the Common Market of the South (MERCOSUR) in 2013 were at double their pre-crisis level, as were inflows to the BRICS (Brazil, the Russian Federation, India, China and South Africa).

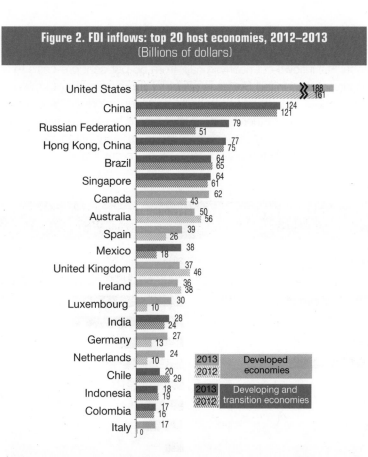

Figure 2. FDI inflows: top 20 host economies, 2012–2013
(Billions of dollars)

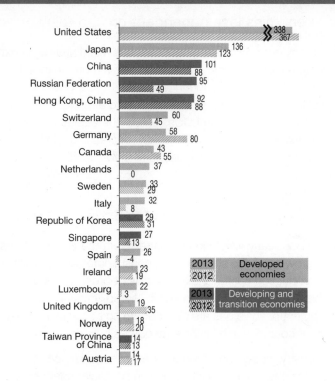

Figure 3. FDI outflows: top 20 home economies, 2012 and 2013
(Billions of dollars)

The three megaregional integration initiatives currently under negotiation – TTIP, TPP and RCEP – show diverging FDI trends. The United States and the EU, which are negotiating the formation of TTIP, saw their combined share of global FDI inflows cut nearly in half, from 56 per cent pre-crisis to 30 per cent in 2013. In TPP, the declining share of the United States is offset by the expansion of emerging economies in the grouping, helping the aggregate share increase from 24 per cent before 2008 to 32 per cent in 2013. The Regional Comprehensive Economic Partnership (RCEP), which is being negotiated between the 10 ASEAN member States and their 6 free trade agreement (FTA) partners, accounted for more than 20 per cent of global FDI flows in recent years, nearly twice as much as the pre-crisis level.

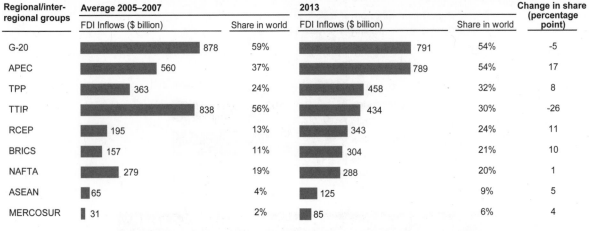

Figure 4. FDI inflows to selected regional and interregional groups, average 2005–2007 and 2013
(Billions of US dollars and per cent)

Regional/inter-regional groups	Average 2005–2007		2013		Change in share (percentage point)
	FDI Inflows ($ billion)	Share in world	FDI Inflows ($ billion)	Share in world	
G-20	878	59%	791	54%	-5
APEC	560	37%	789	54%	17
TPP	363	24%	458	32%	8
TTIP	838	56%	434	30%	-26
RCEP	195	13%	343	24%	11
BRICS	157	11%	304	21%	10
NAFTA	279	19%	288	20%	1
ASEAN	65	4%	125	9%	5
MERCOSUR	31	2%	85	6%	4

Poorest developing economies less dependent on natural resources

Although historically FDI in many poor developing countries has relied heavily on extractive industries, the dynamics of greenfield investment over the last 10 years reveals a more nuanced picture. The share of the extractive industry in the cumulative value of announced cross-border greenfield projects is substantial in Africa (26 per cent) and in LDCs (36 per cent). However, looking at project numbers the share drops to 8 per cent of projects in Africa, and 9 per cent in LDCs, due to the capital intensive nature of the industry. Moreover, the share of the extractive industry is rapidly decreasing. Data on announced greenfield investments in 2013 show that manufacturing and services make up about 90 per cent of the total value of projects both in Africa and in LDCs.

Shale gas is affecting FDI patterns in the Unites States and beyond

The shale gas revolution is now clearly visible in FDI patterns. In the United States oil and gas industry, the role of foreign capital is growing as the shale market consolidates and smaller domestic players need to share development and production costs. Shale gas cross-border M&As accounted for more than 80 per cent of such deals in the oil and gas industry in 2013. United States firms with necessary expertise in the exploration and development of shale gas are also becoming acquisition targets or industrial partners of energy firms based in other countries rich in shale resources.

Beyond the oil and gas industry, cheap natural gas is attracting new capacity investments, including greenfield FDI, to United States manufacturing industries, in particular chemicals and chemical products.

The United States share in global announced greenfield investments in these sectors jumped from 6 per cent in 2011, to 16 per cent in 2012, to 25 per cent in 2013, well above the average United States share across all industries (7 per cent). Some reshoring of United States manufacturing TNCs is also expected.

As the cost advantage of petrochemicals manufacturers in other oil and gas rich countries is being eroded, the effects on FDI are becoming visible also outside the United States, especially in West Asia. TNCs like Chevron Phillips Chemical, Dow Chemical and ExxonMobil Chemical are returning their focus to the United States. Even Gulf Cooperation Council (GCC) petrochemical enterprises such as NOVA chemicals (United Arab Emirates) and Sabic (Saudi Arabia) – are investing in North America.

Pharmaceutical FDI driven by the "patent cliff" and emerging market opportunities

Pharmaceutical TNCs have been divesting non-core business segments and outsourcing R&D activities in recent years, while engaging in M&A activity to secure new revenue streams and low-cost production bases. Global players in this industry have sought access to high-quality, low-cost generic drugs through acquisitions of producers based in developing economies, in response to growing demand. They have also targeted successful research firms and start-ups there. The share of cross-border M&A deals in the sector targeting developing and transition economies increased from less than 4 per cent before 2006, to 10 per cent between 2010 and 2012, jumping to more than 18 per cent in 2013.

The availability of vast reserves of overseas held retained earnings in the top pharmaceutical TNCs facilitates such deals, and signals further activity. During the first quarter of 2014, the transaction value of cross-border M&As ($23 billion in 55 deals) already surpassed the value recorded for all of 2013.

Private equity FDI keeps its powder dry

In 2013, outstanding funds of private equity firms increased further to a record level of $1.07 trillion, an increase of 14 per cent over the previous year. However, their cross-border investment – typically through M&As – was $171 billion ($83 billion on a net basis), a decline of 11 per cent. Private equity accounted for 21 per cent of total gross cross-border M&As in 2013, 10 percentage points lower than at its peak in 2007. With the increasing amount of outstanding funds available for investment (dry powder), and their relatively subdued activity in recent years, the potential for increased private equity FDI is significant.

Most private equity acquisitions are still concentrated in Europe (traditionally the largest market) and the United States. Deals are on the increase in Asia. Though relatively small, developing-country-based private equity firms are beginning to emerge and are involved in deal makings not only in developing countries but also in more mature markets.

FDI by SWFs remains small, State-owned TNCs are heavyweights

Sovereign wealth funds (SWFs) continue to expand in terms of assets, geographical spread and target industries. Assets under management of SWFs approach $6.4 trillion and are invested worldwide, including in sub-Saharan African countries. Oil-producing countries in sub-Saharan Africa have themselves recently created SWFs to manage oil proceeds. Compared to the size of their assets, the level of FDI by SWFs is still small, corresponding to less than 2 per cent of assets under management, and limited to a few major SWFs. In 2013, SWF FDI flows were worth $6.7 billion with cumulative stock reaching $130 billion.

The number of State-owned TNCs (SO-TNCs) is relatively small, but the number of their foreign affiliates and the scale of their foreign assets are significant. According to UNCTAD's estimates, there are at least 550 SO-TNCs – from both developed and developing countries – with more than 15,000 foreign affiliates and estimated foreign assets of over $2 trillion. Some are among the largest TNCs in the world. FDI by State-owned TNCs is estimated to have reached more than $160 billion in 2013, a slight increase after four consecutive years of decline. At that level, although their number constitutes less than 1 per cent of the universe of TNCs, they account for over 11 per cent of global FDI flows.

International production continues its steady growth

International production continued to expand in 2013, rising by 9 per cent in sales, 8 per cent in assets, 6 per cent in value added, 5 per cent in employment, and 3 per cent in exports (table 2). TNCs from developing and transition economies expanded their overseas operations faster than their developed-country counterparts, but at roughly the same rate of their domestic operations, thus maintaining – overall – a stable internationalization index.

Cash holdings by the top 5,000 TNCs remained high in 2013, accounting for more than 11 per cent of their total assets. Cash holdings (including short-term investments) by developed-country TNCs were estimated at $3.5 trillion, while TNCs from developing and transition economies held $1.3 trillion. Developing-country TNCs have held their cash-to-assets ratios relatively constant over the last five years, at about 12 per cent. In contrast, the cash-to-assets ratios of developed-country TNCs increased in recent years, from an average of 9 per cent before the financial crisis to more than 11 per cent in 2013. This increase implies that, at the end of 2013, developed-country TNCs held $670 billion more cash than they would have before – a significant brake on investment.

Table 2. Selected indicators of FDI and international production, 2013 and selected years

Item	Value at current prices (Billions of dollars)				
	1990	2005–2007 pre-crisis average	2011	2012	2013
FDI inflows	208	1 493	1 700	1 330	1 452
FDI outflows	241	1 532	1 712	1 347	1 411
FDI inward stock	2 078	14 790	21 117	23 304	25 464
FDI outward stock	2 088	15 884	21 913	23 916	26 313
Income on inward FDI	79	1 072	1 603	1 581	1 748
Rate of return on inward FDI	3.8	7.3	6.9	7.6	6.8
Income on outward FDI	126	1 135	1 550	1 509	1 622
Rate of return on outward FDI	6.0	7.2	6.5	7.1	6.3
Cross-border M&As	111	780	556	332	349
Sales of foreign affiliates	4 723	21 469	28 516	31 532	34 508
Value added (product) of foreign affiliates	881	4 878	6 262	7 089	7 492
Total assets of foreign affiliates	3 893	42 179	83 754	89 568	96 625
Exports of foreign affiliates	1 498	5 012	7 463	7 532	7 721
Employment by foreign affiliates (thousands)	20 625	53 306	63 416	67 155	70 726
Memorandum:					
GDP	22 327	51 288	71 314	72 807	74 284
Gross fixed capital formation	5 072	11 801	16 498	17 171	17 673
Royalties and licence fee receipts	29	161	250	253	259
Exports of goods and services	4 107	15 034	22 386	22 593	23 160

REGIONAL TRENDS IN FDI

FDI to Africa increases, sustained by growing intra-African flows

FDI inflows to Africa rose by 4 per cent to $57 billion, driven by international and regional market-seeking and infrastructure investments. Expectations for sustained growth of an emerging middle class attracted FDI in consumer-oriented industries, including food, IT, tourism, finance and retail.

The overall increase was driven by the Eastern and Southern African subregions, as others saw falling investments. In Southern Africa flows almost doubled to $13 billion, mainly due to record-high flows to South Africa and Mozambique. In both countries, infrastructure was the main attraction, with investments in the gas sector in Mozambique also playing a role. In East Africa, FDI increased by 15 per cent to $6.2 billion as a result of rising flows to Ethiopia and Kenya. Kenya is becoming a favoured business hub, not only for oil and gas exploration but also for manufacturing and transport; Ethiopian industrial strategy may attract Asian capital to develop its manufacturing base. FDI flows to North Africa decreased by 7 per cent to $15 billion. Central and West Africa saw inflows decline to $8 billion and $14 billion, respectively, in part due to political and security uncertainties.

Intra-African investments are increasing, led by South African, Kenyan, and Nigerian TNCs. Between 2009 and 2013, the share of announced cross-border greenfield investment projects originating from within Africa increased to 18 per cent, from less than 10 per cent in the preceding period. For many smaller, often landlocked or non-oil-exporting countries in Africa, intraregional FDI is a significant source of foreign capital.

Increasing intra-African FDI is in line with leaders' efforts towards deeper regional integration. However, for most subregional groupings, intra-group FDI represent only a small share of intra-African flows. Only in two regional economic cooperation (REC) initiatives does intra-group FDI make up a significant part of intra-African investments – in EAC (about half) and SADC (more than 90 per cent) – largely due to investments in neighbouring countries of the dominant outward investing economies in these RECs, South Africa and Kenya. RECs have thus so far been less effective for the promotion of intraregional investment than a wider African economic cooperation initiative could be.

Intra-African projects are concentrated in manufacturing and services. Only 3 per cent of the value of announced intraregional greenfield projects is in the extractive industries, compared with 24 per cent for extra-regional greenfield projects (during 2009-2013). Intraregional investment could contribute to the build-up of regional value chains. However, so far, African global value chain (GVC) participation is still mostly limited to downstream incorporation of raw materials in the exports of developed countries.

Developing Asia remains the number one investment destination

With total FDI inflows of $426 billion in 2013, developing Asia accounted for nearly 30 per cent of the global total and remained the world's number one recipient region.

FDI inflows to **East Asia** rose by 2 per cent to $221 billion. The stable performance of the subregion was driven by rising FDI inflows to China as well as to the Republic of Korea and Taiwan Province of China. With inflows at $124 billion in 2013, China again ranked second in the world. In the meantime, FDI outflows from China swelled by 15 per cent, to $101 billion, driven by a number of megadeals in developed countries. The country's outflows are expected to surpass its inflows within two to three years. Hong Kong (China) saw its inflows rising slightly to $77 billion. The economy has been highly successful in attracting regional headquarters of TNCs, the number of which reached nearly 1,400 in 2013.

Inflows to **South-East Asia** increased by 7 per cent to $125 billion, with Singapore – another regional headquarters economy – attracting half. The 10 Member States of ASEAN and its 6 FTA partners (Australia, China, India, Japan, the Republic of Korea and New Zealand) have launched negotiations for the RCEP.

In 2013, combined FDI inflows to the 16 negotiating members of RCEP amounted to $343 billion, 24 per cent of world inflows. Over the last 15 years, proactive regional investment cooperation efforts in East and South-East Asia have contributed to a rise in total and intraregional FDI in the region. FDI flows from RCEP now makes up more than 40 per cent of inflows to ASEAN, compared to 17 per cent before 2000. Intraregional FDI in infrastructure and manufacturing in particular is bringing development opportunities for low-income countries, such as the Lao People's Democratic Republic and Myanmar.

Inflows to **South Asia** rose by 10 per cent to $36 billion in 2013. The largest recipient of FDI in the subregion, India, experienced a 17 per cent increase in FDI inflows to $28 billion. Defying the overall trend, investment in the retail sector did not increase, despite the opening up of multi-brand retail in 2012.

Corridors linking South Asia and East and South-East Asia are being established – the Bangladesh-China-India-Myanmar Economic Corridor and the China-Pakistan Economic Corridor. This will help enhance connectivity between Asian subregions and provide opportunities for regional economic cooperation. The initiatives are likely to accelerate infrastructure investment and improve the overall business climate in South Asia.

FDI flows to **West Asia** decreased in 2013 by 9 per cent to $44 billion, failing to recover for the fifth consecutive year. Persistent regional tensions and political uncertainties are holding back investors, although there are differences between countries. In Saudi Arabia and Qatar FDI flows continue to follow a downward trend; in other countries FDI is slowly recovering, although flows remain well below earlier levels, except in Kuwait and Iraq where they reached record levels in 2012 and 2013, respectively.

FDI outflows from West Asia jumped by 64 per cent in 2013, driven by rising flows from the GCC countries. A quadrupling of outflows from Qatar and a near tripling of flows from Kuwait explained most of the increase. Outward FDI could increase further given the high levels of GCC foreign exchange reserves.

Uneven growth of FDI in Latin America and the Caribbean

FDI flows to Latin America and the Caribbean reached $292 billion in 2013. Excluding offshore financial centres, they increased by 5 per cent to $182 billion. Whereas in previous years FDI was driven largely by South America, in 2013 flows to this subregion declined by 6 per cent to $133 billion, after three consecutive years of strong growth. Among the main recipient countries, Brazil saw a slight decline by 2 per cent, despite an 86 per cent increase in flows to the primary sector. FDI in Chile and Argentina declined by 29 per cent and 25 per cent to $20 billion and $9 billion, respectively, due to lower inflows in the mining sector. Flows to Peru also decreased, by 17 per cent to $10 billion. In contrast, FDI flows to Colombia increased by 8 per cent to $17 billion, largely due to cross-border M&As in the electricity and banking industries.

Flows to Central America and the Caribbean (excluding offshore financial centres) increased by 64 per cent to $49 billion, largely due to the $18 billion acquisition of the remaining shares in Grupo Modelo by Belgian brewer AB InBev – which more than doubled inflows to Mexico to $38 billion. Other increases were registered in Panama (61 per cent), Costa Rica (14 per cent), Guatemala and Nicaragua (5 per cent each).

FDI outflows from Latin America and the Caribbean (excluding offshore financial centres) declined by 31 per cent to $33 billion, because of stalled acquisitions abroad and a surge in loan repayments to parent companies by foreign affiliates of Brazilian and Chilean TNCs.

Looking ahead, new opportunities for foreign investors in the oil and gas industry, including shale gas in Argentina and sectoral reform in Mexico, could signal positive FDI prospects. In manufacturing, automotive TNCs are also pushing investment plans in Brazil and Mexico.

The growth potential of the automotive industry appears promising in both countries, with clear differences between the two in government policies and TNC responses. This is reflected in their respective levels and forms of GVC participation. In Mexico, automotive exports are higher, with greater downstream participation, and higher imported value added. Brazil's producers, many of which are TNCs, serve primarily the local market. Although its exports are lower, they contain a higher share of value added produced domestically, including through local content and linkages.

FDI to transition economies at record levels, but prospects uncertain

FDI inflows to transition economies increased by 28 per cent to reach $108 billion in 2013. In South-East Europe, flows increased from $2.6 billion in 2012 to $3.7 billion in 2013, driven by the privatization of remaining State-owned enterprises in the services sector. In the Commonwealth of Independent States (CIS), the 28 per cent rise in flows was due to the significant growth of FDI to the Russian Federation. Although developed countries were the main investors, developing-economy FDI has been on the rise. Prospects for FDI to transition economies are likely to be affected by uncertainties related to regional instability.

In 2013, outward FDI from the region jumped by 84 per cent, reaching a record $99 billion. As in past years, Russian TNCs accounted for the bulk of FDI projects. The value of cross-border M&A purchases by TNCs from the region rose more than six-fold, and announced greenfield investments rose by 87 per cent to $19 billion.

Over the past decade, transition economies have been the fastest-growing host and home region for FDI. EU countries have been the most important partners in this rapid FDI growth, both as investors and recipients. The EU has the largest share of inward FDI stock in the region, with more than two thirds of the total. In the CIS, most of their investment went to natural resources, consumer sectors, and other selected industries as they were liberalized or privatized. In South-East Europe, EU investments have also been driven by privatizations and by a combination of low production costs and the prospect of association with, or membership of the EU. In the same way, the bulk of outward FDI stock from transition economies, mainly from the Russian Federation, is in EU countries. Investors look for strategic assets in EU markets, including downstream activities in the energy industry and value added production activities in manufacturing.

Inflows to developed countries resume growth

After a sharp fall in 2012, inflows to developed economies recovered in 2013 to $566 billion, a 9 per cent increase. Inflows to the European Union were $246 billion (up 14 per cent), less than 30 per cent of their 2007 peak. Among the major economies, inflows to Germany – which had recorded an exceptionally low volume in 2012 – rebounded sharply, but France and the United Kingdom saw a steep decline. In many cases, large swings in intra-company loans were a significant contributing factor. Inflows to Italy and Spain rebounded sharply with the latter becoming the largest European recipient in 2013. Inflows to North America recovered to $250 billion, with the United States – the world's largest recipient – recording a 17 per cent increase to $188 billion.

Outflows from developed countries were $857 billion in 2013 – virtually unchanged from a year earlier. A recovery in Europe and the continued expansion of investment from Japan were weighed down by a contraction of outflows from North America. Outflows from Europe increased by 10 per cent to $329 billion. Switzerland became Europe's largest direct investor. Against the European trend, France, Germany and the United Kingdom registered a large decline in outward FDI. Outflows from North America shed another 10 per cent to $381 billion, partly because United States TNCs transferred funds from Europe, raised in local bond markets, back to the United States. Outflows from Japan grew for the third successive year, rising to $136 billion.

Both inflows and outflows remained at barely half the peak level seen in 2007. In terms of global share, developed countries accounted for 39 per cent of total inflows and 61 per cent of total outflows – both historically low levels.

Although the share of transatlantic FDI flows has declined in recent years, the EU and the United States are important investment partners – much more so than implied by the size of their economies or by volumes of bilateral trade. For the United States, 62 per cent of inward FDI stock is held by EU countries and 50 per cent of outward stock is located in the EU. For the EU, the United States accounts for one third of FDI flows into the region from non-EU countries.

FDI inflows to LDCs up, but LLDCs and SIDS down

FDI inflows to **least developed countries** (LDCs) rose to $28 billion, an increase of 14 per cent. While inflows to some larger host LDCs fell or stagnated, rising inflows were recorded elsewhere. A nearly $3 billion reduction in divestment in Angola contributed most, followed by gains in Bangladesh, Ethiopia, Mozambique, Myanmar, the Sudan and Yemen. The share of inflows to LDCs in global inflows remains small at 2 per cent.

The number of announced greenfield investment projects in LDCs reached a record high, and in value terms they reached the highest level in three years. The services sector, driven by large-scale energy projects, contributed 70 per cent of the value of announced greenfield projects. External sources of finance constitute a major part of the funding behind a growing number of infrastructure projects in LDCs. However, a substantial portion of announced investments has so far not generated FDI inflows, which can be due to structured finance solutions that do not translate into FDI, long gestation periods spreading outlays over many years, or actual project delays or cancellations.

FDI flows to the **landlocked developing countries** (LLDCs) in 2013 fell by 11 per cent to $29.7 billion. The Asian group of LLDCs experienced the largest fall in FDI flows of nearly 50 per cent, mainly due to a decline in investment in Mongolia. Despite a mixed picture for African LLDCs, 8 of the 15 LLDC economies increased their FDI inflows, with Zambia attracting most at $1.8 billion.

FDI remains a relatively more important factor in capital formation and growth for LLDCs than developing countries as a whole. In developing economies the size of FDI flows relative to gross fixed capital formation has averaged 11 per cent over the past decade but in the LLDCs it has averaged almost twice this, at 21 per cent.

FDI inflows to the **small island developing States** (SIDS) declined by 16 per cent to $5.7 billion in 2013, putting an end to two years of recovery. Mineral extraction and downstream-related activities, business and finance, and tourism are the main target industries for FDI in SIDS. Tourism is attracting increasing interest by foreign investors, while manufacturing industries – such as apparel and processed fish – that used to be a non-negligible target for FDI, have been negatively affected by erosion of trade preferences.

INVESTMENT POLICY TRENDS AND KEY ISSUES

New government efforts to prevent divestment and promote reshoring

UNCTAD monitoring shows that, in 2013, 59 countries and economies adopted 87 policy measures affecting foreign investment. National investment policymaking remained geared towards investment promotion and liberalization. At the same time, the overall share of regulatory or restrictive investment policies further increased from 25 to 27 per cent (figure 5).

Investment liberalization measures included a number of privatizations in transition economies. The majority of foreign-investment-specific liberalization measures reported were in Asia; most related to the telecommunications industry and the energy sector. Newly introduced FDI restrictions and regulations included

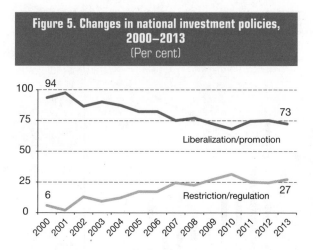

Figure 5. Changes in national investment policies, 2000–2013
(Per cent)

a number of non-approvals of foreign investment projects.

A recent phenomenon is the effort by governments to prevent divestments by foreign investors. Affected by economic crises and persistently high domestic unemployment, some countries have introduced new approval requirements for relocations and lay-offs. In addition, some home countries have started to promote reshoring of overseas investment by their TNCs.

More effective use of investment incentives requires improved monitoring

Incentives are widely used by governments as a policy instrument for attracting investment, despite persistent criticism that they are economically inefficient and lead to misallocations of public funds. In 2013, more than half of new liberalization, promotion or facilitation measures related to the provision of investment incentives.

According to UNCTAD's most recent survey of investment promotion agencies (IPAs), the main objective of investment incentives is job creation, followed by technology transfer and export promotion, while the most important target industry is IT and business services, followed by agriculture and tourism. Despite their growing importance in national and global policy agendas, environmental protection and development of disadvantaged regions do not rank high in current promotion strategies of IPAs.

Linking investment incentives schemes to the SDGs could make them a more effective policy tool to remedy market failures and could offer a response to the criticism raised against the way investment incentives have traditionally been used. Governments should also carefully assess their incentives strategies and strengthen their monitoring and evaluation practices.

Some countries scale up IIA treaty negotiations, others disengage

With the addition of 44 new treaties, the global IIA regime reached close to 3,240 at the end of 2013 (figure 6). The year brought an increasing dichotomy in investment treaty making. An increasing number of developing countries are disengaging from the regime in Africa, Asia and Latin America. At the same time, there is an "up-scaling" trend in treaty making, which manifests itself in increasing dynamism (with more countries participating in ever faster sequenced negotiating rounds) and in an increasing depth and breadth of issues addressed. Today, IIA negotiators increasingly take novel approaches to existing IIA provisions and add new issues to the negotiating agenda. The inclusion of sustainable development features and provisions that bring a liberalization dimension to IIAs and/or strengthen certain investment protection elements are examples in point.

"Megaregional agreements" – systemic implications expected

Negotiations of megaregional agreements have become increasingly prominent in the public debate, attracting both criticism and support from different stakeholders. Key concerns relate to their potential impact on contracting parties' regulatory space and sustainable development. Megaregionals are broad economic agreements among a group of countries that have a significant combined economic weight and

Figure 6. Trends in IIAs signed, 1983–2013

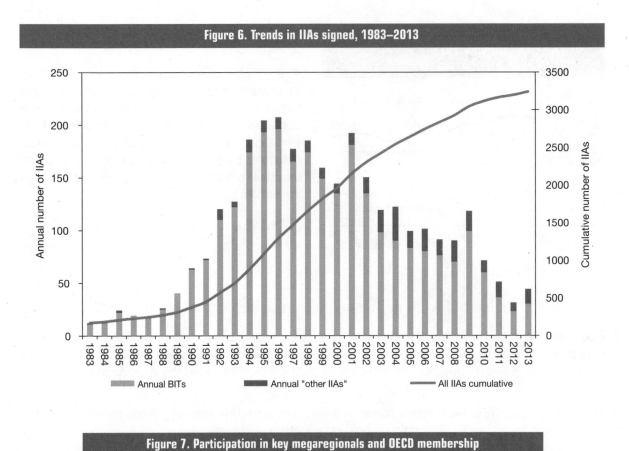

Figure 7. Participation in key megaregionals and OECD membership

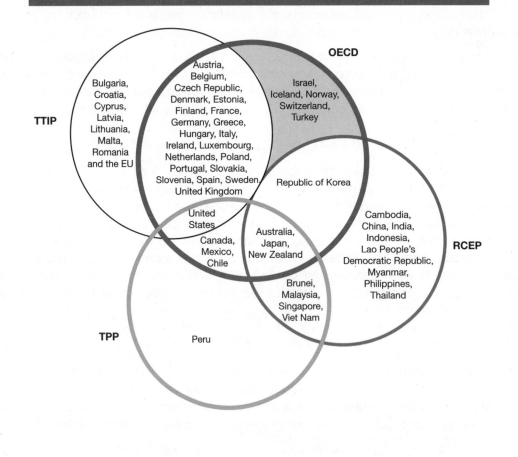

in which investment is one of the key subject areas covered. Taking seven of these negotiations together, they involve a total of 88 developed and developing countries. If concluded, they are likely to have important implications for the current multi-layered international investment regime and global investment patterns.

Megaregional agreements could have systemic implications for the IIA regime: they could either contribute to a consolidation of the existing treaty landscape or they could create further inconsistencies through overlap with existing IIAs – including those at the plurilateral level (figure 7). For example, six major megaregional agreements overlap with 140 existing IIAs but would create 200 new bilateral investment-treaty relationships. Megaregional agreements could also marginalize non-participating third parties. Negotiators need to give careful consideration to these systemic implications. Transparency in rule making, with broad stakeholder engagement, can help in finding optimal solutions and ensure buy-in from those affected by a treaty.

Growing concerns about investment arbitration

The year 2013 saw the second largest number of known investment arbitrations filed in a single year (56), bringing the total number of known cases to 568. Of the new claims, more than 40 per cent were brought against member States of the European Union (EU), with all but one of them being *intra-EU* cases. Investors continued to challenge a broad number of measures in various policy areas, particularly in the renewable energy sector.

The past year also saw at least 37 arbitral decisions – 23 of which are in the public domain – and the second highest known award so far ($935 million plus interest). With the potential inclusion of investment arbitration in "megaregional agreements", investor-State dispute settlement (ISDS) is at the centre of public attention.

A call for reform of the IIA regime

While almost all countries are parties to one or several IIAs, many are dissatisfied with the current regime. Concerns relate mostly to the development dimension of IIAs; the balance between the rights and obligations of investors and States; and the systemic complexity of the IIA regime.

Countries' current efforts to address these challenges reveal four different paths of action: (i) some aim to maintain the status quo, largely refraining from changes in the way they enter into new IIA commitments; (ii) some are disengaging from the IIA regime, unilaterally terminating existing treaties or denouncing multilateral arbitration conventions; and (iii) some are implementing selective adjustments, modifying models for future treaties but leaving the treaty core and the body of existing treaties largely untouched. Finally, (iv) there is the path of systematic reform that aims to comprehensively address the IIA regime's challenges in a holistic manner.

While each of these paths has benefits and drawbacks, systemic reform could effectively address the complexities of the IIA regime and bring it in line with the sustainable development imperative. Such a reform process could follow a gradual approach with carefully sequenced actions: (i) defining the areas for reform (identifying key and emerging issues and lessons learned, and building consensus on what could and should be changed, and on what should and could not be changed), (ii) designing a roadmap for reform (identifying different options for reform, assessing pros and cons, and agreeing on the sequencing of actions), and (iii) implementing it at the national, bilateral and regional levels. A multilateral focal point like UNCTAD could support such a holistic, coordinated and sustainability-oriented approach to IIA reform through its policy analysis, technical assistance and consensus building. The *World Investment Forum* could provide the platform, and the *Investment Policy Framework for Sustainable Development (IPFSD)* the guidance.

Investing in the SDGs: an action plan for promoting private sector contributions

The United Nations' Sustainable Development Goals need a step-change in investment

Faced with common global economic, social and environmental challenges, the international community is defining a set of Sustainable Development Goals (SDGs). The SDGs, which are being formulated by the United Nations together with the widest possible range of stakeholders, are intended to galvanize action worldwide through concrete targets for the 2015–2030 period for poverty reduction, food security, human health and education, climate change mitigation, and a range of other objectives across the economic, social and environmental pillars.

Private sector contributions can take two main forms; good governance in business practices and investment in sustainable development. This includes the private sector's commitment to sustainable development; transparency and accountability in honouring sustainable development practices; responsibility to avoid harm, even if it is not prohibited; and partnership with government on maximizing co-benefits of investment.

The SDGs will have very significant resource implications across the developed and developing world. Estimates for total investment needs in developing countries alone range from $3.3 trillion to $4.5 trillion per year, for basic infrastructure (roads, rail and ports; power stations; water and sanitation), food security (agriculture and rural development), climate change mitigation and adaptation, health and education.

Reaching the SDGs will require a step-change in both public and private investment. Public sector funding capabilities alone may be insufficient to meet demands across all SDG-related sectors. However, today, the participation of the private sector in investment in these sectors is relatively low. Only a fraction of the worldwide invested assets of banks, pension funds, insurers, foundations and endowments, as well as transnational corporations, is in SDG sectors, and even less in developing countries, particularly the poorest ones (LDCs).

At current levels of investment in SDG-relevant sectors, developing countries face an annual gap of $2.5 trillion

At today's level of investment – public and private – in SDG-related sectors in developing countries, an annual funding shortfall of some $2.5 trillion remains (figure 8). Bridging such a gap is a daunting task, but it is achievable. Part of the gap could be covered by the private sector (in a "business as usual scenario") if the current growth rate of private investment continues. For developing countries as a group, including fast-growing emerging economies, the current growth of private investment could be sufficient, approximately, to cover the part of total SDG-related investment needs corresponding to the private sector's current participation in SDG investments. However, at the aggregate level that would still leave a gap of about $1.6 trillion per year, and the relative size of this gap would be far more important in least developing countries and vulnerable economies. Increasing the participation of the private sector in SDG financing in developing countries could potentially cover a larger part of the gap.

At a disaggregated level, the relative size of investment gaps will vary by SDG sector – private sector participation in some sectors is low and likely to remain so – and for different groups of developing countries. The starting levels and growth rates of private investment in SDG sectors in less developed countries are such that the private sector will not even cover the part of investment needs to 2030 that corresponds to its current level of participation.

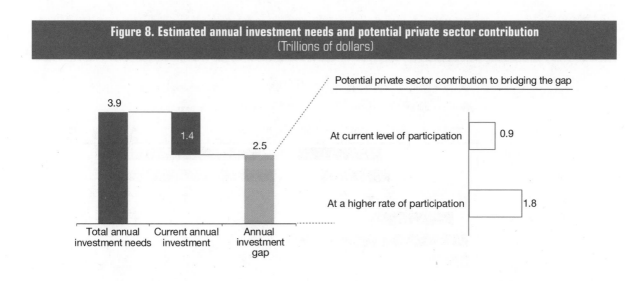

Figure 8. Estimated annual investment needs and potential private sector contribution
(Trillions of dollars)

Structurally weak economies need special attention, LDCs require a doubling of the growth rate of private investment

Investment and private sector engagement across SDG sectors are highly variable across developing countries. Emerging markets face entirely different conditions to vulnerable economies such as LDCs, LLDCs and SIDS. In LDCs, official development assistance (ODA) – currently their largest external source of finance and often used for direct budget support and public spending – will remain of fundamental importance.

At the current rate of private sector participation in investment in SDG sectors, and at current growth rates, a "business as usual" scenario in LDCs will leave a shortfall that would imply a nine-fold increase in public sector funding requirements to 2030. This scenario, with the limited funding capabilities of LDC governments and the fact that much of ODA in LDCs is already used to support current (not investment) spending by LDC governments, is not a viable option. Without higher levels of private sector investment, the financing requirements associated with the prospective SDGs in LDCs may be unrealistic.

A target for the promotion of private sector investment in SDGs in LDCs could be to double the current growth rate of such investment. The resulting contribution would give private investment a meaningful complementary financing role next to public investment and ODA. Public investment and ODA would continue to be fundamental, as covering the remaining funding requirements would still imply trebling their current levels to 2030.

The potential for increased private sector investment contributions is significant, especially in infrastructure, food security and climate change mitigation

The potential for increasing private sector participation is greater in some sectors than in others (figure 9). Infrastructure sectors, such as power and renewable energy (under climate change mitigation), transport and water and sanitation, are natural candidates for greater private sector participation, under the right conditions and with appropriate safeguards. Other SDG sectors are less likely to generate significantly higher amounts of private sector interest, either because it is difficult to design risk-return models attractive to private investors (e.g. climate change adaptation), or because they are at the core of public service responsibilities and highly sensitive to private sector involvement (e.g. education and health care). Therefore, public investment remains fundamental and pivotal. However, because it is unrealistic to expect the public sector to meet all funding demands in many developing countries, the SDGs have to be accompanied by strategic initiatives to increase private sector participation.

Figure 9. Potential private sector contribution to investment gaps at current and high participation levels
(Billions of dollars)

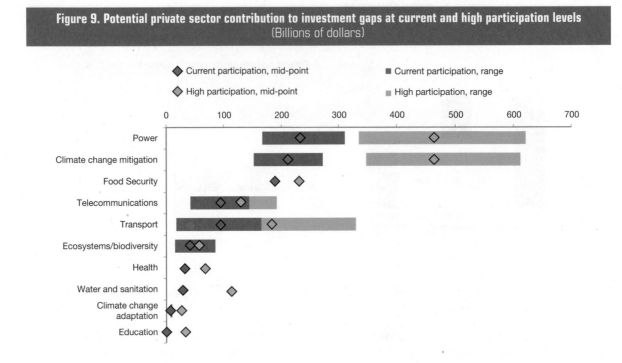

Increasing the involvement of private investors in SDG-related sectors, many of which are sensitive or of a public service nature, leads to policy dilemmas

A first dilemma relates to the risks involved in increased private sector participation in sensitive sectors. Private sector service provision in health care and education in developing countries, for instance, can have negative effects on standards unless strong governance and oversight is in place, which in turn requires capable institutions and technical competencies. Private sector involvement in essential infrastructure industries, such as power or telecommunications can be sensitive in developing countries where this implies the transfer of public sector assets to the private sector. Private sector operations in infrastructure such as water and sanitation are particularly sensitive because of the basic-needs nature of these sectors.

A second dilemma stems from the need to maintain quality services affordable and accessible to all. The fundamental hurdle for increased private sector contributions to investment in SDG sectors is the inadequate risk-return profile of many such investments. Many mechanisms exist to share risks or otherwise improve the risk-return profile for private sector investors. Increasing returns, however, must not lead to the services provided by private investors ultimately becoming inaccessible or unaffordable for the poorest in society. Allowing energy or water suppliers to cover only economically attractive urban areas while ignoring rural needs, or to raise prices of essential services, is not a sustainable outcome.

A third dilemma results from the respective roles of public and private investment. Despite the fact that public sector funding shortfalls in SDG sectors make it desirable that private sector investment increase to achieve the prospective SDGs, public sector investment remains fundamental and pivotal. Governments – through policy and rule making – need to be ultimately accountable with respect to provision of vital public services and overall sustainable development strategy.

A fourth dilemma is the apparent conflict between the particularly acute funding needs in structurally weak economies, especially LDCs, necessitating a significant increase in private sector investment, and the fact that especially these countries face the greatest difficulty in attracting such investment. Without targeted policy intervention and support measures there is a real risk that investors will continue to see operating conditions and risks in LDCs as prohibitive.

UNCTAD proposes a Strategic Framework for Private Investment in the SDGs

A Strategic Framework for Private Investment in the SDGs (figure 10) addresses key policy challenges and solutions, related to:

- Providing *Leadership* to define guiding principles and targets, to ensure policy coherence, and to galvanize action.

- *Mobilizing funds for sustainable development* – raising resources in financial markets or through financial intermediaries that can be invested in sustainable development.

- *Channelling funds to sustainable development projects* – ensuring that available funds make their way to concrete sustainable-development-oriented investment projects on the ground in developing countries, and especially LDCs.

- *Maximizing impact and mitigating drawbacks* – creating an enabling environment and putting in place appropriate safeguards that need to accompany increased private sector engagement in often sensitive sectors.

A set of guiding principles can help overcome policy dilemmas associated with increased private sector engagement in SDG sectors

The many stakeholders involved in stimulating private investment in SDGs will have varying perspectives on how to resolve the policy dilemmas inherent in seeking greater private sector participation in SDG sectors. A common set of principles for investment in SDGs can help establish a collective sense of direction and purpose. The following broad principles could provide a framework.

- *Balancing liberalization and the right to regulate.* Greater private sector involvement in SDG sectors may be necessary where public sector resources are insufficient (although selective, gradual or sequenced approaches are possible); at the same time, such increased involvement must be accompanied by appropriate regulations and government oversight.

- *Balancing the need for attractive risk-return rates with the need for accessible and affordable services.* This requires governments to proactively address market failures in both respects. It means placing clear obligations on investors and extracting firm commitments, while providing incentives to improve the risk-return profile of investment. And it implies making incentives or subsidies conditional on social inclusiveness.

- *Balancing a push for private investment with the push for public investment.* Public and private investment are complementary, not substitutes. Synergies and mutually supporting roles between public and private funds can be found both at the level of financial resources – e.g. raising private sector funds with public sector funds as seed capital – and at the policy level, where governments can seek to engage private investors to support economic or public service reform programmes. Nevertheless, it is important for policymakers not to translate a push for private investment into a policy bias against public investment.

- *Balancing the global scope of the SDGs with the need to make a special effort in LDCs.* While overall financing for development needs may be defined globally, with respect to private sector financing contributions special efforts will need to be made for LDCs, because without targeted policy intervention these countries will not be able to attract the required resources from private investors. Dedicated private sector investment targets for the poorest countries, leveraging ODA for additional private funds, and targeted technical assistance and capacity building to help attract private investment in LDCs are desirable.

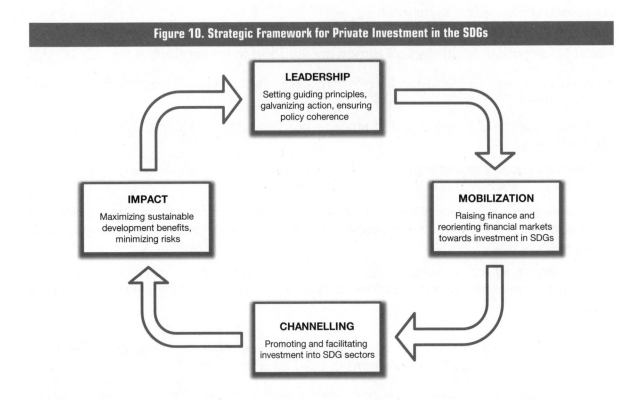

Figure 10. Strategic Framework for Private Investment in the SDGs

LEADERSHIP
Setting guiding principles, galvanizing action, ensuring policy coherence

MOBILIZATION
Raising finance and reorienting financial markets towards investment in SDGs

CHANNELLING
Promoting and facilitating investment into SDG sectors

IMPACT
Maximizing sustainable development benefits, minimizing risks

Increasing private investment in SDGs will require leadership at the global level, as well as from national policymakers

Leadership is needed not only to provide guiding principles to deal with policy dilemmas, but also to: *Set investment targets.* The rationale behind the SDGs, and the experience with the Millennium Development Goals, is that targets help provide direction and purpose. Ambitious investment targets are implied by the prospective SDGs. The international community would do well to make targets explicit, and spell out the consequences for investment policies and investment promotion at national and international levels. Achievable but ambitious targets, including for increasing public and private sector investment in LDCs, are desirable.

Ensure policy coherence and creating synergies. Interaction between policies is important – between national and international investment policies, between investment and other sustainable-development-related policies (e.g. tax, trade, competition, technology, and environmental, social and labour market policies), and between micro- and macroeconomic policies. Leadership is required to ensure that the global push for sustainable development and investment in SDGs has a voice in international macroeconomic policy coordination forums and global financial system reform processes, where decisions will have an fundamental bearing on the prospects for growth in SDG financing.

Establish a global multi-stakeholder platform on investing in the SDGs. A global multi-stakeholder body on investing in the SDGs could provide a platform for discussion on overall investment goals and targets, fostering promising initiatives to mobilize finance and spreading good practices, supporting actions on the ground, and ensuring a common approach to impact measurement.

Create a multi-agency technical assistance facility for investment in the SDGs. Many initiatives aimed at increasing private sector investment in SDG sectors are complex, requiring significant technical capabilities and strong institutions. A multi-agency institutional arrangement could help to support LDCs, advising on, for example, the set-up of SDG project development agencies that can plan, package and promote pipelines of bankable projects; design of SDG-oriented incentive schemes; and regulatory frameworks.

Coordinated efforts to enhance synergies are imperative.

A range of policy options is available to respond to challenges and constraints in mobilizing funds, channelling them into SDG sectors, and ensuring sustainable impact

Challenges to *mobilizing* funds in financial markets include market failures and a lack of transparency on environmental, social and governance performance, misaligned incentives for market participants, and start-up and scaling problems for innovative financing solutions. Policy responses to build a more SDG-conducive financial system might include:

- *Creating fertile soil for innovative SDG-financing approaches.* Innovative financial instruments and funding mechanisms to raise resources for investment in SDGs deserve support to achieve scale. Promising initiatives include SDG-dedicated financial instruments and Impact Investment, funding mechanisms that use public sector resources to catalyse mobilization of private sector resources, and new "go-to-market" channels for SDG investment projects.

- *Building or improving pricing mechanisms for externalities.* Effective pricing mechanisms for social and environmental externalities – either by attaching a cost to such externalities (e.g. through carbon taxes) or through market-based schemes – are ultimately fundamental to put financial markets and investors on a sustainable footing.

- *Promoting Sustainable Stock Exchanges (SSEs).* SSEs provide listed entities with the incentives and tools to improve transparency on ESG performance, and allow investors to make informed decisions on responsible allocation of capital.

- *Introducing financial market reforms.* Realigning rewards in financial markets to favour investment in SDGs will require action, including reform of pay and performance structures, and innovative rating methodologies that reward long-term investment in SDG sectors.

Key constraints to *channelling* funds into SDG sectors include entry barriers, inadequate risk-return ratios for SDG investments, a lack of information and effective packaging and promotion of projects, and a lack of investor expertise. Effective policy responses may include the following.

- *Reducing entry barriers, with safeguards.* A basic prerequisite for successful promotion of SDG investment is a sound overall policy climate, conducive to attracting investment while protecting public interests, especially in sensitive sectors.

- *Expanding the use of risk-sharing tools for SDG investments.* A number of tools, including public-private partnerships, investment insurance, blended financing and advance market commitments, can help improve the risk-return profile of SDG investment projects.

- *Establishing new incentives schemes and a new generation of investment promotion institutions.* SDG investment development agencies could target SDG sectors and develop and market pipelines of bankable projects. Investment incentives could be reoriented, to target investments in SDG sectors and made conditional on social and environmental performance. Regional initiatives can help spur private investment in cross-border infrastructure projects and regional clusters of firms in SDG sectors.

- *Building SDG investment partnerships.* Partnerships between home countries of investors, host countries, TNCs and multilateral development banks can help overcome knowledge gaps as well as generate joint investments in SDG sectors.

Key challenges in maximizing the positive *impact* and minimizing the risks and drawbacks of private investment in SDG sectors include the weak absorptive capacity in some developing countries, social and environmental impact risks, and the need for stakeholder engagement and effective impact monitoring.

Policy responses can include:

- *Increasing absorptive capacity.* A range of policy tools are available to increase absorptive capacity, including the promotion and facilitation of entrepreneurship, support to technology development, human resource and skills development, business development services and promotion of business linkages. Development of linkages and clusters in incubators or economic zones specifically aimed at stimulating businesses in SDG sectors may be particularly effective.

- *Establishing effective regulatory frameworks and standards.* Increased private sector engagement in often sensitive SDG sectors needs to be accompanied by effective regulation. Particular areas of attention include human health and safety, environmental and social protection, quality and inclusiveness of public services, taxation, and national and international policy coherence.

- *Good governance, strong institutions, stakeholder engagement.* Good governance and capable institutions are a key enabler for the attraction of private investment in general, and in SDG sectors in particular. They are also needed for effective stakeholder engagement and management of impact trade-offs.

- *Implementing SDG impact assessment systems.* Monitoring of the impact of investment, especially along social and environmental dimensions, is key to effective policy implementation. A set of core quantifiable impact indicators can help. Impact measurement and reporting by private investors on their social and environmental performance promotes corporate responsibility on the ground and supports mobilization and channelling of investment.

Figure 11 summarizes schematically the key challenges and policy responses for each element of the Strategic Framework. Detailed policy responses are included in UNCTAD's Action Plan for Private Investment in the SDGs.

Figure 11. Key challenges and possible policy responses

	Key challenges	Policy responses
LEADERSHIP *Setting guiding principles, galvanizing action, ensuring policy coherence*	• Need for a clear sense of direction and common policy design criteria • Need for clear objectives to galvanize global action • Need to manage investment policy interactions • Need for global consensus and an inclusive process	• Agree a set of guiding principles for SDG investment policymaking • Set SDG investment targets • Ensure policy coherence and synergies • Multi-stakeholder platform and multi-agency technical assistance facility
MOBILIZATION *Raising finance and re-orienting financial markets towards investment in SDGs*	• Start-up and scaling issues for new financing solutions • Failures in global capital markets • Lack of transparency on sustainable corporate performance • Misaligned investor rewards/pay structures	• Create fertile soil for innovative SDG-financing approaches and corporate initiatives • Build or improve pricing mechanisms for externalities • Promote Sustainable Stock Exchanges • Introduce financial market reforms
CHANNELLING *Promoting and facilitating investment into SDG sectors*	• Entry barriers • Lack of information and effective packaging and promotion of SDG investment projects • Inadequate risk-return ratios for SDG investments • Lack of investor expertise in SDG sectors	• Build an investment policy climate conducive to investing in SDGs, while safeguarding public interests • Expand use of risk sharing mechanisms for SDG investments • Establish new incentives schemes and a new generation of investment promotion institutions • Build SDG investment partnerships
IMPACT *Maximizing sustainable development benefits, minimizing risks*	• Weak absorptive capacity in developing countries • Need to minimize risks associated with private investment in SDG sectors • Need to engage stakeholders and manage impact trade-offs • Inadequate investment impact measurement and reporting tools	• Build productive capacity, entrepreneurship, technology, skills, linkages • Establish effective regulatory frameworks and standards • Good governance, capable institutions, stakeholder engagements • Implement a common set of SDG investment impact indicators and push Integrated Corporate Reporting

A Big Push for private investment in sustainable development

UNCTAD's Action Plan for Private Investment in the SDGs contains a range of policy options to respond to the mobilization, channelling and impact challenges. However, a concerted push by the international community and by policymakers at national levels needs to focus on a few priority actions – or packages. Figure 12 proposes six packages that group actions related to specific segments of the "SDG investment chain" and that address relatively homogenous groups of stakeholders for action. Such a focused set of action packages can help shape a *Big Push* for private investment in sustainable development:

1. *A new generation of investment promotion strategies and institutions.* Sustainable development projects, whether in infrastructure, social housing or renewable energy, require intensified efforts for investment promotion and facilitation. Such projects should become a priority of the work of IPAs and business development organizations.

   The most frequent constraint faced by potential investors in sustainable development projects is the lack of concrete proposals of sizeable, impactful, and bankable projects. Promotion and facilitation of investment in sustainable development should include the marketing of pre-packaged and structured projects with priority consideration and sponsorship at the highest political level. This requires specialist expertise and dedicated units, e.g. government-sponsored "brokers" of sustainable development investment projects. Putting in place such specialist expertise (ranging from project and structured finance expertise to engineering and project design skills) can be supported by technical assistance from a consortium of international organizations and multilateral development banks. Units could also be set up at the regional level to share costs and achieve economies of scale.

   Promotion of investment in SDG sectors should be supported by an international investment policy regime that effectively pursues the same objectives. Currently, IIAs focus on the protection of investment. Mainstreaming sustainable development in IIAs requires, among others, proactive promotion of investment, with commitments in areas such as technical assistance. Other measures include linking investment promotion institutions, facilitating SDG investments through investment insurance and guarantees, and regular impact monitoring.

2. *SDG-oriented investment incentives.* Investment incentive schemes can be restructured specifically to facilitate sustainable development projects. A transformation is needed from purely "location-based" incentives, aiming to increase the competitiveness of a location and provided at the time of establishment, towards "SDG-based" incentives, aiming to promote investment in SDG sectors and conditional upon sustainable performance.

3. *Regional SDG Investment Compacts.* Regional and South-South cooperation can foster SDG investment. Orienting regional cooperation towards the promotion of SDG investment can be especially effective for cross-border infrastructure development and regional clusters of firms operating in SDG sectors (e.g. green zones). This could include joint investment promotion mechanisms, joint programmes to build absorptive capacity, and joint public-private partnership models.

4. *New forms of partnership for SDG investments.* Cooperation between outward investment agencies in home countries and IPAs in host countries could be institutionalized for the purpose of marketing SDG investment opportunities in home countries, provision of investment incentives and facilitation services for SDG projects, and joint monitoring and impact assessment. Outward investment agencies could evolve into genuine business development agencies for investments in SDG sectors in developing countries, raising awareness of investment opportunities, helping investors to bridge knowledge gaps, and practically facilitate the investment process. Concrete tools that might support SDG investment business development services might include online pipelines of bankable projects and opportunities for linkages programmes in developing countries. A multi-agency technical assistance consortium could

Figure 12. A Big Push for private investment in the SDGs: action packages

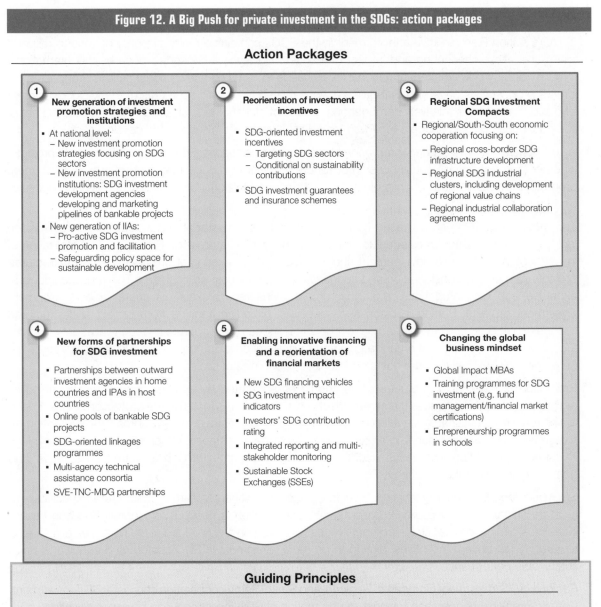

Action Packages

1 New generation of investment promotion strategies and institutions

- At national level:
  - New investment promotion strategies focusing on SDG sectors
  - New investment promotion institutions: SDG investment development agencies developing and marketing pipelines of bankable projects
- New generation of IIAs:
  - Pro-active SDG investment promotion and facilitation
  - Safeguarding policy space for sustainable development

2 Reorientation of investment incentives

- SDG-oriented investment incentives
  - Targeting SDG sectors
  - Conditional on sustainability contributions
- SDG investment guarantees and insurance schemes

3 Regional SDG Investment Compacts

- Regional/South-South economic cooperation focusing on:
  - Regional cross-border SDG infrastructure development
  - Regional SDG industrial clusters, including development of regional value chains
  - Regional industrial collaboration agreements

4 New forms of partnerships for SDG investment

- Partnerships between outward investment agencies in home countries and IPAs in host countries
- Online pools of bankable SDG projects
- SDG-oriented linkages programmes
- Multi-agency technical assistance consortia
- SVE-TNC-MDG partnerships

5 Enabling innovative financing and a reorientation of financial markets

- New SDG financing vehicles
- SDG investment impact indicators
- Investors' SDG contribution rating
- Integrated reporting and multi-stakeholder monitoring
- Sustainable Stock Exchanges (SSEs)

6 Changing the global business mindset

- Global Impact MBAs
- Training programmes for SDG investment (e.g. fund management/financial market certifications)
- Enrepreneurship programmes in schools

Guiding Principles

Balancing liberalization and regulation

Balancing the need for attractive risk-return rates with the need for accessible and affordable services for all

Balancing a push for private funds with the push for public investment

Balancing the global scope of the SDGs with the need to make a special effort in LDCs

help to support LDCs. South-South partnerships could also help spread good practices and lessons learned.

5. *Enabling innovative financing mechanisms and a reorientation of financial markets.* New and existing financing mechanisms, such as green bonds or impact investing, deserve support and an enabling environment to allow them to be scaled up and marketed to the most promising sources of capital. Publicly sponsored seed funding mechanisms and facilitated access to financial markets for SDG projects are further mechanisms that merit attention. Furthermore, reorientation of financial markets towards sustainable development needs integrated reporting on the economic, social and environmental impact of private investors. This is a fundamental step towards responsible investment behavior in financial markets and a prerequisite for initiatives aimed at mobilizing funds for investment in SDGs; integrated reporting is at the heart of Sustainable Stock Exchanges.

6. *Changing the global business mindset and developing SDG investment expertise.* The majority of managers in the world's financial institutions and large multinational enterprises – the main sources of global investment – as well as most successful entrepreneurs tend to be strongly influenced by models of business, management and investment that are commonly taught in business schools. Such models tend to focus on business and investment opportunities in mature or emerging markets, with the risk-return profiles associated with those markets, while they tend to ignore opportunities outside the parameters of these models. Conventional models also tend to be driven exclusively by calculations of economic risks and returns, often ignoring broader social and environmental impacts, both positive and negative. Moreover, a lack of consideration in standard business school teachings of the challenges associated with operating in poor countries, and the resulting need for innovative problem solving, tend to leave managers ill-prepared for pro-poor investments. A curriculum for business schools that generates awareness of investment opportunities in poor countries and that instills in students the problem solving skills needed in developing-country operating environments can have an important long-term impact. Inserting relevant modules in existing training and certification programmes for financial market participants can also help.

The *Action Plan for Private Investment in the SDGs* is meant to serve as a point of reference for policymakers at national and international levels in their discussions on ways and means to implement the SDGs and the formulation of operational strategies for investing in the SDGs. It has been designed as a "living document" and incorporates an online version that aims to establish an interactive, open dialogue, inviting the international community to exchange views, suggestions and experiences. It thus constitutes a basis for further stakeholder engagement. UNCTAD aims to provide the platform for such engagement through its biennial *World Investment Forum*, and online through the *Investment Policy Hub*.

Mukhisa Kituyi
Secretary-General of the UNCTAD

GLOBAL INVESTMENT TRENDS

CHAPTER I

A. CURRENT TRENDS

Global FDI flows rose by 9 per cent in 2013 to $1.45 trillion, up from $1.33 trillion in 2012, despite some volatility in international investments caused by the shift in market expectations towards an earlier tapering of quantitative easing in the United States. FDI inflows increased in all major economic groupings – developed, developing, and transition economies. Although the share of developed economies in total global FDI flows remained low, it is expected to rise over the next three years to 52 per cent (see section B) (figure I.1). Global inward FDI stock rose by 9 per cent, reaching $25.5 trillion, reflecting the rise of FDI inflows and strong performance of the stock markets in many parts of the world. UNCTAD's FDI analysis is largely based on data that exclude FDI in special purpose entities (SPEs) and offshore financial centres (box I.1).

1. FDI by geography

a. FDI inflows

The 9 per cent increase in global FDI inflows in 2013 reflected a moderate pickup in global economic growth and some large cross-border M&A transactions. The increase was widespread, covering all three major groups of economies, though the reasons for the increase differed across the globe. FDI flows to developed countries rose by 9 per cent, reaching $566 billion, mainly through greater retained earnings in foreign affiliates in the European Union (EU), resulting in an increase in FDI to the EU. FDI flows to developing economies reached a new high of $778 billion, accounting for 54 per cent of global inflows. Inflows to transition economies rose to $108 billion – up 28 per cent from the previous year – accounting for 7 per cent of global FDI inflows.

***Developing Asia* remains the world's largest recipient region of FDI flows** (figure I.2). All subregions saw their FDI flows rise except West Asia, which registered its fifth consecutive decline in FDI. The absence of large deals and the worsening of instability in many parts of the region have caused uncertainty and negatively affected investment. FDI inflows to the Association of Southeast Asian Nations (ASEAN) reached a new high of $125 billion – 7 per cent higher than 2012. The high level of flows to East Asia was driven by rising inflows to China, which remained the recipient of the second largest flows in the world (figure I.3).

After remaining almost stable in 2012, at historically high levels, FDI flows to Latin America and the Caribbean registered a 14 per cent increase to $292 billion in 2013. Excluding offshore financial centres, they increased by 6 per cent to $182 billion.

In contrast to the preceding three years, when South America was the main driver of FDI flows to the region, 2013 brought soaring flows to Central America. The acquisition in Mexico of Grupo Modelo by the Belgian brewer Anheuser Busch explains most of the FDI increase in Mexico as well as in the subregion. The decline of inflows to South America resulted mainly from the almost 30 per cent slump noted in Chile, the second largest recipient of FDI in South America in 2012. The decrease was due to equity divestment in the mining sector and lower reinvested earnings by foreign mining companies as a result of the decrease in commodity prices.

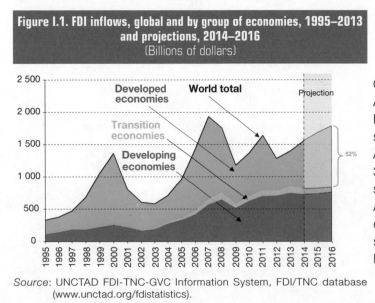

Figure I.1. FDI inflows, global and by group of economies, 1995–2013 and projections, 2014–2016
(Billions of dollars)

Source: UNCTAD FDI-TNC-GVC Information System, FDI/TNC database (www.unctad.org/fdistatistics).

Box I.1. UNCTAD FDI data: treatment of transit FDI

TNCs frequently make use of special purpose entities (SPEs) to channel their investments, resulting in large amounts of capital in transit. For example, an investment by a TNC from country A to create a foreign affiliate in country B might be channeled through an SPE in country C. In the capital account of the balance of payments of investor home and host countries, transactions or positions with SPEs are included in either assets or liabilities of direct investors (parent firms) or direct investment enterprises (foreign affiliates) – indistinguishable from other FDI transactions or positions. Such amounts are considerable and can lead to misinterpretations of FDI data. In particular:

(i) SPE-related investment flows might lead to double counting in global FDI flows (in the example above, the same value of FDI is counted twice, from A to C, and from C to B); and

(ii) SPE-related flows might lead to misinterpretation of the origin of investment, where ultimate ownership is not taken into account (in the example, country B might consider that its inflows originate from country C, rather than from Country A).

In consultation with a number of countries that offer investors the option to create SPEs, and on the basis of information on SPE-related FDI obtained directly from those countries, UNCTAD removes SPE data from FDI flows and stocks, in order to minimize double counting. These countries include Austria, Hungary, Luxembourg, Mauritius and the Netherlands (box table I.1.1).

Box table I.1.1. FDI with and without SPEs reported by UNCTAD, 2013

FDI	Austria		Hungary		Luxembourg		Mauritius		Netherlands	
	With SPE	Without SPE (UNCTAD use)	With SPE	Without SPE (UNCTAD use)	With SPE	Without SPE (UNCTAD use)	With SPE	Without SPE (UNCTAD use)	With SPE	Without SPE (UNCTAD use)
FDI inflows	11.4	11.1	2.4	3.1	367.3	30.1	27.3	0.3	41.3	24.4
FDI ouflows	13.9	13.9	2.4	2.3	363.6	21.6	25.1	0.1	106.8	37.4
Inward FDI stock	286.3	183.6	255.0	111.0	3 204.8	141.4	312.6	3.5	3 861.8	670.1
Outward FDI stock	346.4	238.0	193.9	39.6	3 820.5	181.6	292.8	1.6	4 790.0	1 071.8

Source: UNCTAD, based on data from respective central banks.
Note: Stock data for Mauritius refer to 2012.

Similar issues arise in relation to offshore financial centres such as the British Virgin Islands and Cayman Islands. UNCTAD's FDI data include those economies because no official statistics are available to use in disentangling transit investment from other flows, as in the case of SPEs. However, for the most part UNCTAD excludes flows to and from these economies in interpreting data on investment trends for their respective regions. Offshore financial centres accounted for 8 per cent of global FDI inflows in 2013, with growth rates similar to global FDI; the impact on the analysis of global trends is therefore likely to be limited.

Source: UNCTAD.

FDI inflows to *Africa* rose by 4 per cent to $57 billion. Southern African countries, especially South Africa, experienced high inflows. Persistent political and social tensions continued to subdue flows to North Africa, whereas Sudan and Morocco registered solid growth of FDI. Nigeria's lower levels of FDI reflected the retreat of foreign transnational corporations (TNCs) from the oil industry.

In developed countries, inflows to *Europe* were up by 3 per cent compared with 2012. In the EU, Germany, Spain and Italy saw a substantial recovery

in their FDI inflows in 2013. In Spain, lower labour costs attracted the interests of manufacturing TNCs. The largest declines in inflows were observed in France, Hungary, Switzerland and the United Kingdom.

FDI flows to *North America* grew by 23 per cent as acquisitions by Asian investors helped sustain inflows to the region. The largest deals included the takeover of the Canadian upstream oil and gas company, Nexen, by CNOOC (China) for $19 billion; the acquisition of Sprint Nextel, the third

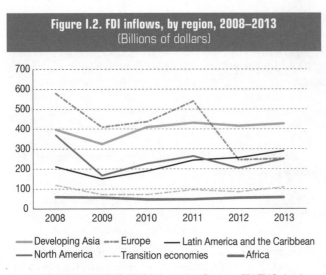

Figure I.2. FDI inflows, by region, 2008–2013
(Billions of dollars)

— Developing Asia　--- Europe　— Latin America and the Caribbean
— North America　---- Transition economies　— Africa

Source: UNCTAD FDI-TNC-GVC Information System, FDI/TNC database (www.unctad.org/fdistatistics).

largest wireless network operator in the United States, by Japanese telecommunications group Softbank for $21.6 billion, the largest deal ever by a Japanese company; and the $4.8 billion acquisition of the pork producer Smithfield by Shuanghui, the largest Chinese takeover of a United States company to date. FDI flows to the United States rose by 17 per cent, reflecting signs of economic recovery in the United States over the past year.

Transition economies experienced a 28 per cent rise in FDI inflows, reaching $108 billion – much of it driven by a single country. The Russian Federation saw FDI inflows jump by 57 per cent to $79 billion, making it the world's third largest recipient of FDI for the first time (figure I.3). The rise was predominantly ascribed to the increase in intracompany loans and the acquisition by BP (United Kingdom) of 18.5 per cent of Rosneft (Russia Federation) as part of Rosneft's $57 billion acquisition of TNK-BP (see box II.4).

In 2013, APEC absorbed half of global flows – on par with the G-20; the BRICS received more than one fifth. Among major regional and interregional groupings, two – Asia-Pacific Economic Cooperation (APEC) countries and the BRICS (Brazil, Russian Federation, India, China and South Africa) countries – saw a dramatic increase in their share of global FDI inflows from the pre-crisis

level (table I.1). APEC now accounts for more than half of global FDI flows, similar to the G-20, while the BRICS jumped to more than one fifth. In ASEAN and the Common Market of the South (MERCOSUR), the level of FDI inflows doubled from the pre-crisis level. Many regional and interregional groups in which developed economies are members (e.g. G-20, NAFTA) are all experiencing a slower recovery.

Mixed trends for the megaregional integration initiatives: TPP and RCEP shares in global flows grew while TTIP shares halved. The three megaregional integration initiatives – the Transatlantic Trade and Investment Partnership (TTIP), the Trans-Pacific Partnership (TPP) and the Regional Comprehensive Economic Partnership (RCEP) – show diverging FDI trends (see chapter II for details). The United States

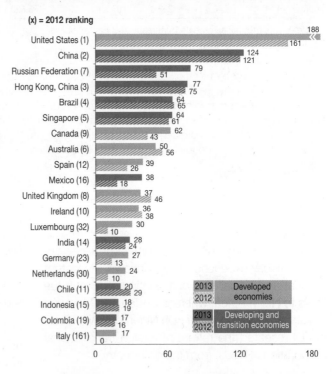

Figure I.3. FDI inflows: top 20 host economies, 2012 and 2013
(Billions of dollars)

Source: UNCTAD FDI-TNC-GVC Information System, FDI/TNC database (www.unctad.org/fdistatistics).

Note: British Virgin Islands is not included in the ranking because of its nature as an offshore financial centre (most FDI is in transit).

Table I.1. FDI inflows to selected regional and interregional groups, average 2005–2007, 2008–2013 (Billions of dollars)							
Regional/inter-regional groups	2005–2007 pre-crisis average	2008	2009	2010	2011	2012	2013
G-20	878	992	631	753	892	694	791
APEC	560	809	485	658	765	694	789
TPP	363	524	275	382	457	402	458
TTIP	838	858	507	582	714	377	434
RCEP	195	293	225	286	337	332	343
BRICS	157	285	201	237	286	266	304
NAFTA	279	396	184	250	287	221	288
ASEAN	65	50	47	99	100	118	125
MERCOSUR	31	59	30	65	85	85	85
Memorandum: percentage share in world FDI flows							
G-20	59	55	52	53	52	52	54
APEC	37	44	40	46	45	52	54
TPP	24	29	23	27	27	30	32
TTIP	56	47	41	41	42	28	30
RCEP	13	16	18	20	20	25	24
BRICS	11	16	16	17	17	20	21
NAFTA	19	22	15	18	17	17	20
ASEAN	4	3	4	7	6	9	9
MERCOSUR	2	3	2	5	5	6	6

Source: UNCTAD FDI-TNC-GVC Information System, FDI/TNC database (www.unctad.org/fdistatistics).
Note: G-20 = 19 individual members economies of the G20, excluding the European Union, which is the 20th member, APEC = Asia-Pacific Economic Cooperation, TTIP = Transatlantic Trade and Investment Partnership, TPP = Trans-Pacific Partnership, RCEP = Regional Comprehensive Economic Partnership, BRICS = Brazil, Russian Federation, India, China and South Africa, NAFTA = North American Free Trade Agreement, ASEAN = Association of Southeast Asian Nations, MERCOSUR = Common Market of the South. Ranked in descending order of the 2013 FDI flows.

and the EU, which are negotiating the formation of TTIP, saw their combined share of global FDI inflows cut nearly in half over the past seven years, from 56 per cent during the pre-crisis period to 30 per cent in 2013. The share of the 12 countries participating in the TPP negotiations was 32 per cent in 2013, markedly smaller than their share in world GDP of 40 per cent. RCEP, which is being negotiated between the 10 ASEAN member States and their 6 FTA partners, accounted for 24 per cent of global FDI flows in recent years, nearly twice as much as before the crisis.

b. FDI outflows

Global FDI outflows rose by 5 per cent to $1.41 trillion, up from $1.35 trillion in 2012. Investors from developing and transition economies continued their expansion abroad, in response to faster economic growth and investment liberalization (chapter III) as well as rising income streams from

high commodity prices. In 2013 these economies accounted for 39 per cent of world outflows; 15 years earlier their share was only 7 per cent (figure I.4). In contrast, TNCs from developed economies continued their "wait and see" approach, and their investments remained at a low level, similar to that of 2012.

FDI flows from developed countries continued to stagnate. FDI outflows from developed countries were unchanged from 2012 – at $857 billion – and still 55 per cent off their peak in 2007. Developed-country TNCs continued to hold large amounts of cash reserves in their foreign affiliates in the form of retained earnings, which constitute part of reinvested earnings, one of the components of FDI flows. This component reached a record level of 67 per cent (figure I.5).

Investments from the largest investor – the United States – dropped by 8 per cent to $338 billion, led by the decline in cross-border merger and acquisition

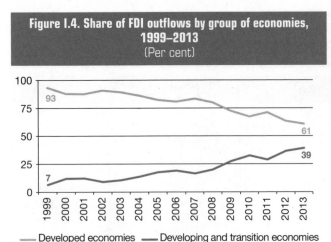

Figure I.4. Share of FDI outflows by group of economies, 1999–2013
(Per cent)

— Developed economies   — Developing and transition economies

Source: UNCTAD FDI-TNC-GVC Information System, FDI/TNC database (www.unctad.org/fdistatistics).

(M&A) purchases and negative intracompany loans. United States TNCs continued to accumulate reinvested earnings abroad, attaining a record level of $332 billion. FDI outflows from the EU rose by 5 per cent to $250 billion, while those from Europe as a whole increased by 10 per cent to $329 billion. With $60 billion, Switzerland became the largest outward investor in Europe, propelled by a doubling of reinvested earnings abroad and an increase in intracompany loans. Countries that had recorded a large decline in 2012, including Italy, the Netherlands and Spain, saw their outflows rebound sharply. In contrast, investments by TNCs from France,

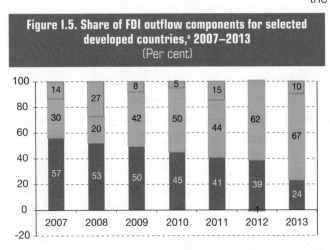

Figure I.5. Share of FDI outflow components for selected developed countries,ᵃ 2007–2013
(Per cent)

■ Equity outflows   ■ Reinvested earnings   ■ Other capital (intra-company loans)

Source: UNCTAD FDI-TNC-GVC Information System, FDI/TNC database (www.unctad.org/fdistatistics).

ᵃ Economies included are Belgium, Bulgaria, the Czech Republic, Denmark, Estonia, Germany, Hungary, Japan, Latvia, Lithuania, Luxembourg, the Netherlands, Norway, Poland, Portugal, Sweden, Switzerland, the United Kingdom and the United States.

Germany and the United Kingdom saw a substantial decline. TNCs from France and the United Kingdom undertook significant equity divestment abroad. Despite the substantial depreciation of the currency, investments from Japanese TNCs continued to expand, rising by over 10 per cent to a record $136 billion.

Flows from developing economies remained resilient, rising by 3 per cent. FDI from these economies reached a record level of $454 billion in 2013. Among developing regions, flows from developing Asia and Africa increased while those from Latin America and the Caribbean declined (figure I.6). Developing Asia remained a large source of FDI, accounting for more than one fifth of the world's total.

Flows from developing Asia rose by 8 per cent to $326 billion with diverging trends among subregions: East and South-East Asia TNCs experienced growth of 7 per cent and 5 per cent, respectively; FDI flows from West Asia surged by almost two thirds; and TNC activities from South Asia slid by nearly three quarters. In East Asia, investment from Chinese TNCs climbed by 15 per cent to $101 billion owing to a surge of cross-border M&As (examples include the $19 billion CNOOC-Nexen deal in Canada and the $5 billion Shuanghui-Smithfield Foods deal in the United States). In the meantime, investments from Hong Kong (China) grew by 4 per cent to $92 billion. The two East Asian economies have consolidated their positions among the leading sources of FDI in the world (figure I.7). Investment flows from the two other important sources in East Asia – the Republic of Korea and Taiwan Province of China – showed contrasting trends: investments by TNCs from the former declined by 5 per cent to $29 billion, while those by TNCs from the latter rose by 9 per cent to $14 billion.

FDI flows from Latin America and the Caribbean decreased by 8 per cent to $115 billion in 2013. Excluding flows to offshore financial centres (box I.1), they declined by 31 per cent to $33 billion. This drop was largely attributable to two developments: a decline in cross-border M&As and a strong increase in loan repayments to parent companies by

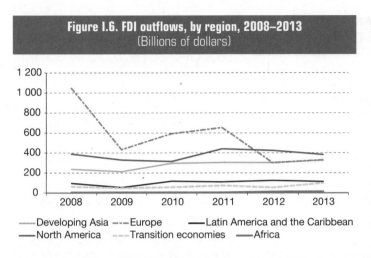

Figure I.6. FDI outflows, by region, 2008–2013
(Billions of dollars)

—— Developing Asia ---- Europe —— Latin America and the Caribbean
—— North America ---- Transition economies —— Africa

Source: UNCTAD FDI-TNC-GVC Information System, FDI/TNC database (www.unctad.org/fdistatistics).

Brazilian and Chilean foreign affiliates abroad. Colombian TNCs, by contrast, bucked the regional trend and more than doubled their cross-border M&As. Investments from TNCs registered in Caribbean countries increased by 4 per cent in 2013, constituting about three quarters of the region's total investments abroad.

FDI flows from transition economies increased significantly, by 84 per cent, reaching a new high of $99 billion. As in past years, Russian TNCs were involved in the most of the FDI projects, followed by TNCs from Kazakhstan and Azerbaijan. The value of cross-border M&A purchases by TNCs from the region rose significantly in 2013 – mainly as a result of the acquisition of TNK-BP Ltd (British Virgin Islands) by Rosneft; however, the number of such deals dropped.

2. FDI by mode of entry

The downward trend observed in 2012 both in FDI greenfield projects[1] and in cross-border M&As reversed in 2013, confirming that the general investment outlook improved (figure I.8). The value of announced greenfield projects increased by 9 per cent – remaining, however, considerably below historical levels – while the value of cross-border M&As increased by 5 per cent.

In 2013, both FDI greenfield projects and cross-border M&As displayed differentiated

patterns among groups of economies. Developing and transition economies largely outperformed developed countries, with an increase of 17 per cent in the values of announced greenfield projects (from $389 billion to $457 billion), and a sharp rise of 73 per cent for cross-border M&As (from $63 billion to $109 billion). By contrast, in developed economies both greenfield investment projects and cross-border M&As declined (by 4 per cent and 11 per cent, respectively). As a result, developing and transition economies accounted for historically high shares of the total values of greenfield investment and M&A projects (68 per cent and 31 per cent respectively).

The importance of developing and transition economies stands out clearly in

Figure I.7. FDI outflows: top 20 home economies, 2012 and 2013
(Billions of dollars)

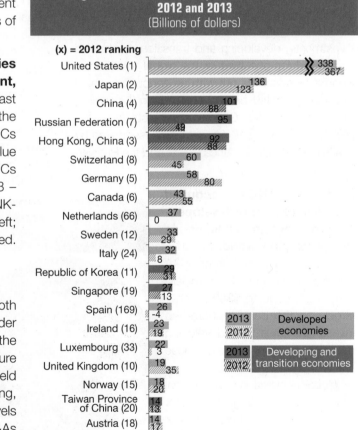

Source: UNCTAD FDI-TNC-GVC Information System, FDI/TNC database (www.unctad.org/fdistatistics).
Note: British Virgin Islands is not included in the ranking because of its nature as an offshore financial centre (most FDI is in transit).

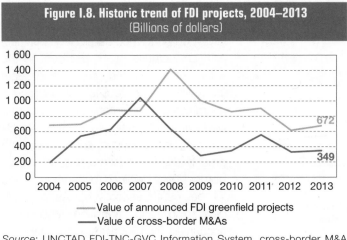

Figure I.8. Historic trend of FDI projects, 2004–2013
(Billions of dollars)

——— Value of announced FDI greenfield projects
——— Value of cross-border M&As

Source: UNCTAD FDI-TNC-GVC Information System, cross-border M&A database for M&As and information from the Financial Times Ltd, fDi Markets (www.fDimarkets.com) for greenfield projects.

their roles as acquirers. Their cross-border M&As rose by 36 per cent to $186 billion, accounting for 53 per cent of global cross-border M&As. Chinese firms invested a record $50 billion. A variety of firms, including those in emerging industries such as information technology (IT) and biotechnology, started to engage in M&As. As to outward greenfield investments, developing and transition economies accounted for one third of the global total. Hong Kong (China) stands out with an announced value of projects of $49 billion, representing 7 per cent of the global total. Greenfield projects from the BRICS registered a 16 per cent increase, driven by TNCs based in South Africa, Brazil and the Russian Federation.

Southern TNCs acquired significant assets of developed-country foreign affiliates in the developing world. In 2013, the value of cross-border M&A purchases increased marginally – by 5 per cent, to $349 billion – largely on the back of increased investment flows from developing and transition economies, whose TNCs captured a 53 per cent share of global acquisitions. The global rankings of the largest investor countries in terms of cross-border M&As reflect this pattern. For example, among the top 20 cross-border M&A investors, 12 were from developing and transition

economies – 7 more than in the case of FDI outflows. More than two thirds of gross cross-border M&As by Southern TNCs were directed to developing and transition economies. Half of these investments involved foreign affiliates of developed-country TNCs (figure I.9), transferring their ownership into the hands of developing-country TNCs.

This trend was particularly marked in the extractive industry, where the value of transactions involving sales by developed-country TNCs to developing-country-based counterparts represented over 80 per cent of gross acquisitions by South-based TNCs in the industry. In Africa as a whole, these purchases accounted for 74 per cent of all purchases on the continent. In the extractive sector, in particular, Asian TNCs have been making an effort to secure upstream reserves in order to satisfy growing domestic demand. At the same time, developed-country TNCs have been divesting assets in some areas, which eventually opens up opportunities for local or other developing-country firms to invest.

The leading acquirer in South-South deals was China, followed by Thailand, Hong Kong (China), Mexico and India. Examples of this trend include several megadeals such as the Italian oil and gas group Eni's sale of its subsidiary in Mozambique to PetroChina for over $4 billion; the oil and gas group

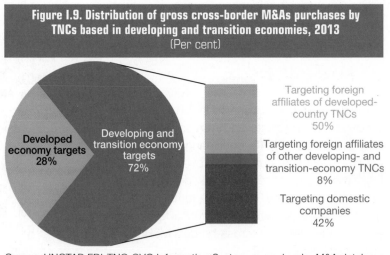

Figure I.9. Distribution of gross cross-border M&As purchases by TNCs based in developing and transition economies, 2013
(Per cent)

Developed economy targets 28%

Developing and transition economy targets 72%

Targeting foreign affiliates of developed-country TNCs 50%

Targeting foreign affiliates of other developing- and transition-economy TNCs 8%

Targeting domestic companies 42%

Source: UNCTAD FDI-TNC-GVC Information System, cross-border M&A database (www.unctad.org/fdistatistics).
Note: "Gross" refer to all cross-border M&As.

Apache's (United States) sale of its subsidiary in Egypt to Sinopec (China) for almost $3 billion; and ConocoPhillips's sale of its affiliates in Algeria to an Indonesian State-owned company, Pertamina, for $1.8 billion.

The banking industry followed the same pattern: for example, in Colombia, Bancolombia acquired the entire share capital of HSBC Bank (Panama) from HSBC (United Kingdom) for $2.1 billion; and in Egypt, Qatar National Bank, a majority-owned unit of the State-owned Qatar Investment Authority, acquired a 77 per cent stake of Cairo-based National Société Générale Bank from Société Générale (France) for $1.97 billion.

This trend – developing countries conducting a high share of the acquisitions of developed-country foreign affiliates – seems set to continue. Whereas in 2007 only 23 per cent of acquisitions from Southern TNCs from developing and transition economies targeted foreign affiliates of developed-country corporations, after the crisis this percentage increased quickly, jumping to 30 per cent in 2010 and 41 per cent in 2011 to half of all acquisitions in 2013.

3. FDI by sector and industry

At the sector level, the types of investment – greenfield activity and cross-border M&As – varied (figure I.10).

Primary sector. Globally, values of greenfield and M&A projects in the primary sector regained momentum in 2013 (increasing by 14 per cent and 32 per cent, respectively), with marked differences between groups of countries. Greenfield activity in the extractive industry by developed and transition economies plummeted to levels near zero, leaving almost all the business to take place in developing countries.

In developing countries the value of announced greenfield projects doubled, from $14 billion in 2012 to $27 billion in 2013; the value of cross-border M&As also increased, from a negative level of -$2.5 billion in 2012 to $25 billion in 2013. Although the value of greenfield projects in developing economies still remains below historic levels, cross-border M&As are back to recent historic highs (2010–2011).

Manufacturing. Investment in manufacturing was relatively stable in 2013, with a limited decrease in the value of greenfield projects (-4 per cent) and a more pronounced increase in the value of cross-border M&As (+11 per cent). In terms of greenfield projects, a sharp rise in investment activity was observed in the *textile and clothing* industry, with the value of announced investment projects totalling more than $24 billion, a historical high and more than twice the 2012 level. Conversely, the *automotive* industry registered a significant decline for the third year in a

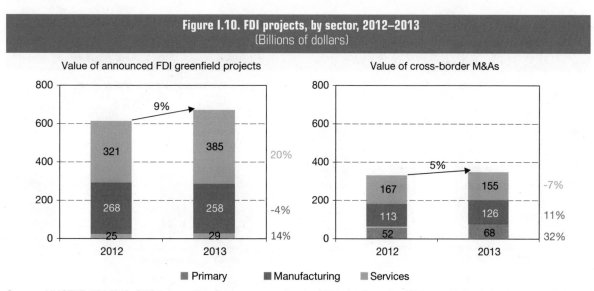

Figure I.10. FDI projects, by sector, 2012–2013
(Billions of dollars)

Value of announced FDI greenfield projects

Value of cross-border M&As

■ Primary   ■ Manufacturing   ■ Services

Source: UNCTAD FDI-TNC-GVC Information System, cross-border M&A database for M&As and information from the Financial Times Ltd, fDi Markets (www.fDimarkets.com) for greenfield projects.

row. As for cross-border M&As, the regional trends display a clear divergence between developed and developing economies. While the value of cross-border M&As in developed economies decreased by more than 20 per cent, developing economies enjoyed a fast pace of growth, seeing the value of such deals double. The growth in momentum was mainly driven by a boom in the value of cross-border M&As in the *food, beverages and tobacco* industry, which jumped from $12 billion in 2012 to almost $40 billion in 2013.

Services. Services continued to account for the largest shares of announced greenfield projects and M&A deals. In 2013, it was the fastest-growing sector in terms of total value of announced greenfield projects, with a significant increase of 20 per cent, while the value of M&A deals decreased moderately. As observed in the primary sector, the increase in greenfield projects took place in developing economies (+40 per cent compared with -5 per cent in developed economies and -7 per cent in transition economies). The growth engines of the greenfield investment activity in developing economies were *business services* (for which the value of announced greenfield project tripled compared with 2012) and *electricity, gas and water* (for which the value of greenfield projects doubled).

The analysis of the past sectoral distribution of new investment projects shows some

important emerging trends in regional investment patterns. In particular, although foreign investments in many poor developing countries historically have concentrated heavily on the extractive industry, analysis of FDI greenfield data in the last 10 years depicts a more nuanced picture: the share of FDI in the extractive industry is still substantial but not overwhelming and, most important, it is rapidly decreasing.

The analysis of the cumulative value of announced greenfield projects in developing countries for the last 10 years shows that investment in the primary sector (almost all of it in extractive industries) is more significant for Africa and least developed countries (LDCs) than for the average developed and developing economies (figure I.11). It also shows that in both Africa and LDCs, investment is relatively balanced among the three sectors. However, looking at greenfield investment in terms of the number of projects reveals a different picture, in which the primary sector accounts for only a marginal share in Africa and LDCs.

Over the past 10 years the share of the primary sector in greenfield projects has been gradually declining in both Africa and LDCs, while that of the services sector has increased significantly (figure I.12). The value share of announced greenfield projects in the primary sector has decreased from 53 per cent in 2004 to 11 per

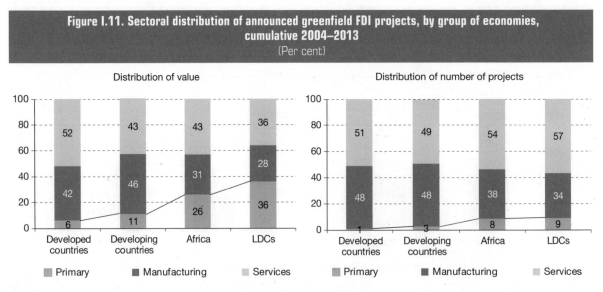

Figure I.11. Sectoral distribution of announced greenfield FDI projects, by group of economies, cumulative 2004–2013
(Per cent)

Source: UNCTAD, based on information from the Financial Times Ltd, fDi Markets (www.fDimarkets.com).

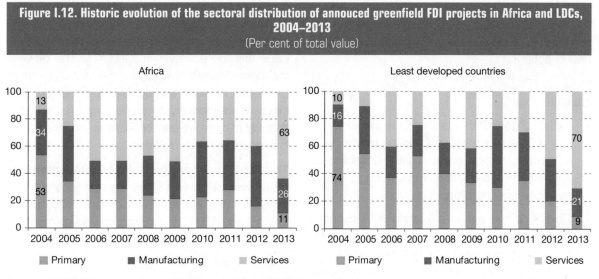

Figure I.12. Historic evolution of the sectoral distribution of annouced greenfield FDI projects in Africa and LDCs, 2004–2013
(Per cent of total value)

Source: UNCTAD, based on information from the Financial Times Ltd, fDi Markets (www.fDimarkets.com).

cent in 2013 for Africa, and from 74 per cent to 9 per cent for LDCs. By comparison, the share for the services sector has risen from 13 per cent to 63 per cent for Africa, and from 10 to 70 per cent for LDCs.

At the global level some industries have experienced dramatic changes in FDI patterns in the face of the uneven global recovery.

- *Oil and gas.* The shale gas revolution in the United States is a major game changer in the energy sector. Although questions concerning its environmental and economic sustainability remain, it is expected to shape the global FDI environment in the oil and gas industry and in other industries, such as petrochemicals, that rely heavily on gas supply.

- *Pharmaceuticals.* Although FDI in this industry remains concentrated in the United States, investments targeting developing economies are edging up. In terms of value, cross-border M&As have been the dominant mode, enabling TNCs to improve their efficiency and profitability and to strengthen their competitive advantages in the shortest possible time.

- *Retail industry.* With the rise of middle classes in developing countries, consumer markets are flourishing. In particular, the retail industry is attracting significant levels of FDI.

a. Oil and gas

The rapid development of shale gas is changing the North American natural gas industry. Since 2007 the production of natural gas in the region has doubled, driven by the boom in shale gas production, which is growing at an average annual rate of 50 per cent.[2] The shale gas revolution is also a key factor in the resurgence of United States manufacturing. The competitive gain produced by falling natural gas prices[3] represents a growth opportunity for the manufacturing sector, especially for industries, such as petrochemicals, that rely heavily on natural gas as a fuel.

The shale gas revolution may change the game in the global energy sector over the next decade and also beyond the United States. However, the realization of its potential depends crucially on a number of factors. Above all, the environmental impact of horizontal drilling and hydraulic fracturing is still a controversial issue, and opposition to the technique is strengthening. An additional element of uncertainty concerns the possibility of replicating the United States success story in other shale-rich countries, such as China or Argentina. Success will require the ability to put in place in the near future the necessary enablers, both "under the ground" (the technical capability to extract shale gas effectively and efficiently) and "above the ground" (a favourable business and investment climate to attract foreign players to share technical and technological know-how). In addition, new evidence suggests that recoverable resources may be less than expected (see chapter II.2.c).

From an FDI perspective, some interesting trends are emerging:

- In the United States oil and gas industry, the role of foreign capital supplied by major TNCs is growing as the shale market consolidates and smaller domestic players need to share development and production costs.

- Cheap natural gas is attracting new capacity investments, including foreign investments, to United States manufacturing industries that are characterized by heavy use of natural gas, such as petrochemicals and plastics. Reshoring of United States manufacturing TNCs is also an expected effect of the lowering of prices in the United States gas market.

- TNCs and State-owned enterprises (SOEs) from countries rich in shale resources, such as China, are strongly motivated to establish partnerships (typically in the form of joint ventures) with United States players to acquire the technical expertise needed to lead the shale gas revolution in their countries.

The FDI impact on the United States oil and gas industry: a market consolidation story. From an FDI perspective, the impact of the shale revolution on the United States oil and gas industry is an M&A story. In the start-up (greenfield) stage, the shale revolution was led by North American independents rather than oil and gas majors. Greenfield data confirm that, despite the shale gas revolution, FDI greenfield activity in the United States oil and gas industry has collapsed in the last five years, from almost $3 billion in 2008 (corresponding to some 5 per cent of all United States greenfield activity) to $0.5 billion in 2013 (or 1 per cent of all greenfield activity).[4] Only in a second stage will the oil and gas majors enter the game, either engaging in M&A operations or establishing partnerships, typically joint ventures, with local players who are increasingly eager to share the development costs and ease the financial pressure.[5]

Analysis of cross-border M&A deals in the recent years (figure I.13) shows that deals related to shale

gas have been a major driver of cross-border M&A activity in the United States oil and gas industry, accounting for more than 70 per cent of the total value of such activity in the industry. The peak of the consolidation wave occurred in 2011, when the value of shale-related M&As exceeded $30 billion, corresponding to some 90 per cent of the total value of cross-border M&As in the oil and gas industry in the United States.

The FDI impact on the United States chemical industries: a growth story. The collapse of North American gas prices, down by one third to one fourth since 2008, is boosting new investments in United States chemical industries.

Unlike in the oil and gas industry, a significant part of the foreign investment in the United States chemical industry goes to greenfield investment projects. A recent report by the American Chemical Council[6] confirms the trend toward new capacity investments. On the basis of investment projects that had been announced by March 2013, the report estimates the cumulative capital expenditure in the period 2010–2020 attributable to the shale gas revolution at $71.7 billion. United States TNCs such as ExxonMobil, Chevron and Dow Chemicals will play a significant role in this expenditure, with investments already planned for several billion dollars.

These operations may also entail a reshoring of current foreign business, with a potential negative

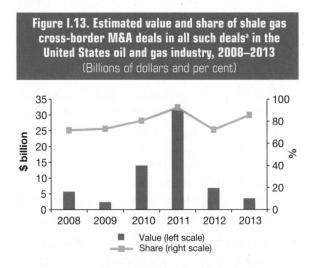

Figure I.13. Estimated value and share of shale gas cross-border M&A deals in all such deals[a] in the United States oil and gas industry, 2008–2013
(Billions of dollars and per cent)

- ■ Value (left scale)
- ■ Share (right scale)

Source: UNCTAD FDI-TNC-GVC Information System, cross-border M&A database for M&As; other various sources.
[a] Includes changes of ownership.

impact (through divestments) on inward FDI to traditionally cheap production locations such as West Asia or China (see chapter II.2.c). TNCs from other countries are also actively seeking investment opportunities in the United States. According to the Council's report, nearly half of the cumulative $71.7 billion in investments is coming from foreign companies, often through the relocation of plants to the United States. The investment wave involves not only TNCs from the developed world; those from developing and transition economies are also increasingly active, aiming to capture the United States shale opportunity.[7]

As a consequence, the most recent data show a significant shift in global greenfield activity in chemicals towards the United States: in 2013 the country's share in chemical greenfield projects (excluding pharmaceutical products) reached a record high of 25 per cent, from historical levels between 5 and 10 per cent – well above the average United States share for all other industries (figure I.14).

The FDI impact on other shale-rich countries (e.g. China): a knowledge-sharing story. TNCs, including SOEs from countries rich in shale resources, are strongly motivated to establish partnerships with the United States and other international players to acquire the technical know-how to replicate the success of the United States shale revolution in their home countries. In terms of FDI, this is likely to have a twofold effect:

- Outward FDI flows to the United States are expected to increase as these players proactively look for opportunities to acquire know-how in the field through co-management (with domestic companies) of United States shale projects. Chinese companies have been among the most active players. In 2013, for example, Sinochem entered into a $1.7 billion joint venture with Pioneer Natural Resources to acquire a stake in the Wolcamp Shale in Texas.

- Foreign capital in shale projects outside the United States is expected to grow as companies from shale-rich countries are seeking partnerships with foreign companies to develop their domestic shale projects. In China the two giant State oil and gas companies,

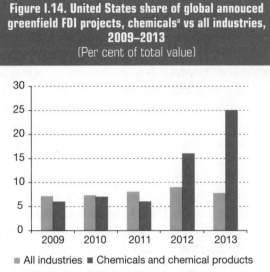

Figure I.14. United States share of global annouced greenfield FDI projects, chemicals[a] vs all industries, 2009–2013
(Per cent of total value)

■ All industries ■ Chemicals and chemical products

Source: UNCTAD FDI-TNC-GVC Information System, information from the Financial Times Ltd, fDi Markets (www.fDimarkets.com).
[a] Excluding the pharmaceutical industry.

PetroChina and CNOOC, have signed a number of agreements with major western TNCs, including Shell. In some cases these agreements involve only technical assistance and support; in others they also involve actual foreign capital investment. This is the case with the Shell-PetroChina partnership in the Sichuan basin, which entails a $1 billion investment from Shell. In other shale-rich countries such as Argentina and Australia the pattern is similar, with a number of joint ventures between domestic companies and international players.

b. Pharmaceuticals

A number of factors caused a wave of restructuring and new market-seeking investments in the pharmaceuticals industry. They include the "patent cliff" faced by some large TNCs,[8] increasing demand for generic drugs, and growth opportunities in emerging markets. A number of developed-country TNCs are divesting non-core business segments and outsourcing research and development (R&D) activities,[9] while acquiring or merging with firms in both developed and developing economies to secure new streams of revenues and to optimize costs. Global players in this industry are keen to gain access to high-quality, low-cost generic drug manufacturers.[10] To save time and resources, instead of developing new products from scratch, TNCs are looking for acquisition opportunities in successful research start-ups and generics firms (UNCTAD 2011b). Some focus on smaller biotechnology firms that are open to in-licensing activities and collaboration. Others look for deals to develop generic versions of medicines.[11] Two other factors – the need to deploy vast reserves of retained earnings held overseas and the desire for tax savings – are also driving developed-country TNCs to acquire assets abroad. A series of megadeals over the last two decades has reshaped the industry.[12]

FDI in pharmaceuticals[13] has been concentrated in developed economies, especially in the United States – the largest pharmaceuticals market for FDI.[14] Although the number of greenfield FDI projects announced was similar to the number of cross-border M&As,[15] the transaction values of the M&As (figure I.15) were notably greater than the announced values of the greenfield projects for the entire period (figure I.16). The impact of M&A deals in biological products on the overall transaction volume became more prominent since 2009. After a rise in 2011, these cross-border M&A activities – both in value and in the number of deals – dropped in 2012–2013. The slowdown also reflects a smaller number of megadeals involving large TNCs in developed economies.

Announced greenfield investments in developing economies have been relatively more important than developed-country projects since 2009, when they hit a record $5.5 billion (figure I.16). In 2013, while greenfield FDI in developed economies stagnated ($3.8 billion), announced greenfield investments in developing economies ($4.3 billion) represented 51 per cent of global greenfield FDI in pharmaceuticals (compared with an average of 40 per cent for the period 2003–2012).

Pharmaceutical TNCs are likely to continue to seek growth opportuni-

ties through acquisitions, pursuing growth in emerging markets and opportunities for new product development and marketing.[16] Restructuring efforts by developed-country TNCs are gaining momentum, and further consolidation of the global generic market is highly likely.[17] During the first quarter of 2014, the transaction value of cross-border M&As ($22.8 billion in 55 deals) already surpassed the value recorded for all of 2013.[18] Announcements of potential deals strongly suggest a return of megadeals,[19] led by cash-rich TNCs holding record amounts of cash reserves in their foreign affiliates.[20]

The increasing interest of pharmaceuticals TNCs in emerging markets can also be witnessed in the trends in cross-border M&As. In developing economies, the transaction value of cross-border M&A deals in pharmaceuticals, including biological products, soared in 2008 (from $2.2 billion in 2007 to $7.9 billion),[21] driven by the $5.0 billion acquisition of Ranbaxy Laboratories (India) by Daiichi Sankyo (Japan).[22] It hit another peak ($7.5 billion) in 2010, again led by a $3.7 billion deal that targeted India.[23] As shown in figure I.15, transaction volumes in developing and transition economies remain a fraction of global cross-border M&A activities in this industry, but their shares are expanding. In 2013, at $6.6 billion,[24] their share in global pharmaceutical deals reached the highest on record (figure I.17).[25]

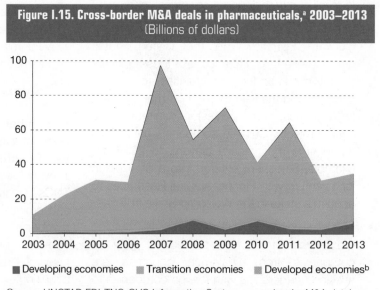

Figure I.15. Cross-border M&A deals in pharmaceuticals,[a] 2003–2013
(Billions of dollars)

■ Developing economies   ■ Transition economies   ■ Developed economies[b]

Source: UNCTAD FDI-TNC-GVC Information System, cross-border M&A database.
a   Includes biological products.
b   A substantial part of pharmaceuticals in developed countries is accounted for by biological products.

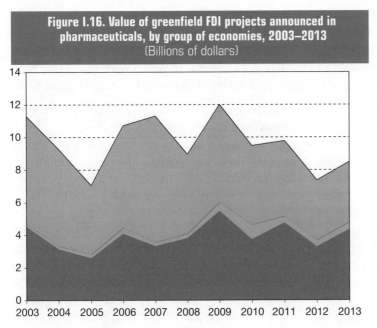

Figure I.16. Value of greenfield FDI projects announced in pharmaceuticals, by group of economies, 2003–2013
(Billions of dollars)

■Developing economies ■Transition economies ■Developed economies

Source: UNCTAD, based on information from the Financial Times Ltd, fDi Markets (www.fDimarkets.com).

Pharmaceutical TNCs' growing interest in emerging markets as a new platform for growth will expand opportunities for developing and transition economies to attract investment. In Africa, for example, where the growing middle class is making the market more attractive to the industry, the scale and scope of manufacturing and R&D investments are likely to expand to meet increasing demands for drugs to treat non-communicable diseases.[26] At the same time, TNCs may become more cautious about their operations and prospects in emerging markets as they face shrinking margins for generics[27] as well as bribery investigations,[28] concerns about patent protection of branded drugs,[29] and failures of acquired developing-country firms to meet quality and regulatory compliance requirements.[30]

For some developing and transition economies, the changing global environment in this industry poses new challenges. For example, as India and other generic-drug-manufacturing countries start to export more drugs to developed economies, one possible scenario is a supply shortage in poor countries, leading to upward pressures on price,

which will adversely affect access to inexpensive, high-quality generic drugs by people in need (UNCTAD 2013a). In Bangladesh, where the domestic manufacturing base for generics has been developed by restricting FDI and benefitting from TRIPS exemptions, the Government will have to make substantial changes in its policies and in development strategies pertaining to its pharmaceutical industry in order to achieve sustainable growth.[31]

c. Retail

Changing industrial context. The global retail industry is in the midst of an industrial restructuring, driven by three important changes. First, the rise of e-commerce is changing consumers' purchasing behaviour and exerts strong pressures on the traditional retail sector, particularly in developed countries and high-income developing countries. Second, strong economic growth and the rapid expansion of the middle class have created important retail markets in not only large emerging

Figure I.17. Cross-border M&A deals in pharmaceuticals[a] targeted at developing and transition economies, 2004–2013

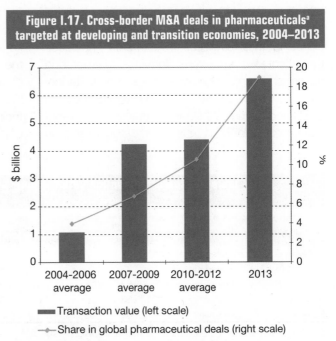

■Transaction value (left scale)
◆Share in global pharmaceutical deals (right scale)

Source: UNCTAD FDI-TNC-GVC Information System, cross-border M&A database.
[a] Includes biological products.

markets but also other relatively small developing countries. Third, competition has intensified, and margins narrowed, as market growth has slowed. In some large emerging markets, foreign retailers now face difficulties because of the rising number of domestic retailers and e-commerce companies alike, as well as rising operational costs due to higher real estate prices, for example.

These changes have significantly affected the internationalization strategies and practices of global retailers. Some large retail chains based in developed countries have started to optimize the scale of their businesses to fewer stores and smaller formats. They do this first in their home countries and other developed-country markets, but now the reconfiguration has started to affect their operations in emerging markets. In addition, their internationalization strategies have become more selective: a number of the world's largest retailers have slowed their expansion in some large markets (e.g. Brazil, China) and are giving more attention to other markets with greater growth potential (e.g. sub-Saharan Africa).

Global retailers slow their expansion in large emerging markets. Highly internationalized, the top five retail TNCs (table I.2) account for nearly 20 per cent of the total sales of the world's 250 largest retailers, and their share in total foreign sales is more than 30 per cent.[32] The latest trends in their overseas investments showcase the effects of an overall industry restructuring on firms' international operations. For instance, the expansion of Wal-Mart (United States) in Brazil and China has slowed. After years of rapid expansion, Wal-Mart has nearly 400 stores in

China, accounting for about 11 per cent of Chinese hypermarket sales. In October 2013, the company announced that it would close 25 underperforming stores, some of which were gained through the acquisition of Trust-Mart (China) in 2007.[33]

A number of companies undertake divestments abroad in order to raise cash and shore up balance sheets,[34] and it seems that regional and national retailers have accordingly taken the opportunity to expand their market shares, including through the acquisition of assets sold by TNCs. Carrefour (France) sold $3.6 billion in assets in 2012, withdrawing from Greece, Colombia and Indonesia. In 2013, the French retailer continued to downsize and divest internationally. In April, it sold a 12 per cent stake in a joint venture in Turkey to its local partner, Sabanci Holding, for $79 million. In May, it sold a 25 per cent stake in another joint venture in the Middle East to local partner MAF for $680 million. Carrefour has also closed a number of stores in China.

New growth markets stand out as a focus of international investment. Some relatively low-income countries in South America, sub-Saharan Africa and South-East Asia have become increasingly attractive to FDI by the world's top retailers. After the outbreak of the global financial crisis, the international expansion of large United States and European retailers slowed owing to economic recession and its effects on consumer spending in many parts of the world. Retailers' expansion into large emerging markets also slowed, as noted above. However, Western retailers continued to establish and expand their presence in the new growth markets, because of their strong economic growth, burgeoning middle

Table I.2. Top 5 TNCs in the retail industry, ranked by foreign assets, 2012
(Billions of dollars and number of employees)

Corporation	Home economy	Sales		Assets		Employment		Countries of operation	Transnationality Index[a]
		Foreign	Total	Foreign	Total	Foreign	Total		
Wal-Mart Stores Inc	United States	127	447	84	193	800 000	2 200 000	28	0.76
Tesco PLC	United Kingdom	35	103	39	76	219 298	519 671	33	0.84
Carrefour SA	France	53	98	34	61	267 718	364 969	13	0.57
Metro AG	Germany	53	86	27	46	159 344	248 637	33	0.62
Schwarz Group[b]	Germany	49	88	..	..	..	..	26	0.56

Source: UNCTAD, based on data from Thomson ONE.

[a] The Transnationality Index is calculated as the average of the following three ratios: foreign to total assets, foreign to total sales and foreign to total employment, except for Schwarz Group which is based on the foreign to total sales ratio.

[b] Data of 2011.

class, increasing purchasing power and youthful populations.

Africa has the fastest-growing middle class in the world: according to the African Development Bank, the continent's middle class numbers about 120 million now and will grow to 1.1 billion by 2060. Wal-Mart plans to open 90 new stores across sub-Saharan Africa over the next three years, as it targets growth markets such as Nigeria and Angola. As Carrefour retreats from other foreign markets, it aims to open its first store in Africa in 2015, in Côte d'Ivoire, followed by seven other countries (Cameroon, Congo, the Democratic Republic of the Congo, Gabon, Ghana, Nigeria and Senegal). In the luxury goods segment as well, some of the world's leading companies are investing in stores and distribution networks in Africa (chapter II.1).

More and more cross-border M&As, including in e-commerce. Global retailers invest internationally through both greenfield investments and cross-border M&As, and sometimes they operate in foreign markets through non-equity modes, most notably franchising. Available data show that, since 2009, international greenfield investment in retail dropped for three years before a recent pickup; by contrast, the value of cross-border M&As in the sector has increased continuously. In 2012, driven by the proactive international expansion of some large TNCs, total global sales of cross-border M&As surpassed the pre-crisis level, and that amount continued to rise in 2013.

A number of megadeals have been undertaken in industrialized economies over the past few years.[35] At the same time, the world's leading retailers have expanded into emerging markets more and more through cross-border M&As. For instance, in 2009, Wal-Mart (United States) acquired a 58 per cent stake in DYS, Chile's largest food retailer, with an investment of $1.5 billion; and in 2012, it acquired South Africa's Massmart for $2.4 billion. International M&As have also targeted e-commerce companies in key markets, particularly China, where online retail sales have reached almost the same level as in the United States. Apart from foreign e-commerce companies, international private equity investors such as Bain Capital and IDG Capital Partners (both from the United States) and sovereign wealth funds (SWFs) such as Temasek

Company	Foreign investors	Investment ($ million)	Year
Alibaba	Sequoia Capital, Silver Lake, Temasek	3 600	2011, 2012
JD.com	Tiger Fund, HilhouseCapitalManagement	1 500	2011
Yougou	Belly International	443	2011
Gome	Bain Capital	432	2010
VANCL	Temasek, IDG Capital	230	2011

Source: UNCTAD, based on ChinaVenture (www.chinaventure.com.cn).

(Singapore) have invested in leading Chinese e-commerce companies, including in Alibaba and JD.com before their planned initial public offering (IPO) in the United States (table I.3).

4. FDI by selected types of investors

This subsection discusses recent trends in FDI by private equity funds, SWFs and SOEs.

a. Private equity firms

In 2013, the unspent outstanding funds of private equity firms (so-called dry powder) grew further to a record level of $1.07 trillion, an increase of 14 per cent over the previous year. Firms thus did not use funds for investment despite the fact that they could raise more money for leverage owing to quantitative easing and low interest rates. This is reflected also in lower levels of FDI by such firms. In 2013, their new cross-border investment (usually through M&As due to the nature of the business) was only $171 billion ($83 billion net of divestments), accounting for 21 per cent of gross cross-border M&As. This was 10 percentage points lower than in the peak year of 2007 (table I.4). Private equity markets remain muted. In addition, private equity firms are facing increasing scrutiny from regulatory and tax authorities, as well as rising pressure to find cost savings in their operations and portfolio firms.

Private equity firms are becoming relatively more active in emerging markets (figure I.18). In particular, in Asia they acquired more companies, pushing up the value of M&As. Examples include the acquisitions

Table I.4. Cross-border M&As by private equity firms, 1996–2013						
(Number of deals and value)						
	Number of deals		Gross M&As		Net M&As	
Year	Number	Share in total (%)	Value ($ billion)	Share in total (%)	Value ($ billion)	Share in total (%)
1996	989	16	44	16	18	12
1997	1 074	15	58	15	18	10
1998	1 237	15	63	9	29	8
1999	1 466	15	81	9	27	5
2000	1 478	14	83	6	30	3
2001	1 467	17	85	11	36	8
2002	1 329	19	72	14	14	6
2003	1 589	23	91	23	31	19
2004	1 720	22	134	25	62	31
2005	1 892	20	209	23	110	20
2006	1 898	18	263	23	118	19
2007	2 108	17	541	31	292	28
2008	2 015	18	444	31	109	17
2009	2 186	24	115	18	70	25
2010	2 280	22	147	19	68	20
2011	2 026	19	161	15	69	12
2012	2 300	23	192	23	67	20
2013	2 043	24	171	21	83	24

Source: UNCTAD FDI-TNC-GVC Information System, cross-border M&A database (www.unctad.org/fdistatistics).

Note: Value on a net basis takes into account divestments by private equity funds. Thus it is calculated as follows: Purchases of companies abroad by private equity funds (-) Sales of foreign affiliates owned by private equity funds. The table includes M&As by hedge and other funds (but not sovereign wealth funds). Private equity firms and hedge funds refer to acquirers as "investors not elsewhere classified". This classification is based on the Thomson ONE database on M&As.

of Ping An Insurance of China by a group of investors from Thailand for $9.4 billion and Focus Media Holding (China) by Giovanna Acquisition (Cayman Islands) for $3.6 billion. Outside Asia, some emerging economies, such as Brazil, offer opportunities for the growth of private equity activity. For example, in Latin America, where Latin America-based private equity firms invested $8.9 billion in 2013, with $3.5 billion going to infrastructure, oil and energy.[36] In addition, FDI by foreign private equity firms for the same year was $6 billion. In contrast, slow M&A growth in regions such as Europe meant fewer opportunities for private equity firms to pick up assets that might ordinarily be sold off during or after an acquisition. Furthermore, the abundance of cheap credit and better asset performance in areas such as real estate made private equity less attractive.

In 2013, private equity funds attracted attention with their involvement in delisting major public companies such as H. J. Heinz and Dell (both United States), and with large cross-border M&As such as the acquisition of Focus Media Holding, as mentioned above. Furthermore, increases in

both club deals – deals involving several private equity funds – and secondary buyouts, in which investments change hands from one private equity fund to another, may signal a diversification of strategies in order to increase corporate value in the context of the generally low investment activity by private equity firms.

Secondary buyouts have been increasingly popular also as an exit route in 2013, particularly in Western Europe. Some of the largest private equity deals of the year were sales to other buyout firms. For example, Springer Science+Business Media (Germany), owned by EQT Partners (United States) and the Government of Singapore Investment Corporation (GIC), was sold to BC Partners (United Kingdom) for $4.4 billion. Nevertheless, there is still an overhang of assets that were bought before the financial crisis that have yet to realize their expected value and have not been sold.

Although emerging market economies appear to provide the greater potential for growth, developed countries still offer investment targets, in particular

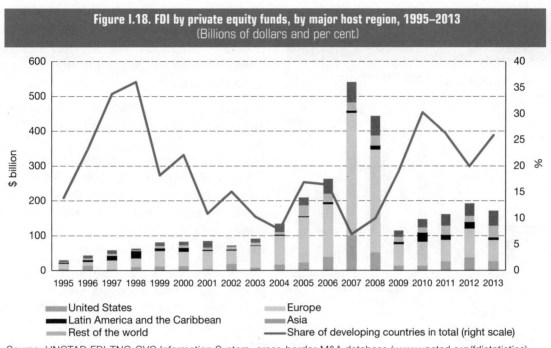

Figure I.18. FDI by private equity funds, by major host region, 1995–2013
(Billions of dollars and per cent)

■ United States
■ Latin America and the Caribbean
■ Rest of the world
■ Europe
■ Asia
— Share of developing countries in total (right scale)

Source: UNCTAD FDI-TNC-GVC Information System, cross-border M&A database (www.unctad.org/fdistatistics).
Note: Data refer to gross values of M&As by private equity firms; they are not adjusted to exclude FDI by SWFs.

in small and medium-size enterprises (SMEs), which are crucial to economic recovery and to the absorption of unemployment. In the EU, where one of the dominant concerns for SMEs is access to finance – a concern that was further aggravated during the crisis[37] – private equity funds are an important alternative source of finance.

b. SWFs

SWFs continue to grow, spread geographically, but their FDI is still small. Assets under management of more than 70 major SWFs approached $6.4 trillion based in countries around the world, including in sub-Saharan Africa. In addition to the $150 billion Public Investment Corporation of South Africa, SWFs were established recently in Angola, Nigeria and Ghana, with oil proceeds of $5 billion, $1 billion and $500 million, respectively. Since 2010, SWF assets have grown faster than the assets of any other institutional investor group, including private equity and hedge funds. In the EU, for example, between 15 and 25 per cent of listed companies have SWF shareholders. In 2013, FDI flows of SWFs, which had remained subdued after the crisis, reached $6.7 billion, with cumulative flows of $130 billion (figure I.19).

FDI by SWFs is still small, corresponding to less than 2 per cent of total assets under management and represented mostly by a few major SWFs. Nevertheless, the geographical scope of their investment has recently been expanding to markets such as sub-Saharan Africa. In 2011, China Investment Corporation (CIC) bought a 25 per cent stake in Shanduka Groupe (South Africa) for $250 million, and in late 2013 Temasek (Singapore's SWF) paid $1.3 billion to buy a 20 per cent stake in gas fields in the United Republic of Tanzania.

SWFs' investment portfolios are expanding across numerous sectors, including the retail and consumer sectors, where Temasek's acquisition of a 25 per cent stake in AS Watson (Hong Kong, China) for $5.7 billion in early 2014 is an example. SWFs are also expanding their investment in real estate markets in developed countries. For example, in early 2014, the Abu Dhabi Investment Authority and Singapore's GIC purchased an office building in New York for $1.3 billion, and China's CIC spent £800 million for an office area in London. In December 2013, GIC and Kuwait's government real estate company bought office buildings in London for £1.7 billion. Norway's Government Pension Fund Global, the largest SWF, also started

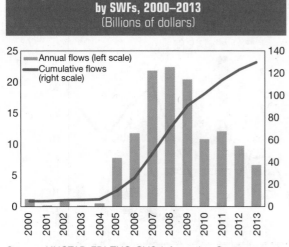

Figure I.19. Annual and cumulative value of FDI by SWFs, 2000–2013
(Billions of dollars)

Source: UNCTAD FDI-TNC-GVC Information System, cross-border M&A database for M&As and information from the Financial Times Ltd, fDi Markets (www.fDimarkets.com) for greenfield projects.

Note: Data include value of flows for both cross-border M&As and greenfield FDI projects and only investments by SWFs which are the sole and immediate investors. Data do not include investments made by entities established by SWFs or those made jointly with other investors. In 2003–2013, cross-border M&As accounted for about 80 per cent of total.

to invest in real estate outside Europe in 2013, with up to 5 per cent of its total funds. Global real estate investment by SWFs is expected to run to more than $1 trillion in 2014, a level similar to the pre-crisis position seven years ago.[38]

SWF motives and types of investment targets differ. The share of investment by SWFs in the Gulf region, for example, has been increasing in part due to external factors, such as the euro crisis, but also in support of boosting public investment at home. Gulf-based SWFs are increasingly investing in their domestic public services (health, education and infrastructure), which may lower their level of FDI further. For countries with SWFs, public investment is increasingly seen as having better returns (financial and social) than portfolio investment abroad. Chapter IV looks at ways that countries without SWFs may be able to tap into this public-services investment expertise.

By contrast, Malaysia's SWF, Khazanah, like many other SWFs,[39] views itself more as a strategic development fund. Although 35 per cent of its assets are invested abroad, it targets the bulk of its investment

at home to strategic development sectors, such as utilities, telecommunications and other infrastructure, which are relevant for sustainable development, as well as trying to crowd in private-sector investment.[40]

In an effort to source funds widely and attract private investment for public investment, some SWFs are engaged in public offerings. For example, in 2013, Doha Global Investment Company (backed by the Qatari SWF) decided to launch an IPO. The IPO will offer shares only to Qatari nationals and private Qatari companies, thereby sharing some of the benefits of Qatari sovereign investments directly with the country's citizens and companies.

SWFs are undertaking more joint activity with private equity fund managers and management companies, in part as a function of the decline of private equity activity since the crisis. SWFs are also taking larger stakes in private equity firms as the funds look for greater returns following declining yields on their traditional investments (e.g. government bonds). SWFs may also be favouring partnerships with private equity firms as a way of securing managerial expertise in order to support more direct involvement in their acquisitions; for example, Norway's Government Pension Fund Global, which is a shareholder of Eurazeo (France), Ratos (Sweden), Ackermans en Van Haaren (Belgium) and other companies; and the United Arab Emirates' Mubadala, which is a shareholder in The Carlyle Group (United States). These approaches by SWFs to using and securing funds for further investment provide useful lessons for other financial firms in financing for development.

c. SOEs

State-owned TNCs (SO-TNCs) represent a small part of the global TNC universe,[41] but the number of their foreign affiliates and the scale of their foreign assets are significant. According to UNCTAD's estimates, there are at least 550 SO-TNCs; their foreign assets are estimated at more than $2 trillion.[42] Both developed and developing countries have SO-TNCs, some of them among the largest TNCs in the world (table I.5). A number of European countries, such as Denmark, France and Germany, as well as the BRICS, are home to the most important SO-TNCs.

Table I.5. The top 15 non-financial State-owned TNCs,[a] ranked by foreign assets, 2012
(Billions of dollars and number of employees)

SO-TNCs	Home country	Industry	State share	Assets Foreign	Assets Total	Sales Foreign	Sales Total	Employment Foreign	Employment Total	Transnationality Index[b]
GDF Suez	France	Utilities	36	175	272	79	125	110 308	219 330	0.59
Volkswagen Group	Germany	Motor vehicles	20	158	409	199	248	296 000	533 469	0.58
Eni SpA	Italy	Oil and gas	26	133	185	86	164	51 034	77 838	0.63
Enel SpA	Italy	Utilities	31	132	227	66	109	37 588	73 702	0.57
EDF SA	France	Utilities	84	103	331	39	93	30 412	154 730	0.31
Deutsche Telekom AG	Germany	Telecommunications	32	96	143	42	75	113 502	232 342	0.58
CITIC Group	China	Diversified	100	72	515	10	52	30 806	140 028	0.18
Statoil ASA	Norway	Oil and gas	67	71	141	28	121	2 842	23 028	0.29
General Motors Co	United States	Motor vehicles	16	70	149	65	152	108 000	213 000	0.47
Vattenfall AB	Sweden	Utilities	100	54	81	19	25	23 864	32 794	0.72
Orange S.A.	France	Telecommunications	27	54	119	24	56	65 492	170 531	0.42
Airbus Group	France	Aircraft	12	46	122	67	73	88 258	140 405	0.64
Vale SA	Brazil	Metal mining	3[c]	46	131	38	48	15 680	85 305	0.45
COSCO	China	Transport and storage	100	40	52	19	30	7 355	130 000	0.50
Petronas	Malaysia	Oil and gas	100	39	150	43	73	8 653	43 266	0.35

Source: UNCTAD.

[a] These TNCs are at least 10 per cent owned by the State or public entities, or the State/public entity is the largest shareholder.

[b] The Transnationality Index is calculated as the average of the following three ratios: foreign to total assets, foreign to total sales and foreign to total employment.

[c] State owns 12 golden shares that give it veto power over certain decisions.

In line with the industrial characteristics of SOEs in general, SO-TNCs tend to be active in industries that are capital-intensive, require monopolistic positions to gain the necessary economies of scale or are deemed to be of strategic importance to the country. Therefore, their global presence is considerable in the extractive industries (oil and gas exploration and metal mining), infrastructure industries and public utilities (electricity, telecommunication, transport and water), and financial services. The oil and gas industry offers a typical example of the prominence of SOEs, particularly in the developing world: SOEs control more than three fourths of global crude oil reserves. In addition, some of the world's largest TNCs in the oil and gas industry are owned and controlled by developing-country governments, including CNPC, Sinopec and CNOOC in China, Gazprom in the Russian Federation, Petronas in Malaysia, Petrobras in Brazil and Saudi Aramco in Saudi Arabia.

Owing to the general lack of data on FDI by companies with different ownership features, it is difficult to assess the global scale of FDI flows related to SO-TNCs. However, the value of FDI projects, including both cross-border M&A purchases and

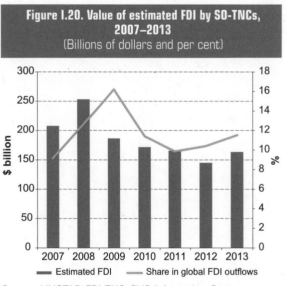

Figure I.20. Value of estimated FDI by SO-TNCs, 2007–2013
(Billions of dollars and per cent)

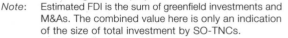

Source: UNCTAD FDI-TNC-GVC Information System, cross-border M&A database for M&As and information from the Financial Times Ltd, fDi Markets (www.fDimarkets.com) for greenfield projects.

Note: Estimated FDI is the sum of greenfield investments and M&As. The combined value here is only an indication of the size of total investment by SO-TNCs.

announced greenfield investments, can provide a rough picture of such FDI flows and their fluctuation over the years (figure I.20). Overall, FDI by SO-TNCs had declined in every year after the global financial crisis, but in 2013 such investment started to pick up, and the upward trend is likely to be sustained in 2014, driven partly by rising investments in extractive industries.

Rising FDI by SO-TNCs from emerging economies, especially the BRICS, contributed to the growth in FDI flows in 2013. The internationalization of Chinese SOEs accelerated, driving up FDI outflows from China. In extractive industries, Chinese SO-TNCs have been very active in cross-border acquisitions: for instance, CNOOC spent $15 billion to acquire Nexen in Canada, the largest overseas deal ever undertaken by a Chinese oil and gas company; and Minmetal bought the Las Bambas copper mine in Peru for $6 billion. Furthermore, Chinese SOEs in manufacturing and services, especially finance and real estate, have increasingly invested abroad. Indian SO-TNCs in the extractive industries have become more proactive in overseas investment as well. For example, ONGC Videsh Limited, the overseas arm of the State-owned Oil and Natural Gas Corporation, is to invest heavily in Rovuma Area I Block, a project in Mozambique.

In the Russian Federation, State ownership has increased as Rosneft, Russia's largest oil and gas company, acquired BP's 50 per cent interest in TNK-BP for $28 billion (part in cash and part in Rosneft shares) in March 2013. This deal made Rosneft the world's largest listed oil company by output. In the meantime, Rosneft has expanded its global presence by actively investing abroad: its subsidiary Neftegaz America Shelf LP acquired a 30 per cent interest in 20 deep-water exploration blocks in the Gulf of Mexico held by ExxonMobil (United States). In December, Rosneft established a joint venture in cooperation with ExxonMobil to develop shale oil reserves in western Siberia.

Compared with their counterparts from the BRICS, SO-TNCs from developed countries have been less active in investing abroad and their international investment remains sluggish. This is partly because of the weak economic performance of their home countries in the Eurozone. However, a number of large M&A projects undertaken by these firms, such as those of EDF (France) and Vattenfall (Sweden), were recorded in infrastructure industries. In addition, emerging investment opportunities in utilities and transport industries in Europe may increase FDI by SO-TNCs in these industries.

B. PROSPECTS

The gradual improvement of macroeconomic conditions, as well as recovering corporate profits and the strong performance of stock markets, will boost TNCs' business confidence, which may lead to a rise in FDI flows over the next three years. On the basis of UNCTAD's survey on investment prospects of TNCs and investment promotion agencies (IPAs), results of UNCTAD's FDI forecasting model and preliminary 2014 data for cross-border M&As and greenfield activity, UNCTAD projects that FDI flows could rise to $1.62 trillion in 2014, $1.75 trillion in 2015 and $1.85 trillion in 2016 (see figure I.1).

The world economy is expected to grow by 3.6 per cent in 2014 and 3.9 per cent in 2015 (table I.6). Gross fixed capital formation and trade are projected to rise faster in 2014–2015 than in 2013. Those improvements could prompt TNCs to gradually transform their record levels of cash holdings into new investments. The slight rise in TNC profits in 2013 (figure I.21) will also have a positive impact on their capacity to invest.

Table I.6. Annual growth rates of global GDP, trade, GFCF and employment, 2008–2015
(Per cent)

Variable	2008	2009	2010	2011	2012	2013[a]	2014[b]	2015[b]
GDP	2.8	-0.4	5.2	3.9	3.2	3.0	3.6	3.9
Trade	3.1	-10.6	12.5	6.0	2.5	3.6	5.3	6.2
GFCF	2.0	-4.6	5.6	4.6	4.3	3.1	4.4	5.1
Employment	1.1	0.5	1.3	1.5	1.3	1.3	1.3	1.3

Source: UNCTAD based on IMF for GDP, trade and GFCF, and ILO for employment.
[a] Estimation.
[b] Projections.
Note: GFCF = gross fixed capital formation.

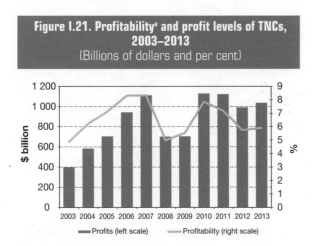

Figure I.21. Profitability[a] and profit levels of TNCs, 2003–2013
(Billions of dollars and per cent)

■ Profits (left scale)   ━ Profitability (right scale)

Source: UNCTAD, based on data from Thomson ONE.
[a] Profitability is calculated as the ratio of net income to total sales.

UNCTAD's econometric model (*WIR11*) projects that FDI flows will pick up in 2014, rising 12.5 per cent to reach $1.62 trillion (table I.7), mainly owing to the strengthening of global economic activity. Much of the impetus will come from developed countries, where FDI flows are expected to rise by 35 per cent.

FDI flows to developing countries will remain high in the next three years. Concerns about economic growth and the ending of quantitative easing raise the risk of slow growth in FDI inflows in emerging markets. Following the recent slowdown in growth of FDI inflows in developing countries (a 6 per cent increase in 2013 compared with an average of 17 per cent in the last 10 years), FDI in these countries is expected to remain flat in 2014 and then increase slightly in 2015 and 2016 (table I.7).

In light of this projection, the pattern of FDI by economic grouping may tilt in favour of developed countries. The share of developing and transition economies would decline over the next three years (figure I.22).

However, the results of the model are based mainly on economic fundamentals – projections which are subject to fluctuation. Furthermore, the model does not take into account risks such as policy uncertainty and regional conflict, which are difficult to quantify. It also does not take into account megadeals such as the $130 billion buy-back of shares by Verizon (United States) from Vodafone (United Kingdom) in 2014), which will reduce the equity component of FDI inflows to the United States and affect the global level of FDI inflows.

Although the introduction of quantitative easing appears to have had little impact on FDI flows in developing countries, this might not be the case for the ending of those measures. Although there seems to be a strong relationship between the easing of monetary policy

Table I.7. Summary of econometric medium-term baseline scenarios of FDI flows, by groupings
(Billions of dollars and per cent)

	Averages		2012	2013	Projections		
	2005–2007	2009–2011			2014	2015	2016
Global FDI flows	**1 493**	**1 448**	**1 330**	**1 452**	**1 618**	**1 748**	**1 851**
Developed economies	978	734	517	566	763	887	970
Developing economies	455	635	729	778	764	776	799
Transition economies	60	79	84	108	92	85	82

Memorandum	Average growth rates		Growth rates		Growth rate projections		
	2005–2007	*2009–2011*	*2012*	*2013*	*2014*	*2015*	*2016*
Global FDI flows	***39.6***	***1.0***	***- 21.8***	***9.1***	***12.5***	***8.0***	***5.9***
Developed economies	46.5	- 0.4	- 41.3	9.5	35.1	16.3	9.5
Developing economies	27.8	4.4	0.6	6.7	- 0.2	1.6	2.9
Transition economies	47.8	- 1.9	- 11.3	28.3	- 15.3	- 7.6	- 3.9

Source: UNCTAD.

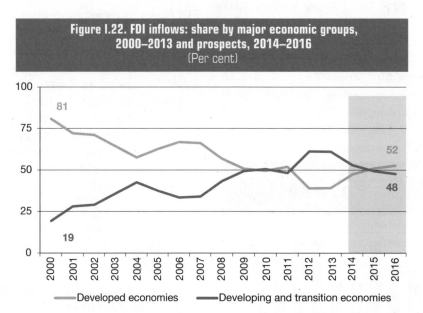

Figure I.22. FDI inflows: share by major economic groups, 2000–2013 and prospects, 2014–2016
(Per cent)

Source: UNCTAD FDI-TNC-GVC Information System, FDI database (www.unctad.org/fdistatistics); and UNCTAD estimates.

in developed countries and portfolio capital flows to emerging economies, quantitative easing had no visible impacts on FDI flows (figure I.23). FDI projects have longer gestation periods and are thus less susceptible to short-term fluctuations in exchange rates and interest rates. FDI generally involves a long-term commitment to a host economy. Portfolio and other investors, by contrast, may liquidate their investments when there is a drop in confidence in the currency, economy or government.

Although quantitative easing had little impact on FDI flows in the period 2009–2013, this might change

with the ending of unconventional measures, judging by developments when the tapering was announced and when it began to be implemented. During the first half of 2013 and the beginning of 2014, there is evidence of a sharp decrease in private external capital flows and a depreciation of the currencies of emerging economies.

FDI inflows to the countries affected by the tapering could see the effect of more company assets offered for sale, given the heavy indebtedness of domestic firms and their reduced access to liquidity. Increases in cross-border

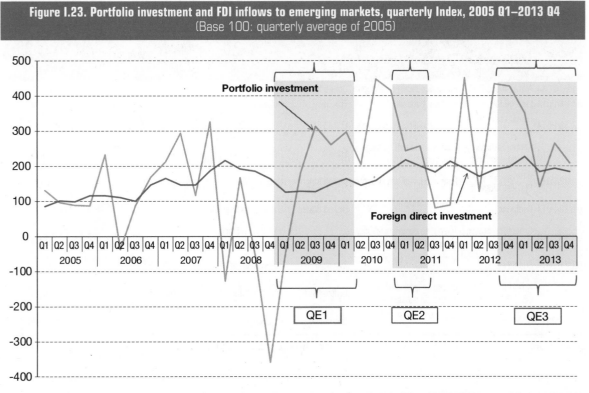

Figure I.23. Portfolio investment and FDI inflows to emerging markets, quarterly Index, 2005 Q1–2013 Q4
(Base 100: quarterly average of 2005)

Source: UNCTAD FDI-TNC-GVC Information System, FDI/TNC database (www.unctad.org/fdistatistics); IMF for portfolio investment.
Note: 2013 Q4 is estimated.
Countries included are Argentina, Brazil, Bulgaria, Chile, Colombia, Ecuador, Hong Kong (China), Hungary, India, Indonesia, Kazakhstan, the Republic of Korea, Malaysia, Mexico, the Philippines, Poland, the Russian Federation, South Africa, Thailand, Turkey, Ukraine and the Bolivarian Republic of Venezuela.

M&As in emerging markets in late 2013 and the beginning of 2014 may reflect this phenomenon. Foreign investors may also see the crisis as an opportunity to pick up assets at relatively low cost. Furthermore, some affected developing countries (e.g. Indonesia) have intensified their efforts to attract long-term capital flows or FDI to compensate for the loss in short-term flows. Their efforts essentially concentrate on further promoting and facilitating inward FDI (chapter III). The impact of tapering on FDI flows may evolve differently by type of FDI.

- *Export-oriented FDI:* Currency depreciation, if continued, can increase the attractiveness of affected emerging economies to foreign investors by lowering the costs of production and increasing export competitiveness.

- *Domestic market-oriented FDI:* Reduced demand and slower growth could lead to some downscaling or delay of FDI in the countries

most affected. The impact on domestic-market-oriented affiliates varies by sector and industry. Foreign affiliates in the services sector are particularly susceptible to local demand conditions.

Reviving M&A activity in the beginning of 2014. An overall increase of FDI inflows and the rise of developed countries as FDI hosts are apparent in the value of cross-border M&As announced in the beginning of 2014. For the first four months of 2014, the global market for cross-border M&As was worth about $500 billion (including divestments), the highest level since 2007 and more than twice the value during the same period in 2013 (figure I.24). The deals in this period were financed either by stocks or by cash held in the form of retained earnings abroad. The 10 largest deals announced in the first quarter of 2014 all targeted companies in developed countries (table I.8); in 2013 only 5 of the top 10 deals were invested in developed countries.

Table I.8. Top 10 largest cross-border M&A announcements by value of transaction, January–April 2014

Date announced	Target company	Target industry	Target nation	Acquiror name	Value of transaction ($ million)	Acquiror ultimate parent firm	Acquiror ultimate parent nation
04/28/2014	AstraZeneca PLC	Pharmaceutical preparations	United Kingdom	Pfizer Inc	106 863	Pfizer Inc	United States
04/04/2014	Lafarge SA	Cement, hydraulic	France	Holcim Ltd	25 909	Holcim Ltd	Switzerland
02/18/2014	Forest Laboratories Inc	Pharmaceutical preparations	United States	Actavis PLC	25 110	Actavis PLC	Ireland
04/30/2014	Alstom SA-Energy Businesses	Turbines and turbine generator sets	France	GE	17 124	GE	United States
04/22/2014	GlaxoSmithKline PLC-Oncology	Pharmaceutical preparations	United Kingdom	Novartis AG	16 000	Novartis AG	Switzerland
01/13/2014	Beam Inc	Wines, brandy, and brandy spirits	United States	Suntory Holdings Ltd	13 933	Kotobuki Realty Co Ltd	Japan
03/17/2014	Grupo Corporativo ONO SA	Telephone communications, except radiotelephone	Spain	Vodafone Holdings Europe SLU	10 025	Vodafone Group PLC	United Kingdom
02/21/2014	Scania AB	Motor vehicles and passenger car bodies	Sweden	Volkswagen AG	9 162	Porsche Automobil Holding SE	Germany
04/22/2014	Novartis AG-Vaccines Business	Biological products, except diagnostic substances	Switzerland	GlaxoSmithKline PLC	7 102	GlaxoSmithKline PLC	United Kingdom
03/16/2014	RWE Dea AG	Crude petroleum and natural gas	Germany	L1 Energy	7 099	LetterOne Holdings SA	Luxembourg

Source: UNCTAD FDI-TNC-GVC Information System, cross-border M&A database.

Figure I.24. Global markets for cross-border M&As on announcement basis January–April of each year of 2007–2014, by group of economies
(Billions of dollars)

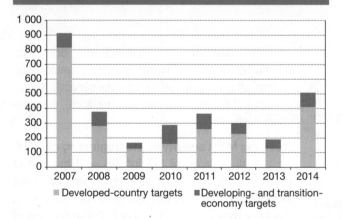

Developed-country targets   Developing- and transition-economy targets

Source: UNCTAD FDI-TNC-GVC Information System, cross-border M&A database.

Responses to this year's World Investment Prospects Survey (WIPS) support an optimistic scenario. This year's survey generated responses from 164 TNCs, collected between February and April 2014, and from 80 IPAs in 74 countries. Respondents revealed that they are still uncertain about the investment outlook for 2014 but had a bright forecast for the following two years (figure I.25). For 2016, half of the respondents had positive expectations and almost none felt pessimistic about the investment climate. When asked about their intended FDI expenditures, half of the respondents forecasted an increase over the 2013 level in each of the next three years (2014–2016). Among the factors positively affecting FDI over the next three years, respondents most frequently cited the state of the economies of the United States, the BRIC (Brazil, Russian Federation, India and China), and the EU-28. Negative factors remain the pending sovereign debt issues and fear of rising protectionism in trade and investment.

In the medium term, FDI expenditures are set to increase in all sectors. However, low-tech manufacturing industries are expected to see FDI decreases in 2014. According to the WIPS responses, TNCs across all sectors will either maintain or increase FDI in 2015 and 2016. In contrast, for 2014 investors expressed some uncertainties about their plans, with respondents from some low-tech industries in the manufacturing sector forecasting decreases of expenditures.

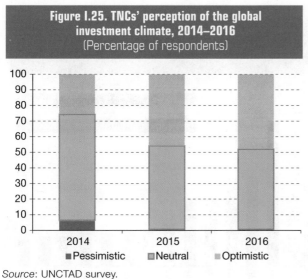

Figure I.25. TNCs' perception of the global investment climate, 2014–2016
(Percentage of respondents)

■ Pessimistic ■ Neutral ■ Optimistic

Source: UNCTAD survey.
Note: Based on responses from 164 companies.

Respondents from manufacturing industries such as textiles, wood and wood products, construction products, metals and machinery indicated a fall in investments in 2014. By 2016, almost half of TNCs in all sectors expect to see an increase in their FDI expenditures, in line with their rising optimism about the global investment environment.

Echoing the prospects perceived by TNCs, IPAs also see more investment opportunities in services than in manufacturing. Indeed, few IPAs selected a manufacturing industry as one of the top three promising industries. However, the view from IPAs differs for inward FDI by region (figure I.26). IPAs in developed economies anticipate good prospects for FDI in machinery, business services, such as computer programming and consultancy, and transport and communication, especially telecommunications. African IPAs expect further investments in the extractive and utilities industries, while Latin American IPAs emphasize finance and tourism services. Asian IPAs refer to positive prospects in construction, agriculture and machinery. IPAs in transition economies have high expectations in construction, utilities and textiles.

FDI expenditures are set to grow, especially from developing countries, and to be directed more to other developing countries. This year's survey results show diverging trends across groups of economies with regard to investment expenditures. More than half of the respondents from the developing and transition economies

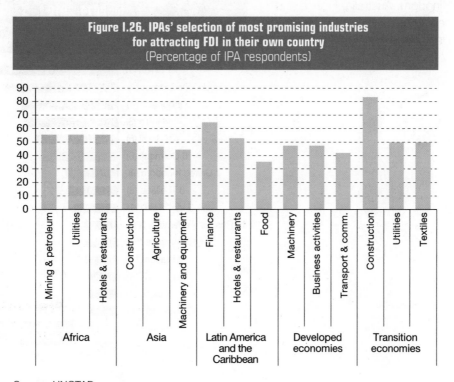

Figure I.26. IPAs' selection of most promising industries for attracting FDI in their own country
(Percentage of IPA respondents)

Mining & petroleum, Utilities, Hotels & restaurants — Africa
Construction, Agriculture, Machinery and equipment — Asia
Finance, Hotels & restaurants, Food — Latin America and the Caribbean
Machinery, Business activities, Transport & comm. — Developed economies
Construction, Utilities, Textiles — Transition economies

Source: UNCTAD survey.
Note: Based on responses from 80 IPAs. Aggregated by region or economic grouping to which responding IPAs belong.

foresaw an increase in FDI expenditures in 2014 (57 per cent) and in the medium term (63 per cent). In contrast, TNCs from developed countries expected to increase their investment budgets in only 47 per cent of cases, in both the short and medium terms.

Developed economies remain important sources of FDI but are now accompanied by major developing countries such as the BRIC, the United Arab Emirates, the Republic of Korea and Turkey. Indeed, China is consistently ranked the most promising source of FDI, together with the United States (figure I.27). Among the developed economies, the United States, Japan, the United Kingdom, Germany and France are ranked as the most promising developed-economy investors, underscoring their continuing role in global FDI flows. As to host economies, this year's ranking is largely consistent with past ones, with only minor changes. South-East Asian countries such as Viet Nam, Malaysia and Singapore, and some developed economies, such as the United Kingdom, Australia, France and Poland, gained some positions, while Japan and Mexico lost some (figure I.28).

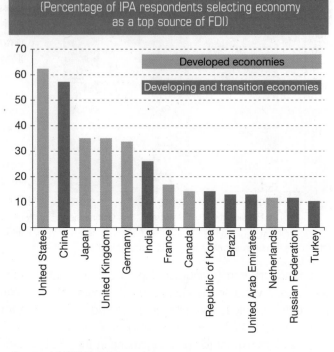

Figure I.27. IPAs' selection of most promising investor home economies for FDI in 2014–2016
(Percentage of IPA respondents selecting economy as a top source of FDI)

Source: UNCTAD survey.
Note: Based on responses from 80 IPAs.

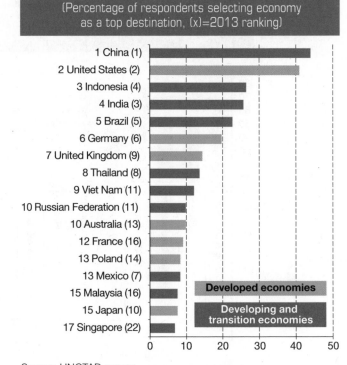

Figure I.28. TNCs' top prospective host economies for 2014–2016
(Percentage of respondents selecting economy as a top destination, (x)=2013 ranking)

Source: UNCTAD survey.
Note: Based on responses from 164 companies.

C. TRENDS IN INTERNATIONAL PRODUCTION

International production continued to gain strength in 2013, with all indicators of foreign affiliate activity rising, albeit at different growth rates (table I.9). Sales rose the most, by 9.4 per cent, mainly driven by relatively high economic growth and consumption in developing and transition economies. The growth rate of 7.9 per cent in foreign assets reflects the strong performance of stock markets and, indeed, is in line with the growth rate of FDI outward stock. Employment and value added of foreign affiliates grew at about the same rate as FDI outflows – 5 per cent – while exports of foreign affiliates registered only a small increase of 2.5 per cent. For foreign employment, the 5 per cent growth rate represents a positive trend, consolidating the increase in 2012 following some years of stagnation in the growth of the workforce, both foreign and national. By contrast, a 5.8 per cent growth rate for value added represents a slower trend since 2011, when value added rebounded after the financial crisis. These patterns suggest that international production is growing more slowly than before the crisis.

Cash holdings for the top 5,000 TNCs remained high in 2013, accounting for more than 11 per cent of their total assets (figure I.29), a level similar to 2010, in the immediate aftermath of the crisis. At the end of 2013, the top TNCs from developed economies had cash holdings, including short-term investments, estimated at $3.5 trillion, compared with roughly $1.0 trillion for firms from developing and transition economies. However, while developing-country TNCs have held their cash-to-assets ratios relatively constant over time at about 12 per cent, developed-country TNCs have increased their ratios since the crisis, from an average of 9 per cent in 2006–2008 to more than 11 per cent in 2010, and they maintained that ratio through 2013. This shift may reflect the greater risk aversion of developed-economy corporations, which are adopting cash holding ratios similar to the ones prevalent in the developing world. Taking the average cash-to-assets ratio in 2006–2008 as a benchmark, developed-country TNCs in 2013 had an estimated additional amount of cash holdings of $670 billion.

Given the easy access to finance enjoyed by large firms, partly thanks to the intervention of central banks in the aftermath of the crisis, financial constraints might not be the only reason for the slow recovery of investments. However, easy money measures did not lead to a full recovery of debt financing to its pre-crisis level (figure I.30); in 2013, net debt issuance amounted to just under $500 billion, almost a third less than the level in 2008. At the same time, corporations did increase share buy-backs and dividend payments, producing total cash outflows of about $1 trillion in 2013. Two factors underlie this behaviour: on the one hand, corporations are repaying debt and rewarding their shareholders to achieve greater stability in an economic environment still perceived as uncertain, and on the other hand, depending in which industry they operate, they are adopting a very cautious attitude toward investment because of weak demand.

Figure I.30 shows sources and uses of cash at an aggregate level for the biggest public TNCs, which hides important industry-specific dynamics. In fact, overall capital expenditures (for both domestic and foreign activities) have increased in absolute terms over the last three years; at the same time, expenditures for acquisition of business have decreased. However, there are wide differences across industries. TNCs in the oil and gas, telecommunications and utilities industries all significantly increased their expenditures (capital expenditures plus acquisitions), especially in 2013. In contrast, investments in industries such as consumer goods, and industrials (defined as transport, aerospace and defence, and electronic and electrical equipment) fell after the crisis and have remained low. This is largely consistent with the level of cash holdings observed by industry. These industries accumulated cash holdings of $440 billion and $511 billion between the pre-crisis period and 2013 (figure I.31). This represents a jump of more than three and two percentage points, respectively, to 12.8 and 11.5 per cent. This suggests that the companies operating in these industries are the ones most affected by the slow

Table I.9. Selected indicators of FDI and international production, 2013 and selected years

Item	Value at current prices (Billions of dollars)				
	1990	2005–2007 (pre-crisis average)	2011	2012	2013
FDI inflows	208	1 493	1 700	1 330	1 452
FDI outflows	241	1 532	1 712	1 347	1 411
FDI inward stock	2 078	14 790	21 117	23 304	25 464
FDI outward stock	2 088	15 884	21 913	23 916	26 313
Income on inward FDI [a]	79	1 072	1 603	1 581	1 748
Rate of return on inward FDI [b]	3.8	7.3	6.9	7.6	6.8
Income on outward FDI [a]	126	1 135	1 550	1 509	1 622
Rate of return on outward FDI [b]	6.0	7.2	6.5	7.1	6.3
Cross-border M&As	111	780	556	332	349
Sales of foreign affiliates	4 723	21 469	28 516	31 532[c]	34 508[c]
Value-added (product) of foreign affiliates	881	4 878	6 262	7 089[c]	7 492[c]
Total assets of foreign affiliates	3 893	42 179	83 754	89 568[c]	96 625[c]
Exports of foreign affiliates	1 498	5 012[d]	7 463[d]	7 532[d]	7 721[d]
Employment by foreign affiliates (thousands)	20 625	53 306	63 416	67 155[c]	70 726[c]
Memorandum:					
GDP	22 327	51 288	71 314	72 807	74 284
Gross fixed capital formation	5 072	11 801	16 498	17 171	17 673
Royalties and licence fee receipts	29	161	250	253	259
Exports of goods and services	4 107	15 034	22 386	22 593[e]	23 160[e]

Source: UNCTAD.

[a] Based on data from 179 countries for income on inward FDI and 145 countries for income on outward FDI in 2013, in both cases representing more than 90 per cent of global inward and outward stocks.

[b] Calculated only for countries with both FDI income and stock data.

[c] Data for 2012 and 2013 are estimated using a fixed effects panel regression of each variable against outward stock and a lagged dependent variable for the period 1980–2010.

[d] Data for 1995–1997 are based on a linear regression of exports of foreign affiliates against inward FDI stock for the period 1982–1994. For 1998–2013, the share of exports of foreign affiliates in world exports in 1998 (33.3 per cent) was applied to obtain values.

[e] Data from IMF, *World Economic Outlook*, April 2014.

Note: Not included in this table are the values of worldwide sales by foreign affiliates associated with their parent firms through non-equity relationships and of the sales of the parent firms themselves. Worldwide sales, gross product, total assets, exports and employment of foreign affiliates are estimated by extrapolating the worldwide data of foreign affiliates of TNCs from Australia, Austria, Belgium, Canada, the Czech Republic, Finland, France, Germany, Greece, Israel, Italy, Japan, Latvia, Lithuania, Luxembourg, Portugal, Slovenia, Sweden, and the United States for sales; those from the Czech Republic, France, Israel, Japan, Portugal, Slovenia, Sweden, and the United States for value added (product); those from Austria, Germany, Japan and the United States for assets; those from the Czech Republic, Japan, Portugal, Slovenia, Sweden, and the United States for exports; and those from Australia, Austria, Belgium, Canada, Czech Republic, Finland, France, Germany, Italy, Japan, Latvia, Lithuania, Luxembourg, Macao (China), Portugal, Slovenia, Sweden, Switzerland, and the United States for employment, on the basis of three-year average shares of those countries in worldwide outward FDI stock.

economic recovery and related persistent demand slack in developed countries.

The other industries with bulging cash holdings are computer services and software (here represented by technology), which in 2013 saw an increase in cash holdings of $319 billion over the pre-crisis level (figure I.31). On the one hand, firms with more growth opportunities and with high R&D expenditures have higher cash holdings than the average because returns on research activities are highly risky and unpredictable; hence firms prefer to rely on cash generated in-house rather than on external resources. On the other hand, these technology industries – as well as health care industries – often move intellectual property and drug patents to low-tax jurisdictions, letting earnings from those assets pile up offshore to avoid paying high home taxes. This adds significantly to corporate cash stockpiles.

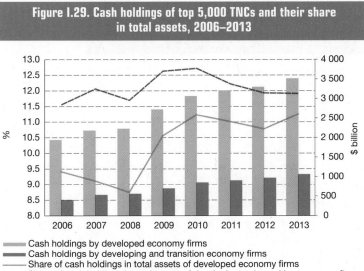

Figure I.29. Cash holdings of top 5,000 TNCs and their share in total assets, 2006–2013

- Cash holdings by developed economy firms
- Cash holdings by developing and transition economy firms
- Share of cash holdings in total assets of developed economy firms
- Share of cash holdings in total assets of developing and transition economy firms

Source: UNCTAD, based on data from Thomson ONE.
Note: Data based on records of 5,309 companies of which 3,472 were in developed countries. These do not include non-listed companies such as many developing country SO-TNCs.

For example, Apple (United States) has added $103 billion to its cash holdings since 2009. Other United States corporations in these industries such as Microsoft, Google, Cisco Systems and Pfizer, are all holding record-high cash reserves.

The cash-to-assets ratios in these industries are thus normally much higher and have also increased the most over the years, from 22 to 26 per cent for technology and from 15 to 16 per cent for health care. By contrast, oil and gas production, basic materials, utilities and telecommunications are the industries in which cash holdings have been low during the period considered (with an average cash-to-assets ratio of 6–8 per cent). In the oil and gas industry, not only have large investments been made in past years, but United States oil and gas production and capital spending on that production have continued to rise, boosted by the shale gas revolution. Similarly, big investments have been required in telecommunications (e.g. 4G wireless networks, advanced television and internet services).

The degree of internationalization of the world's largest TNCs remained flat. Data for the top 100 TNCs, most of them from developed economies, show that their domestic production – as measured by domestic assets, sales and employment – grew faster than their foreign production. In particular, their ratio of foreign to total employment fell for the second consecutive year (table I.10). Lower internationalization may be partly explained by onshoring and relocation of production to home countries by these TNCs *(WIR13)*.

Similarly, the internationalization level of the largest 100 TNCs domiciled in developing and transition economies remained stable. However, this was not due to divestments or relocation of international businesses, but to larger domestic investment. Thus, while the foreign assets of TNCs from these economies rose 14 per cent in 2012 – faster than the rate of the world's largest 100 TNCs – the rise was similar to the increase in domestic

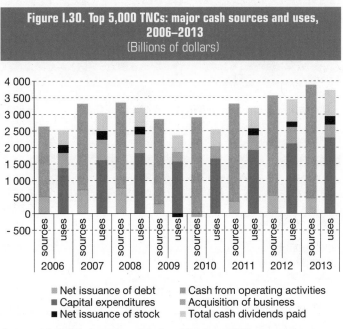

Figure I.30. Top 5,000 TNCs: major cash sources and uses, 2006–2013
(Billions of dollars)

- Net issuance of debt
- Capital expenditures
- Net issuance of stock
- Cash from operating activities
- Acquisition of business
- Total cash dividends paid

Source: UNCTAD, based on data from Thomson ONE.
Note: Based on records of 5,108 companies, of which 3,365 were in developed countries. Both domestic and foreign activities are covered. These companies do not include non-listed companies such as SOEs.

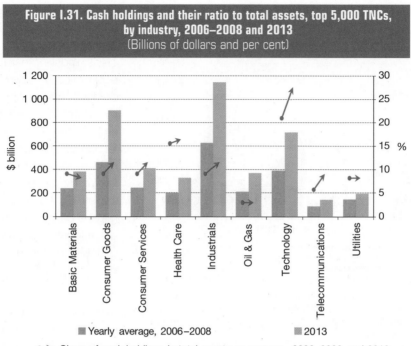

Figure I.31. Cash holdings and their ratio to total assets, top 5,000 TNCs, by industry, 2006–2008 and 2013
(Billions of dollars and per cent)

■ Yearly average, 2006–2008   ■ 2013

↔ Share of cash holdings in total assets on average, 2006–2008 and 2013

Source: UNCTAD, based on data from Thomson ONE.
Note: Data based on records of 5,309 companies, of which 3,472 were in developed countries.

Table I.10. Internationalization statistics of the 100 largest non-financial TNCs worldwide and from developing and transition economies
(Billions of dollars, thousands of employees and per cent)

Variable	100 largest TNCs worldwide					100 largest TNCs from developing and transition economies		
	2011	2012 [a]	2011–2012 % Change	2013 [b]	2012–2013 % Change	2011	2012	% Change
Assets								
Foreign	7 634	7 888	3	8 035	2	1 321	1 506	14
Domestic	4 897	5 435	11	5 620	3	3 561	4 025	13
Total	12 531	13 323	6	13 656	2	4 882	5 531	13
Foreign as % of total	61	59	-2[c]	59	0[c]	27	27	0[c]
Sales								
Foreign	5 783	5 900	2	6 057	3	1 650	1 690	2
Domestic	3 045	3 055	0	3 264	7	1 831	2 172	19
Total	8 827	8 955	1	9 321	4	3 481	3 863	11
Foreign as % of total	66	66	0[c]	65	-1[c]	47	44	-4[c]
Employment								
Foreign	9 911	9 821	-1	9 810	0	3 979	4 103	3
Domestic	6 585	7 125	8	7 482	5	6 218	6 493	4
Total	16 496	16 946	3	17 292	2	10 197	10 596	4
Foreign as % of total	60	58	-2[c]	57	-1[c]	39	39	0[c]

Source: UNCTAD.
[a] Revised results.
[b] Preliminary results.
[c] In percentage points.
Note: From 2009 onwards, data refer to fiscal year results reported between 1 April of the base year to 31 March of the following year. Complete 2013 data for the 100 largest TNCs from developing and transition economies are not yet available.

assets (13 per cent) (table I.10). The growth of sales and foreign employment at home outpaced foreign sales. In particular, the 19 per cent growth in domestic sales demonstrates the strength of developing and transition economies.

Notes

1   Greenfield investment projects data refer to announced ones. The value of a greenfield investment project indicates the capital expenditure planned by the investor at the time of the announcement. Data can be substantially different from the official FDI data as companies can raise capital locally and phase their investments over time, and the project may be cancelled or may not start in the year when it is announced.

2   United States Energy Information Administration.

3   United States natural gas prices dropped from nearly $13 per MMBtu (million British thermal units) in 2008 to $4 per MMBtu in 2013 (two to three times lower than European gas prices and four times lower than Japanese prices for liquefied natural gas).

4   According to UNCTAD database, based on information from the Financial Times Ltd, fDi Markets (www.fDimarkets.com).

5   Both United States and foreign companies benefit from these deals. United States operators get financial support, while foreign companies gain experience in horizontal drilling and hydraulic fracturing that may be transferable to other regions. Most of the foreign investment in these joint ventures involves buying a percentage of the host company's shale acreages through an upfront cash payment with a commitment to cover a portion of the drilling cost. Foreign investors in joint ventures pay upfront cash and commit to cover the cost of drilling extra wells within an agreed-upon time frame, usually between 2 and 10 years.

6   American Chemical Council, "Shale Gas Competitiveness, and new US chemical industry investment: an analysis based on announced projects", May 2013.

7   As examples, South African Sasol is investing some $20 billion in Louisiana plants that turn gas into plastic, in the largest-ever manufacturing project by a foreign direct investor in the United States; Formosa Plastics from Taiwan Province of China plans two new factories in Texas to make ethylene and propylene, key components in the manufacture of plastics and carpets; EuroChem, a Russian company that makes fertilizers, is building an ammonia plant in Louisiana, where proximity to the Mississippi River provides easy access to Midwest farms. Recently the CEO of Saudi Basic Industries Corporation (SABIC), the world's biggest petrochemicals maker by market value, disclosed company plans to enter the United States shale market.

8   The potential sharp decline in revenues as a firm's patents on one or more leading products expire from the consequent opening up of the market to generic alternatives.

9   Innovation used to drive this industry, but outsourcing of R&D activities has become one of the key industry trends in the past decade as a result of big TNCs shifting their R&D efforts in the face of patent cliffs and cost pressures (IMAP, *Global Pharma & Biotech M&A Report 2014*, www.imap.com, accessed on 2 April 2014).

10   "India approves $1.6bn acquisition of Agila Specialties by Mylan", 4 September 2014, www.ft.com.

11   "Pharma & biotech stock outlook – Dec 2013 – industry outlook", 3 December 2013, www.nasdaq.com.

12   "Big pharma deals are back on the agenda", *Financial Times*, 22 April 2014.

13   In the absence of global FDI data specific to the pharmaceutical industry, trends in cross-border M&A deals and greenfield FDI projects are used to represent the global FDI trends in this industry. Subindustries included in M&A deals are the manufacture of pharmaceuticals, medicinal chemical products, botanical products and biological products. In greenfield FDI projects, pharmaceuticals and biotechnology.

14   In the United States, FDI inflows to this industry represented about one quarter of manufacturing FDI in 2010–2012 ("Foreign direct investment in the United States", 23 October 2013, www.whitehouse.gov).

15   For the period 2003–2013, the number of greenfield FDI projects was between 200 and 290, with an annual average of 244, while that of cross-border M&As was between 170 and 280, with an annual average of 234.

16   PwC (2014), *Pharmaceutical and Life Science Deals Insights Quarterly*, quoted in "Strong Q4 pharmaceutical & life sciences M&A momentum expected to continue into 2014, according to PwC" (PwCUS, press release, 10 February 2014).

17   "Why did one of the world's largest generic drug makers exit China?", *Forbes*, 3 February 2014, www.forbes.com.

18   The largest deals reported in the first quarter of 2014 were a $4.3 billion acquisition of Bristol-Myers Squibb (United States) by AstraZeneca (United Kingdom) through its Swedish affiliate, followed by a $4.2 billion merger between Shire (Ireland) and ViroPharma (United States).

19   Among them, the largest so far was a bid made by Pfizer (United States) for AstraZeneca (United Kingdom) (table I.8). Even though Pfizer walked away, AstraZeneca may look for another merger option with a smaller United States company ("Big pharma deals are back on the agenda", *Financial Times*, 22 April 2014).

20   "Corporate takeovers: Return of the big deal", *The Economist*, 3 May 2014.

21   In 2008, no information on transaction value was available for transition economies.

22   Daiichi Sankyo plans to divest in 2014.

23   Abbott Laboratories (United States) acquired the Healthcare Solutions business of Piramal Healthcare (India). In transition economies, only $7 million was recorded in 2010.

24   The largest deal was a $1.9 billion acquisition of Agila Specialties, a Bangalore-based manufacturer of pharmaceuticals, from Strides Arcolab (United States) by Mylan (United States).

25   When deals in biological products are excluded, the share of developing and transition economies in 2013 exceeded 30 per cent.

26   GlaxoSmithKline (United Kingdom) has announced plans to invest over $200 million in sub-Saharan Africa in the next five years to expand its existing manufacturing capacities in Kenya, Nigeria and South Africa and to build new factories in Ethiopia, Ghana and/or Rwanda, as well as the world's first open-access R&D laboratory for non-communicable diseases in Africa, creating 500 new jobs ("Drugmaker GSK to invest $200 mln in African factories, R&D", 31 March 2014, www.reuters.com).

27   "The world of pharma in 2014 – serialization, regulations, and rising API costs", 23 January 2014, www.thesmartcube.com.

28   IMAP, *Global Pharma & Biotech M&A Report 2014*, www.imap.com, accessed on 2 April 2014.

29   For example, "Low-Cost Drugs in Poor Nations Get a Lift in Indian Court", *The New York Times*, 1 April 2013.

30 See, for example, "What does Mylan get for $1.6 billion? A vaccine maker with a troubled factory", 24 September 2013, www.forbes.com; "US drug regulator slams poor maintenance of Ranbaxy plant", 27 January 2014, http://indiatoday.intoday.in.

31 See UNCTAD (2013a) for details.

32 Data on the world's top 250 retailers show that these companies receive about one quarter of their revenues from abroad (Deloitte, 2013).

33 Laurie Burkitt and Shelly Banjo, "Wal-Mart Takes a Pause in China ", *Wall Street Journal*, 16 October 2013.

34 Reuters, "Carrefour sells stake in Middle East venture for $683m", *Al Arabiya News*, 22 May 2013.

35 In 2011, for example, Aldi (Germany) took over Walgreen's and Home Depot in the United States.

36 Latin American Private Equity & Venture Capital Association, as quoted in "LatAm investment hit six-year high", Private Equity International, 20 February 2014, and "PE drives LatAM infrastructure", 16 December 2013, Financial Times.

37 European Central Bank, *2013 SMEs' Access to Finance Survey*, http://ec.europa.eu.

38 Forecast by Cushman & Wakefield.

39 As reported in an interview with the managing director of Kazanah: "We have a mandate to 'crowd-in' and catalyze some parts of the economy, hence we tend to find our natural home in those areas where there is a strategic benefit, perhaps in providing an essential service or key infrastructure, and where there are high barriers to entry for the private sector, inter alia very long investment horizons or large balance sheet requirements."

40 Available at http://blogs.cfainstitute.org/investor/2013/07/30/malaysias-khazanah-not-just-a-swf-but-a-nation-building-institution/.

41 In UNCTAD's definition, SO-TNCs are TNCs that are at least 10 per cent owned by the State or public entities, or in which the State or public entity is the largest shareholder or has a "golden share".

42 UNCTAD has revamped the SO-TNC database by strictly applying its definition, thereby shortening the list of SO-TNCs. In addition, some majority privately owned TNCs, in which the State has acquired a considerable share through financial investment, are no longer considered State-owned. See, e.g., Karl P. Sauvant and Jonathan Strauss, "State-controlled entities control nearly US$ 2 trillion in foreign assets", *Columbia FDI Perspectives*, No. 64 April 2, 2012.

Nihic tem, Ti. Effre, voltis, nostra traci iaelut fat orum ine

REGIONAL INVESTMENT TRENDS

CHAPTER II

INTRODUCTION

In 2013, foreign direct investment (FDI) inflows increased in all three major economic groups – developed, developing and transition economies (table II.1) – although at different growth rates.

FDI flows to *developing economies* reached a new high of $778 billion, accounting for 54 per cent of global inflows in 2013. Flows to most developing subregions were up. Developing Asia remained the largest host region in the world. FDI flows to *transition economies* recorded a 28 per cent increase, to $108 billion. FDI flows to *developed countries* increased by 9 per cent to $566 billion – still only 60 per cent of their pre-crisis average during 2005–2007. FDI flows to the *structurally weak, vulnerable and small economies* fell by 3 per cent in 2013, from $58 billion in 2012 to $57 billion, as the growth of FDI to least developed countries

(LDCs) was not enough to offset the decrease of FDI to small island developing States (SIDS) and landlocked developing countries (LLDCs) (table II.1). Their share in the world total also fell, from 4.4 per cent in 2012 to 3.9 per cent.

Outward FDI from developed economies stagnated at $857 billion in 2013, accounting for a record low share of 61 per cent in global outflows. In contrast, flows from developing economies remained resilient, rising by 3 per cent to reach a new high of $454 billion. Flows from developing Asia and Africa rose while those from Latin America and the Caribbean declined. Developing Asia remained a large source of FDI, accounting for more than one fifth of the global total. And flows from transition economies rose significantly – by 84 per cent – reaching a new high of $99 billion.

Table II.1. FDI flows, by region, 2011–2013
(Billions of dollars and per cent)

Region	FDI inflows			FDI outflows		
	2011	2012	2013	2011	2012	2013
World	**1 700**	**1 330**	**1 452**	**1 712**	**1 347**	**1 411**
Developed economies	880	517	566	1 216	853	857
European Union	490	216	246	585	238	250
North America	263	204	250	439	422	381
Developing economies	725	729	778	423	440	454
Africa	48	55	57	7	12	12
Asia	431	415	426	304	302	326
East and South-East Asia	333	334	347	270	274	293
South Asia	44	32	36	13	9	2
West Asia	53	48	44	22	19	31
Latin America and the Caribbean	244	256	292	111	124	115
Oceania	2	3	3	1	2	1
Transition economies	95	84	108	73	54	99
Structurally weak, vulnerable and small economies[a]	**58**	**58**	**57**	**12**	**10**	**9**
LDCs	22	24	28	4	4	5
LLDCs	36	34	30	6	3	4
SIDS	6	7	6	2	2	1
Memorandum: percentage share in world FDI flows						
Developed economies	51.8	38.8	39.0	71.0	63.3	60.8
European Union	28.8	16.2	17.0	34.2	17.7	17.8
North America	15.5	15.3	17.2	25.6	31.4	27.0
Developing economies	42.6	54.8	53.6	24.7	32.7	32.2
Africa	2.8	4.1	3.9	0.4	0.9	0.9
Asia	25.3	31.2	29.4	17.8	22.4	23.1
East and South-East Asia	19.6	25.1	23.9	15.8	20.3	20.7
South Asia	2.6	2.4	2.4	0.8	0.7	0.2
West Asia	3.1	3.6	3.0	1.3	1.4	2.2
Latin America and the Caribbean	14.3	19.2	20.1	6.5	9.2	8.1
Oceania	0.1	0.2	0.2	0.1	0.1	0.1
Transition economies	5.6	6.3	7.4	4.3	4.0	7.0
Structurally weak, vulnerable and small economies[a]	**3.4**	**4.4**	**3.9**	**0.7**	**0.7**	**0.7**
LDCs	1.3	1.8	1.9	0.3	0.3	0.3
LLDCs	2.1	2.5	2.0	0.4	0.2	0.3
SIDS	0.4	0.5	0.4	0.1	0.2	0.1

Source: UNCTAD, FDI-TNC-GVC Information System, FDI/TNC database (www.unctad.org/fdistatistics).
[a]Without double counting.

A. REGIONAL TRENDS

1. Africa

Table A. Distribution of FDI flows among economies, by range,[a] 2013

Range	Inflows	Outflows
Above $3.0 billion	South Africa, Mozambique, Nigeria, Egypt, Morocco, Ghana and Sudan	South Africa
$2.0 to $2.9 billion	Democratic Republic of the Congo and the Congo	Angola
$1.0 to $1.9 billion	Equatorial Guinea, United Republic of Tanzania, Zambia, Algeria, Mauritania, Uganda, Tunisia and Liberia	Nigeria
$0.5 to $0.9 billion	Ethiopia, Gabon, Madagascar, Libya, Namibia, Niger, Sierra Leone, Cameroon, Chad and Kenya	Sudan and Liberia
$0.1 to $0.4 billion	Mali, Zimbabwe, Burkina Faso, Côte d'Ivoire, Benin, Senegal, Djibouti, Mauritius, Botswana, Seychelles, Malawi, Rwanda and Somalia	Democratic Republic of the Congo, Morocco, Egypt, Zambia, Libya, Cameroon and Mauritius
Below $0.1 billion	Togo, Swaziland, Lesotho, Eritrea, São Tomé and Principe, Gambia, Guinea, Cabo Verde, Guinea-Bissau, Comoros, Burundi, Central African Republic and Angola	Gabon, Burkina Faso, Malawi, Benin, Togo, Côte d'Ivoire, Senegal, Zimbabwe, Tunisia, Lesotho, Rwanda, Mali, Ghana, Seychelles, Kenya, Mauritania, Cabo Verde, Guinea, Swaziland, Guinea-Bissau, São Tomé and Principe, Botswana, Mozambique, Uganda, Niger, Namibia and Algeria

[a] Economies are listed according to the magnitude of their FDI flows.

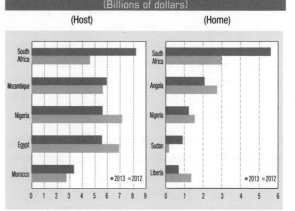

Figure A. FDI flows, top 5 host and home economies, 2012–2013
(Billions of dollars)

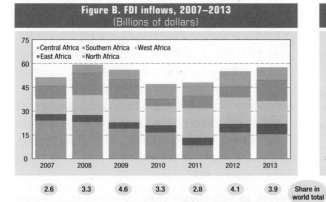

Figure B. FDI inflows, 2007–2013
(Billions of dollars)

Share in world total: 2.6 3.3 4.6 3.3 2.8 4.1 3.9

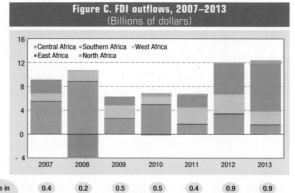

Figure C. FDI outflows, 2007–2013
(Billions of dollars)

Share in world total: 0.4 0.2 0.5 0.5 0.4 0.9 0.9

Table B. Cross-border M&As by industry, 2012–2013
(Millions of dollars)

Sector/industry	Sales		Purchases	
	2012	2013	2012	2013
Total	**-1 254**	**3 848**	**629**	**3 019**
Primary	**-1 125**	**135**	**308**	**289**
Mining, quarrying and petroleum	-1 148	135	286	289
Manufacturing	**231**	**3 326**	**1 518**	**1 632**
Food, beverages and tobacco	634	1 023	185	244
Chemicals and chemical products	17	16	-162	-
Pharmaceuticals, medicinal chemical & botanical prod.	42	567	502	1 310
Non-metallic mineral products	-25	1 706	81	-
Services	**-360**	**387**	**-1 197**	**1 098**
Transportation and storage	2	27	2	27
Information and communication	-750	-207	-11	105
Financial and insurance activities	335	240	-1 688	653
Business services	24	104	374	135

Table C. Cross-border M&As by region/country, 2012–2013
(Millions of dollars)

Region/country	Sales		Purchases	
	2012	2013	2012	2013
World	**-1 254**	**3 848**	**629**	**3 019**
Developed economies	**-3 500**	**-8 953**	**635**	**2 288**
European Union	841	-4 831	1 261	1 641
North America	-1 622	-5 196	19	-17
Australia	-1 753	141	-645	664
Developing economies	**2 172**	**12 788**	**-7**	**731**
Africa	126	130	126	130
Asia	2 050	13 341	145	596
China	1 580	7 271	-	78
India	22	419	410	233
Indonesia	-	1 753	212	-
Singapore	271	543	-615	167
Transition economies	**-**	**-**	**-**	**-**

Table D. Greenfield FDI projects by industry, 2012–2013
(Millions of dollars)

Sector/industry	Africa as destination		Africa as investors	
	2012	2013	2012	2013
Total	**47 455**	**53 596**	**7 764**	**15 807**
Primary	**7 479**	**5 735**	**455**	**7**
Mining, quarrying and petroleum	7 479	3 795	455	7
Manufacturing	**21 129**	**13 851**	**4 013**	**7 624**
Food, beverages and tobacco	2 227	1 234	438	373
Textiles, clothing and leather	206	1 750	34	128
Non-metallic mineral products	1 067	3 616	674	2 896
Motor vehicles and other transport equipment	2 316	1 593	-	108
Services	**18 847**	**34 010**	**3 296**	**8 177**
Electricity, gas and water	6 401	11 788	60	-
Construction	3 421	3 514	-	1 005
Transport, storage and communications	3 147	7 652	1 221	2 558
Business services	1 892	7 096	889	2 662

Table E. Greenfield FDI projects by region/country, 2012–2013
(Millions of dollars)

Partner region/economy	Africa as destination		Africa as investors	
	2012	2013	2012	2013
World	**47 455**	**53 596**	**7 764**	**15 807**
Developed economies	**17 541**	**27 254**	**1 802**	**2 080**
European Union	8 114	16 308	370	960
United States	4 844	2 590	1 362	1 076
Japan	708	1 753	39	-
Developing economies	**29 847**	**26 234**	**5 962**	**13 652**
Africa	4 019	12 231	4 019	12 231
Nigeria	711	2 261	161	2 729
South Africa	1 397	4 905	396	344
Asia	25 586	13 807	1 474	1 337
China	1 771	303	102	140
India	7 747	5 628	149	68
Transition economies	**67**	**108**	**-**	**76**

FDI inflows to Africa rose by 4 per cent to $57 billion, driven by international and regional market-seeking flows, and infrastructure investments. Expectations for sustained economic and population growth continue to attract market-seeking FDI into consumer-oriented industries. Intraregional investments are increasing, led by South African, Kenyan and Nigerian corporations. Most of the outflows were directed to other countries in the continent, paving the way for investment-driven regional integration.

Consumer-oriented sectors are beginning to drive FDI growth. Expectations for further sustained economic and population growth underlie investors' continued interest not only in extractive industries but also in consumer-market-oriented sectors that target the rising middle-class population (*WIR13*).[1] This group is estimated to have expanded 30 per cent over the past decade, reaching 120 million people. Reflecting this change, FDI is starting to diversify into consumer-market-oriented industries, including consumer products such as foods, information technology (IT), tourism, finance and retail. Similarly, driven by the growing trade and consumer markets, infrastructure FDI showed strong increases in transport and in information and communication technology (ICT).

Data on announced greenfield investment projects (table D) show that the services sector is driving inflows (see also chapter I). In particular, investments are targeting construction, utilities, business services and telecommunications. The fall in the value of greenfield investment projects targeting the manufacturing sector was caused by sharply decreasing flows in resource-based industries such as coke and petroleum products, and metal and metal products, both of which fell by about 70 per cent. By contrast, announced greenfield projects show rising inflows in the textile industry and high interest by international investors in motor vehicle industries. Data on cross-border merger and acquisition (M&A) sales show a sharp increase in the manufacturing sector, targeting the food processing industry, construction materials (non-metallic mineral products) and pharmaceutical industries (table B).

Some foreign TNCs are starting to invest in research and development (R&D) in agriculture in the continent, motivated by declining yields, global warming, concerns about supply shortages and the sectoral need for a higher level of technological development. For example, in 2013, Dupont (United States) gained a majority stake in the seed company Pannar by promising to invest $6.2 million by 2017 to establish an R&D hub in South Africa to develop new seed technology for the region. Similarly, Barry Callebaut (Switzerland) inaugurated its Cocoa Centre of Excellence to promote advanced agricultural techniques in Côte d'Ivoire, the world's largest cocoa-producing country. That investment is estimated at $1.1 million.

Technology firms have also started to invest in innovation in Africa. In November 2013, IBM opened its first African research laboratory, on the outskirts of Nairobi, with an investment of more than $10 million for the first two years. The facility reflects IBM's interest in a continent where smartphones are becoming commonplace. Kenya has become a world leader in payment by mobile phone, stirring hope that Africa can use technology to leapfrog more established economies. In October, Microsoft announced a partnership with three African technology incubation hubs to develop businesses based on cloud-computing systems. In the last few years, Google has funded start-up hubs in Nigeria, Kenya and South Africa, as part of a push to invest in innovation in Africa.

Trends in FDI flows vary by subregion. Flows to North Africa decreased by 7 per cent to $15.5 billion (figure B). However, with this relatively high level of FDI, investors appear to be ready to return to the region. FDI to Egypt fell by 19 per cent but remained the highest in the subregion at $5.6 billion. In fact, many foreign investors, especially producers of consumer products, remain attracted by Egypt's large population (the largest in the subregion) and cheap labour costs. Most of the neighbouring countries saw increasing flows. Morocco attracted increased investment of $3.4 billion – especially in the manufacturing sector, with Nissan alone planning to invest about $0.5 billion in a new production site – as well as in the real estate, food processing and utility sectors. In Algeria, the Government is intensifying efforts to reform the market and attract more foreign investors. As an example, State-owned Société de Gestion des Participations Industries Manufacturières concluded an agreement with Taypa Tekstil Giyim (Turkey), to construct a multimillion-dollar centre in the textile-clothing industry. Among other objectives, the partnership aims to promote public-private joint ventures in Algeria and to create employment opportunities for more than 10,000 people, according to the Algerian Ministry of Industry.

FDI flows to West Africa declined by 14 per cent, to $14.2 billion, much of that due to decreasing flows to Nigeria. Uncertainties over the long-awaited petroleum industry bill and security issues triggered a series of asset disposals from foreign TNCs. National champions and other developing-country TNCs are taking over the assets of the retreating TNCs. Examples are two pending megadeals that will see Total (France) and ConocoPhillips (United States) sell their Nigerian assets to Sinopec Group (China) and local Oando PLC for $2.5 billion and $1.8 billion, respectively. By contrast, in 2013 Ghana and Côte d'Ivoire started to produce oil, attracting considerable investment from companies such as Royal Dutch Shell (United Kingdom), ExxonMobil (United States), China National Offshore Oil Company (CNOOC) and China National Petroleum Corporation (CNPC), as well as from State-owned petroleum companies in Thailand and India.

Central Africa attracted $8.2 billion of FDI in 2013, a fall of 18 per cent from the previous year. Increasing political turmoil in the Central African Republic and the persisting armed conflict in the Democratic Republic of the Congo could have negatively influenced foreign investors. In East Africa, flows surged by 15 per cent to $6.2 billion, driven by rising flows to Kenya and Ethiopia. Kenya is developing as the favoured business hub, not only for oil and gas exploration in the subregion but also for industrial production and transport. The country is set to develop further as a regional hub for energy, services and manufacturing over the next decade. Ethiopia's industrial strategy is attracting Asian capital to develop its manufacturing base. In 2013, Huanjin Group (China) opened its first factory for shoe production, with a view to establishing a $2 billion hub for light manufacturing. Early in the year, Julphar (United Arab Emirates), in conjunction with its local partner, Medtech, officially inaugurated its first pharmaceutical manufacturing facility in Africa in Addis Ababa. Julphar's investment in the

construction of the plant is estimated at around $8.5 million. Uganda, the United Republic of Tanzania and Madagascar maintained relatively high inward flows, thanks to the development of their gas and mineral sectors.

FDI flows to Southern Africa almost doubled in 2013, jumping to $13.2 billion from $6.7 billion in 2012, mainly owing to record-high flows to South Africa and Mozambique. In both countries, infrastructure was the main attraction. In Mozambique, investments in the gas sector also played a role. Angola continued to register net divestments, albeit at a lower rate than in past years. Because foreign investors in that country are asked to team with local partners, projects are failing to materialize for lack of those partners, despite strong demand.[2]

Outward FDI flows from Africa rose marginally to $12 billion. The main investors were South Africa, Angola and Nigeria, with flows mostly directed to neighbouring countries. South African outward FDI almost doubled, to $5.6 billion, powered by investments in telecommunications, mining and retail. Nigeria outflows were concentrated in building materials and financial services. A few emerging TNCs expanded their reach over the continent. In addition to well-known South African investors (such as Bidvest, Anglo Gold Ashanti, MTN, Shoprite, Pick'n'Pay, Aspen Pharmacare and Naspers), some other countries' conglomerates are upgrading their cross-border operations first in neighbouring countries and then across the whole continent. For example, Sonatrach (Algeria) is present in many African countries in the oil and gas sector. Other examples include the Dangote and Simba Groups (Nigeria), which are active in the cement, agriculture and oil-refining industries. Orascom (Egypt), active in the building materials and chemicals industries, is investing in North African countries. Sameer Group (Kenya) is involved in industries that include agriculture, manufacturing, distribution, high-tech, construction, transport and finance. The Comcraft Group (Kenya), active in the services sector, is extending its presence beyond the continent into Asian markets.

Regional integration efforts intensified. African leaders are seeking to accelerate regional integration, which was first agreed to in the 1991 Abuja Treaty. The treaty provided for the African

Economic Community to be set up through a gradual process, which would be achieved by coordinating, harmonizing and progressively integrating the activities of regional economic communities (RECs).[3] Recent efforts in this direction include a summit of African Union leaders in January 2012 that endorsed a new action plan to establish a Continental Free Trade Area. In addition, several RECs plan to establish monetary unions as part of a broader effort to promote regional integration.

Another example of these integration efforts was the launch of negotiations on the COMESA-EAC-SADC Free Trade Area in 2011, between the Common Market for East and Southern Africa (COMESA), the East African Community (EAC) and the Southern African Development Community (SADC). The Tripartite Free Trade Agreement (FTA) involves 26 African countries in the strategic objective of consolidating RECs to achieve a common market as well as a single investment area. In the Tripartite Roadmap, Phase I covers the implementation of the FTA for trade in goods.[4] Phase II will discuss infrastructure and industrial development, addressing investment issues as well as services, intellectual property rights, competition policy, and trade development and competitiveness.

Although Phase II plans to address investment issues, the primary impact on FDI will most likely occur through tariff and non-tariff measures, especially non-tariff barriers, the main remaining impediment to the free and competitive flow of goods and services on the continent.

Raising intraregional FDI supports African leaders' efforts to achieve deeper regional integration. The rapid economic growth of the last decade underlies the rising dynamism of African firms on the continent, in terms of both trade and foreign investment.[5] Led by the cross-border operations of TNCs based in the major economies of the continent, this trend is sustaining African leaders' efforts. Intra-African investments are trending up, driven by a continuous rise in South African FDI into the continent, as well as by increases of flows since 2008 from Kenya, Nigeria, and Northern African countries.[6]

Between 2009 and 2013, the share of cross-border greenfield projects – the major investment type in Africa – originating from other African countries has increased to 18 per cent, from about 10 per cent in the period 2003–2008 (figure II.1). All major investors – South Africa (7 per cent), Kenya (3 per cent) and Nigeria (2 per cent) – more than doubled their shares. Over the same five years, the gross value of cross-border intra-African acquisitions grew from less than 3 per cent of total investments in 2003–2008 to more than 9 per cent in the next five years. Growing consumer markets are a key force enabling these trends, given that an increasing amount of FDI into Africa – from abroad and by region – goes to consumer-facing industries, led by banking and telecommunications.

Compared with other foreign investment, intra-African projects are concentrated in manufacturing and services; the extractive industries play a very marginal role (figure II.2). Comparing the sectoral distribution across sources shows that 97 per cent of intra-African investments target non-primary sectors compared with 76 per cent of investments from the rest of the world, with a particularly high difference in the share that targets the manufacturing sector. Intra-African investments in the manufacturing sector concentrate in agri-processing, building materials, electric and electronic equipment, and textiles, while in the services sector African TNCs have been attracted to telecommunications and retail industries, especially in rapidly growing economies like those in Nigeria, Ghana, Uganda and Zambia. Other very active industries for intraregional investments are finance, especially banking, and business services, where investors from South Africa, Kenya, Togo and Nigeria are expanding in the neighbouring countries. In finance, low-technology consumer products and wood furniture, intra-African investments accounted for roughly 40 per cent of all greenfield investments by number of projects. In residential construction and in hotels and restaurants services, TNCs from South Africa, Kenya and Egypt were the leading investors in Africa by number of cross-border acquisitions deals. The high shares of intra-African investment targeting the manufacturing sector accord with evidence from trade statistics showing that the industry products that are most traded intraregionally are manufactured goods – especially those entailing low and medium levels of processing (UNCTAD, 2013b). These industries could thus benefit the most from

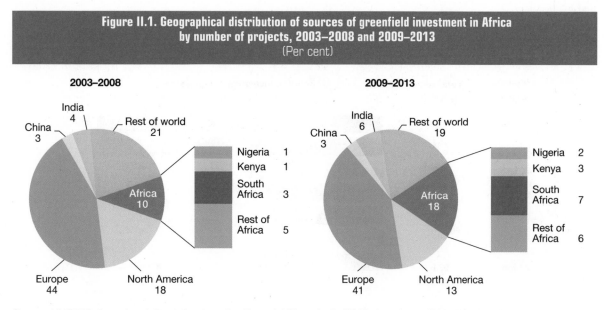

Figure II.1. Geographical distribution of sources of greenfield investment in Africa by number of projects, 2003–2008 and 2009–2013
(Per cent)

Source: UNCTAD, based on information from the Financial Times Ltd., fDi Markets (www.fDimarkets.com).

regional integration measures; an enlarged market could provide companies enough scope to grow and create incentives for new investments.

The share of intra-African FDI in the manufacturing and services sectors varies widely across RECs. In some RECs, such as ECOWAS and EAC, intraregional FDI in these sectors represents about 36 per cent of all investments; in others, such as UMA, it is marginal (figure II.3). Furthermore, excluding SADC, investments from all of Africa

usually represents a much higher share of FDI than intra-REC investments do.

The gap between intra-African and intra-REC FDI indicates that cross-REC investment flows are relatively common and suggests the importance of viewing RECs as building blocks of a continental FTA. Because RECs' market size is limited and not all RECs have advanced TNC members that can drive FDI, the integration of RECs into a single Africa-wide market will benefit most the economies of the smallest and less industrially diversified groups such as the Economic Community of Central African States (ECCAS).

Intraregional FDI is a means to integrate smaller African countries into global production processes. Smaller African economies rely more heavily on regional FDI (figure II.4). For many smaller countries, often landlocked or non-oil-exporting ones, intraregional FDI is a critical source of foreign capital.

For smaller countries such as Benin, Burkina Faso, Guinea-Bissau, Lesotho, Rwanda and Togo, investments from other African countries represented at least 30 per cent of their FDI stocks. Similarly, Southern African countries such as Malawi, Mozambique, Namibia, Uganda and the United Republic of Tanzania received a sizeable

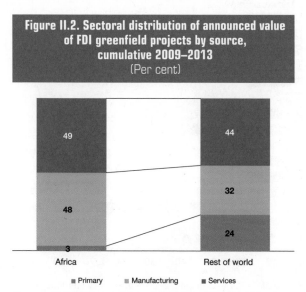

Figure II.2. Sectoral distribution of announced value of FDI greenfield projects by source, cumulative 2009–2013
(Per cent)

■ Primary ■ Manufacturing ■ Services

Source: UNCTAD, based on information from the Financial Times Ltd., fDi Markets (www.fDimarkets.com).

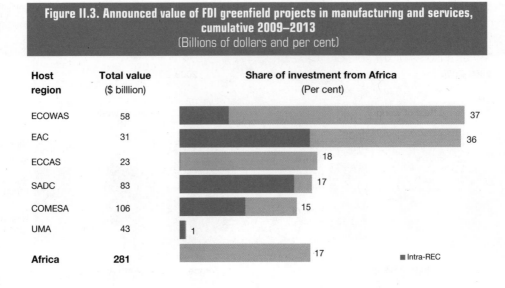

Figure II.3. Announced value of FDI greenfield projects in manufacturing and services, cumulative 2009–2013
(Billions of dollars and per cent)

Host region	Total value ($ billion)	Share of investment from Africa (Per cent)
ECOWAS	58	37
EAC	31	36
ECCAS	23	18
SADC	83	17
COMESA	106	15
UMA	43	1
Africa	**281**	17

Intra-REC

Source: UNCTAD, based on information from the Financial Times Ltd., fDi Markets (www.fDimarkets.com).

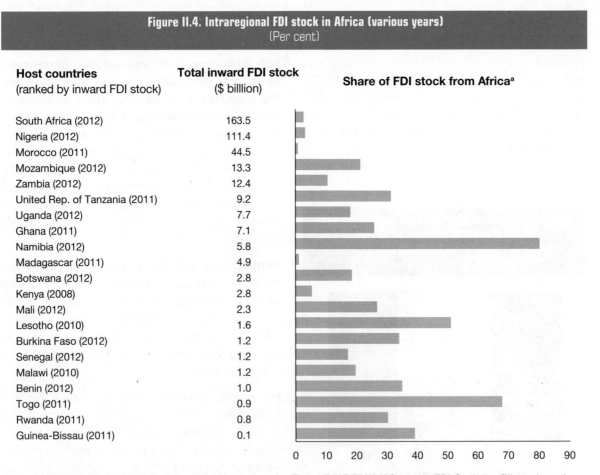

Figure II.4. Intraregional FDI stock in Africa (various years)
(Per cent)

Host countries (ranked by inward FDI stock)	Total inward FDI stock ($ billion)	Share of FDI stock from Africa[a]
South Africa (2012)	163.5	
Nigeria (2012)	111.4	
Morocco (2011)	44.5	
Mozambique (2012)	13.3	
Zambia (2012)	12.4	
United Rep. of Tanzania (2011)	9.2	
Uganda (2012)	7.7	
Ghana (2011)	7.1	
Namibia (2012)	5.8	
Madagascar (2011)	4.9	
Botswana (2012)	2.8	
Kenya (2008)	2.8	
Mali (2012)	2.3	
Lesotho (2010)	1.6	
Burkina Faso (2012)	1.2	
Senegal (2012)	1.2	
Malawi (2010)	1.2	
Benin (2012)	1.0	
Togo (2011)	0.9	
Rwanda (2011)	0.8	
Guinea-Bissau (2011)	0.1	

Source: UNCTAD, Bilateral FDI Statistics (http://unctad.org/en/Pages/DIAE/FDI%20Statistics/FDI-Statistics-Bilateral.aspx).
[a] Mauritius was excluded from the calculation of the African share as it acts as an investment platform for many extraregional investors.

amount of their FDI stock from the region (excluding stock from Mauritius), most of that from South Africa. By contrast, African investments in North African countries such as Morocco are minimal; the bulk of investments there come from neighbouring countries in Europe and the Middle East.

Intraregional FDI is one of the most important mechanisms through which Africa's increasing demand can be met by a better utilization of its own resources. Furthermore, intra-African investment helps African firms enhance their competitiveness by increasing their scale, developing their production know-how and providing access to better and cheaper inputs. Several of the most prominent African TNCs that have gone global, such as Anglo American and South African Breweries (now SABMiller), were assisted in developing their international competitiveness through first expanding regionally.

The rising intra-African investments have not yet triggered the consolidation of regional value chains. In terms of participation in global value chains (GVCs), Africa ranks quite high in international comparisons: its GVC participation rate in 2011 was 56 per cent compared with the developing-country average of 52 per cent and the global average of 59 per cent (figure II.5). However, the analysis of the components of the GVC participation rate shows that the African down-stream component (exports that are incorporated in other products and re-exported) represents a much higher share than the upstream component (foreign

value added in exports). This high share reflects the important contribution of African natural resources to other countries' exports.

Natural resources are mainly traded with extraregional countries, do not require much transformation (nor foreign inputs), and thus contribute little to African industrial development and its capacity to supply the growing internal demand. The high share of commodities in the region's exports together with inadequate transport, energy and telecommunications infrastructure is also a key factor hampering the development of regional value chains. Among the world's regions, Africa relies the least on regional interactions in the development of GVCs. On both the upstream side (the foreign value added) and the downstream side (the domestic value added included in other countries' exports), the share of intra-African value chain links is very limited compared with all other regions (figure II.6). In terms of sectors, manufacturing and services appear to be more regionally integrated than the primary sector. One of the industries most integrated regionally is agri-processing, where Africa benefits from economies of scale – deriving from regional integration measures – in processing raw materials. However, further development and upscaling of the regional value chains in this industry remains difficult as long as intra-African investments are local market-oriented FDI.

Across RECs, regional value chains seem to be most developed in the three RECs that are

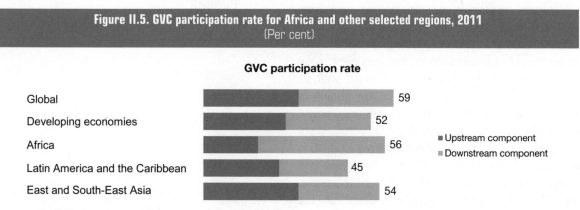

Figure II.5. GVC participation rate for Africa and other selected regions, 2011
(Per cent)

GVC participation rate

Global	59
Developing economies	52
Africa	56
Latin America and the Caribbean	45
East and South-East Asia	54

■ Upstream component
■ Downstream component

Source: UNCTAD-EORA GVC Database.
Note: GVC participation rate indicates the share of a country's exports that is part of a multi-stage trade process; it is the foreign value added (FVA) used in a country's exports (the upstream component) plus the value added supplied to other countries' exports (the downstream component, or DVX), divided by total exports.

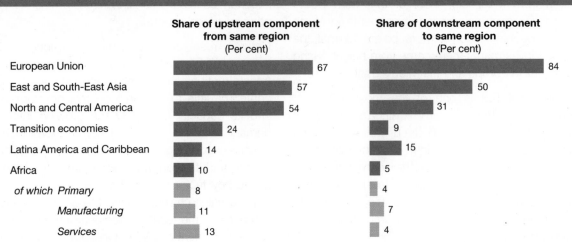

Figure II.6. Regional value chain participation, 2011

Source: UNCTAD-EORA GVC Database.
Note: The upstream component is defined as the foreign value added used in a country's exports; the downstream component
         is defined as the domestic value added supplied to other countries' exports.

planning to create the Tripartite FTA (COMESA, EAC and SADC). This suggests that the economies in this subregion are a step ahead in the regional integration process. Northern African countries that belong to UMA are the least involved in regional value chains, while the participation of ECCAS and ECOWAS in regional value chains is relatively in the average of the continent.

Future prospects for regional integration and industrial development. The Tripartite FTA that COMESA, EAC and SADC members aim to establish could be a useful model for other regional communities to use in boosting their efforts to bring Africa's small and fragmented economies together into a single market. By deepening regional integration, resources will be pooled and local markets enlarged, thus stimulating production and investment and improving prospects for growth and development in the continent. One of the main obstacles to integration as well as to the development of regional value chains is inadequate and poor infrastructure. Insufficient and nonexistent transport and energy services are common problems that affect all firms operating in Africa.[7] To tackle some infrastructure gaps and make further economic development possible, international support is needed. In particular, the sustainable development goals (SDGs) (chapter IV) offer an opportunity to increase FDI that targets the continent's major needs.

The sharp increase in the number of Asian businesses engaging in Africa (through both trade and FDI), as well as the new investments from North America and Europe in R&D and consumer industries, could provide an extraregional impetus to the development of regional value chains and GVCs. With declining wage competitiveness, China, for example, may relocate its labour-intensive industries to low-income countries while upgrading its industry towards more sophisticated products with higher value added (Lin 2011, Brautigam 2010).[8] The relocation of even a small part of China's labour-intensive industries could support industrial development in Africa, providing a much-needed source of employment for the burgeoning working-age population.[9]

2. Asia

Asia continues to be the world's top FDI spot, accounting for nearly 30 per cent of global FDI inflows. Thanks to a significant increase in cross-border M&As, total inflows to the region as a whole amounted to $426 billion in 2013, 3 per cent higher than in 2012. The growth rates of FDI inflows to the East, South-East and South Asia subregions ranged between 2 and 10 per cent, while inflows to West Asia declined by 9 per cent (figure II.7). FDI outflows from subregions showed more diverging trends: outflows from East and South-East Asia experienced growth of 7 and 5 per cent, respectively; outflows from West Asia increased

by about two thirds; and those from South Asia plummeted to a negligible level (figure II.7).

For some low-income countries in the region, weak infrastructure has long been a major challenge in attracting FDI and promoting industrial development. Today, rising intraregional FDI in infrastructure industries, driven by regional integration efforts (section a) and enhanced connectivity through the establishment of corridors between subregions (section b), is likely to accelerate infrastructure build-up, improve the investment climate and promote economic development.

Figure II.7. FDI in and out of developing Asia, by subregion, 2012–2013
(Billions of dollars)

FDI inflows

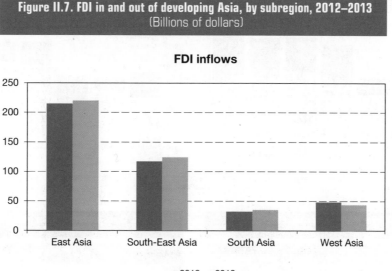

■2012 ■2013

FDI outflows

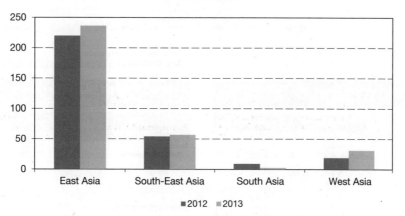

■2012 ■2013

Source: UNCTAD FDI-TNC-GVC Information System, FDI/TNC database (www.unctad.org/fdistatistics).

a. East and South-East Asia

Table A. Distribution of FDI flows among economies, by range,ª 2013

Range	Inflows	Outflows
Above $50 billion	China, Hong Kong (China) and Singapore	China and Hong Kong (China)
$10 to $49 billion	Indonesia, Thailand, Malaysia and Republic of Korea	Republic of Korea, Singapore, Taiwan Province of China and Malaysia
$1.0 to $9.9 billion	Viet Nam, Philippines, Taiwan Province of China, Myanmar, Macao (China), Mongolia and Cambodia	Thailand, Indonesia, Philippines and Viet Nam
$0.1 to $0.9 billion	Brunei Darussalam, Lao People's Democratic Republic and Democratic People's Republic of Korea	..
Below $0.1 billion	Timor-Leste	Mongolia, Macao (China), Cambodia, Timor-Leste, Lao People's Democratic Republic and Brunei Darussalam

ª Economies are listed according to the magnitude of their FDI flows.

Figure A. FDI flows, top 5 host and home economies, 2012–2013
(Billions of dollars)

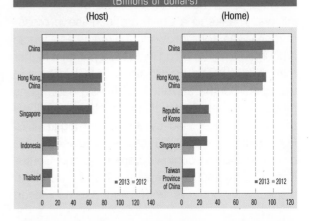

Figure B. FDI inflows, 2007–2013
(Billions of dollars)

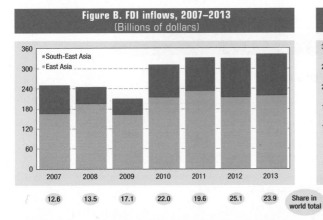

| 12.6 | 13.5 | 17.1 | 22.0 | 19.6 | 25.1 | 23.9 | Share in world total |

Figure C. FDI outflows, 2007–2013
(Billions of dollars)

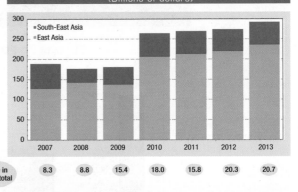

| 8.3 | 8.8 | 15.4 | 18.0 | 15.8 | 20.3 | 20.7 |

Table B. Cross-border M&As by industry, 2012–2013
(Millions of dollars)

Sector/industry	Sales 2012	Sales 2013	Purchases 2012	Purchases 2013
Total	**22 377**	**40 655**	**78 736**	**98 217**
Primary	**831**	**-3 489**	**10 578**	**10 902**
Mining, quarrying and petroleum	421	-3 492	11 982	10 845
Manufacturing	**12 702**	**19 017**	**12 956**	**6 376**
Food, beverages and tobacco	7 197	13 411	4 820	5 701
Basic metal and metal products	281	919	2 822	-2 339
Computer, electronic optical prod. & elect. equipment	712	1 239	2 878	1 635
Machinery and equipment	1 830	196	1 525	1 897
Services	**8 844**	**25 128**	**55 203**	**80 939**
Electricity, gas, water and waste management	858	1 216	2 761	4 873
Information and communications	4 379	104	4 827	2 827
Financial and insurance activities	709	14 977	46 321	66 826
Business services	1 056	10 149	452	3 704

Table C. Cross-border M&As by region/country, 2012–2013
(Millions of dollars)

Region/country	Sales 2012	Sales 2013	Purchases 2012	Purchases 2013
World	**22 377**	**40 655**	**78 736**	**98 217**
Developed economies	**5 357**	**6 065**	**54 514**	**50 844**
European Union	2 686	-5 814	24 286	8 927
United Kingdom	-2 958	721	15 364	3 033
Canada	-290	-32	7 778	20 805
United States	-1 149	5 038	7 608	11 289
Australia	580	-270	11 050	6 861
Japan	3 821	9 005	2 969	1 676
Developing economies	**16 040**	**32 148**	**23 966**	**45 213**
Africa	-386	334	1 861	9 728
Asia and Oceania	16 339	30 619	16 614	32 610
Latin America and the Caribbean	87	1 194	5 491	2 875
Transition economies	**-**	**597**	**256**	**2 160**

Table D. Greenfield FDI projects by industry, 2012–2013
(Millions of dollars)

Sector/industry	East and South-East Asia as destination 2012	East and South-East Asia as destination 2013	East and South-East Asia as investors 2012	East and South-East Asia as investors 2013
Total	**147 303**	**146 465**	**110 393**	**106 067**
Primary	**363**	**593**	**3 022**	**2 195**
Mining, quarrying and petroleum	363	372	3 022	2 195
Manufacturing	**70 298**	**76 193**	**43 738**	**22 285**
Food, beverages and tobacco	6 260	5 012	4 028	2 181
Chemicals and chemical products	9 946	13 209	10 770	3 301
Electrical and electronic equipment	9 361	7 571	11 562	5 492
Motor vehicles and other transport equipment	17 212	16 855	4 844	3 293
Services	**76 641**	**69 679**	**63 632**	**81 588**
Electricity, gas and water	4 507	17 925	14 392	7 979
Construction	19 652	11 179	29 147	13 388
Finance	13 658	9 080	6 109	4 951
Business services	9 611	9 553	2 184	42 666

Table E. Greenfield FDI projects by region/country, 2012–2013
(Millions of dollars)

Partner region/economy	East and South-East Asia as destination 2012	East and South-East Asia as destination 2013	East and South-East Asia as investors 2012	East and South-East Asia as investors 2013
World	**147 303**	**146 465**	**110 393**	**106 067**
Developed economies	**98 785**	**100 261**	**35 998**	**15 789**
European Union	38 453	41 127	19 012	8 230
Germany	12 036	13 189	468	401
United Kingdom	8 443	7 632	15 003	4 079
United States	27 637	23 173	13 417	3 943
Japan	24 252	27 191	677	1 728
Developing economies	**47 849**	**45 721**	**69 027**	**88 723**
Asia	47 327	44 652	59 632	36 904
East Asia	23 966	17 753	25 144	21 185
South-East Asia	19 728	14 094	18 549	10 662
South Asia	2 386	2 627	8 211	3 016
Transition economies	1 247	10 178	7 728	2 041

Against the backdrop of a sluggish world economy and a regional slowdown in growth, total FDI inflows to East and South-East Asia reached $347 billion in 2013, 4 per cent higher than in 2012. Inflows to East Asia rose by 2 per cent to $221 billion, while those to South-East Asia increased by 7 per cent to $125 billion. FDI outflows from the overall region rose by 7 per cent to $293 billion. In late 2012, the 10 member States of the Association for Southeast Asian Development (ASEAN) and their 6 FTA partners (Australia, China, India, Japan, the Republic of Korea and New Zealand) launched negotiations for the Regional Comprehensive Economic Partnership (RCEP). In 2013, combined FDI inflows to the 16 negotiating members amounted to $343 billion, accounting for 24 per cent of global FDI flows. The expansion of free trade areas in and beyond the region is likely to further increase the dynamism of FDI growth and deliver associated development benefits.

China's outflows grew faster than inflows. FDI inflows to China have resumed their growth since late 2012. With inflows at $124 billion in 2013, the country again ranked second in the world (figure I.3) and narrowed the gap with the largest host country, the United States. China's 2 per cent growth in 2013 was driven by rising inflows in services, particularly trade and real estate. As TNCs invest in the country increasingly through M&As, the value of cross-border M&A sales surged, from $10 billion in 2012 to $27 billion in 2013.

In the meantime, China has strengthened its position as one of the leading sources of FDI, and its outflows are expected to surpass its inflows within two years. During 2013, FDI outflows swelled by 15 per cent, to an estimated $101 billion, the third highest in the world. Chinese companies made a number of megadeals in developed countries, such as the $15 billion CNOOC-Nexen deal in Canada and the $5 billion Shuanghui-Smithfield deal in the United States – the largest overseas deals undertaken by Chinese firms in the oil and gas and the food industries, respectively. As China continues to deregulate outward FDI,[10] outflows to both developed and developing countries are expected to grow further. For instance, Sinopec, the second largest Chinese oil company, plans to invest $20 billion in Africa in the next five years,[11] while Lenovo's recent acquisitions of IBM's X86 server business ($2.3 billion) and Motorola Mobile ($2.9 billion) will boost Chinese FDI in the United States.

High-income economies in the region performed well in attracting FDI. Inflows to the Republic of Korea reached $12 billion, the highest level since the mid-2000s, thanks to rising foreign investments in shipbuilding and electronics – industries in which the country enjoys strong international competitiveness – as well as in the utility industries. In 2013, FDI inflows to Taiwan Province of China grew by 15 per cent, to $4 billion, as economic cooperation with Mainland China helped improve business opportunities in the island economy.[12] In 2013, FDI outflows from the Republic of Korea declined by 5 per cent to $29 billion, while those from Taiwan Province of China rose by 9 per cent to $14 billion.

Hong Kong (China) and Singapore – the other two high-income economies in the region – experienced relatively slow growth in FDI inflows. Inflows to Hong Kong (China) increased by 2 per cent to $77 billion. Although this amount is still below the record level of $96 billion in 2011, it is higher than the three-year averages before the crisis ($49 billion) and after the crisis ($68 billion). In 2012, annual FDI inflows to Singapore rose above $60 billion for the first time. A number of megadeals in 2013, such as the acquisition of Fraser & Neave by TCC Assets for about $7 billion, drove FDI inflows to a record $64 billion. As the recipients of the second and third largest FDI in developing Asia, Hong Kong (China) and Singapore have competed for the regional headquarters of TNCs with each other, as well as with some large Chinese cities, in recent years (box II.1).

FDI growth in ASEAN slowed, particularly in some lower-income countries. FDI inflows to ASEAN rose by 7 per cent in 2013, to $125 billion. It seems that the rapid growth of FDI inflows to ASEAN during the past three years – from $47 billion in 2009 to $118 billion in 2012 – has slowed, but the balance between East Asia and South-East Asia continued to shift in favour of the latter (figure B).

Among the ASEAN member States, Indonesia was most affected by the financial turmoil in emerging economies in mid-2013. However, FDI inflows remained stable, at about $18 billion.

Box II.1. Attracting regional headquarters of TNCs: competition among Asian economies

Hong Kong (China) and Singapore are very attractive locations for the regional headquarters of TNCs. The two economies are similar in terms of specific criteria that are key for attracting regional headquarters (European Chamber, 2011). As highly open economies, strong financial centres and regional hubs of commerce, both are very successful in attracting such headquarters. The number of TNC headquarters based in Hong Kong (China), for example, had reached about 1,380 by the end of 2013. Its proximity to Mainland China may partly explain its competitive edge. The significant presence of such headquarters has helped make the two economies the major recipients of FDI in their subregions: Hong Kong (China) is second only to Mainland China in East Asia, while Singapore is the largest host in South-East Asia.

The two economies now face increasing competition from large cities in Mainland China, such as Beijing and Shanghai. By the end of October 2013, for example, more than 430 TNCs had established regional headquarters in Shanghai, as well as 360 R&D centres.[13] However, the TNCs establishing these headquarters have targeted mainly the Chinese market, while Hong Kong (China) and Singapore remain major destinations for the headquarters of TNCs targeting the markets of Asia and the Pacific at large.

In March 2014, the Chinese Government decided to move the headquarters of CIFIT Group, China's largest TNC in terms of foreign assets, from Beijing to Hong Kong (China). This decision shows the Government's support for the economy of Hong Kong (China) and is likely to enhance the city's competitive advantages for attracting investment from leading TNCs, including those from Mainland China.

Source: UNCTAD.

In Malaysia, another large FDI recipient in ASEAN, inflows increased by 22 per cent to $12 billion as a result of rising FDI in services. In Thailand, inflows grew to $13 billion; however, about 400 FDI projects were shelved in reaction to the continued political instability, and the prospects for inflows to the country remain uncertain.[14] Nevertheless, Japanese investment in manufacturing in Thailand has risen significantly during the past few years and is likely to continue to drive up FDI to the country. FDI inflows to the Philippines were not affected by 2013's typhoon Haiyan; on the contrary, total inflows rose by one fifth, to $4 billion – the highest level in its history. The performance of ASEAN's low-income economies varied: while inflows to Myanmar increased by 17 per cent to $2.6 billion, those to Cambodia, the Lao People's Democratic Republic and Viet Nam remained at almost the same levels.

FDI outflows from ASEAN increased by 5 per cent. Singapore, the regional group's leading investor, saw its outward FDI double, rising from $13 billion in 2012 to $27 billion in 2013. This significant increase was powered by large overseas acquisitions by Singaporean firms and the resultant surge in the amount of transactions. Outflows from Malaysia and Thailand, the other two important investing countries in South-East Asia, dropped by 21 per cent and 49 per cent, to $14 billion and $7 billion, respectively.

Prospects remain positive. Economic growth has remained robust and new liberalization measures have been introduced, such as the launch of the China (Shanghai) Pilot Free Trade Zone. Thus, East Asia is likely to enjoy an increase of FDI inflows in the near future. The performance of South-East Asia is expected to improve as well, partly as a result of the accelerated regional integration process (see below). However, rising geopolitical tensions have become an important concern in the region and may add uncertainties to the investment outlook.

As part of a renewed effort to bring about economic reform and openness, new policy measures are being introduced in trade, investment and finance in the newly established China (Shanghai) Pilot Free Trade Zone. In terms of inward FDI administration, a new approach based on pre-establishment national treatment has been adopted in the zone, and a negative list announced. Specific segments in six service industries – finance, transport, commerce and trade, professional services, cultural services and public services – have been opened to foreign investors (chapter III). FDI inflows to the zone and to Shanghai in general are expected to grow as a result.[15]

Accelerated regional integration contributes to rising FDI flows

Regional economic integration in East and South-East Asia has accelerated in recent years. This has contributed to enhanced competitiveness in attracting FDI and TNC activities across different industries. In particular, investment cooperation among major economies has facilitated international investment and operation by regional TNCs in their neighbouring countries, contributing to greater intraregional FDI flows and stronger regional production networks. Low-income countries in the region have benefited significantly from such flows in building up their infrastructure and productive capacities. The geographical expansion of free trade areas in and beyond the region is likely to further extend the dynamism of FDI growth and deliver associated development benefits.

A comprehensive regional partnership in the making. ASEAN was the starting point of regional economic integration in East and South-East Asia, and has always been at the centre of the integration process. Established in 1967, ASEAN initially involved Indonesia, Malaysia, the Philippines, Singapore and Thailand. Subsequently, Brunei Darussalam, Viet Nam, the Lao People's Democratic Republic, Myanmar and Cambodia joined. Since its establishment, ASEAN has made efforts to widen as well as deepen the regional integration process, contributing to improved regional connectivity and interaction. Its economic links with the rest of the world have increasingly intensified and its intraregional links have strengthened.

Over time, ASEAN has broadened the scope of regional economic integration alongside its major partners – China, the Republic of Korea and Japan – through the ASEAN+3 Cooperation.[16] The East Asia Summit involves these three countries as well, in addition to Australia, India and New Zealand.[17] ASEAN has signed FTAs with all six countries. In November 2012, the 10 ASEAN member States and the six ASEAN FTA partners launched negotiations for RCEP, which aims to establish the largest free trade area in the world by population. In

2013, combined FDI inflows to the 16 negotiating members amounted to $343 billion, or 24 per cent of global FDI inflows.

Proactive investment cooperation. Investment cooperation is an important facet of these regional economic integration efforts. In 1998, ASEAN members signed the Framework Agreement on the ASEAN Investment Area (AIA). In 2009, the ASEAN Comprehensive Investment Agreement (ACIA) consolidated the 1998 AIA Agreement and the 1987 Agreement for the Promotion and Protection of Investments (also known as the ASEAN Investment Guarantee Agreement). At the ASEAN Economic Ministers Meeting in August 2011, member States agreed to accelerate the implementation of programmes towards the ASEAN Economic Community in 2015, focusing on initiatives that would enhance investment promotion and facilitation.

In addition, various investment agreements have been signed under general FTA frameworks in East and South-East Asia. In recent years significant progress has been made, involving leading economies in Asia, including China, India, Japan and the Republic of Korea. For instance, ASEAN and China signed their investment agreement in August 2009. In May 2012, China, Japan and the Republic of Korea signed a tripartite investment agreement, which represented a crucial step in establishing a free trade bloc among the three East Asian countries.

Within the overall framework of regional integration, these investment agreements aim to facilitate international investment in general but may also promote cross-border investment by regional TNCs in particular. In addition, ASEAN has established effective institutional mechanisms of investment facilitation and promotion, aiming to coordinate national efforts within the bloc and compete effectively with other countries in attracting FDI.

Rising intraregional FDI flows. Proactive regional investment cooperation efforts in East and South-East Asia have contributed to a rise in FDI inflows to the region in general and intraregional FDI flows in particular. ASEAN has seen intraregional flows rise over the past decade, and for some of its member States, inflows from neighbouring countries have increased significantly. During 2010–2012, the RCEP-negotiating countries (or ASEAN+6 countries) provided on average 43 per cent of FDI flows to ASEAN, compared with an average of 17 per cent during 1998–2000 (figure II.8).

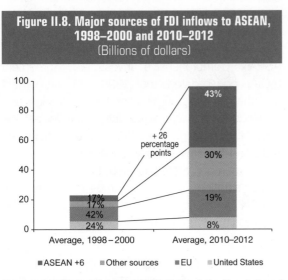

Figure II.8. Major sources of FDI inflows to ASEAN, 1998–2000 and 2010–2012
(Billions of dollars)

Source: UNCTAD, Bilateral FDI Statistics (http://unctad.org/en/Pages/DIAE/FDI%20Statistics/FDI-Statistics-Bilateral.aspx).

China, India, Japan and the Republic of Korea, as well as Singapore, Malaysia and Thailand have made considerable advances as sources of FDI to ASEAN. It seems that this has taken place mainly at the cost of the United States and the European Union (EU). Singapore is an important source of FDI for other countries in ASEAN, as well as for other major Asian economies, such as China and India.[18] Japan has been one of the leading investors in South-East Asia, and ASEAN as a whole accounted for more than one tenth of all Japanese outward FDI stock in 2012. In 2013, Japanese investors spent nearly $8 billion in ASEAN, which is replacing China as the most important target of Japanese FDI. In recent years, FDI flows from China to ASEAN countries have rapidly increased, and the country's outward FDI stock in ASEAN as a whole had exceeded $25 billion by the end of 2012 (figure II.9). The establishment of the China-ASEAN Free Trade Area in early 2010 has strengthened regional economic cooperation and contributed to the promotion of two-way FDI flows, particularly from China to ASEAN. Accordingly, the share of ASEAN in China's total outward FDI stock rose to 5.3 per cent in 2012.

Emerging industrial patterns and development implications. Rising intraregional FDI flows have focused increasingly on infrastructure and manufacturing. Low-income countries in the region have gained in particular.

- **Manufacturing.** Rising intraregional FDI in manufacturing has helped South-East Asian countries build their productive capacities in both capital- and labour-intensive industries. TNCs from Japan have invested in capital-intensive manufacturing industries such as automotive and electronics. For instance, Toyota has invested heavily in Thailand in recent years, making the country its third largest production base. Attracted by low labour costs and good growth prospects, Japanese companies invested about $1.8 billion in Viet Nam in 2011, and $4.4 billion of Japanese investment was approved in 2012. FDI from Japan is expected to increase in other ASEAN member States as well, particularly Myanmar. China's investment in manufacturing in ASEAN covers a broad range of industries but is especially significant in labour-intensive manufacturing.

- **Infrastructure.** TNCs from Singapore have been important investors in infrastructure industries in the region, accounting for about 20 per cent of greenfield investments. In recent years, Chinese companies have invested in Indonesia and Viet Nam.[19] In transport, Chinese investment is expected to increase in railways, including in the Lao People's Democratic Republic and Myanmar. In November 2013, China and Thailand signed a memorandum of understanding on a large project that is part of a planned regional network of high-speed railways linking China and Singapore. In the meantime, other ASEAN member States have begun to open some transport industries to foreign participation, which may lead to more intraregional FDI (including from Chinese companies). For example, Indonesia has recently allowed foreign investment in service industries such as port management.[20] As more countries in South-East Asia announce ambitious long-term plans, total investment in infrastructure in this subregion between 2011 and 2020 is expected to exceed $1.5 trillion.[21] Fulfilling this huge amount of investment will require mobilizing various sources of funding, in which TNCs and financial institutions within East and South-East Asia can

Figure II.9. China: outward FDI stock in ASEAN member States and share of ASEAN in total, 2005–2012
(Billions of dollars and per cent)

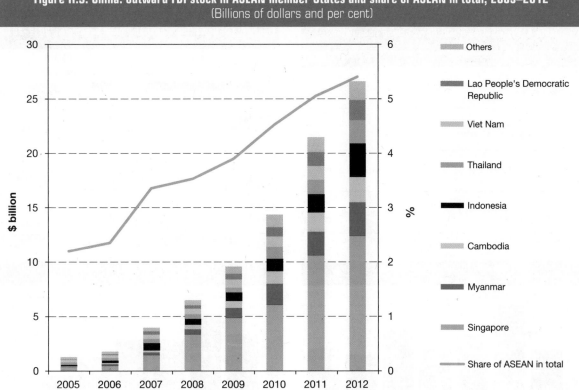

Source: UNCTAD, Bilateral FDI Statistics (http://unctad.org/en/Pages/DIAE/FDI%20Statistics/FDI-Statistics-Bilateral.aspx).

play an important role, through both equity- and non-equity modes.

For most of the low-income countries in the region, intraregional flows account for a major share of FDI inflows, contributing to a rapid build-up of infrastructure and productive capacities. For instance, Indonesia and the Philippines have seen higher capital inflows to infrastructure industries, such as electricity generation and transmission, through various contractual arrangements. Cambodia and Myanmar, the two LDCs in South-East Asia, have recently emerged as attractive locations for investment in labour-intensive industries, including textiles, garments and footwear. Low-income South-East Asian countries have benefited from rising production costs in China and the subsequent relocation of production facilities.

Outlook. The negotiation of RCEP started in May 2013 and is expected to be completed in 2015. It is likely to promote FDI inflows and associated development benefits for economies at different levels of development in East and South-East Asia, through improved investment climates, enlarged markets, and the build-up of infrastructure and productive capacities. RCEP is not the only integration mechanism that covers a large range of economies across Asia and the Pacific. As the Asia Pacific Economic Cooperation and the Trans-Pacific Partnership (chapter I) extend beyond the geographical scope of the region, so may the development benefits related to increased flows of both trade and investment.

b. South Asia

Table A. Distribution of FDI flows among economies, by range,ᵃ 2013

Range	Inflows	Outflows
Above $10 billion	India	..
$1.0 to $9.9 billion	Islamic Republic of Iran, Bangladesh and Pakistan	India
$0.1 to $0.9 billion	Sri Lanka and Maldives	Islamic Republic of Iran and Pakistan
Below $0.1 billion	Nepal, Afghanistan and Bhutan	Sri Lanka and Bangladesh

ᵃ Economies are listed according to the magnitude of their FDI flows.

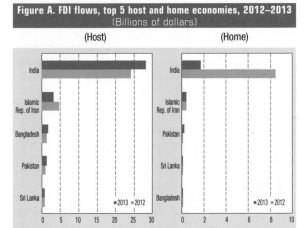

Figure A. FDI flows, top 5 host and home economies, 2012–2013
(Billions of dollars)

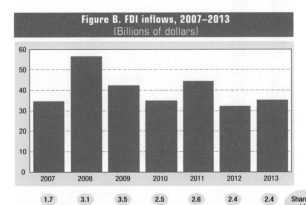

Figure B. FDI inflows, 2007–2013
(Billions of dollars)

	2007	2008	2009	2010	2011	2012	2013
Share in world total	1.7	3.1	3.5	2.5	2.6	2.4	2.4

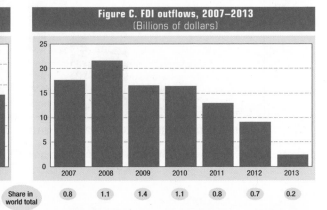

Figure C. FDI outflows, 2007–2013
(Billions of dollars)

	2007	2008	2009	2010	2011	2012	2013
	0.8	1.1	1.4	1.1	0.8	0.7	0.2

Table B. Cross-border M&As by industry, 2012–2013
(Millions of dollars)

Sector/industry	Sales		Purchases	
	2012	2013	2012	2013
Total	2 821	4 784	3 104	1 621
Primary	130	28	-70	1 482
Mining, quarrying and petroleum	130	2	-70	1 482
Manufacturing	1 232	4 608	718	920
Food, beverages and tobacco	355	1 173	-2	-34
Chemicals and chemical products	-207	3 620	12	246
Pharmaceuticals, medicinal chemical & botanical prod.	138	3 148	502	551
Basic metal and metal products	124	-4 068	116	65
Services	1 459	148	2 456	-781
Electricity, gas, water and waste management	40	-677	-	-
Information and communications	-430	-209	414	85
Financial and insurance activities	1 597	-298	675	-691
Business services	-59	621	56	350

Table C. Cross-border M&As by region/country, 2012–2013
(Millions of dollars)

Region/country	Sales		Purchases	
	2012	2013	2012	2013
World	2 821	4 784	3 104	1 621
Developed economies	1 350	3 367	2 421	1 883
European Union	467	1 518	669	1 734
France	1 051	144	-	108
United Kingdom	-791	1 110	62	510
United States	627	1 368	1 759	387
Japan	1 077	382	7	-
Switzerland	-1 011	-62	357	-
Developing economies	1 456	1 212	683	-262
Africa	431	233	22	419
Asia and Oceania	1 026	979	542	-1 240
Latin America and the Caribbean	-	-	119	559
Transition economies	-	-	-	-

Table D. Greenfield FDI projects by industry, 2012–2013
(Millions of dollars)

Sector/industry	South Asia as destination		South Asia as investors	
	2012	2013	2012	2013
Total	39 525	24 499	27 714	15 789
Primary	165	23	4 602	47
Mining, quarrying and petroleum	165	23	4 602	47
Manufacturing	16 333	11 220	11 365	6 842
Chemicals and chemical products	1 786	1 161	1 668	900
Metals and metal products	3 317	896	2 178	886
Motor vehicles and other transport equipment	4 248	1 969	2 941	2 386
Other manufacturing	1 089	1 008	103	509
Services	23 027	13 256	11 747	8 900
Electricity, gas and water	6 199	2 044	4 236	3 069
Transport, storage and communications	7 210	3 265	1 442	2 121
Finance	3 264	1 906	726	722
Business services	2 805	2 389	2 048	2 021

Table E. Greenfield FDI projects by region/country, 2012–2013
(Millions of dollars)

Partner region/economy	South Asia as destination		South Asia as investors	
	2012	2013	2012	2013
World	39 525	24 499	27 714	15 789
Developed economies	23 579	17 495	8 598	4 115
European Union	12 962	6 543	2 895	2 593
Germany	4 291	1 137	847	500
United Kingdom	2 748	2 386	1 765	1 733
United States	5 559	4 718	829	1 308
Japan	3 147	2 801	84	45
Developing economies	15 694	6 928	18 736	10 802
Africa	149	871	9 315	5 799
Asia and Oceania	15 511	6 031	8 815	4 717
East and South-East Asia	8 211	3 016	2 386	2 627
West Asia	4 972	2 293	4 100	1 367
Transition economies	252	76	380	872

FDI inflows to South Asia rose by 10 per cent to $36 billion in 2013. Outflows from the region slid by nearly three fourths, to $2 billion. Facing old challenges and new opportunities, South Asian countries registered varied performance in attracting FDI. At the regional level, renewed efforts to enhance connectivity with other parts of Asia are likely to help build up infrastructure and improve the investment climate. India has taken various steps to open its services sector to foreign investors, most notably in the retail industry. It seems that the opening up of single-brand retail in 2006 has led to increased FDI inflows; that of multi-brand retail in 2012 has so far not generated the expected results.

Trends in M&As and announced greenfield projects diverged. In 2013, the total amount of announced greenfield investments in South Asia dropped by 38 per cent, to $24 billion (table D). In manufacturing, greenfield projects in metals and metal products and in the automotive industry experienced considerable drops; in services, a large decline took place in infrastructure industries and financial services. Most major recipients of FDI in the region experienced a significant decline in greenfield projects, except for Sri Lanka, where they remained at a high level of about $1.3 billion.

In contrast, the total amount of cross-border M&A sales rose by 70 per cent, to $5 billion. The value of M&As boomed in manufacturing, particularly in food and beverage, chemical products and pharmaceuticals (table B). A number of large deals took place in these industries. For instance, in food and beverage, Relay (Netherlands) acquired a 27 per cent stake in United Sprits (India) for $1 billion, and, in pharmaceuticals, Mylan (United States) took over Agila (India) for $1.9 billion. Some smaller deals also took place in other South Asian countries, including Bangladesh, Pakistan and Sri Lanka.

FDI inflows rose in India, but macroeconomic uncertainties remain a major concern. The dominant recipient of FDI in South Asia, India, experienced a 17 per cent increase in inflows in 2013, to $28 billion (table A). The value of greenfield projects by TNCs declined sharply in both manufacturing and services. Flows in the form of M&As from the United Kingdom and the United States increased, while those from Japan declined considerably. In the meantime, the value of greenfield projects from

these countries all dropped, but only slightly. The main manufacturing industries targeted by foreign investors were food and beverage, chemical products, and pharmaceuticals.

Macroeconomic uncertainties in India continue to be a concern for foreign investors. The annual rate of GDP growth in that country has slowed to about 4 per cent, and the current account deficit has reached an unprecedented level – nearly 5 per cent of GDP. The Indian rupee depreciated significantly in mid-2013. High inflation and the other macroeconomic problems have cast doubts on prospects for FDI, despite the Government's ambitious goal to boost foreign investment. Policy responses to macroeconomic problems will play an important role in determining FDI prospects in the short to medium run.[22]

For Indian companies, domestic economic problems seemed to have deterred international expansion, and India saw its outward FDI drop to merely $1.7 billion in 2013. The slide occurred mainly as a result of reversed equity investment – from $2.2 billion to -2.6 billion – and large divestments by Indian TNCs accounted for much of the reverse. Facing a weak economy and high interest rates at home, some Indian companies with high financial leverage sold equity or assets in order to improve cash flows.[23]

Facing old challenges as well as new opportunities, other countries reported varied performance. Bangladesh experienced significant growth in FDI inflows: from $1.3 billion in 2012 to about $1.6 billion in 2013. Manufacturing accounted for a major part of inflows and contributed significantly to employment creation (UNCTAD, 2013a). The country has emerged as an important player in the manufacturing and export of ready-made garments (RMG) and has become a sourcing hotspot with its advantages of low cost and capacity (*WIR13*). However, the industry in Bangladesh has faced serious challenges, including in labour standards and skill development (box II.2).

FDI inflows to Pakistan increased to $1.3 billion, thanks to rising inflows to services in 2013. The country recently held its first auction for 3G and 4G networks of mobile telecommunications. China Mobile was the winning bidder and now plans to invest $1.5 billion in Pakistan in the next four years.

Box II.2. Challenges facing the garment industry of Bangladesh: roles of domestic and foreign companies

Bangladesh has been recognized as one of the "Next 11" emerging countries to watch, following the BRICS countries (Brazil, Russian Federation, India, China, and South Africa) and listed among the "Frontier Five" emerging economies, along with Kazakhstan, Kenya, Nigeria and Viet Nam. The RMG industry has been the major driver of the country's economic development in recent decades and is still fundamental to the prospects of the Bangladesh economy. This industry is considered the "next stop" for developed-country TNCs that are moving sourcing away from China. Such opportunity is essential for development, as Bangladesh needs to create jobs for its growing labour force (ILO, 2010).

With the prediction of further growth in the industry and the willingness of developed-country firms to source from Bangladesh, the picture on the demand side seems promising. However, realizing that promise requires the country to address constraints on the supply side. At the national level, poor infrastructure continues to deter investment in general and FDI in particular (UNCTAD, 2013a). At the firm level, one issue concerns the need for better compliance with labour legislation, as illustrated by several tragedies in the country's garment industry. Besides strengthening such compliance, the industry needs to develop its capabilities, not only by consolidating strengths in basic garment production but also by diversifying into higher-value activities along the RMG value chain.

Currently, Bangladesh's garment firms compete predominantly on price and capacity. The lack of sufficient skills remains a major constraint, and both domestic and foreign-invested firms need to boost their efforts in this regard. A recent UNCTAD study shows the dominance of basic and on-the-job training, which links directly to established career trajectories within firms. However, high labour turnover hampers skill development at the firm level. On-the-job training is complemented by various initiatives supported by employer organizations, which have training centres but often cooperate with governmental and non-governmental organizations.

FDI has accounted for a relatively small share of projects in the Bangladesh RMG industry in recent years. During 2003–2011, only 11 per cent of investment projects registered in the industry were foreign-originated. Nevertheless, owing to the larger scale of such projects, they account for a significantly high share of employment and capital formation, and they can be an important catalyst for skills development in the labour force.

Source: UNCTAD (2014a).

FDI to the Islamic Republic of Iran focuses heavily on oil exploration and production, and economic sanctions have had negative effects on those inflows, which declined by about one third in 2013, to $3 billion.

Services have attracted increasing attention from TNCs, as countries open new sectors to foreign investment. However, as demonstrated in India's retail industry (see next subsection), some of the new liberalization efforts have not yet been able to boost FDI inflows as governments expected. One reason is the uncertain policy environment. For instance, responses from foreign investors to the Indian Government's liberalization efforts have been mixed.

Enhanced regional connectivity improves FDI prospects in South Asia. Poor infrastructure has long been a major challenge in attracting FDI and promoting industrial development in the region. Policy developments associated with enhanced connectivity with East Asia, especially the potential establishment of the Bangladesh-China-India-

Myanmar Economic Corridor and the China-Pakistan Economic Corridor (box II.3), are likely to accelerate infrastructure investment in South Asia, and to improve the overall investment climate. As a result of interregional initiatives, China has shown its potential to become an important source of FDI in South Asia, particularly in infrastructure and manufacturing industries. The Chinese Government has started negotiating with the Indian Government on setting up an industrial zone in India to host investments from Chinese companies. China is the third country to consider such country-specific industrial zones in India, following Japan and the Republic of Korea (*WIR13*).

New round of retail liberalization has not yet brought expected FDI inflows to India

Organized retailing, such as supermarkets and retail chains, has expanded rapidly in emerging markets.[25] In India, organized retail has become a $28 billion sector and is expected to grow to

Box II.3. International economic corridors and FDI prospects in South Asia

Two international economic corridors linking South Asia and East and South-East Asia are to be established: the Bangladesh-China-India-Myanmar (BCIM) Economic Corridor and the China-Pakistan Economic Corridor. Countries involved in the two initiatives have drawn up specific timetables for implementation. For the BCIM Economic Corridor, for example, the four countries have agreed to build transport, energy and telecommunication networks connecting each other.[24]

Box figure II.3.1. The Bangladesh-China-India-Myanmar Economic Corridor and the China-Pakistan Economic Corridor: the geographical scope

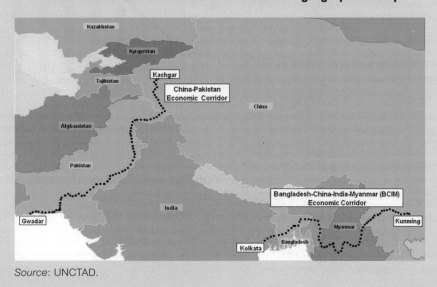

Source: UNCTAD.

The two initiatives will help enhance connectivity between Asian subregions and foster regional economic cooperation. In particular, these initiatives will facilitate international investment, enhancing FDI flows between participating countries and benefiting low-income countries in South Asia. Significant investment in infrastructure, particularly for land transportation, is expected to take place along these corridors, strengthening the connectedness of the three subregions. In addition, industrial zones will be built along these corridors, leading to rising investment in manufacturing in the countries involved. This is likely to help South Asian countries benefit from the production relocation that is under way in China.

Source: UNCTAD.

a market worth $260 billion by 2020, according to forecasts of the Boston Consulting Group. As part of an overall reform programme and in order to boost investment and improve efficiency in the industry, the Indian Government opened up single-brand and multi-brand retail in 2006 and 2012, respectively. However, the two rounds of liberalization have had different effects on TNCs' investment decisions, and the recent round has not yet generated the expected results.

Two rounds of retail liberalization. The liberalization of the Indian retail sector has encountered significant political resistance from domestic interest groups, such as local retailers and

small suppliers (Bhattacharyya, 2012). In response, the Government adopted a gradual approach to opening up the sector – first the single-brand segment and then the multi-brand one. When the Government opened single-brand retail to foreign investment in 2006, it allowed 51 per cent foreign ownership; five years later, it allowed 100 per cent. In September 2012, the Government started to allow 51 per cent foreign ownership in multi-brand retail.

However, to protect relevant domestic stakeholders and to enhance the potential development benefits of FDI, the Government has simultaneously introduced specific regulations. These regulations cover important issues, such as the minimum amount of investment, the location of operation, the mode of entry and the share of local sourcing. For instance, single-brand retailers must source 30 per cent of their goods from local small and medium-size enterprises. Multi-brand retailers may open stores only in cities with populations greater than 1 million and must invest at least $100 million. In addition, the Government recently clarified that foreign multi-brand retailers may not acquire existing Indian retailers.

The opening up of single-brand retail in 2006 led to increased FDI inflows. Since the initial opening up of the retail sector, a number of the world's leading retailers, such as Wal-Mart (United States) and Tesco (United Kingdom), have taken serious steps to enter the Indian market. These TNCs have started doing businesses of wholesale and single-brand retailing, sometimes through joint ventures with local conglomerates. For instance, jointly with Bharti Group, Wal-Mart opened about 20 stores in more than a dozen major cities. Tesco's operations include sourcing and service centres, as well as a franchise arrangement with Tata Group. It has also signed an agreement to supply Star Bazaar with exclusive access to Tesco's retail expertise and 80 per cent of the stock of the local chain.

Thanks to policy changes in 2006, annual FDI inflows to the trade sector in general jumped from an average of $60 million during 2003–2005 to about $600 million during 2007–2009. Inflows have fluctuated between $390 million and $570 million in recent years (figure II.10). The share of the sector in total FDI inflows rose from less than 1 per cent in 2005 to about 3 per cent during 2008–2009. However, that share has declined as investment encouraged by the first round of investment liberalization lost momentum.

The opening up of multi-brand retail in 2012 has not generated the expected results. Policy-related uncertainties continue to hamper the expansion plans of foreign chains. Although foreign investment continues to flow into single-brand retail, no new investment projects have been recorded in multi-brand retail and in fact divestments have taken place. Major TNCs that entered the Indian market after the first round of liberalization have taken steps to get out of the market. For instance,

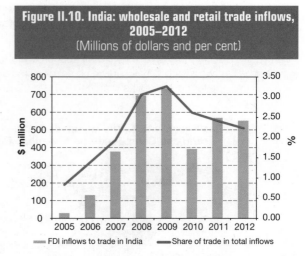

Figure II.10. India: wholesale and retail trade inflows, 2005–2012
(Millions of dollars and per cent)

Source: UNCTAD FDI-TNC-GVC Information System, FDI/TNC database (www.unctad.org/fdistatistics).

Wal-Mart (United States) recently abandoned its plan to open full-scale retail outlets in India and dissolved its partnership with Bharti.

TNCs' passive and even negative reactions to the second round of retail liberalization in India were due partly to the strict operational requirements and continued policy uncertainties. As the two rounds of policy changes encountered significant political resistance, compromises have been made at both national and local levels to safeguard local interests by regulating issues related to the location of operations, the mode of entry and the share of local sourcing required.

The way forward. A different policy approach could be considered for better leveraging foreign investment for the development of Indian retail industry. For example, in terms of mode of entry, franchising and other non-equity forms of TNC participation can be options. Through such arrangements, the host country can benefit from foreign capital and know-how while minimizing potential tensions between foreign and local stakeholders.

c. West Asia

Table A. Distribution of FDI flows among economies, by range,ᵃ 2013

Range	Inflows	Outflows
Above $10 billion	Turkey and United Arab Emirates	..
$5.0 to $9.9 billion	Saudi Arabia	Kuwait and Qatar
$1.0 to $4.9 billion	Iraq, Lebanon, Kuwait, Jordan and Oman	Saudi Arabia, Turkey, United Arab Emirates, Oman and Bahrain
Below $1.0 billion	Bahrain, State of Palestine, Yemen and Qatar	Lebanon, Iraq, Yemen, Jordan and State of Palestine

ᵃ Economies are listed according to the magnitude of their FDI flows.

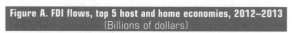
Figure A. FDI flows, top 5 host and home economies, 2012–2013
(Billions of dollars)

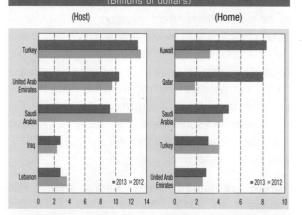

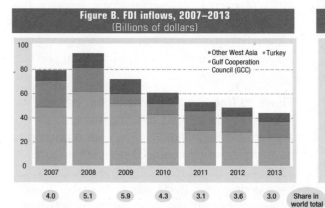
Figure B. FDI inflows, 2007–2013
(Billions of dollars)

Figure C. FDI outflows, 2007–2013
(Billions of dollars)

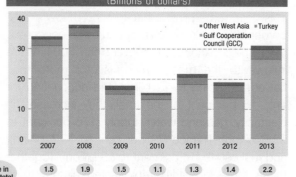

Table B. Cross-border M&As by industry, 2012–2013
(Millions of dollars)

Sector/industry	Sales 2012	Sales 2013	Purchases 2012	Purchases 2013
Total	8 219	2 065	11 390	8 077
Primary	233	357	21	476
Mining, quarrying and petroleum	233	344	21	466
Manufacturing	2 568	451	1 668	61
Food, beverages and tobacco	1 019	186	1 605	-
Pharmaceuticals, medicinal chem. & botanical prod.	700	40	27	-
Services	5 419	1 257	9 700	7 540
Electricity, gas and water	284	140	-	1 908
Construction	125	14	1 126	-47
Transportation and storage	874	55	-132	483
Information and communications	3 357	21	2 803	1 137
Financial and insurance activities	- 298	465	6 543	3 972
Business services	1 039	371	73	184

Table C. Cross-border M&As by region/country, 2012–2013
(Millions of dollars)

Region/country	Sales 2012	Sales 2013	Purchases 2012	Purchases 2013
World	8 219	2 065	11 390	8 077
Developed economies	-1 083	406	5 223	2 739
European Union	-3 007	714	5 319	1 312
Germany	72	3 456	-584	-654
United Kingdom	-214	390	1 318	1 527
United States	1 700	-573	-244	67
Developing economies	4 228	1 160	4 585	4 913
Egypt	-	-	9	3 150
West Asia	3 855	1 039	3 855	1 039
Iraq	-14	-	1 503	630
Qatar	3 357	449	-	-
Transition economies	4 023	3	1 582	425
Russian Federation	3 873	3	1 582	425

Table D. Greenfield FDI projects by industry, 2012–2013
(Millions of dollars)

Sector/industry	West Asia as destination 2012	West Asia as destination 2013	West Asia as investors 2012	West Asia as investors 2013
Total	44 668	56 527	35 069	39 240
Primary	2	5 990	37	1 701
Mining, quarrying and petroleum	2	5 990	37	1 701
Manufacturing	20 249	18 692	12 401	17 880
Coke, petroleum products and nuclear fuel	5 002	3 769	5 768	9 666
Chemicals and chemical products	6 181	4 178	103	202
Motor vehicles and other transport equipment	1 019	5 750	130	111
Services	24 417	31 845	22 630	19 659
Electricity, gas and water	2 608	13 761	601	1 777
Construction	6 693	3 253	5 105	4 313
Hotels and restaurants	3 809	3 555	3 302	3 142
Finance	2 226	1 641	3 993	2 305
Business services	2 038	6 155	588	3 953

Table E. Greenfield FDI projects by region/country, 2012–2013
(Millions of dollars)

Partner region/economy	West Asia as destination 2012	West Asia as destination 2013	West Asia as investors 2012	West Asia as investors 2013
World	44 668	56 527	35 069	39 240
Developed economies	15 652	27 253	2 054	4 572
Europe	9 883	15 801	1 640	2 509
North America	5 102	10 009	342	1 976
Developing economies	25 860	16 496	30 874	31 016
North Africa	1 047	109	10 511	3 906
Egypt	1 047	86	7 403	1 552
East Asia	4 901	1 058	820	500
South-East Asia	2 827	984	427	9 678
South Asia	4 100	1 367	4 972	2 293
West Asia	12 746	12 729	12 746	12 729
Transition economies	3 156	12 779	2 140	3 653
Russian Federation	122	12 710	313	1 345

FDI flows to West Asia decreased in 2013 by 9 per cent, to $44 billion, the fifth consecutive decline since 2009 and a return to the level they had in 2005. Persistent tensions in the region continued to hold off foreign direct investors in 2013. Since 2009, FDI flows to Saudi Arabia and Qatar have maintained a downward trend. During this period, flows to a number of other countries have started to recover, although that recovery has been bumpy in some cases. Flows have remained well below the levels reached some years ago, except in Kuwait and Iraq, where they reached record levels in 2012 and 2013, respectively.

Turkey remained West Asia's main FDI recipient in 2013, although flows decreased slightly, remaining at almost the same level as in the previous year – close to $13 billion (figure A). This occurred against a background of low cross-border M&A sales, which dropped by 68 per cent to $867 million, their lowest level since 2004. While inflows to the manufacturing sector more than halved, dropping to $2 billion and accounting for only 16 per cent of the total, they increased in electricity, gas and water supply (176 per cent to $2.6 billion), finance (79 per cent to $3.7 billion), and real estate (16 per cent to $3 billion). Together these three industries represented almost three quarters of total FDI to the country.

FDI flows to the United Arab Emirates continued their recovery after the sharp decline registered in 2009, increasing in 2013 for the fourth consecutive year and positioning this country as the second largest recipient of FDI after Turkey. Flows increased by 9 per cent to $10.5 billion, remaining however well below their level in 2007 ($14.2 billion). This FDI recovery coincided with the economy rebounding from the 2009 debt crisis, driven by both oil and non-oil activities. Among the latter, the manufacturing sector expanded, led by heavy industries such as aluminium and petrochemicals; tourism and transport benefited from the addition of more routes and capacity by two local airlines; and the property market recovered, thanks to the willingness of banks to resume loans to real estate projects, which brought new life to the construction business, the industry that suffered most from the financial crisis and has taken the longest to recover. That industry got further impetus in November

2013, when Dubai gained the right to host the World Expo 2020.

Flows to Saudi Arabia registered their fifth consecutive year of decline, decreasing by 24 per cent to $9.3 billion, and moving the country from the second to the third largest host economy in the region. This decline has taken place despite the large capital projects under way in infrastructure and in downstream oil and gas, mainly refineries and petrochemicals. However, the Government remains the largest investor in strategically important sectors, and the activities of many private firms (including foreign ones) depend on government contracts (non-equity mode) or on joint ventures with State-owned companies. The departure in 2013 of over 1 million expatriate workers has exacerbated the mismatch of demand and supply in the private job market that has challenged private businesses since the 2011 launch of the policy of "Saudization" (*WIR13*).

Flows to Iraq reached new highs. Despite high levels of instability in Iraq, affecting mainly the central area around Baghdad, FDI flows are estimated to have increased by about 20 per cent in 2013, to $2.9 billion. The country's economic resurgence has been underpinned by its vast hydrocarbon wealth. Economic growth has been aided by substantial increases in government spending to compensate for decades of war, sanctions and underinvestment in infrastructure and basic services. In addition, work on several large oilfields has gathered speed since the award of the largest fields to foreign oil TNCs. A significant development for the industry in 2013 was the start of operations of the first stage of a long-delayed gas-capture project run by Basra Gas Company (State-owned South Gas Company (51 per cent), Shell (44 per cent) and Mitsubishi (5 per cent)). The project captures associated gas that was being flared from three oil fields in southern Iraq and processes it for liquefied petroleum gas (LPG), natural gas liquids and condensate for domestic markets.

FDI flows to Kuwait are estimated to have decreased by 41 per cent in 2013, after having reached record highs in 2012 owing to a one-off acquisition deal worth $1.8 billion (see *WIR13*). FDI to Jordan increased by 20 per cent to $1.8 billion, despite regional unrest and sluggish economic growth.

Because of the country's geostrategic position, countries and foreign entities have been extending considerable new funding in the form of aid, grants, guarantees, easy credit and investment.[26] FDI to Lebanon is estimated to have fallen by 23 per cent, with most of the flows still focused on the real estate market, which registered a significant decrease in investments from the Gulf Cooperation Council (GCC) countries.

Prospects for the region's inward FDI remain bleak, as rising political uncertainties are a strong deterrent to FDI, even in countries not directly affected by unrest and in those registering robust economic growth. The modest recovery in FDI flows recorded recently in some countries would have been much more substantial in the absence of political turmoil, given the region's vast hydrocarbon wealth.

FDI outflows from West Asia soared by 64 per cent to $31 billion in 2013, boosted by rising flows from the GCC countries, which enjoy a high level of foreign exchange reserves derived from their accumulation of surpluses from export earnings. Although each of these countries augmented its investment abroad, the quadrupling of outflows from Qatar and the 159 per cent growth in flows from Kuwait explain most of the increase. Given the high levels of their foreign exchange reserves and the relatively small sizes of their economies, GCC countries are likely to continue to increase their direct investment abroad.

New challenges faced by the GCC petrochemicals industry. With the goal of diversifying their economies by leveraging their abundant oil and gas and their capital to develop industrial capabilities and create jobs where they enjoy competitive advantages, GCC Governments have embarked since the mid-2000s on the development of large-scale petrochemicals projects in joint ventures with international oil companies (see *WIR12*). These efforts have significantly expanded the region's petrochemicals capacities.[27] And they continue to do so, with a long list of plants under development, including seven megaprojects distributed between Saudi Arabia, the United Arab Emirates, Qatar and Oman (table II.2). The industry has been facing new challenges, deriving among others from the shale gas production under way in North America (see chapter I), which has affected the global strategy of petrochemicals TNCs.

TNC focus on the United States. The shale gas revolution in North America, combined with gas shortages in the GCC region,[28] has reduced the cost advantage of the GCC petrochemicals players and introduced new competition. By driving down gas prices in the United States,[29] the shale revolution is reviving that country's petrochemicals sector.[30] Some companies have been looking again to the United States, which offers a huge consumer base and the opportunity to spread companies' business risks. Global petrochemicals players that have engaged in several multibillion-

Table II.2. Selected mega-petrochemicals projects under development in the GCC countries

Project/Company name	Partners	Location	Start Up	Capital expenditure ($ million)
Sadara	Aramco (65%) and Dow Chemical (35%)	Jubail, Saudi Arabia	2016	20 000
Chemaweyaat	Abu Dhabi Investment Council (40%); International Petroleum Investment Company (IPIC) (40%) and Abu Dhabi National Oil Company (ADNOC) (20%)	Al-Gharbia UAE	2018	11 000–20 000
Petro Rabigh 2	Aramco (37.5%) and Sumitomo (37.5%)	Rabigh, Saudi Arabia	2016	7 000
Al Karaana	Qatar Petroleum (80%) and Shell (20%)	Ras, Laffan, Qatar	2017	6 400
Al-Sejeel	Qatar Petroleum (80%) and Qatar Petrochemical (Qapco) (20%)	Ras Laffan, Qatar	2018	5 500
Liwa Plastics	Oman Oil Refineries and Petroleum Industries (Orpic)	Sohar, Oman	2018	3 600
Kemya	SABIC (50%) and Exxon Mobil (50%)	Jubail, Saudi Arabia	2015	3 400

Source: UNCTAD, based on various newspaper accounts.

dollar megaprojects in GCC countries in the last 10 years – including Chevron Phillips Chemical, Dow Chemical and ExxonMobil Chemical – have been considering major projects in the United States. For example, Chevron Phillips is planning to build a large-scale ethane cracker and two polyethylene units in Texas.[31] Dow Chemical has restarted its idled Saint Charles plant in Louisiana and is undertaking a major polyethylene and ethylene expansion in its plant in Texas.[32] As of March 2014, the United States chemical industry had announced investment projects valued at about $70 billion and linked to the plentiful and affordable natural gas from domestic shale formations. About half of the announced investment is by firms based outside the United States (see chapter III).

Shale technology is being transferred through cross-border M&As to Asian TNCs. United States technology has been transferred to Asian countries rich in shale gas through M&A deals, which should eventually help make these regions more competitive producers and exporters for chemicals. Government-backed Chinese and Indian companies have been aggressively luring or acquiring partners in the United States and Canada to gather the required production techniques, with a view to developing their own domestic resources.[33]

GCC petrochemicals and energy enterprises have also invested in North America. The North American shale gas boom has also attracted investment from West Asian petrochemicals companies: NOVA Chemicals (fully owned by Abu Dhabi's State-owned International Petroleum Investment Company) is among the first to build a plant to exploit low-cost North American ethylene.[34] SABIC (Saudi Arabia) is also moving to harness the shale boom in the United States. The company – which already has a presence in the United States through SABIC Americas, a chemicals and fertilizer producer and a petrochemicals research centre – is looking to seal a deal to invest in a petrochemicals project as well.[35] The boom has also pushed State-owned Qatar Petroleum (QP) to establish small footholds in North America's upstream sector. Because QP is heavily dependent on Qatar's North Field, it has invested to diversify risk geographically. In April 2013, its affiliate, Qatar Petroleum International (QPI), signed a memorandum of understanding with ExxonMobil for future joint investment in unconventional gas and natural gas liquids in the United States, which suggests a strategy of strengthening ties with TNCs that invest in projects in Qatar[36] and reflects joint interest in expanding the partnership both domestically and internationally. QPI also announced a $1 billion deal with Centrica (United Kingdom) to purchase oil and gas assets and exploration acreage in Alberta from oil sands producer Suncor Energy (Canada). However, new evidence suggests that the outlook for the shale gas industry may be less bright than was thought.[37]

Petrochemicals producers in the Middle East should nonetheless build on this experience to develop a strategy of gaining access to key growth markets beyond their diminishing feedstock advantage. Rather than focusing on expanding capacity, they need to leverage their partnership with petrochemicals TNCs to strengthen their knowledge and skills base in terms of technology, research and efficient operations, and to establish linkages with the global manufacturing TNCs that use their products. Efforts towards that end have been undertaken, for example, by SABIC, which has opened R&D centres in Saudi Arabia, China and India, and is developing a strategy to market its chemicals to international manufacturing giants.

3. Latin America and the Caribbean

Table A. Distribution of FDI flows among economies, by range,ᵃ 2013

Range	Inflows	Outflows
Above $10 billion	British Virgin Islands, Brazil, Mexico, Chile, Colombia, Cayman Islands and Peru	British Virgin Islands, Mexico, Cayman Islands and Chile
$5.0 to $9.9 billion	Argentina and Venezuela (Bolivarian Republic of)	Colombia
$1.0 to $4.9 billion	Panama, Uruguay, Costa Rica, Dominican Republic, Bolivia (Plurinational State of), Trinidad and Tobago, Guatemala, Bahamas and Honduras	Venezuela (Bolivarian Republic of) and Argentina
$0.1 to $0.9 billion	Nicaragua, Ecuador, Jamaica, Paraguay, Barbados, Guyana, Haiti, Aruba, El Salvador, Antigua and Barbuda, Saint Vincent and the Grenadines, Suriname and Saint Kitts and Nevis	Trinidad and Tobago, Panama, Bahamas, Costa Rica and Peru
Less than $0.1 billion	Belize, Saint Lucia, Grenada, Sint Maarten, Anguilla, Curaçao, Dominica and Montserrat	Nicaragua, Ecuador, Guatemala, Honduras, Saint Lucia, Aruba, Antigua and Barbuda, Barbados, El Salvador, Grenada, Sint Maarten, Saint Kitts and Nevis, Belize, Montserrat, Dominica, Saint Vincent and the Grenadines, Suriname, Jamaica, Uruguay, Curaçao, Dominican Republic and Brazil

ᵃ Economies are listed according to the magnitude of their FDI flows.

Figure A. FDI flows, top 5 host and home economies, 2012–2013 (Billions of dollars)

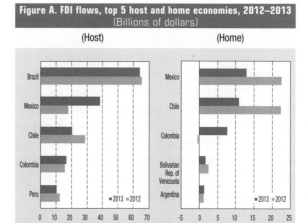

Note: Not including offshore financial centres.

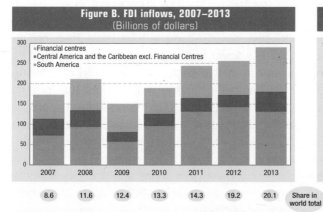

Figure B. FDI inflows, 2007–2013 (Billions of dollars)

Share in world total: 8.6 | 11.6 | 12.4 | 13.3 | 14.3 | 19.2 | 20.1

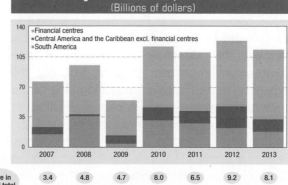

Figure C. FDI outflows, 2007–2013 (Billions of dollars)

3.4 | 4.8 | 4.7 | 8.0 | 6.5 | 9.2 | 8.1

Table B. Cross-border M&As by industry, 2012–2013 (Millions of dollars)

Sector/industry	Sales 2012	Sales 2013	Purchases 2012	Purchases 2013
Total	24 050	61 613	33 673	18 479
Primary	-2 550	28 245	823	309
Mining, quarrying and petroleum	-2 844	28 238	868	309
Manufacturing	9 573	25 138	4 849	7 153
Food, beverages and tobacco	3 029	23 848	235	4 644
Basic metal and metal products	4 367	-34	1 326	39
Non-metallic mineral products	-	-	66	1 936
Services	17 027	8 230	28 001	11 017
Electricity, gas, water and waste management	-73	3 720	398	85
Transportation and storage	4 550	1 520	3 443	628
Information and communications	1 146	252	-10	345
Financial and insurance activities	5 121	2 189	19 586	9 931
Business services	3 043	-488	960	-23

Table C. Cross-border M&As by region/country, 2012–2013 (Millions of dollars)

Region/country	Sales 2012	Sales 2013	Purchases 2012	Purchases 2013
World	24 050	61 613	33 673	18 479
Developed economies	1 699	-7 188	17 146	7 274
Belgium	1 237	15 096	-	-60
Spain	-1 996	-7 083	1 109	422
United Kingdom	-4 592	-30 530	932	-213
United States	8 717	6 299	4 642	2 250
Developing economies	22 011	14 168	16 705	10 818
Brazil	1 138	21	8 555	2 909
Chile	9 445	2 769	608	617
Colombia	2 277	4 815	4 260	1 500
Mexico	-134	2 700	448	214
Transition economies	-	53 916	-178	387
Russian Federation	-	53 916	-178	370

Table D. Greenfield FDI projects by industry, 2012–2013 (Millions of dollars)

Sector/industry	LAC as destination 2012	LAC as destination 2013	LAC as investors 2012	LAC as investors 2013
Total	69 731	145 066	9 508	18 257
Primary	5 557	12 485	159	4 000
Mining, quarrying and petroleum	5 557	12 485	159	4 000
Manufacturing	32 236	34 630	3 745	4 292
Food, beverages and tobacco	3 605	3 844	692	1 493
Chemicals and chemical products	1 790	3 038	157	362
Metals and metal products	5 226	3 913	823	89
Motor vehicles and other transport equipment	12 409	11 794	523	114
Services	31 939	97 952	5 605	9 966
Electricity, gas and water	11 802	17 454	1 040	809
Transport, storage and communications	4 150	14 205	560	4 703
Finance	2 138	5 770	413	923
Business services	9 553	49 961	1 993	1 501

Table E. Greenfield FDI projects by region/country, 2012–2013 (Millions of dollars)

Partner region/economy	LAC as destination 2012	LAC as destination 2013	LAC as investors 2012	LAC as investors 2013
World	69 731	145 066	9 508	18 257
Developed economies	56 709	80 421	2 172	1 249
Europe	27 786	37 739	385	653
Italy	8 106	6 013	-	-
Spain	6 799	11 875	62	121
North America	22 852	30 687	1 780	585
Japan	3 250	6 420	-	-
Developing economies	12 684	63 790	7 336	16 912
East Asia	4 582	45 538	99	693
Latin America and the Caribbean	6 576	15 730	6 576	15 730
Brazil	2 706	5 926	1 895	3 022
Mexico	1 260	4 144	790	1 113
Transition economies	337	855	-	96

FDI flows to Latin America and the Caribbean reached $292 billion in 2013 (figure B). Excluding the offshore financial centres, they increased by 6 per cent to $182 billion. Flows to Central America and the Caribbean increased by 64 per cent to $49 billion, boosted by a mega-acquisition in Mexico. Whereas in previous years FDI growth was driven largely by South America, in 2013 flows to this subregion declined by 6 per cent to $133 billion, as the decline in metal prices dampened FDI growth in the metal mining industry of some countries. FDI outflows reached $115 billion in 2013. Excluding financial centres, they declined by 31 per cent to $33 billion.

Central America and the Caribbean drove FDI growth to the region. The purchase by the Belgian brewer AB InBev of the remaining shares in Grupo Modelo for $18 billion more than doubled inflows to Mexico to $38 billion (figure A), and is largely behind the strong increase of FDI to Central America and the Caribbean. Flows also increased in Panama (61 per cent to $4.7 billion) – Central America's second largest recipient after Mexico – on the back of large infrastructure investment projects, including the expansion of the Panama Canal and of the capital city's metro rail system, both part of ambitions to develop the country into a regional logistical hub and expand its capacity for assembly operations. Flows to Costa Rica rose by 14 per cent to $2.7 billion, boosted by a near tripling of real estate acquisitions by non-residents, accounting for 43 per cent of total FDI to the country. The growth of FDI to Guatemala and to Nicaragua slowed in 2013, with flows growing by only 5 per cent after registering substantial increases in the last few years. The growth was powered primarily by surges in FDI in the mining and banking industries in Guatemala, and in free trade zones and offshore assembly manufacturing in Nicaragua.

In the Caribbean, flows to the Dominican Republic fell by 37 per cent to $2 billion, after two years of strong recovery which had driven them to $3.1 billion in 2012. This fall is due to both the predictable decline of cross-border M&As in 2013 – after the one-off acquisition of the country's largest brewer for $1.2 billion in 2012 – and the completion of the Barrick Gold mining investment project, which started production in 2012. FDI in Trinidad and Tobago – highly concentrated in the oil and gas extractive industry, which attracted more than 70 per cent of total inflows to the country in 2001–2011 (see section B.3) – decreased by 30 per cent to $1.7 billion, owing to the halving of reinvested earnings as natural gas prices remained weak.

After three consecutive years of strong growth, FDI to South America declined (figure B). Among the main recipient countries, Brazil saw only a slight decline from 2012 – 2 per cent to $64 billion (figure A) – but with highly uneven growth by sector. Flows to the primary sector soared by 86 per cent to $17 billion, powered primarily by the oil and gas extractive industry (up 144 per cent to $11 billion), while flows to the manufacturing and services sectors decreased by 17 and 14 per cent, respectively. FDI to the automobile and electronics industries bucked the trend of the manufacturing sector, rising by 85 and 120 per cent, respectively. FDI to Chile declined by 29 per cent to $20 billion, driven mainly by decreasing flows to the mining industry, which accounted for more than half of total FDI flows to this country in 2006–2012. The decrease in this sector is due to the completion of a number of investment projects that started production in 2013 and to the indefinite suspension of Barrick Gold's (Canada) $8.5 billion Pascua-Lama gold-mining mega-project, located on the Chilean-Argentinian border.[38] The suspension, prompted mainly by lower gold prices and Barrick's financial strains, has also affected FDI to Argentina, which declined by 25 per cent. Flows to Peru decreased by 17 per cent to $10 billion, following a strong decline of reinvested earnings (by 41 per cent to $4.9 billion) and of equity capital (by 48 per cent to $2.4 billion), partly compensated by the increase in intracompany loans. The Bolivarian Republic of Venezuela saw its FDI inflows more than double, to $7 billion. Inflows to Colombia increased by 8 per cent to $17 billion (figure A), largely on the back of cross-border M&A sales in the electricity and banking industries.

Decreasing cross-border purchases and increasing loan repayments caused a slide of outward FDI from the region. FDI outflows reached $115 billion in 2013 (figure C). Excluding offshore financial centres, they declined by 31 per cent to $33 billion. The decline is the result of both a 47 per cent decrease in cross-border acquisitions from the high value reached during 2012 ($31 billion) and a strong increase in loan repayments to parent companies by foreign affiliates of Brazilian and Chilean TNCs.[39] Colombian TNCs clearly bucked the region's declining trend in cross-border M&As, more than doubling the value of their net purchases abroad to over $6 billion, mainly in the banking, oil and gas, and food industries.

FDI prospects in the region are likely to be led by developments in the primary sector. New opportunities are opening for foreign TNCs in the region's oil and gas industry, namely in Argentina and in Mexico.

Argentina's vast shale oil and gas resources[40] and the technical and financial needs of Yacimientos Petrolíferos Fiscales (YPF), the majority State-owned energy company, to exploit them open new horizons for FDI in this industry. The agreement reached in 2014 with Repsol (Spain) regarding compensation for the nationalization of its majority stake in YPF[41] removed a major hurdle to the establishment of joint ventures between YPF and other foreign companies for the exploitation of shale resources. YPF has already secured some investment, including a $1.2 billion joint venture with Chevron (United States) for the exploitation of the Vaca Muerta shale oil and gas field. Total (France) will also participate in a $1.2 billion upstream joint venture.

In Mexico, FDI in the oil and gas industry is likely to receive a powerful boost after the approval of the long-disputed energy reform bill that ended a 75-year State oil monopoly and opened the Mexican energy industry to greater participation by international energy players in the upstream, midstream and downstream oil and gas sectors (see chapter III).

The sectoral composition of FDI stock in Latin America and the Caribbean shows similarities and differences by countries and subregions. The services sector is the main target of FDI both in South America and in Central America and the Caribbean (figure II.11), albeit relatively more important in the latter. The prominence of this sector is the result of the privatizations and the removal of restrictions on FDI that took place in both subregions in the last two decades. The manufacturing sector is the second most important target in both subregions, but more important in Central America and the Caribbean. The primary sector is relatively more important in South America but marginal in the other subregion. In Brazil and Mexico – the two biggest economies, where the region's FDI to the manufacturing sector is concentrated – FDI is driven by two different strategies; export-oriented in Mexico (efficiency-seeking) and domestic-market-oriented in Brazil (market-seeking).

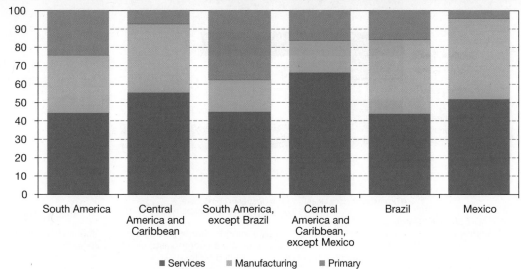

Figure II.11. Latin America and the Caribbean: share of FDI stock by main sectors, subregions and countries, 2012
(Per cent)

■ Services ■ Manufacturing ■ Primary

Source: UNCTAD FDI-TNC-GVC Information System, FDI/TNC database.

These different patterns of FDI flows and the different strategies of TNCs have shaped the different export structures of the two subregions, with primary products and commodity-based manufactures predominating in South America's exports and manufactured products predominating in Central America and the Caribbean's exports, resulting in two distinct GVC participation patterns. A closer look at the industry level also shows significant differences in GVC patterns within the same manufacturing activities, resulting from different industrialization strategies.

Different patterns of GVC integration. In 2011, the share of Latin American exports dependent on GVCs was 45 per cent, but the subregional figures differ strongly. In Central America and the Caribbean, GVC participation derives primarily from the relatively high imported foreign value added in exports (upstream component), while the downstream component is low. This occurs because most exports are made up of medium- and high-skill technology-intensive products (e.g. automobiles, electronics) as well as low-technology products (e.g. textiles) near the end of the value

chain. In South America, by contrast, there is low upstream but high downstream participation in GVCs (figure II.12). This is due to the predominance of primary products and commodity-based manufactures in exports, which use few foreign inputs and, because they are at the beginning of the value chain, are themselves used as intermediate goods in third countries' exports.

The same phenomenon can be observed in the value added exports of the manufacturing sector. While GVC participation in this sector in South America was 34 per cent in 2010 – shared equally between imported value added and downstream use of exports (at 17 per cent each) – participation was much higher in Central America and the Caribbean (50 per cent) and highly imbalanced in favour of imported value added in exports (44 per cent), while downstream use represented only 6 per cent (figure II.13). Differences between the two subregions are more accentuated in industries such as electronics, motor vehicles, machinery and equipment, and textiles and clothing (table II.3).

This different degree and pattern of participation in GVCs between the two subregions – in the same

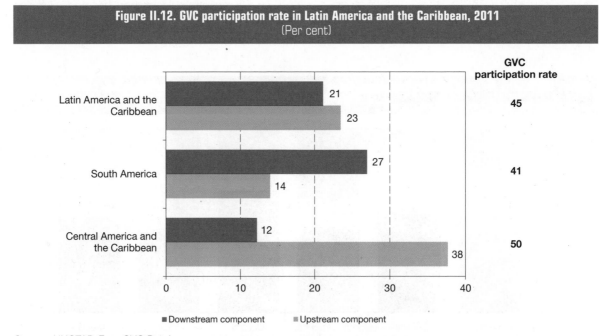

Figure II.12. GVC participation rate in Latin America and the Caribbean, 2011
(Per cent)

■ Downstream component   ■ Upstream component

Source: UNCTAD-Eora GVC Database.

Note: GVC participation rate indicates the share of a country's exports that is part of a multi-stage trade process; it is the foreign value added (FVA) used in a country's exports (the upstream component) plus the value added supplied to other countries' exports (the downstream component, or DVX), divided by total exports.
        The share of foreign value added in Central America and the Caribbean's exports is under-estimated because the UNCTAD-EORA data do not take into account the high import content of production in the maquiladora industry.

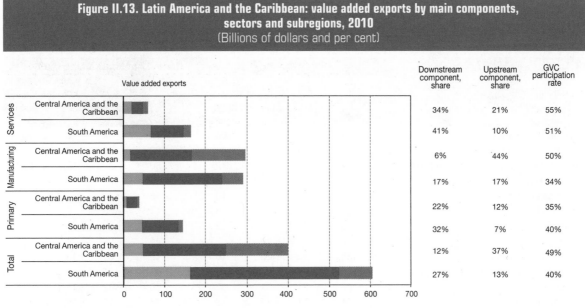

Figure II.13. Latin America and the Caribbean: value added exports by main components, sectors and subregions, 2010
(Billions of dollars and per cent)

		Downstream component, share	Upstream component, share	GVC participation rate
Services	Central America and the Caribbean	34%	21%	55%
Services	South America	41%	10%	51%
Manufacturing	Central America and the Caribbean	6%	44%	50%
Manufacturing	South America	17%	17%	34%
Primary	Central America and the Caribbean	22%	12%	35%
Primary	South America	32%	7%	40%
Total	Central America and the Caribbean	12%	37%	49%
Total	South America	27%	13%	40%

- Domestic value added incorporated in other countries' exports (downstream component) ■ Domestic value added exports that are not re-exported (final market)
- Foreign value added in exports (upstream component)

Source: UNCTAD-Eora GVC Database.
Note: GVC participation rate indicates the share of a country's exports that is part of a multi-stage trade process; it is the foreign value added (FVA) used in a country's exports (the upstream component) plus the value added supplied to other countries' exports (the downstream component, or DVX), divided by total exports.
Total exports as calculated in GVCs (sum of the three components) are not necessarily the same as reported in the national account of exports of goods and services.

manufacturing activities – derives from their position in the value chain, the nature of end markets, the linkages between export activities and the local economy, the nature of industrial policy, and the degree of intraregional integration. Central American and Caribbean countries rely heavily on the United States as both an export market for manufacturing products (76 per cent of all such exports) (figure II.14) and a GVC partner, especially in the upstream part of the chain, contributing 55 per cent of the imported value added in those exports (table II.4). However, their intraregional trade links and GVC interaction are weak: the subregion absorbs only 5 per cent of its own manufacturing exports (see figure II.4) and accounts for a small part of its upstream and downstream GVC links in the manufacturing sector (2 per cent and 6 per cent respectively) (see table II.4).

By contrast, intraregional trade links in South America are much stronger, accounting for 49 per cent of the subregion's manufacturing exports, 24 per cent of its upstream GVC manufacturing links, and 13 per cent of its downstream links

(table II.4). Finally, South America's manufacturing exports integrate a much lower share of imported value added (17 per cent) than do those of Central America (44 per cent) (table II.4).

In the manufacturing sector in particular, the differences between South America and Central America in patterns of GVC participation derive mostly from two sources: different industrialization strategies and different modes of integration in international trade of Latin America's biggest economies, Brazil and Mexico.[42] This is illustrated by the example of the automobile industry, which, in both countries, is dominated by almost the same foreign vehicle-assembly TNCs but shows very different patterns of GVC participation.

Two ways to participate in GVCs: the automobile industry in Brazil and Mexico. Brazil and Mexico are respectively the seventh and eighth largest automobile producers and the fourth and sixteenth largest car markets, globally.[43] Almost all of their motor vehicle production is undertaken

Table II.3. Latin America and the Caribbean manufacturing sector: GVC participation, components and share in total value added manufacturing exports by main industry, 2010
(Per cent)

Industry	South America				Central America and the Caribbean			
	GVC participation rate	FVA share	DVX share	Share in total manu-facturing exports	GVC participation rate	FVA share	DVX share	Share in total manu-facturing exports
Manufacturing sector	**34**	**17**	**17**	**100**	**50**	**44**	**6**	**100**
Electrical and electronic equipment	40	24	16	4	63	59	4	33
Motor vehicles and other transport equipment	34	25	9	12	50	47	4	25
Food, beverages and tobacco	20	13	8	17	25	21	4	6
Chemicals and chemical products	42	22	20	16	38	20	18	5
Textiles, clothing and leather	27	16	11	8	41	38	2	10
Metal and metal products	43	16	27	12	55	29	26	4
Machinery and equipment	27	16	12	7	41	38	4	5
Wood and wood products	35	13	22	8	45	31	14	2
Coke, petroleum products and nuclear fuel	40	9	31	5	42	31	11	3
Rubber and plastic products	42	21	21	3	56	42	14	1
Non-metallic mineral products	29	11	18	3	27	12	15	2

Source: UNCTAD-Eora GVC Database.

Note: GVC participation rate indicates the share of a country's exports that is part of a multi-stage trade process; it is the foreign value added (FVA) used in a country's exports (the upstream component) plus the value added supplied to other countries' exports (the downstream component, or DVX), divided by total exports.

Figure II.14. Latin America and the Caribbean: geographical distribution of export of manufactured goods by destination, 2010
(Per cent)

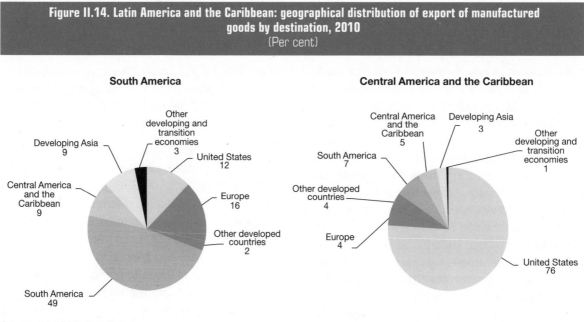

Source: UNCTAD GlobStat.

by global vehicle assemblers, most of which – including Ford, General Motors, Honda, Nissan, Renault, Toyota and Volkswagen – have assembly plants in both countries. This shared characteristic notwithstanding, clear differences exist between the industries in the two countries. The most significant one is that the Brazilian automobile value chain has the domestic market as its main end market, whereas the Mexican one is largely export-oriented and directed mainly to the United States as its end

Table II.4. Latin America and the Caribbean: GVC upstream and downstream links in the manufacturing sector by subregion and by geographical origin and destination, 2010

(Per cent)

Partner region	FVA share (by origin)		DVX share (by destination)		GVC participation rate (by origin and destination)	
	South America	Central America and the Caribbean	South America	Central America and the Caribbean	South America	Central America and the Caribbean
Developed countries	**55**	**76**	**64**	**76**	**59**	**76**
North America	23	54	14	35	19	52
Europe	27	16	46	38	36	19
Other developed	5	6	4	3	5	6
Developing and transition economies	**45**	**24**	**36**	**24**	**41**	**24**
Latin America and the Caribbean	26	7	18	10	22	7
South America	24	5	13	4	19	5
Central America and the Caribbean	2	2	5	6	3	2
Asia and Oceania	15	15	15	11	15	15
Other developing and transition economies	4	2	3	3	4	2
World	**100**	**100**	**100**	**100**	**100**	**100**
Amount ($ billion)	50	130	48	19	98	149
Share in total value added manufacturing exports	17	44	17	6	34	50

Source: UNCTAD-Eora GVC Database.

Note: GVC participation rate indicates the share of a country's exports that is part of a multi-stage trade process; it is the foreign value added (FVA) used in a country's exports (the upstream component) plus the value added supplied to other countries' exports (the downstream component, or DVX), divided by total exports.

market. In 2012, the Mexican automobile industry exported, for example, 82 per cent of its vehicle production[44] – 64 per cent of it to the United States. By contrast, only 13 per cent of vehicle production in Brazil was exported, with MERCOSUR absorbing 67 per cent of exports by value.[45]

The inward/outward orientation of the motor vehicle industries in the two countries is also reflected by the much lower GVC participation of Brazil's motor vehicle exports – 26 per cent, compared with 58 per cent for Mexico's exports. This difference is explained mainly by the much lower imported content in Brazil's exports (21 per cent versus 47 per cent in Mexico) and also – but to a lesser extent – by the lower participation of Brazil's motor vehicle exports in other countries' exports (5 per cent, compared with 11 per cent) (table II.5).

Another difference is the major interaction of Brazil's automotive industry with other Latin American countries – mainly Argentina, with which Brazil has an agreement on common automotive policy.[46] Mexico's industry relies strongly on developed countries, mainly the United States; its few linkages

with other Latin American countries are with neighbours that do not have significant activity in the automotive industry. Indeed, whereas Latin America and the Caribbean accounts for only 4 per cent of GVC participation in Mexico's motor vehicle exports, in Brazil its share is 12 per cent. More tellingly, Brazil represents an important step in Argentina's motor vehicle value chain: it accounts for 34 per cent of GVC participation in Argentina's motor vehicle exports (table II.5) and absorbs 77 per cent of the value of those exports.[47]

Different TNC strategies and different government industrial policies have resulted in distinct GVC integration patterns with different implications in each country for business linkages, innovation and technology. Mexico opted for an export-oriented strategy that allows companies operating under the IMMEX programme[48] to temporarily import goods and services that will be manufactured, transformed or repaired, and then re-exported, with no payment of taxes, no compensatory quotas and other specific benefits.[49] This strategy relies mainly on

Table II.5. Latin America: GVC upstream and downstream links in the motor vehicle industry, selected countries,by geographical origin and destination, 2010								
(Per cent)								

Partner region/country	FVA share (by origin)			DVX share (by destination)			GVC participation rate (by origin and destination)		
	Brazil	Mexico	Argentina	Brazil	Mexico	Argentina	Brazil	Mexico	Argentina
Developed countries	**79**	**89**	**43**	**70**	**81**	**50**	**72**	**83**	**48**
United States	36	72	18	24	56	17	27	59	17
Europe	33	10	20	37	16	27	36	15	26
Other developed	9	7	5	9	9	6	9	8	6
Developing and transition economies	**21**	**11**	**57**	**30**	**19**	**50**	**28**	**17**	**52**
Latin America and the Caribbean	12	4	49	12	4	37	12	4	40
South America	11	4	49	11	4	36	11	4	39
Argentina	9	0	0	6	0	0	7	0	0
Brazil	0	3	42	0	2	31	0	2	34
Central America and the Caribbean	1	0	1	1	0	1	1	0	1
Mexico	1	0	1	1	0	1	1	0	1
Asia and Oceania	9	7	7	14	13	12	13	12	11
China	4	3	4	6	5	6	6	5	5
Other developing and transitional economies	1	0	0	3	2	2	3	1	1
World	**100**	**100**	**100**	**100**	**100**	**100**	**100**	**100**	**100**
Amount ($ billion)	5.7	33.2	2.2	1.4	8.1	0.7	7.0	41.2	2.9
Share in total value added motor vehicle exports (%)	21	47	50	5	11	15	26	58	65

Source: UNCTAD-Eora GVC Database.

Note: GVC participation rate indicates the share of a country's exports that is part of a multi-stage trade process; it is the foreign value added (FVA) used in a country's exports (the upstream component) plus the value added supplied to other countries' exports (the downstream component, or DVX), divided by total exports.
UNCTAD-Eora's estimates of foreign and domestic value added in Mexico's gross exports do not take into account the high import content of production in the Maquiladora and PITEX programmes, likely leading to a significant under-estimation of the share of foreign value added in its exports. UNCTAD-Eora's data, based on a country's input-output table, relies on the assumption that the intensity in the use of imported inputs is the same between production for exports and production for domestic sales. This assumption does not hold for countries, like Mexico, hosting significant processing exports characterized by favourable tax treatment for temporary imports to produce export goods. This implies a significant difference in the intensity of imported intermediate inputs between the production of processing exports on the one hand and the production for normal exports and domestic sales on the other hand. Estimates using an input-output table for the maquiladora industry for 2003, found a foreign value added share of about 74 per cent for the transportation equipment industry (NICS 336) in 2003 (De la Cruz et al. (2011), while UNCTAD-Eora's estimates for the same year are 41 per cent for the manufacture of motor vehicles trailers and semi-trailers and other transport equipment (ISIC D34 and D35).

the low cost of labour as a fundamental factor of competitiveness and GVC integration. It has resulted in the development of an extensive network of maquiladora-type producers, including carmakers and automobile suppliers, mostly foreign owned, that has transformed Mexico into a significant export hub. However, it has not necessarily forged strong linkages with local suppliers (Sturgeon et al., 2010).[50] The weak linkages with local suppliers in the automobile value chain may also be attested to by the high level of foreign value added in the industry's exports (table II.5).

In contrast, the automotive value chain in Brazil has benefited from the advantages offered by a large internal and regional market, and thus has expanded into more complex and diverse activities, generating local innovation. Brazilian affiliates of TNC carmakers have increased their technological capabilities through the search for solutions to meet local demand, related to technical differences in materials, fuels and road conditions or to distinct consumer preferences. Thus, the capabilities of Brazilian automotive engineering have been formed through a learning process of adapting and, more recently, designing and developing vehicles suitable for local conditions. This process has generated opportunities to involve locally owned component producers, local research and engineering services institutions, and other smaller suppliers of parts and components, which may have specific local knowledge not available in multinational engineering firms (Quadros, 2009; Quadros et al., 2009).[51]

Although the size of the Brazilian car market was one of the main factors behind the wave of investment in the 1990s and the progressive delegation of innovation activities to Brazilian affiliates and their local suppliers, Government policies have been a strong determinant in the attraction of new vehicle assemblers and in the expansion of innovation and R&D activities. In contrast to Mexico, where since the 1990s, Government policy has moved towards free trade and investment rules, automotive policy in Brazil maintains high tariffs on automotive products imported from outside MERCOSUR. Brazil also introduced a series of incentives for exports and for investment in new plants. In 2011, faced with an increase in imported models favoured by the expanding internal market, an overvalued local currency and depressed export markets in developed countries, the Government introduced an internal tax on car purchases. However, it exempted carmakers that sourced at least 65 per cent of their parts from MERCOSUR partners or from Mexico (with which Brazil has an automotive deal). This reduced vehicle imports from a peak of 27 per cent in December 2011 to 19 per cent in October 2013. In 2012, the Government renegotiated the bilateral deal with Mexico, imposing import quotas. A new automotive regime for 2013–2017 (Inovar Autos), introduced in 2012, set new rules that are intended to boost local content, energy efficiency, innovation and R&D. Companies that achieve specific targets in production steps located in Brazil and in investment in product development and R&D will benefit from additional tax incentives.[52]

Both Brazil and Mexico continue to attract significant foreign investment in their automobile sector. In Brazil, the new automobile regime, combined with the continued expansion of the car market in Brazil and Argentina, has encouraged foreign investors to step up investment plans and increase local content.[53] In Mexico, low labour costs, an increasingly dense and capable foreign-owned supply chain, and a global web of FTAs are driving a production surge in the automotive industry, much of it from Japanese and German manufacturers.[54]

The growth potential of the automotive industry appears promising in both countries, despite clear differences between the two in government policies and TNC strategies. Mexico has successfully leveraged its strategic proximity to the United States market and its trade agreements with more than 40 countries to attract important amounts of FDI to its automobile industry, which has transformed the country into a major export base, creating significant job opportunities. However, the country's competitiveness is still based primarily on low wages, and the industry – strongly export-oriented – has developed only weak linkages with local suppliers. In Brazil, the exports are lower but the advantages represented by the large internal and regional markets have attracted FDI to the automobile industry. The need to adapt to the specificities of this market, coupled with a government policy introduced in the 2000s to provide greater incentives for innovation, R&D and development of domestic productive capacity, have led to more integration of local suppliers into the automobile value chain, and the development of local innovation and R&D capabilities.

4. Transition economies

Table A. Distribution of FDI flows among economies, by range,ᵃ 2013

Range	Inflows	Outflows
Above $5.0 billion	Russian Federation and Kazakhstan	Russian Federation
$1.0 to $4.9 billion	Ukraine, Turkmenistan, Azerbaijan, Belarus, Albania, Uzbekistan, Serbia and Georgia	Kazakhstan and Azerbaijan
$0.5 to $0.9 billion	Kyrgyzstan	..
Below $0.5 billion	Montenegro, Armenia, the former Yugoslav Republic of Macedonia, Bosnia and Herzegovina, Republic of Moldova and Tajikistan	Ukraine, Belarus, Georgia, Albania, Republic of Moldova, Montenegro, Armenia, Serbia, Kyrgyzstan, the former Yugoslav Republic of Macedonia, and Bosnia and Herzegovina

ᵃ Economies are listed according to the magnitude of their FDI flows.

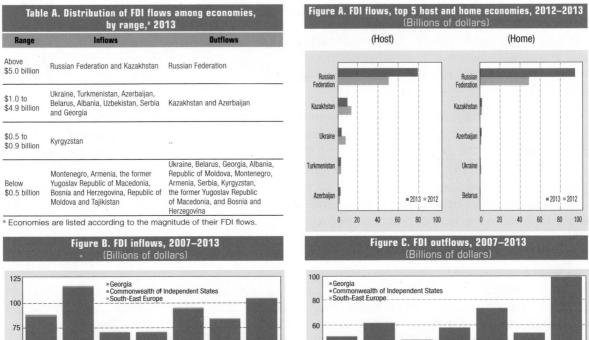

Figure A. FDI flows, top 5 host and home economies, 2012–2013 (Billions of dollars)

Figure B. FDI inflows, 2007–2013 (Billions of dollars)

Figure C. FDI outflows, 2007–2013 (Billions of dollars)

Share in world total (inflows): 4.4, 6.5, 5.8, 5.0, 5.6, 6.3, 7.4
Share in world total (outflows): 2.2, 3.1, 4.1, 3.9, 4.3, 4.0, 7.0

Table B. Cross-border M&As by industry, 2012–2013 (Millions of dollars)

Sector/industry	Sales 2012	Sales 2013	Purchases 2012	Purchases 2013
Total	6 852	-3 820	9 296	56 970
Primary	-1 193	-3 726	2 173	55 687
Mining, quarrying and petroleum	-1 212	-3 726	2 173	55 687
Manufacturing	340	2 813	-547	-24
Food, beverages and tobacco	6	189	-40	4
Chemicals and chemical products	281	2 000	-	30
Basic metal and metal products	5	425	-182	-59
Motor vehicles and other transport equipment	-390	60	-	-
Services	7 705	-2 907	7 669	1 307
Electricity, gas, water and waste management	-451	857	-	597
Transport and storage	2 148	348	1 291	652
Information and communications	6 714	-4 106	23	-
Financial and insurance activities	-168	-164	6 314	-17

Table C. Cross-border M&As by region/country, 2012–2013 (Millions of dollars)

Region/country	Sales 2012	Sales 2013	Purchases 2012	Purchases 2013
World	6 852	-3 820	9 296	56 970
Developed economies	4 746	-7 591	4 848	1 682
European Union	3 709	-3 987	5 164	243
Cyprus	7 988	-234	-	-
Sweden	-1 747	-3 384	-	15
United States	-212	-3 580	-283	30
Developing economies	1 661	2 972	4 023	54 516
Africa	-	-	-	-
Latin America and the Caribbean	-178	387	-	53 916
West Asia	1 582	425	4 023	3
South, East and South-East Asia	256	2 160	-	597
China	200	2 000	-	-
Transition economies	424	771	424	771

Table D. Greenfield FDI projects by industry, 2012–2013 (Millions of dollars)

Sector/industry	Transition economies as destination 2012	2013	Transition economies as investors 2012	2013
Total	39 389	27 868	9 950	18 611
Primary	2 604	560	145	3 146
Mining, quarrying and petroleum	2 604	560	145	3 146
Manufacturing	18 134	10 041	6 496	2 462
Food, beverages and tobacco	2 348	725	201	248
Coke, petroleum products and nuclear fuel	424	501	3 747	714
Chemicals and chemical products	5 316	995	186	396
Motor vehicles and other transport equipment	4 229	2 027	1 682	673
Services	18 651	17 267	3 310	13 003
Electricity, gas and water	3 984	5 076	594	10 389
Construction	2 908	3 069	31	-
Transport, storage and communications	4 051	2 698	893	676
Finance	2 056	2 359	1 134	1 330

Table E. Greenfield FDI projects by region/country, 2012–2013 (Millions of dollars)

Partner region/economy	Transition economies as destination 2012	2013	Transition economies as investors 2012	2013
World	39 389	27 868	9 950	18 611
Developed economies	29 092	19 633	3 060	2 327
European Union	20 338	14 719	2 337	2 186
Germany	4 329	2 767	29	157
United Kingdom	2 538	563	540	80
United States	4 610	2 570	279	41
Developing economies	7 888	6 253	4 481	14 302
Africa	-	76	67	108
East and South-East Asia	5 368	1 556	668	483
South Asia	380	872	252	76
West Asia	2 140	3 653	3 156	12 779
Latin America and the Caribbean	-	96	337	855
Transition economies	2 409	1 982	2 409	1 982

FDI flows to and from transition economies reached record levels in 2013. The Russian Federation was the world's third largest recipient of FDI and the world's fourth largest investor, mostly due to a single large deal. In South-East Europe, most of the increase in inflows was driven by the privatization of remaining State-owned enterprises in the services sector. FDI in the transition economies is likely to be affected by uncertainties related to regional conflict; FDI linkages between the transition economies and the EU may be particularly impacted.

FDI inflows to the transition economies increased by 28 per cent in 2013, to $108 billion (figure B). The FDI performance of both transition subgroups was significant: in South-East Europe, flows increased by 43 per cent, from $2.6 billion in 2012 to $3.7 billion in 2013, reflecting a rise of investments in the services sector; in the Commonwealth of Independent States (CIS), the 28 per cent rise in flows was due to the significant growth of FDI to the Russian Federation, which made it the world's third largest recipient of inflows for the first time. Large countries in the region continued to account for the lion's share of inward FDI, with the top two destinations (Russian Federation and Kazakhstan) accounting for 82 per cent of the flows (figure A).

The Russian Federation saw FDI flows grow by 57 per cent, reaching $79 billion. Foreign investors were motivated by continued strong growth in the domestic market coupled with productivity gains. They primarily used intracompany loans from parent companies to finance these investments. Investors

also continued to be attracted by high returns in energy and other natural-resource-related projects, as illustrated by partnership deals in "hard to access" oil projects, for which tax relief is offered. The FDI surge was also due to the acquisition by BP (United Kingdom) of an 18.5 per cent equity stake in Rosneft (Russia Federation) as part of a bigger deal between those two companies (box II.4). As a result, in 2013 the United Kingdom was the largest investor in the Russian Federation for the first time, accounting for an estimated 23 per cent of FDI to the country.

FDI inflows to Kazakhstan declined by 29 per cent, to $10 billion, as investments in financial services slowed, with some foreign banks divesting their assets. For example, Unicredit (Italy) sold its affiliate ATF bank to a domestic investor. Political uncertainties since 2013 have halved FDI flows to *Ukraine* to $3.8 billion, partly due to a number of divestments – in particular, in the banking sector.

In South-East Europe, most of the FDI inflows were driven by privatizations in the services sector. In Albania, FDI inflows reached $1.2 billion, owing mainly to the privatization of four hydropower plants and to the acquisition of a 70 per cent share of the main oil-refining company ARMO by Heaney Assets Corporation (Azerbaijan). In Serbia, the jump in FDI can be ascribed to some major acquisitions. The private equity group KKR (United States) acquired pay-TV and broadband group SBB/Telemach, for $1 billion. Abu Dhabi's Etihad Airways acquired a 49 per cent stake in Jat Airways, the Serbian national flag

---

Box II.4. The Rosneft-BP transactions

In March 2013, Rosneft, the Russian Federation's State-owned and largest oil company, completed the acquisition of TNK-BP. Rosneft paid $55 billion to the two owners: BP (United Kingdom) and A.A.R. Consortium, an investment vehicle based in the British Virgin Islands that represented the Russian co-owners of TNK-BP. A.A.R. was paid all in cash, while BP received $12.5 billion in cash and an 18.5 per cent stake in Rosneft, valued at $15 billion. The payment by Rosneft was reflected as direct equity investment abroad in the balance-of-payment statistics of the Russian Federation, while the acquisition by BP of the stake in Rosneft was reflected as direct equity inflow. The remainder of the acquisition was funded by borrowing from foreign banks (reported at $29.5 billion) and from domestic banks. The Rosneft-BP transactions raised FDI inflows in the first quarter of 2013 by $15 billion in the Russian Federation. It raised foreign borrowing by about $29.5 billion, while boosting FDI outflows by $55 billion in the British Virgin Islands.

Source: UNCTAD, based on conversation with the Central Bank of Russia; Institute of International Finance, "Private capital flows to emerging market economies", June 2013.

carrier, as part of the offloading of loss-making State-owned enterprises.

Although developed countries were the main investors in the region, developing-economy FDI has been on the rise. Chinese investors, for example, have expanded their presence in the CIS by acquiring either domestic or foreign assets. Chengdong Investment Corporation acquired a 12 per cent share of Uralkali (Russian Federation), the world's largest potash producer. CNPC acquired ConocoPhillips' shares in the Kashagan oil-field development project in Kazakhstan for $5 billion.

In 2013, outward FDI from the region jumped by 84 per cent, reaching $99 billion. As in past years, Russian TNCs accounted for most FDI projects, followed by TNCs from Kazakhstan and Azerbaijan. The value of cross-border M&A purchases by TNCs from the region rose more than six-fold, mainly owing to the acquisition of TNK-BP Ltd (British Virgin Islands) by Rosneft (box II.4). Greenfield investments also rose by 87 per cent to $19 billion.

Prospects. FDI in the transition economies is expected to decline in 2014 as uncertainties related to regional conflict deter investors – mainly those from developed countries. However, regional instability has not yet affected investors from developing countries. For example, in the Russian Federation, the government's Direct Investment Fund – a $10 billion fund to promote FDI in the country – has been actively deployed in collaboration with foreign partners, for example, to fund a deal with Abu Dhabi's Finance Department to invest up to $5 billion in Russian infrastructure. In South-East Europe, FDI is expected to rise – especially in pipeline projects in the energy sector. In Serbia, the South Stream project, valued at about €2 billion, is designed to transport natural gas from the Russian Federation to Europe. In Albania, the Trans-Adriatic pipeline will generate one of that country's largest FDI projects, with important benefits for a number of industries, including manufacturing, utilities and transport. The pipeline will enhance Europe's energy security and diversity by providing a new source of gas.[55]

Interregional FDI with the EU

FDI linkages between the East (transition economies) and the West (EU) were strong until 2013, but the deepening stand-off between the EU and the Russian Federation over Ukraine might affect their FDI relationship.

Over the past 10 years, transition economies have been the fastest-growing hosts for FDI worldwide, overtaking both developed and all developing groups (figure II.15). During 2000–2013, total FDI in these economies – in terms of stocks as well as flows – rose at roughly 10 times the rate of growth of total global FDI. Similarly, outflows from transition economies rose by more than 17 times between 2000 and 2013, an increase unrivalled by any other regional grouping. EU countries have been important partners, both as investors and recipients, in this evolution.

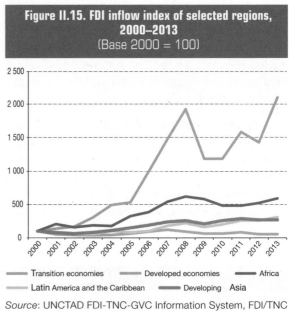

Figure II.15. FDI inflow index of selected regions, 2000–2013
(Base 2000 = 100)

Source: UNCTAD FDI-TNC-GVC Information System, FDI/TNC database (www.unctad.org/fdistatistics).

In transition economies, the EU has the largest share of inward FDI stock, accounting for more than two thirds of the total. North America has consistently accounted for a lower share of inward FDI to transition economies (3 per cent), while the share of developing economies has been on the rise to 17 per cent. In the CIS, EU investors are motivated by a desire to gain access to natural resources and growing local consumer markets, and to benefit from business opportunities arising from the liberalization of selected industries. In South-East Europe, most of the EU investments are driven by the privatization of State-owned enterprises and by large projects benefiting from a combination of low production costs in the region and the prospect of association with or membership in the EU. Among the EU countries, Germany has the largest stock of FDI, followed by France, Austria, Italy and the United Kingdom (figure II.16).

Data on individual FDI projects show a similar pattern: In terms of cross-border M&As, TNCs from the Netherlands are the largest acquirers (31 per cent), followed by those from Germany and Italy. In greenfield projects, German investors have the largest share (19 per cent), followed by those from the United Kingdom and Italy. With regard to target countries, about 60 per cent of the region's M&As and announced greenfield projects took place in the Russian Federation, followed by Ukraine.

Data on cross-border M&As indicate that EU investments in transition economies are more concentrated in finance; electricity, gas and water,

information and communication; and mining and quarrying (figure II.17). Construction; transport, storage and communication; motor vehicles and other transport equipment; coke and petroleum products; and electricity, gas and water are the main recipient industries of announced greenfield

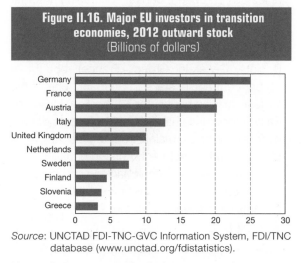

Figure II.16. Major EU investors in transition economies, 2012 outward stock
(Billions of dollars)

Source: UNCTAD FDI-TNC-GVC Information System, FDI/TNC database (www.unctad.org/fdistatistics).

Note: Data as reported by the investor countries.

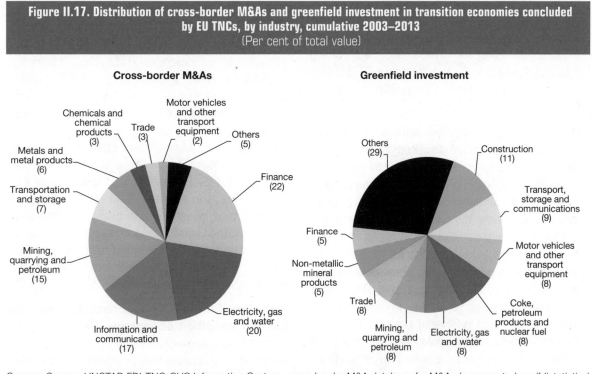

Figure II.17. Distribution of cross-border M&As and greenfield investment in transition economies concluded by EU TNCs, by industry, cumulative 2003–2013
(Per cent of total value)

Cross-border M&As

Chemicals and chemical products (3)
Motor vehicles and other transport equipment (2)
Trade (3)
Others (5)
Metals and metal products (6)
Finance (22)
Transportation and storage (7)
Mining, quarrying and petroleum (15)
Electricity, gas and water (20)
Information and communication (17)

Greenfield investment

Others (29)
Construction (11)
Transport, storage and communications (9)
Finance (5)
Non-metallic mineral products (5)
Motor vehicles and other transport equipment (8)
Trade (8)
Coke, petroleum products and nuclear fuel (8)
Mining, quarrying and petroleum (8)
Electricity, gas and water (8)

Source: Source: UNCTAD FDI-TNC-GVC Information System, cross-border M&A database for M&As (www.unctad.org/fdistatistics) and information from the Financial Times Ltd, fDi Markets (www.fDimarkets.com) for greenfield projects.
Note: M&A data cover only those deals that involved an acquisition of an equity stake of more than 10 per cent. Greenfield data refer to estimated amounts of capital investment.

projects by EU investors. Salient FDI trends in some of these industries are as follows:

- The relaxation of foreign ownership restrictions in the *financial services* industry and accession to the WTO of some transition economies facilitated the entry of EU investors. It also reflected European banks' increasing interest in growth opportunities outside their traditional markets. For example, UniCredit (Italy) acquired Ukrsotsbank (Ukraine) for $2.1 billion and Société Générale Group (France) bought a 20 per cent equity stake in Rosbank, one of the largest Russian banks, for $1.7 billion. In South-East Europe, the share of banking assets owned by foreign entities, mainly from the EU, has risen to more than 90 per cent. Foreign banks (mainly Austrian, Italian and Greek banking groups) have either acquired local banks or established local affiliates or regional branches.

- The need for structural reform to enable the *electricity* industry to meet the growing demand for electric power in the Russian Federation prompted the unbundling and reorganization of State-owned Unified Energy Systems. This restructuring and sales of assets have provided opportunities for foreign investors to enter the industry. A number of the stakes have been acquired by European TNCs, such as Fortum (Finland), Enel (Italy), E.ON (Germany), CEZ Group (Czech Republic), RWE Group (Germany) and EDF (France).

- Driven by high expected returns, EU TNCs increased their investments in *energy and natural-resource-related projects,* mainly through two channels. First, the European companies entered transition economies' oil and gas markets through asset-swap deals by which those companies obtained minority participation in exploration and extraction projects in exchange for allowing firms from transition economies to enter downstream markets in the EU. For example, Wintershall (Germany) acquired a stake in the Yuzhno-Russkoye gas field in Siberia; in return, Gazprom (Russian Federation) could acquire parts of Wintershall's European assets in hydrocarbons transportation, storage and distribution. Second, in some "hard to access" oil and gas projects requiring cutting-edge technology, such as the

development of the Yamal and Shtokman fields, EU TNCs·were invited to invest.

- Among announced greenfield projects, the increased activity in the *automotive industry* in transition economies was fuelled by EU manufacturers' search for low-cost, highly skilled labour and access to a growing market. Many EU car manufacturers – among them, Fiat, Volkswagen, Opel, Peugeot and Renault – have opened production facilities in transition economies, mainly in the Russian Federation. Car assembly plants have already created a sufficient critical mass to encourage the entry of many types of component suppliers.

The bulk of outward FDI stock from transition economies is in EU countries. Virtually all (95 per cent) of the outward stock from South-East Europe and CIS countries is due to the expansion abroad of Russian TNCs. These investors increasingly look for strategic assets in EU markets, including downstream activities in the energy industry and value added production activities in metallurgy, to build global and regional value chains through vertical integration. Much of the outward FDI has been undertaken by relatively few major TNCs with significant exports, aiming to reinforce their overseas business activities through investment. Russian oil and gas TNCs made some market-seeking acquisitions of processing activities, distribution networks, and storage and transportation facilities across Europe. For example, Gazprom concluded an agreement with OMV (Austria) for the purchase of 50 per cent of its largest Central European gas distribution terminal and storage facility, and Lukoil acquired a 49 per cent stake in the Priolo oil refinery of ISAB (Italy) for $2.1 billion (table II.6). Russian TNCs in iron and steel also continued to increase their investments in developed countries. For M&As, the United Kingdom was the main target with almost one third of all investment; for greenfield projects, Germany accounted for 36 per cent of investments from transition economies (figure II.18).

Prospects for the FDI relationship between the EU and transition economies. Since the global economic crisis, several Russian TNCs have had to sell foreign companies they acquired through M&As as the values of their assets declined (an example is Basic Element, which lost some of its foreign assets in machinery and construction in Europe).

Year	Value ($ million)	Acquired company	Host economy	Industry of the acquired company	Ultimate acquiring company	Ultimate home economy	Industry of the ultimate acquiring company

Table II.6. The 20 largest cross-border M&A deals in EU countries by transition economy TNCs, 2005–2013

Year	Value ($ million)	Acquired company	Host economy	Industry of the acquired company	Ultimate acquiring company	Ultimate home economy	Industry of the ultimate acquiring company
2008	2 098	ISAB Srl	Italy	Crude petroleum and natural gas	NK LUKOIL	Russian Federation	Crude petroleum and natural gas
2005	2 000	Nelson Resources Ltd	United Kingdom	Gold ores	NK LUKOIL	Russian Federation	Crude petroleum and natural gas
2009	1 852	MOL Magyar Olaj es Gazipari Nyrt	Hungary	Crude petroleum and natural gas	Surgutneftegaz	Russian Federation	Crude petroleum and natural gas
2007	1 637	Strabag SE	Austria	Industrial buildings and warehouses	KBE	Russian Federation	Investors, nec
2011	1 600	Ruhr Oel GmbH	Germany	Petroleum refining	Rosneftegaz	Russian Federation	Crude petroleum and natural gas
2009	1 599	Lukarco BV	Netherlands	Pipelines, nec	NK LUKOIL	Russian Federation	Crude petroleum and natural gas
2008	1 524	Oriel Resources PLC	United Kingdom	Ferroalloy ores, except vanadium	Mechel	Russian Federation	Iron and steel forgings
2007	1 427	Strabag SE	Austria	Industrial buildings and warehouses	KBE	Russian Federation	Investors, nec
2006	1 400	PetroKazakhstan Inc	United Kingdom	Crude petroleum and natural gas	NK KazMunaiGaz	Kazakhstan	Crude petroleum and natural gas
2010	1 343	Kazakhmys PLC	United Kingdom	Copper ores	Kazakhstan	Kazakhstan	National government
2009	1 200	Rompetrol Group NV	Netherlands	Crude petroleum and natural gas	NK KazMunaiGaz	Kazakhstan	Crude petroleum and natural gas
2012	1 128	BASF Antwerpen NV-Fertilizer Production Plant	Belgium	Nitrogenous fertilizers	MKHK YevroKhim	Russian Federation	Chemical and fertilizer mineral mining, nec
2012	1 024	Gefco SA	France	Trucking, except local	RZhD	Russian Federation	Railroads, line-haul operating
2009	1 001	Sibir Energy PLC	United Kingdom	Crude petroleum and natural gas	Gazprom	Russian Federation	Crude petroleum and natural gas
2008	940	Formata Holding BV	Netherlands	Grocery stores	Pyaterochka Holding NV	Russian Federation	Grocery stores
2012	926	Bulgarian Telecommunications Co AD	Bulgaria	Telephone communications, except radiotelephone	Investor Group	Russian Federation	Investors, nec
2011	744	Sibir Energy PLC	United Kingdom	Crude petroleum and natural gas	Gazprom	Russian Federation	Crude petroleum and natural gas
2012	738	Volksbank International AG {VBI}	Austria	Banks	Sberbank Rossii	Russian Federation	Banks
2009	725	Total Raffinaderij Nederland NV	Netherlands	Crude petroleum and natural gas	NK LUKOIL	Russian Federation	Crude petroleum and natural gas
2006	700	Lucchini SpA	Italy	Steel works, blast furnaces, and rolling mills	Kapital	Russian Federation	Steel foundries, nec

Source: UNCTAD FDI-TNC-GVC Information System, cross-border M&A database (www.unctad.org/fdistatistics).

Note: The data cover only deals that involved acquisition of an equity stake greater than 10 per cent.

The regional conflict might affect FDI flows to and from transition economies. The outlook for developed-country TNCs investing in the region appears gloomier. For Russian TNCs investing abroad, an important concern is the risk of losing access to foreign loans. Banks in developed countries may be reluctant to provide fresh finance. Although some Russian State banks might fill the gap left by foreign lenders, some Russian TNCs depend on loans from developed countries.

Furthermore, additional scrutiny of Russian investments in Europe, including an asset swap between Gazprom and BASF (Germany), may slow down the vertical integration process that Russian TNCs have been trying to establish.[56]

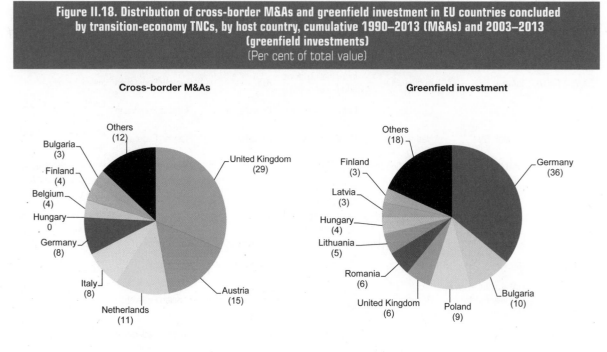

Figure II.18. Distribution of cross-border M&As and greenfield investment in EU countries concluded by transition-economy TNCs, by host country, cumulative 1990–2013 (M&As) and 2003–2013 (greenfield investments)
(Per cent of total value)

Source: UNCTAD FDI-TNC-GVC Information System, cross-border M&A database (www.unctad.org/fdistatistics) for M&As and information from the Financial Times Ltd, fDi Markets (www.fDimarkets.com) for greenfield projects.
Note: The data cover only those deals that involved an acquisition of an equity stake of more than 10 per cent.

5. Developed countries

Table A. Distribution of FDI flows among economies, by range,ᵃ 2013

Range	Inflows	Outflows
Above $100 billion	United States	United States and Japan
$50 to $99 billion	Canada	Switzerland and Germany
$10 to $49 billion	Australia, Spain, United Kingdom, Ireland, Luxembourg, Germany, Netherlands, Italy, Israel and Austria	Canada, Netherlands, Sweden, Italy, Spain, Ireland, Luxembourg, United Kingdom, Norway and Austria
$1 to $9 billion	Norway, Sweden, Czech Republic, France, Romania, Portugal, Hungary, Greece, Japan, Denmark and Bulgaria	Denmark, Australia, Israel, Finland, Czech Republic, Hungary and Portugal
Below $1 billion	New Zealand, Estonia, Latvia, Slovakia, Croatia, Cyprus, Lithuania, Iceland, Gibraltar, Bermuda, Slovenia, Finland, Malta, Belgium, Switzerland and Poland	New Zealand, Iceland, Estonia, Latvia, Cyprus, Bulgaria, Romania, Lithuania, Slovenia, Bermuda, Malta, Croatia, Slovakia, Greece, France, Poland and Belgium

ᵃ Economies are listed according to the magnitude of their FDI flows.

Figure A. FDI flows, top 5 host and home economies, 2012–2013
(Billions of dollars)

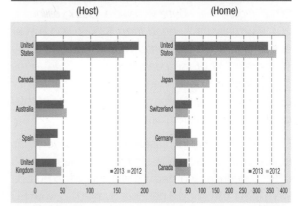

Figure B. FDI inflows, 2007–2013
(Billions of dollars)

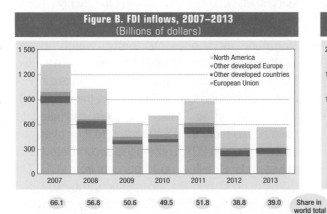

Share in world total: 66.1 | 56.8 | 50.6 | 49.5 | 51.8 | 38.8 | 39.0

Figure C. FDI outflows, 2007–2013
(Billions of dollars)

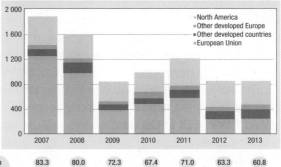

Share in world total: 83.3 | 80.0 | 72.3 | 67.4 | 71.0 | 63.3 | 60.8

Table B. Cross-border M&As by industry, 2012–2013
(Millions of dollars)

Sector/industry	Sales 2012	Sales 2013	Purchases 2012	Purchases 2013
Total	268 652	239 606	183 914	151 752
Primary	50 161	39 346	-10 406	-41 903
Mining, quarrying and petroleum	43 032	37 906	-10 411	-42 154
Manufacturing	109 481	86 617	117 068	79 993
Food, beverages and tobacco	20 616	19 708	24 945	25 231
Chemicals and chemical products	16 411	21 132	19 705	4 822
Pharmaceuticals, medicinal chem. & botanical prod.	11 638	742	17 951	20 443
Computer, electronic optical prod. & electrical equipt.	22 061	10 776	23 909	11 808
Services	109 010	113 643	77 252	113 662
Trade	12 581	7 406	19 537	-2 067
Information and communications	22 395	29 374	9 372	22 476
Financial and insurance activities	9 905	9 081	27 461	64 741
Business services	31 406	35 965	16 865	22 220

Table C. Cross-border M&As by region/country, 2012–2013
(Millions of dollars)

Region/country	Sales 2012	Sales 2013	Purchases 2012	Purchases 2013
World	268 652	239 606	183 914	151 752
Developed economies	175 408	165 650	175 408	165 650
Europe	45 246	34 225	93 865	112 545
North America	103 729	85 138	67 732	40 618
Other developed countries	26 432	45 287	13 811	12 487
Japan	-32 276	44 872	-1 548	2 576
Developing economies	79 982	65 035	3 760	-6 307
Africa	635	2 288	-3 500	-8 953
Latin America and the Caribbean	17 146	7 274	1 699	-7 188
Asia and Oceania	62 201	55 473	5 561	9 833
China	27 009	37 405	3 251	6 201
Singapore	-1 039	2 745	6 004	4 386
Transition economies	4 848	1 682	4 746	-7 591

Table D. Greenfield FDI projects by industry, 2012–2013
(Millions of dollars)

Sector/industry	Developed countries as destination 2012	Developed countries as destination 2013	Developed countries as investors 2012	Developed countries as investors 2013
Total	224 604	215 018	413 541	458 336
Primary	9 222	1 687	16 979	17 878
Mining, quarrying and petroleum	9 220	1 683	16 977	15 712
Manufacturing	88 712	92 748	186 278	197 086
Textiles, clothing and leather	6 579	13 711	10 080	18 269
Chemicals and chemical products	13 165	15 615	26 090	32 542
Electrical and electronic equipment	10 604	13 853	15 108	20 716
Motor vehicles and other transport equipment	21 423	15 944	52 736	49 247
Services	126 670	120 584	210 285	243 372
Electricity, gas and water	27 023	25 463	41 758	69 487
Transport, storage & communications	17 070	19 436	40 067	41 630
Finance	11 120	10 260	23 106	21 309
Business services	31 316	33 689	50 188	56 767

Table E. Greenfield FDI projects by region/country, 2012–2013
(Millions of dollars)

Partner region/economy	Developed countries as destination 2012	Developed countries as destination 2013	Developed countries as investors 2012	Developed countries as investors 2013
World	224 604	215 018	413 541	458 336
Developed economies	170 919	184 887	170 919	184 887
Europe	107 093	112 784	109 572	107 921
North America	47 082	54 615	45 010	57 582
Other developed countries	16 744	17 488	16 337	19 383
Japan	9 818	11 212	4 317	7 920
Developing economies	50 625	27 804	213 530	253 816
Africa	1 802	2 080	17 541	27 254
Asia and Oceania	46 650	24 475	139 280	146 140
China	6 232	9 171	50 451	48 894
India	8 553	3 530	21 249	13 571
Latin America and the Caribbean	2 172	1 249	56 709	80 421
Transition economies	3 060	2 327	29 092	19 633

After the sharp fall in 2012, overall FDI of the 39 developed economies[57] resumed its recovery in 2013, albeit marginally in the case of outflows. Inflows were $566 billion, rising 9 per cent over 2012 (figure B). Outflows were $857 billion in 2013, virtually unchanged from $852 billion a year earlier (figure C). Both inflows and outflows were still barely half of the peak level in 2007. In terms of global share, developed countries accounted for 39 per cent of total inflows and 61 per cent of total outflows – both historically low levels.

Despite the overall increase in inflows, recovery was concentrated in a smaller set of economies; only 15 of 39 economies registered a rise. Inflows to Europe were $251 billion (up 3 per cent over 2012), with EU countries accounting for the bulk, at $246 billion. Inflows to Italy and Spain made a robust recovery, with the latter receiving the largest flows in Europe in 2013 (figure A). Inflows to North America rebounded to $250 billion with a 23 per cent increase, making the United States and Canada the recipients of the largest flows to developed countries in 2013 (figure A). The increase was primarily due to large inflows from Japan in the United States and a doubling of United States FDI in Canada. Inflows to Australia and New Zealand together declined by 12 per cent, to $51 billion.

The recovery of outflows from developed countries was more widely shared, with an increase in 22 economies. Outflows from Europe rose by 10 per cent to $328 billion, of which $250 billion was from the EU countries. Switzerland became Europe's largest direct investor (figure A). In contrast, outflows from North America shed another 10 per cent, slipping to $381 billion. The effect of greater cash hoarding abroad by United States TNCs (i.e. an increase in reinvested earnings) was countered by the increasing transfer of funds raised in Europe back to the home country (i.e. a decline in intracompany loans). Outflows from Japan grew for the third successive year, rising to $136 billion. In addition to investment in the United States, market-seeking FDI in South-East Asia helped Japan consolidate its position as the second largest direct investor (figure A).

Diverging trends among major European countries. European FDI flows have fluctuated considerably from year to year. Among the major

economies, Germany saw inflows more than double from $13 billion in 2012 to $27 billion in 2013. In contrast, inflows to France declined by 80 per cent to $5 billion and those to the United Kingdom declined by 19 per cent to $37 billion. In all cases, large swings in intracompany loans were a significant contributing factor. Intracompany loans to Germany, which had fallen by $39 billion in 2012, bounced back by $20 billion in 2013. Intracompany loans to France fell from $5 billion in 2012 to -$14 billion in 2013, implying that foreign TNCs pulled funds out of their affiliates in France. Similarly, intracompany loans to the United Kingdom fell from -$2 billion to -$10 billion. Other European countries that saw a large change in inflows of intracompany loans in 2012 were Luxembourg (up $22 billion) and the Netherlands (up $16 billion).

Negative intracompany loans weigh down outflows from the United States. In 2013, two types of transactions had opposite effects on FDI outflows from the Unites States. On the one hand, the largest United States TNCs are estimated to have added more than $200 billion to their overseas cash holdings in 2013, raising the accumulated total to just under $2 trillion, up 12 per cent from 2012. On the other hand, non-European issuers (mostly United States but also Asian TNCs) reportedly sold euro-denominated corporate bonds worth $132 billion (a three-fold increase from 2011) and transferred some of the proceeds to the United States to meet funding needs there.[58] Rather than repatriating retained earnings, United States TNCs often prefer to meet funding needs through additional borrowing so as to defer corporate income tax liabilities.[59] Favourable interest rates led them to raise those funds in Europe. As a consequence, the United States registered negative outflows of intracompany loans (-$6.1 billion) in 2013, compared with $21 billion in 2012.

TTIP under negotiation. The Transatlantic Trade and Investment Partnership (TTIP) is a proposed FTA between the EU and the United States. Talks started in July 2013 and are expected to finish in 2015 or early 2016. If successfully concluded, TTIP would create the world's largest free trade area. Its key objective is to harmonize regulatory regimes and reduce non-tariff "behind the border" barriers to trade and investment.[60] Aspects of TTIP could have implications for FDI.

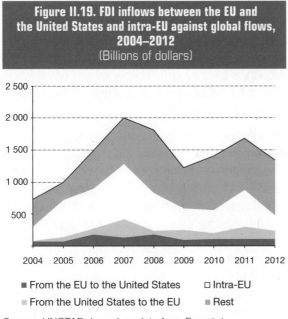

Figure II.19. FDI inflows between the EU and the United States and intra-EU against global flows, 2004–2012
(Billions of dollars)

- From the EU to the United States
- From the United States to the EU
- Intra-EU
- Rest

Source: UNCTAD, based on data from Eurostat.

The EU and the United States together constitute more than 45 per cent of global GDP. FDI flows within the TTIP bloc accounted for, on average, half of global FDI flows over the period 2004–2012 (figure II.19). Intra-EU FDI has tended to be volatile, but FDI flows between the EU and the United States have remained relatively stable in recent years.

Viewed from the United States, the EU economies make up about 30 per cent of the outside world in terms of GDP. The EU's importance as a destination for United States FDI has been much more significant, with its share in flows ranging from 41 per cent to 59 per cent over 2004–2012, and its share in outward stocks at over 50 per cent by the end of that period.[61] In contrast, the EU's share in United States exports averaged only 25 per cent over the same period. Major host countries of United States FDI are listed in table II.7.

The industry breakdown shows that about four fifths of United States FDI stock in the EU is in services, in which "Holding Companies (nonbank)" account for 60 per cent and "Finance (except depository institutions) and insurance" for another 20 per cent. Manufacturing takes up 12 per cent.

From the EU's perspective, much of the inflows to EU countries arrive from other EU countries. Over the period 2004–2012, on average, 63 per cent of FDI flows to the region came from other EU

countries and 15 per cent from the United States. The combined share of the EU and the United States in FDI stock in the EU at the end of 2012 was 76 per cent. Considering the EU as a single block, the United States was the largest investment partner, accounting for one third of all investment flows from outside the EU.

For the United States, the share of the EU in its

Table II.7. United States FDI stock abroad, by major recipient economies, 2012

Destination	FDI stock ($ million)	Share (%)
Netherlands	645 098	14.5
United Kingdom	597 813	13.4
Luxembourg	383 603	8.6
Canada	351 460	7.9
Ireland	203 779	4.6
Singapore	138 603	3.1
Japan	133 967	3.0
Australia	132 825	3.0
Switzerland	130 315	2.9
Germany	121 184	2.7
European Union	2 239 580	50.3
All countries total	4 453 307	100.0

Source: UNCTAD, Bilateral FDI Statistics (http://unctad.org/en/Pages/DIAE/FDI%20Statistics/FDI-Statistics-Bilateral.aspx).
Note: Excludes Bermuda and United Kingdom Caribbean islands (British Antilles, British Virgin Islands, Cayman Islands, Montserrat).

inflows ranged from 45 per cent to 75 per cent over the period 2004–2012. In terms of FDI stock, the EU's share was 62 per cent at the end of 2012 (table II.8). The top investors include the larger economies in the EU, such as France and Germany, along with the United Kingdom. Luxembourg and the Netherlands rank high as source countries of FDI in the United States, too. One explanation for the high share of these economies is that they have become preferred locations for incorporating global companies. The merger between two of the largest suppliers of chip-making equipment, Applied Materials (United States) and Tokyo Electron (Japan), in 2013 illustrates the case. To implement the merger, the two companies set up a holding company in the Netherlands. The existing companies became United States and Japanese affiliates of the Dutch holding company through share swaps.

Table II.8. FDI stock in the United States, by major source economy, 2012		
Source	**FDI stock ($ million)**	**Share (%)**
United Kingdom	486 833	18.4
Japan	308 253	11.6
Netherlands	274 904	10.4
Canada	225 331	8.5
France	209 121	7.9
Switzerland	203 954	7.7
Luxembourg	202 338	7.6
Germany	199 006	7.5
Belgium	88 697	3.3
Spain	47 352	1.8
Australia	42 685	1.6
European Union	1 647 567	62.2
All countries total	2 650 832	100.0

Source: UNCTAD, Bilateral FDI Statistics (http://unctad.org/en/Pages/DIAE/FDI%20Statistics/FDI-Statistics-Bilaleral.aspx).

Note: Excludes Bermuda and United Kingdom Caribbean islands (British Antilles, British Virgin Islands, Cayman Islands, Montserrat).

Booming inflows to Israel. One beneficiary of the growing cash holdings among TNCs seems to be Israel, which hosts a vibrant pool of venture-capital-backed start-up companies, especially in knowledge-intensive industries. These companies have become acquisition targets of global TNCs. In 2013, foreign TNCs are estimated to have spent $6.5 billion on Israeli companies,[62] raising inflows to Israel to the record high of $12 billion. High-profile examples include the acquisitions of Waze by Google for $966 million, Retalix by NCR for $735 million and Intucell by Cisco for $475 million. Berkshire Hathaway paid $2.05 billion to take full control of its Israeli affiliate IMC. A Moody's report noted that, at 39 per cent at the end of 2013, the technology industry had the largest hoard (domestic and offshore) of total corporate cash of non-financial United States companies; the health-care and pharmaceuticals industries followed.[63] This concentration of cash in knowledge-intensive industries may signal further deals in the making for Israel.

A shift towards consumer-oriented industries. As the weight of developing countries in the global economy increases, their effects on both the inward and outward FDI patterns of developed countries are becoming more apparent. The growth of more affluent, urbanized populations in developing economies presents significant market potential that TNCs around the world are keen to capture. For example, the shift in emphasis in the Chinese economy from investment-led to consumption-led growth is beginning to shape investment flows in consumer-oriented industries such as food (tables B and D).

On the one hand, TNCs from developed countries are entering the growing food market in China. The Japanese trading house Marubeni, the largest exporter of soya beans to China, finalized a $2.7 billion deal to acquire the grain merchant Gavilon (United States) after the deal was approved by China's competition authority. On the other hand, the trend is also shaping investment flows in the other direction: in the largest takeover of a United States company by a Chinese company, Shuanghui acquired pork producer Smithfield for $4.7 billion. Shuanghui's strategy is to export meat products from the United States to China and other markets. Another example of Chinese investment in agri-processing occurred in New Zealand, where Shanghai Pengxin proposed to acquire Synlait Farms, which owns 4,000 hectares of farmland, for $73 million.[64] The company had already acquired the 8,000-hectare Crafar farms for $163 million in 2012.

A slowdown in investment in extractive industries. Earlier optimism in the mining industry, fuelled by surging demand from China, has been replaced by a more cautious approach. Rio Tinto (United Kingdom/Australia) announced that its capital expenditure would fall gradually from over $17 billion in 2012 to $8 billion in 2015. BHP Billiton (Australia) also announced its intent to reduce its capital and exploration budget. Glencore Xstrata (Switzerland) announced it would reduce its total capital expenditures over 2013–2015 by $3.5 billion. The investment slowdown in mining has affected developed countries that are rich in natural resources, an effect that was particularly apparent in cross-border M&As (table B). Net M&A sales (analogous to inward FDI) of developed countries in mining and quarrying were worth $110 billion at the peak of the commodity boom in 2011 but declined to $38 billion in 2013. For example, in the United States they fell from $46 billion in 2011 to $2 billion in 2013 and in Australia from $24 billion in 2011 to $5 billion in 2013. Similarly, net cross-border purchases (analogous to outward FDI) by developed-country TNCs in this industry declined from $58 billion in 2011 to a net divestment of -$42 billion in 2013.

TNCs eyeing growth markets. Growing consumer markets in emerging economies remain a prime target for developed-country TNCs. The Japanese beverages group Kirin Holdings, which bought control of Brazil's Schincariol in 2011, announced its plan to invest $1.5 billion during 2014 to expand its beer-brewing capacity in the country. Japanese food and beverage group Suntory acquired the United States spirits company Beam Inc. for $13.6 billion and the drinks brands Lucozade and Ribena of GlaxoSmithKline for $2.1 billion. These deals give the Japanese group not only a significant presence in the United States and the United Kingdom, but also access to distribution networks in India, the Russian Federation and Brazil in the case of Beam, and Nigeria and Malaysia in the case of Lucozade and Ribena.

Growing urban populations are driving a rapid expansion of power generation capacity in emerging economies, which is drawing investment from developed-country TNCs. In October 2013, an international consortium comprising Turkish Electricity Generation Corporation, Itochu (Japan), GDF Suez (France) and the Government of Turkey signed a framework agreement to study the feasibility of constructing a nuclear power plant in Sinop, Turkey.[65] GDF Suez (France) also teamed up with Japanese trading house Mitsui and Moroccan energy company Nareva Holdings to form the joint venture Safi Energy Company, which was awarded a contract to operate a coal-fired power plant in Morocco in September 2013.[66] Another European power company, Eon (Germany), acquired a 50 per cent stake in the Turkish power company Enerjisa and increased its stake in the Brazilian power generation company MPX in 2013, in an effort to build a presence in emerging markets.

The pursuit of "next emerging markets" has led TNCs to target lower-income countries, too. For instance, the Japanese manufacturer Nissin Food invested in a joint venture with the Jomo Kenyatta University of Agriculture and Technology in Kenya,

initially to market imported packaged noodles, but also to start local production in 2014. The joint venture aims to source agricultural input from local producers and to export packaged noodles to neighbouring countries, taking advantage of free trade within EAC.

Facilitating investment in Africa. In June 2013, the Government of the United States announced Power Africa – an initiative to double the number of people in sub-Saharan Africa with access to power. For the first phase over 2013–2018, the Government has committed more than $7 billion in financial support and loan guarantees, which has resulted in the leveraging of commitments by private sector partners, many of them TNCs, to invest over $14.7 billion in the power sectors of the target countries. In a different sector, the Government of Japan announced a $2 billion support mechanism for its TNCs to invest in natural resource development projects in Africa.[67] One of the projects earmarked for support is Mitsui's investment – expected to be worth $3 billion – in natural gas in Mozambique.

General optimism might not be reflected in FDI statistics in 2014. UNCTAD's forecast based on economic fundamentals suggests that FDI flows to developed economies could rise by 35 per cent in 2014 (chapter I). As an early indication, M&A activities picked up significantly in the first quarter of 2014. Furthermore, shareholder activism is likely to intensify in North America, adding extra impetus to spend the accumulated earnings. However, reasons to expect declines in FDI flows are also present. The divestment by Vodafone (United Kingdom) of its 45 per cent stake in Verizon Wireless (United States) was worth $130 billion, appearing in statistics as negative FDI inflows to the United States.

B. TRENDS IN STRUCTURALLY WEAK, VULNERABLE AND SMALL ECONOMIES

1. Least developed countries

Table A. Distribution of FDI flows among economies, by range,ᵃ 2013

Range	Inflows	Outflows
Above $2.0 billion	Mozambique, Sudan Myanmar and Democratic Republic of the Congo	Angola
$1.0 to $1.9 billion	Equatorial Guinea, United Republic of Tanzania, Zambia, Bangladesh, Cambodia, Mauritania, Uganda and Liberia	..
$0.5 to $0.9 billion	Ethiopia, Madagascar, Niger, Sierra Leone and Chad	Sudan and Liberia
$0.1 to $0.4 billion	Mali, Burkina Faso, Benin, Senegal, Lao People's Democratic Republic, Djibouti, Haiti, Malawi, Rwanda, Somalia and Solomon Islands	Democratic Republic of the Congo and Zambia
Below $0.1 billion	Togo, Nepal, Afghanistan, Lesotho, Eritrea, Vanuatu, São Tomé and Principe, Samoa, Gambia, Guinea, Bhutan, Timor-Leste, Guinea-Bissau, Comoros, Kiribati, Burundi, Central African Republic, Yemen and Angola	Burkina Faso, Yemen, Malawi, Benin, Cambodia, Togo, Bangladesh, Senegal, Lesotho, Rwanda, Timor-Leste, Mali, Mauritania, Solomon Islands, Guinea, Vanuatu, Guinea-Bissau, São Tomé and Principe, Samoa, Kiribati, Mozambique, Uganda, Niger and Lao People's Democratic Republic

ᵃ Economies are listed according to the magnitude of their FDI flows.

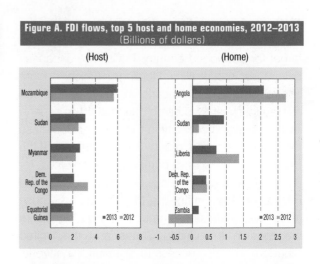

Figure A. FDI flows, top 5 host and home economies, 2012–2013
(Billions of dollars)

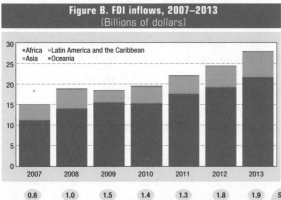

Figure B. FDI inflows, 2007–2013
(Billions of dollars)

Share in world total: 0.8 | 1.0 | 1.5 | 1.4 | 1.3 | 1.8 | 1.9

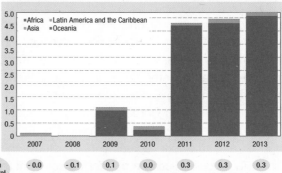

Figure C. FDI outflows, 2007–2013
(Billions of dollars)

Share in world total: - 0.0 | - 0.1 | 0.1 | 0.0 | 0.3 | 0.3 | 0.3

Table B. Cross-border M&As by industry, 2012–2013
(Millions of dollars)

Sector/industry	Sales 2012	Sales 2013	Purchases 2012	Purchases 2013
Total	374	26	-102	-12
Primary	11	16	-	-12
Mining, quarrying and petroleum	11	16	-	-12
Manufacturing	342	37	-185	-
Food, beverages and tobacco	351	20	-	-
Textiles, clothing and leather	-	2	-	-
Chemicals and chemical products	-	-	-185	-
Pharmaceuticals, medicinal chem. & botanical prod.	-	15	-	-
Non-metallic mineral products	90	-	-	-
Services	22	-27	83	-
Information and communications	18	3	-	-
Financial and insurance activities	1	-42	83	-
Business services	-	12	-	-

Table C. Cross-border M&As by region/country, 2012–2013
(Millions of dollars)

Region/country	Sales 2012	Sales 2013	Purchases 2012	Purchases 2013
World	374	26	-102	-12
Developed economies	-1 217	-4 020	88	2
Cyprus	-	-155	-	-
Italy	-	-4 210	-	-
Switzerland	-	761	-	-
Canada	-1 258	-353	-	-
Australia	-115	-36	-	-
Developing economies	1 591	4 046	-190	-14
Nigeria	-	-	-185	-
Panama	-	-430	-	-
China	1 580	4 222	-	-14
Malaysia	-	176	-	-
Transition economies	-	-	-	-

Table D. Greenfield FDI projects by industry, 2012–2013
(Millions of dollars)

Sector/industry	LDCs as destination 2012	LDCs as destination 2013	LDCs as investors 2012	LDCs as investors 2013
Total	21 923	39 943	1 005	1 528
Primary	4 390	3 461	-	7
Agriculture, hunting, forestry and fisheries	-	1 940	-	-
Mining, quarrying and petroleum	4 390	1 520	-	7
Manufacturing	6 727	8 100	91	395
Coke, petroleum products and nuclear fuel	1 970	1 764	-	-
Non-metallic mineral products	1 265	3 379	-	262
Motor vehicles and other transport equipment	397	812	-	-
Services	10 806	27 482	914	1 126
Electricity, gas and water	3 905	17 902	-	-
Transport, storage and communications	2 234	4 819	168	92
Finance	1 920	1 523	327	593
Business services	725	1 224	418	37

Table E. Greenfield FDI projects by region/country, 2012–2013
(Millions of dollars)

Partner region/economy	LDCs as destination 2012	LDCs as destination 2013	LDCs as investors 2012	LDCs as investors 2013
World	21 923	39 043	1 005	1 528
Developed economies	8 822	24 806	32	122
Finland	18	1 942	-	-
United Kingdom	1 289	2 152	-	-
Iceland	-	4 000	-	-
United States	3 251	1 194	-	-
Japan	1 371	11 322	-	-
Developing economies	13 072	14 237	973	1 366
Nigeria	691	1 833	-	17
South Africa	786	2 360	8	-
Malaysia	342	1 059	1	2
India	4 383	3 479	-	41
Transition economies	30	-	-	39

FDI flows to LDCs rose to $28 billion in 2013. Greenfield investments in LDCs rebounded to a three-year high, driven by announced projects in the services sector. External finance constitutes an important part of the financing of infrastructure projects in LDCs, but a substantial portion of announced investments has not generated FDI inflows. Growing official development finance to support infrastructure projects in LDCs is encouraging, but LDCs' estimated investment needs are much greater. Mobilization of resources for infrastructure development in LDCs remains a challenge.

FDI inflows to LDCs increased by 14 per cent to $28 billion. While inflows to some larger LDCs fell or stagnated (figure A), rising inflows were recorded elsewhere. A $2.6 billion reduction in divestment (negative inflows) in Angola contributed most to this trend, followed by gains in Ethiopia ($0.7 billion or 242 per cent), Myanmar ($0.4 billion or 17 per cent), the Sudan ($0.6 billion or 24 per cent) and Yemen (a $0.4 billion or 75 per cent fall in divestment). The share of inflows to LDCs in global inflows continued to be small (figure B). Among the developing economies, the share of inflows to LDCs increased to 3.6 per cent of FDI inflows to all developing economies compared with 3.4 per cent in 2012.

As in 2012, developed-economy TNCs continued selling their assets in LDCs to other foreign investors. The net sales value of cross-border M&As in LDCs (table B) masks the fact that more than 60 such deals took place in 2013. While the value of net sales to developed-economy investors continued to decline in 2013 (table C) – indicating the highest-ever divestments in LDCs by those economies – net sales to developing-economy investors rose to a record level, mainly through the acquisition of assets divested by developed economies. Examples include the $4.2 billion divestment of a partial stake in the Italian company Eni's oil and gas exploration and production affiliate in Mozambique, which was acquired by the China National Petroleum Corporation. Other such deals include a series of acquisitions by Glencore (Switzerland) in Chad and the Democratic Republic of the Congo, which were recorded as a $0.4 billion divestment by Canada and a $0.4 billion divestment by Panama (table C).[68]

Announced greenfield FDI rebounded, driven by large-scale energy projects. The number of announced new projects reached a record high,[69] and the value of announced investments reached their highest level in three years. The driving force was robust gains in the services sector (table D), contributing 70 per cent of total greenfield investments. Greenfield investments in energy (in 11 projects) and in transport, storage and communications (in 59 projects) both hit their highest levels in 2013 (table D). Announced greenfield FDI from developed economies was at a 10-year high, led by record-high investments from Iceland and Japan to LDCs (table E). A single large electricity project from each of these home countries boosted greenfield investments in LDCs.

The largest fossil fuel electric power project from Japan (table II.9) was linked with the development of a newly established special economic zone (SEZ) in Myanmar (box II.2). Iceland's $4 billion geothermal power project in Ethiopia (see also table II.9) received support from the Government of the United States as part of its six-nation Power Africa initiative, a $7 billion commitment to double the number of people with access to electricity in Africa.[70] In this, the largest alternative energy project ever recorded in LDCs, Rejkavik Geothermal (Iceland) will build and operate up to 1,000 megawatts of geothermal power in the next 8–10 years.

India continued to lead greenfield FDI from developing economies to LDCs, with South Africa and Nigeria running second and third. Among investors from developing economies, India remained the largest, despite a 21 per cent fall in the value of announced investments in LDCs (table E). Announced greenfield investments from India were mostly in energy – led by Jindal Steel & Power – and telecommunications projects – led by the Bharti Group – in African LDCs. In Asia, Bangladesh was the only LDC in which Indian greenfield FDI projects were reported in 2013.[71] Announced greenfield investments from South Africa and Nigeria to LDCs showed a strong increase (table E). The fourth largest project in Mozambique (table II.9) accounted for two thirds of announced greenfield FDI from South Africa to LDCs. Announced greenfield FDI projects from Nigeria to LDCs hit a record high, led by the Dangote Group's cement and concrete projects in five African LDCs and Nepal ($1.8 billion in total). Greenfield projects from Nigeria also boosted greenfield investments in non-metallic mineral products in LDCs (table D).

Table II.9. The five largest greenfield projects announced in LDCs, 2013				
Host economy (destination)	**Industry segment**	**Investing company**	**Home economy**	**Estimated investment ($ million)**
Myanmar	Fossil fuel electric power	Mitsubishi	Japan	9 850
Ethiopia	Geothermal electric power	Reykjavik Geothermal	Iceland	4 000
Mozambique	Forestry and logging	Forestal Oriental	Finland	1 940
Mozambique	Petroleum and coal products	Beacon Hill Resources	South Africa	1 641
Cambodia	Biomass power	Wah Seong	Malaysia	1 000

Source: UNCTAD, based on information from the Financial Times Ltd, fDi Markets (www.fDimarkets.com).

External finance constitutes an important part of the financing of a growing number of infrastructure projects announced in LDCs. The surge in announced greenfield investments in energy, transport, storage and communications (table D) indicates increasing foreign engagement in infrastructure projects in LDCs. From 2003 to 2013, nearly 290 infrastructure projects[72] – including domestic and non-equity modes of investment – were announced in LDCs.[73] The cumulative costs amounted to $332 billion (about $30 billion a year),[74] of which 43 per cent ($144 billion) was attributed to 142 projects that were announced to be financed partly or fully by foreign sponsors (including public entities, such as bilateral and multilateral development agencies) and almost half ($164 billion) was attributed to 110 projects whose sponsors were unspecified.[75] Energy projects have been the driver, accounting for 61 per cent of the estimated cost of all foreign participating projects (and 71 per cent of the total project costs with unspecified sponsors).

Over the past decade, the number of announced infrastructure projects in LDCs rose from an annual average of 15 in 2003–2005 to 34 in 2011–2013. Growth in total announced project costs nearly quadrupled (from an annual average of $11 billion in 2003–2005 to $43 billion in 2011–2013). The total value of announced infrastructure projects hit an exceptionally high level twice: first in 2008 and then in 2012 (figure II.20). In both cases, the driver was the announcement of a single megaproject – in the Democratic Republic of the Congo ($80 billion in energy)[76] in 2008 and in Myanmar ($50 billion in transportation) in 2012. Not only did the number of projects increase to their highest level in 2013, but

the total value of announced projects also made significant gains, in 2012–2013 (figure II.20). This was due to a sharp increase in transport projects in Africa, led by a $10 billion project for an oil and gas free port zone in the United Republic of Tanzania, as well as a $4 billion rail line project and a $3 billion rail and port project in Mozambique.[77]

A substantial portion of announced infrastructure investments has not generated FDI inflows. Judging from the level of current FDI stock in LDCs (annex table II.2) and the average annual FDI inflows to all LDCs ($16.7 billion in 2003–2013), a substantial portion of foreign and unspecified contributions to announced infrastructure projects (about $29 billion annually, of which $15 billion was attributed to unspecified sponsors) did not generate FDI inflows. Project costs could be shared among different types of sponsors, so that not all were funded by foreign investors alone. Also, the FDI statistics do not capture a large part of foreign sponsors' investment commitments, which were financed with non-equity modes of investments by TNCs (*WIR08* and *WIR11*), debts, structured finance, or bilateral or multilateral donor funding.[78] It is also possible that some announced projects may have been cancelled or never realized. Another possible explanation is that the year when a project is announced does not correspond to the year when the host LDC receives FDI.[79] The status of two megaprojects announced in 2008 and 2012 (boxes II.5 and II.6) reflects these gaps between announced project costs and their impacts on FDI flows. Neither project has yet triggered the announced levels of foreign or domestic investment.

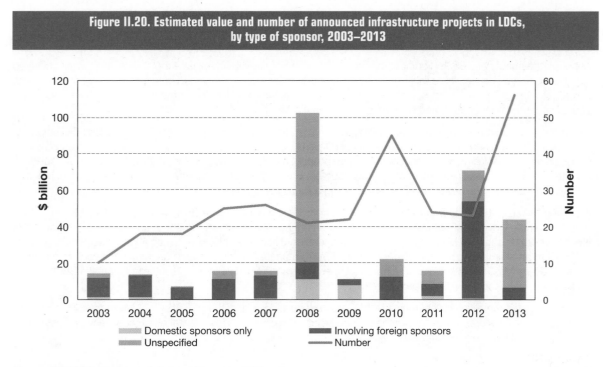

Figure II.20. Estimated value and number of announced infrastructure projects in LDCs, by type of sponsor, 2003–2013

Domestic sponsors only
Unspecified
Involving foreign sponsors
Number

Source: UNCTAD, based on data from Thomson ONE.

Box II.5. The Grand Inga Hydroelectric Power Station Project: no foreign investment secured to start first phase

When the $80 billion Grand Inga hydroelectric project was recorded in 2008, the Democratic Republic of the Congo was one of five African countries (with Angola, Botswana, Namibia and South Africa) that agreed to develop this project under the management of the Western Power Corridor, a consortium of five national utility companies representing each of the five States sharing 20 per cent of the equity. The host country had already secured an agreement with BHP Billiton (Australia) to jointly develop a $3 billion aluminium smelter to use 2,000 megawatts of electricity to be generated by the first phase of the project, "Inga III".[80] In 2009, however, seeking a greater controlling share in the project, the Democratic Republic of the Congo withdrew from the agreement and went alone to develop Inga III.[81] BHP Billiton was then selected to build a $5 billion smelter, along with a 2,500-megawatt plant for $3.5 billion. In early 2012, citing economic difficulties, the company abandoned both plans and withdrew from Inga III.

In May 2013, the stalled project was revived as a 4,800-megawatt project at an estimated cost of $12 billion, to be managed by Eskom (South Africa) and Société Nationale d'Electricité (Democratic Republic of the Congo). By the end of 2013, a cooperation treaty had been sealed between the Democratic Republic of the Congo and South Africa, in which South Africa committed to buy more than half of the electricity generated. With financial and technical assistance from the African Development Bank ($33 million) and the World Bank ($73 million),[82] feasibility studies were conducted for the base chute development. Other bilateral development agencies and regional banks expressed interest in funding the project, but no firm commitments have been made.

Three consortiums, including TNCs from Canada, China, the Republic of Korea and Spain, have been prequalified to bid for this $12 billion project, and a winning bidder will be selected in the summer of 2014.[83] This will result in an expansion in both FDI and non-equity modes of activity by TNCs, though the exact amounts will depend on which consortium wins and the configuration of the project. Construction is scheduled to start in early 2016, to make the facility operational by 2020.

Source: UNCTAD based on "Grand Inga Hydroelectric Project: An Overview", www.internationalrivers.org, and "The Inga 3 Hydropower Project", 27 January 2014, www.icafrica.org.

> ### Box II.6. Dawei Special Economic Zone: $10 billion secured, search continues for new investors to finance remaining $40 billion
>
> Although the announced $50 billion build-operate-own project in Dawei, Myanmar – the Dawei SEZ – was registered as a transportation project, it is a multisectoral infrastructure project: a two-way road between Myanmar and Thailand, a seaport, steel mills, oil refineries, petrochemical factories, power plants, telecommunication lines, water supply, a wastewater treatment system, and housing and commercial facilities.
>
> When this project was announced in late 2012, Thailand's largest construction group, Italian-Thailand Development (ITD), was in charge under a 75-year concession. ITD was responsible for implementing the first phase, estimated at $8 billion, and construction was scheduled to start in April 2014.[84] However, due to ITD's failure to secure sufficient investments and reach an agreement on the development of energy infrastructure, the Governments of Myanmar and of Thailand took over the project in 2013, establishing a joint special purpose vehicle (SPV).[85]
>
> Stressing the potential for Dawei to grow into a new production hub in the ASEAN region, the Thai-Myanmar SPV approached the Government of Japan, which had been engaged in the development of another SEZ in Thilawa.[86] In November 2013, the Thai-Myanmar SPV involved a leading Japanese TNC in a 7-megawatt power station project in Dawei at an estimated cost of $9.9 billion (table II.9). To manage this project, a Thai-Japan joint venture has been established by Mitsubishi Corporation (Japan) (30 per cent) and two Thai firms – Electricity Generating Authority of Thailand (50 per cent) and ITD (20 per cent).[87]
>
> To implement the remaining six segments of infrastructure development in the SEZ, the Thai-Myanmar SPV continues to look for new investors. The viability of the SEZ depends on successful implementation of the planned infrastructure developments. Until the remaining $40 billion is secured, therefore, its fate is on hold.
>
> *Source:* UNCTAD.

The growth in development finance to support infrastructure projects in LDCs is encouraging, but the estimated investment needs in these countries are much greater. Along with FDI and non-equity modes, official development assistance (ODA) from the OECD Development Assistance Committee (DAC) has been the important external source of finance for infrastructure projects in LDCs. Because ODA can act as a catalyst for boosting FDI in infrastructure development in LDCs (*WIR10*), synergies between ODA disbursements and FDI inflows to LDCs should be encouraged to strengthen productive capacities in LDCs.[88]

Led by transport and storage, gross disbursements of official development finance (ODF) to selected infrastructure sectors[89] in LDCs are growing steadily (figure II.21). ODF includes both ODA and non-concessional financing[90] from multilateral development banks. In cumulative terms, however, gross ODF disbursements to infrastructure projects in LDCs amounted to $41 billion,[91] or an annual average of $4 billion, representing 0.9 per cent of average GDP in 2003–2012.

Relatively small infrastructure financing by DAC donors is not unique to LDCs.[92] Yet, considering that low-income countries had to spend 12.5 per cent of GDP (or about $60 billion for LDCs) annually to develop infrastructure to meet the Millennium Development Goals (MDGs),[93] ODF of $4 billion a year (7 per cent of the estimated $60 billion) for all LDCs appears to fall short of their investment requirements. Given the structural challenges such countries face, where the domestic private sector is underdeveloped, it is a daunting task to bridge the gap between ODF and investment needs for achieving the SDGs (see chapter IV).

For instance, in water supply and sanitation, where hardly any foreign investments in announced projects have been recorded in the last decade, the highest level of gross ODF disbursements to LDCs ($1.8 billion in 2012) would cover no more than 10 per cent of the estimated annual capital that LDCs need ($20 billion a year for 2011–2015) to meet the MDG water supply and sanitation target ($8 billion) and universal coverage target (an additional $12 billion).[94] With the current level of external finance, therefore, the remaining $18 billion must be secured in limited domestic sources in LDCs.

Prospects. Announced projects suggest that FDI inflows to infrastructure projects in LDCs

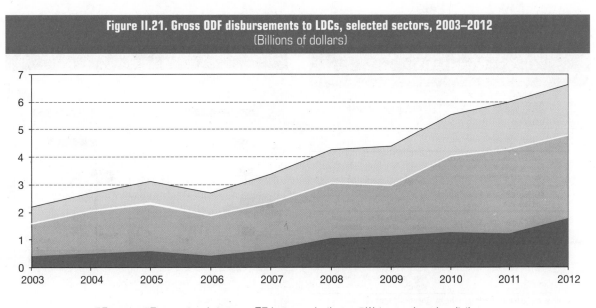

Figure II.21. Gross ODF disbursements to LDCs, selected sectors, 2003–2012
(Billions of dollars)

■ Energy   ■ Transport and storage   □ Telecommunications   ■ Water supply and sanitation

Source: UNCTAD, based on selected sectoral data available from the OECD Creditor Reporting System.
Note: Excludes disbursements to finance–related training, policy, administration and management projects in these four sectors.

are growing, which is imperative for sustainable economic growth. FDI inflows to LDCs in the ASEAN region are likely to grow further by attracting not only large-scale infrastructure investments but also FDI in a range of industries in the manufacturing and services sectors (section A.2.a). As infrastructure investments tend to flow more into larger resource-rich LDCs than into smaller resource-scarce ones, there is a risk that uneven distributions of FDI among LDCs may intensify.

Mobilization of available resources for improving infrastructure in LDCs remains a great challenge. Along with the international aid target for LDCs, donor-led initiatives for leveraging private finance in infrastructure development in developing economies – such as some DAC donors' explicit support for public-private partnerships (PPPs),[95] EU blending facilities,[96] and the G-20's intent to identify appropriate actions to increase infrastructure investment in low-income countries (OECD, 2014, p. 27) – can generate more development finance for LDCs. The promotion of impact investments and private-sector investments in economic and social infrastructure for achieving the SDGs (chapter IV) will lead to opportunities for some LDCs. The increasing importance of FDI and development finance from the South to LDCs[97] is also encouraging.

The extent of FDI growth and sustainable economic development in LDCs largely depends on the successful execution and operation of infrastructure projects in the pipeline. In this respect, domestic and foreign resources should be mobilized more efficiently and effectively. Although international development partners are stepping up their efforts to deliver on their commitments for better development outcomes, LDCs are also expected to increase domestic investments in infrastructure.[98]

2. Landlocked developing countries

Table A. Distribution of FDI flows among economies, by range,[a] 2013

Range	Inflows	Outflows
Above $1 billion	Kazakhstan, Turkmenistan, Azerbaijan, Mongolia, Zambia, Bolivia (Plurinational State of), Uganda and Uzbekistan	Kazakhstan and Azerbaijan
$500 to $999 million	Ethiopia, Kyrgyzstan, Niger and Chad	..
$100 to $499 million	Mali, Zimbabwe, Paraguay, Burkina Faso, Armenia, the Former Yugoslav Republic of Macedonia, Lao People's Democratic Republic, Republic of Moldova, Botswana, Malawi, Rwanda and Tajikistan	Zambia
$10 to $99 million	Nepal, Afghanistan, Swaziland, Lesotho and Bhutan	Burkina Faso, Mongolia, Malawi, Republic of Moldova, Zimbabwe, Lesotho, Armenia and Rwanda
Below $10 million	Burundi and Central African Republic	Mali, Swaziland, Kyrgyzstan, Botswana, Uganda, the Former Yugoslav Republic of Macedonia, Niger and Lao People's Democratic Republic

[a] Economies are listed according to the magnitude of their FDI flows.

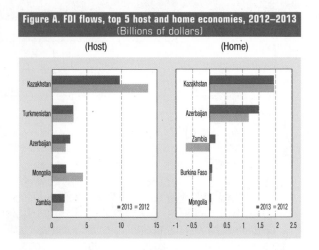

Figure A. FDI flows, top 5 host and home economies, 2012–2013
(Billions of dollars)

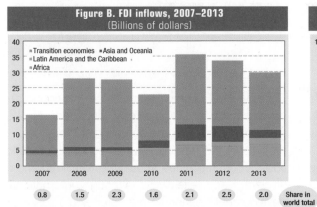

Figure B. FDI inflows, 2007–2013
(Billions of dollars)

	2007	2008	2009	2010	2011	2012	2013
Share in world total	0.8	1.5	2.3	1.6	2.1	2.5	2.0

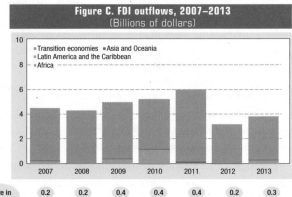

Figure C. FDI outflows, 2007–2013
(Billions of dollars)

	2007	2008	2009	2010	2011	2012	2013
Share in world total	0.2	0.2	0.4	0.4	0.4	0.2	0.3

Table B. Cross-border M&As by industry, 2012–2013
(Millions of dollars)

Sector/industry	Sales 2012	Sales 2013	Purchases 2012	Purchases 2013
Total	-574	258	544	6
Primary	-2 612	-22	160	2
Mining, quarrying and petroleum	-2 614	-22	160	2
Manufacturing	468	257	-183	-
Food, beverages and tobacco	377	177	-	-
Chemicals and chemical products	-	5	-185	-
Motor vehicles and other transport equipment	-	60	-	-
Non-metallic mineral products	90	-	-	-
Services	1 570	23	566	3
Trade	-	-	20	-
Information and communications	1 542	20	-	-
Financial and insurance activities	17	3	598	3
Public administration and defence, compulsory social sec.	-	-	-52	-

Table C. Cross-border M&As by region/country, 2012–2013
(Millions of dollars)

Region/country	Sales 2012	Sales 2013	Purchases 2012	Purchases 2013
World	-574	258	544	6
Developed economies	-804	99	445	2
European Union	-823	72	435	2
Other developed Europe	-5	331	-	-
Canada	2	-298	10	-
United States	-22	-	-	-
Other developed countries	44	-6	-	-
Developing economies	191	160	-35	3
Africa	106	-	-185	3
Latin America and the Caribbean	-150	-	-	-
West Asia	-	6	150	-
South, East and South-East Asia	235	154	-	-
Transition economies	23	-	133	-

Table D. Greenfield FDI projects by industry, 2012–2013
(Millions of dollars)

Sector/industry	LLDCs as destination 2012	LLDCs as destination 2013	LLDCs as investors 2012	LLDCs as investors 2013
Total	17 931	17 211	4 005	1 033
Primary	1 443	1 207	-	-
Mining, quarrying and petroleum	1 443	1 207	-	-
Manufacturing	8 931	5 273	3 276	407
Chemicals and chemical products	4 781	128	-	92
Non-metallic mineral products	66	1 624	18	75
Metals and metal products	1 784	279	-	70
Electrical and electronic equipment	246	587	-	-
Services	7 558	10 730	729	626
Electricity, gas and water	2 300	5 213	-	-
Trade	400	467	197	133
Transport, storage and communications	1 823	2 349	168	139
Finance	1 306	1 301	240	332

Table E. Greenfield FDI projects by region/country, 2012–2013
(Millions of dollars)

Partner region/economy	LLDCs as destination 2012	LLDCs as destination 2013	LLDCs as investors 2012	LLDCs as investors 2013
World	17 931	17 211	4 005	1 033
Developed economies	5 279	9 879	178	188
European Union	3 109	3 618	128	150
Other developed Europe	12	4 346	-	-
United States	1 131	502	50	3
Other developed countries	431	1 060	-	35
Developing economies	11 853	6 163	3 587	507
Africa	679	2 872	308	174
East and South-East Asia	5 561	1 249	244	36
South Asia	3 643	776	-	116
West Asia	1 962	582	3 034	114
Latin America and the Caribbean	10	684	-	66
Transition economies	799	1 168	240	338

FDI flows to the landlocked developing countries (LLDCs) fell by 11 per cent to $29.7 billion in 2013 after the 2012 figure was revised slightly downward to $33.5 billion. Investment to the group was still concentrated in the transition-economy LLDCs, which accounted for 62 per cent of FDI inflows. In African LLDCs, FDI flows increased by 10 per cent but the picture was mixed: 7 of the 15 countries . experienced falls and 8 countries, predominantly mineral-exporting economies, saw increases. In contrast to 2012, when the Republic of Korea and the West Asian economies led investments, in 2013 developed-economy investors took the lead (in particular Europe), which increased their share in the group from 29 per cent in 2012 to 57 per cent. Services continued to attract strong investor interest, especially in the electricity, water and gas sectors and the transport sector.

FDI inflows to LLDCs as a group registered a decline of 11 per cent in 2013, to $29.7 billion. This follows revised figures for 2012 that show a slight fall, making 2013 the first year in which FDI has fallen two years in a row for this group of economies. The Asian group of LLDCs experienced the largest fall, nearly 50 per cent, mainly due to a precipitous decline in investment in Mongolia. As reported in UNCTAD's Investment Policy Review of Mongolia (UNCTAD, 2014), this fall was linked to an investment law introduced in early 2012 which was thought to have concerned many investors, especially those who were already cautious.[99] The law was amended in November 2013. The more than 12 per cent drop in FDI to the transition LLDCs is accounted for mainly by a tailing off of investment to Kazakhstan in 2013, despite strong performance in Azerbaijan, where inflows rose by 31 per cent.

In other subregions, FDI performance was positive in 2013. Inflows to the Latin American LLDCs increased by 38 per cent, as a result of the steadily increasing attractiveness of the Plurinational State of Bolivia to foreign investors. African LLDCs saw their share of total LLDC inflows increase from 18 to 23 per cent, with strong performance in Zambia, where flows topped $1.8 billion. Nevertheless, inflows to LLDCs in 2013 remained comparatively small, representing just 2 per cent of global flows – a figure which has shrunk since 2012 and illustrates the continuing economic marginalization of many of these countries.

LLDC outflows, which had surged to $6.1 billion in 2011, declined in 2012 but recovered to $3.9 billion last year, up 44 per cent. Historically, Kazakhstan has accounted for the bulk of LLDC outflows and, together with Azerbaijan, it accounted for almost all outward investment last year.

Greenfield and M&A figures reveal a changed pattern of investment in 2013 in terms of sectors and source countries. In 2012, the major investors in LLDCs were developing economies, primarily the Republic of Korea and India. However, in 2013, developing-economy flows to LLDCs fell by almost 50 per cent from $11.9 billion in 2012 to $6.2 billion – albeit with some notable exceptions such as Nigeria, which was the second largest investor in LLDCs in 2013. Europe was the major investor, accounting for 46 per cent of FDI in terms of source; as investors in LLDCs, developed economies as a whole increased their share from 29 per cent in 2012 to 57 per cent in 2013.

In terms of investors' sectoral interests, services remain strong: in 2013, announced greenfield investments in this sector increased 42 per cent from the previous year. Investment in infrastructure doubled, in particular to the electricity, water and gas sectors, primarily on the back of an announced greenfield project in the geothermal sector in Ethiopia by Reykjavik Geothermal, valued at $4 billion (see previous section on LDCs); FDI to the transport sector rose 29 per cent. With regard to M&As, the pattern of divestment in the primary sector – especially by European firms – that was seen in 2012 continued, albeit more slowly, and European firms registered a positive number for total M&As in 2013.

a. FDI in the LLDCs – a stock-taking since Almaty I (2003)

The Almaty Programme of Action for the LLDCs, adopted in 2003, addressed transport and transit cooperation to facilitate the integration of LLDCs into the global economy. The follow-up Second United Nations Conference on Landlocked Developing Countries, to be held in November 2014, will examine LLDC performance in this respect and assess their infrastructure needs, in particular those that can improve trade links, reduce transport costs and generate economic development. Recognizing

Table II.10. Selected FDI and GVC indicators, 2004–2013
(Per cent)

Indicator	LLDCs	Developing countries	World
FDI inflows, annual growth	10	12	8
Inward FDI stock as % of GDP, 10-year average	34	29	30
FDI inflows as % of GFCF, 10-year average	21	11	11
GVC participation, annual growth[a]	18	12	10

Source: UNCTAD FDI-TNC-GVC Information System, FDI/TNC/database (www.unctad.org/fdistatistics) and UNCTAD-Eora GVC Database.
Note: Annual growth computed as compound annual growth rate over the period considered.
GVC participation indicates the part of a country's exports that is part of a multi-stage trade process; it is the foreign value added (FVA) used in a country's exports (the upstream component) plus the value added supplied to other countries' exports (the downstream component, or DVX).
[a] 2004–2011.

the critical role that the private sector can play, it will be essential for LLDCs to adopt measures to boost investment, in particular investment in infrastructure for transport, telecommunications and utilities.

An analysis of FDI indicators (table II.10) over the past 10 years reveals a mixed performance in LLDCs. In terms of FDI growth, they fared better than the global average but worse than other developing countries as a group. Among LLDCs, FDI growth in the Latin American and African subregions was stronger than in the transition economies and Asian subregion. Looking at the importance of FDI for LLDC economies, in terms of the share of FDI stock in GDP, it has averaged 5 percentage points higher than in developing countries, revealing the importance of foreign investment for growth in the LLDCs. In terms of the ratio of FDI to gross fixed capital formation (GFCF) – one of the building blocks of development – FDI's role was again more important for LLDCs than for developing economies over the previous 10 years. And LLDCs registered a much stronger growth rate in GVC participation than either the developing-country or the global average.

b. FDI inflows over the past decade

Since 2004, FDI inflows to LLDCs have generally followed a rising trajectory, with the exception of declines in 2005 and following the global economic crisis in 2009 and 2010. Figures for 2012 and 2013 also show a decline in inward investment to the group, but FDI has nevertheless stabilized around the previous three-year average (figure II.22).

At 10 per cent, the compound annual growth rate (CAGR) for FDI inflows to LLDCs was higher

than the world rate of 8 per cent but lower than for developing countries as a whole, at 12 per cent (table II.10). Although the transition LLDCs accounted for the bulk of the increase in FDI in value terms, the subregion's CAGR was in fact the lowest of all LLDC regions over the period (table II.11). The Asian and Latin American economies experienced the strongest FDI growth in terms of their CAGR, which dampens the effects of volatility in flows. However, the picture in Latin America is distorted by the presence of only two landlocked economies, and in Asia by the impact of Mongolia's natural resources boom, which attracted significantly increased FDI over the past decade.

Another distortion therefore concerns the weight of the mineral-exporting economies that mainly form part of the transition-economy subregion, and in particular, Kazakhstan. As a group, the transition-economy LLDCs accounted for the bulk of FDI inflows over the period 2004–2013, with an average share of almost 70 per cent. Indeed, just six mineral-exporting countries – Kazakhstan, Turkmenistan

Table II.11. FDI inflows to LLDCs, 2004–2013
(Millions of dollars and per cent)

Subregion	2004	2013	Growth
LLDCs Subregion	12 290	29 748	10
LLDCs-Africa	2 464	6 800	12
LLDCs-Latin America and the Caribbean	113	2 132	39
LLDCs-Asia and Oceania	305	2 507	26
LLDCs-Transition economies	9 408	18 309	8

Source: UNCTAD FDI-TNC-GVC Information System, FDI-TNC-GVC Information System, FDI/TNC database (www.unctad.org/fdistatistics).
Note: Growth computed as compound annual growth rate over the period.

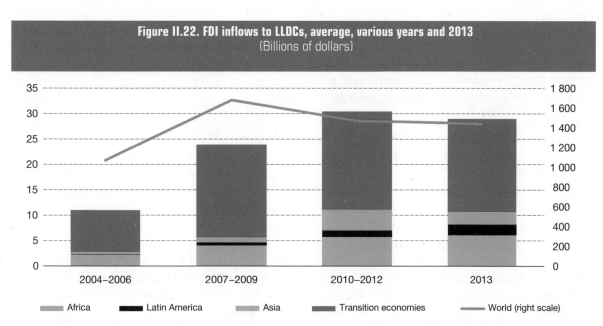

Figure II.22. FDI inflows to LLDCs, average, various years and 2013
(Billions of dollars)

Legend: Africa | Latin America | Asia | Transition economies | World (right scale)

Source: UNCTAD FDI-TNC-GVC Information System, FDI/TNC database (www.unctad.org/fdistatistics).

and Azerbaijan, plus the non-transition - economies of Mongolia, Uganda and Zambia – accounted for almost three quarters of all LLDC inflows. Although trends have remained broadly similar over the past decade, several countries have attracted increasing flows, largely as a result of the development of their natural resource sectors, among them Mongolia, Turkmenistan and Uganda. All three countries started to attract large increases in FDI in the past five years. Kazakhstan, which accounted for over 60 per cent of LLDC FDI during the boom years of 2006–2008, has since seen its share of inflows decline to about 41 per cent and to just under a third in 2013.

However, as a share of global flows, FDI inflows to LLDCs remain small, having grown from 1.7 per cent of global flows in 2004 to a high of 2.5 per cent in 2012, and retreated to just 2 per cent this year.

c. FDI's contribution to economic growth and capital formation

With the caveat that FDI trends in LLDCs remain skewed by the dominance of the mineral-exporting economies of Central Asia, it is clear that FDI has made a significant contribution to economic development in LLDCs. As a percentage of GDP, inflows have been relatively more important for this group of countries than for the global average or for

developing countries as a group. FDI flows peaked at over 6 per cent of GDP in 2004 and remained an important source of investment at 5 per cent of GDP in 2012. Even ignoring Kazakhstan, and latterly Mongolia, FDI as a percentage of GDP has remained above the world and developing-country averages (1.04 percentage points higher than developing countries without Kazakhstan, and 0.53 percentage point higher without Kazakhstan and Mongolia, averaged over the past decade.)

The story repeats itself when FDI stocks are used instead of flows (figure II.23). Despite having fallen

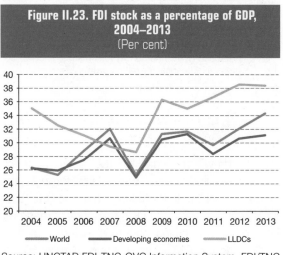

Figure II.23. FDI stock as a percentage of GDP, 2004–2013
(Per cent)

Legend: World | Developing economies | LLDCs

Source: UNCTAD FDI-TNC-GVC Information System, FDI/TNC database (www.unctad.org/fdistatistics).

below the world and developing-country averages in 2007, FDI stocks as a percentage of GDP have since risen steeply and now represent a value equivalent to 38 per cent of GDP, compared with 31 per cent for developing countries as a whole.

This picture is reinforced by the role of FDI in gross fixed capital formation (GFCF) – one of the essential building blocks of long-term investment and development. In LLDCs, FDI can potentially contribute to GFCF: it plays a far more important role in GFCF than in the global average or in developing countries generally (figure II.24). The average ratio of FDI to GFCF peaked at over 27 per cent in 2004; after a dramatic fall in 2005, it climbed steadily to more than 20 per cent in 2012. What is significant, however, is the difference between the relative importance of FDI for GFCF for LLDCs: the average ratio of FDI to GFCF is almost twice that for other developing countries and for all economies, both of which have hovered around 10 per cent in the past five years.

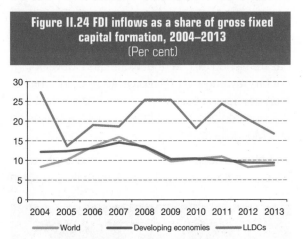

Figure II.24 FDI inflows as a share of gross fixed capital formation, 2004–2013
(Per cent)

Source: UNCTAD FDI-TNC-GVC Information System, FDI/TNC database (www.unctad.org/fdistatistics) and IMF for gross fixed capital formation data.

d. The role of investment in LLDC GVC patterns

WIR13 drew attention to the links between investment and trade, particularly through the GVCs of TNCs. It is striking that, despite their structural constraints, LLDCs do not differ markedly from other developing countries in terms of their participation in GVCs: as a group, almost 50 per cent of their exports form part of a multistage trade

process – not far below the developing-country average of 52 per cent (figure II.25).

LLDCs have a much smaller share in the upstream component of GVC participation, reflecting the role that natural resources play in several countries' exports. Consequently, the average LLDC upstream component – 18 per cent in 2011 – is lower than the average developing-country share – 25 per cent. However, the growth of LLDC participation in GVCs in all subregions in the past decade looks very different: the compound annual growth rate has averaged more than 18 per cent from 2004 to 2011. This compares with a global growth rate in GVC participation of 10 per cent and a developing-country growth rate of 12 per cent. In view of the rising rates of foreign investment in this group of countries over the past decade, a relationship can be inferred between increasing FDI flows, principally from TNCs, and rapid growth in GVC participation.

e. M&As and greenfield investments in the LLDCs – a more nuanced picture

Like FDI as a whole, M&As in the LLDC group are dominated by Kazakhstan. Of the 73 M&A deals worth over $100 million completed in the LLDCs over the last 10 years, almost half were in Kazakhstan, including 8 of the top $10 billion-plus deals. Of these, all but two were in the mineral and gas sectors. However, the telecommunications sector also produced a number of large deals, not only in Kazakhstan but also in Zambia, Uganda and Uzbekistan.

From 2004 through 2013, the average value of announced greenfield investments has been greater than that of M&As and more diversified across the group. Of the 115 largest greenfield investments worth more than $500 million, just over a quarter were in Kazakhstan, a significantly smaller proportion than the country's share of M&As. Kazakhstan also took a similar proportion of the $42 billion-plus investments. However, in terms of sectoral distribution, greenfield projects were even more concentrated in the mineral and gas sectors than were M&As.

Focusing specifically on investment in infra-structure (in this case in electricity generation, telecommunications and transportation), where LLDCs have particular needs, shows that greenfield

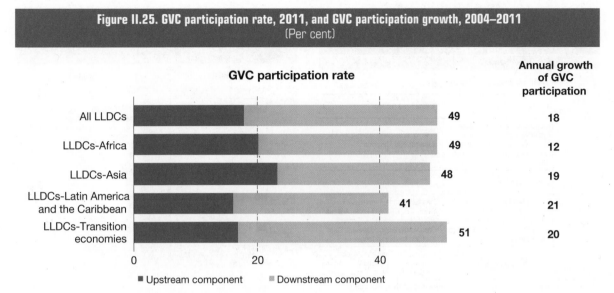

Figure II.25. GVC participation rate, 2011, and GVC participation growth, 2004–2011
(Per cent)

GVC participation rate | Annual growth of GVC participation

	GVC participation rate	Annual growth of GVC participation
All LLDCs	49	18
LLDCs-Africa	49	12
LLDCs-Asia	48	19
LLDCs-Latin America and the Caribbean	41	21
LLDCs-Transition economies	51	20

■ Upstream component ■ Downstream component

Source: UNCTAD-EORA GVC Database.
Note: GVC participation rate indicates the share of a country's exports that is part of a multi-stage trade process; it is the foreign value added (FVA) used in a country's exports (the upstream component) plus the value added supplied to other countries' exports (the downstream component, or DVX), divided by total exports.

investment has been relatively more distributed geographically over the past decade. Although Kazakhstan still accounts for 9 per cent of greenfield projects in infrastructure worth over $100 million, this share is lower than its shares in M&As in infrastructure and in large greenfield FDI projects (figure II.26). Of the 133 greenfield projects in infrastructure worth over $100 million in the past decade, 99 were in the Asian and transition economy LLDCs, 29 were in Africa and 5 were in South America.

M&A and greenfield data portray a more nuanced picture of the geographical spread of foreign investment deals and projects in LLDCs. For example, they do not all take place in Kazakhstan and a small number of Central Asian economies. The data also reveal the concentration of investment in two sectors: minerals and gas, where investment is primarily resource seeking, and telecommunications, where it is primarily market seeking.

The indicators of FDI performance in LLDCs since 2004 (table II.10) show that LLDCs performed relatively well compared with developing countries and with the global economy on all indicators, even when Kazakhstan and Mongolia are excluded from the analysis. However, it is clear that to speak of LLDCs as a homogenous group is misleading and disguises regional and country differences. As

LLDCs prepare for the follow-up Global Review Conference in 2014, policymakers and the international community must reflect on how to spread the benefits of FDI to other members of the grouping and beyond a relatively narrow set of sectors, as well as how to promote FDI attraction in those LLDCs, while minimizing any negative impacts.[100]

Figure II.26. Kazakhstan: share of LLDC M&As, greenfield investment projects and greenfield infrastructure projects, 2004–2013
(Per cent)

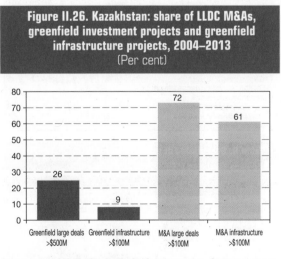

Greenfield large deals >$500M	Greenfield infrastructure >$100M	M&A large deals >$100M	M&A infrastructure >$100M
26	9	72	61

Source: UNCTAD FDI-TNC-GVC Information System, cross-border M&A database for M&As and information from the Financial Times Ltd., fDiMarkets (www.fDimarkets.com) for greenfield projects.

3. Small island developing States

Table A. Distribution of FDI flows among economies, by range,[a] 2013

Range	Inflows	Outflows
Above $1 billion	Trinidad and Tobago and Bahamas	..
$500 to $999 million	Jamaica	Trinidad and Tobago
$100 to $499 million	Barbados, Maldives, Fiji, Mauritius, Seychelles, Antigua and Barbuda, Saint Vincent and the Grenadines, Saint Kitts and Nevis and Solomon Islands	Bahamas and Mauritius
$50 to $99 million	Saint Lucia and Grenada	..
$1 to $49 million	Vanuatu, São Tomé and Principe, Samoa, Marshall Islands, Timor-Leste, Cabo Verde, Papua New Guinea, Dominica, Comoros, Tonga, Kiribati and Palau	Marshall Islands, Timor-Leste, Seychelles, Fiji, Saint Lucia, Antigua and Barbuda, Barbados, Grenada, Cabo Verde, Solomon Islands, Saint Kitts and Nevis and Tonga
Below $1 million	Federated States of Micronesia	Vanuatu, São Tomé and Principe, Samoa, Dominica, Saint Vincent and the Grenadines, Kiribati and Jamaica

[a] Economies are listed according to the magnitude of their FDI flows.

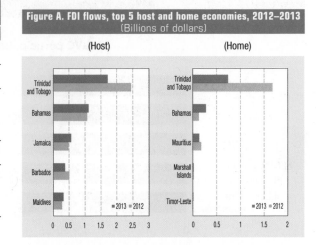

Figure A. FDI flows, top 5 host and home economies, 2012–2013
(Billions of dollars)

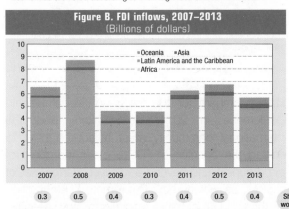

Figure B. FDI inflows, 2007–2013
(Billions of dollars)

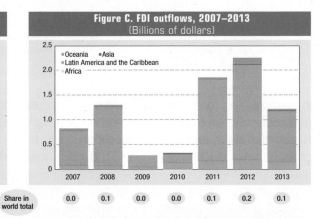

Figure C. FDI outflows, 2007–2013
(Billions of dollars)

Table B. Cross-border M&As by industry, 2012–2013
(Millions of dollars)

Sector/industry	Sales 2012	Sales 2013	Purchases 2012	Purchases 2013
Total	**97**	**-596**	**-2**	**-266**
Primary	**110**	**-600**	**25**	**-14**
Agriculture, forestry and fishing	-	-	20	-
Mining, quarrying and petroleum	110	-600	5	-14
Manufacturing	**-47**	**-5**	**-**	**10**
Food, beverages and tobacco	-47	-	-	-
Basic metal and metal products	-	-	-	10
Services	**33**	**9**	**-27**	**-262**
Electricity, gas, water and waste management	-	-	228	-
Transportation and storage	20	-	-	-
Information and communications	-	4	-	108
Financial and insurance activities	13	-	-254	-369
Business services	-	5	-	-

Table C. Cross-border M&As by region/country, 2012–2013
(Millions of dollars)

Region/country	Sales 2012	Sales 2013	Purchases 2012	Purchases 2013
World	**97**	**-596**	**-2**	**-266**
Developed economies	**-42**	**-604**	**5**	**-219**
Germany	-	285	-	-
Switzerland	-	-285	-	-
United States	-37	-600	-	103
Developing economies	**119**	**3**	**-7**	**-47**
Latin America and the Caribbean	-	-272	330	-86
Guatemala	-	-	228	-
Cayman Islands	-	-272	-	-86
India	115	-	66	38
Indonesia	-	-	189	-
Singapore	7	331	-655	9
Transition economies	**-**	**-**	**-**	**-**

Table D. Greenfield FDI projects by industry, 2012–2013
(Millions of dollars)

Sector/industry	SIDS as destination 2012	SIDS as destination 2013	SIDS as investors 2012	SIDS as investors 2013
Total	**2 298**	**6 506**	**205**	**3 809**
Primary	**8**	**2 532**	**-**	**-**
Mining, quarrying and petroleum	8	2 532	-	-
Manufacturing	**1 169**	**1 986**	**130**	**-**
Coke, petroleum products and nuclear fuel	929	1 048	-	-
Chemical and chemical products	-	850	-	-
Services	**1 121**	**1 988**	**75**	**3 809**
Electricity, gas and water	156	-	-	-
Construction	-	1 350	-	-
Hotels and restaurants	505	65	30	-
Transport, storage and communications	116	477	-	1 871
Finance	201	22	12	190
Business services	77	46	33	1 749

Table E. Greenfield FDI projects by region/country, 2012–2013
(Millions of dollars)

Partner region/economy	SIDS as destination 2012	SIDS as destination 2013	SIDS as investors 2012	SIDS as investors 2013
World	**2 298**	**6 506**	**205**	**3 809**
Developed economies	**1 493**	**2 814**	**26**	**3**
Europe	307	255	26	3
United States	181	1 379	-	-
Australia	1 005	316	-	-
Japan	-	863	-	-
Developing economies	**805**	**3 691**	**179**	**3 806**
Kenya	-	-	-	450
Nigeria	-	-	-	2 296
China	-	3 250	-	164
Latin America and the Caribbean	30	13	30	457
Small island developing states (SIDS)	30	-	30	-
Transition economies	**-**	**-**	**-**	**-**

FDI in small island developing States – a decade in review

FDI inflows to the SIDS declined by 16 per cent to $5.7 billion in 2013, putting an end to a two-year recovery. Flows decreased in all subregions, but unevenly. African SIDS registered the highest decline (41 per cent to $499 million), followed by Latin American SIDS (14 per cent to $4.3 billion). SIDS in Asia and Oceania registered a slight 3 per cent decline to $853 million. This trend is examined in a long-term context.

SIDS face unique development challenges that are formally recognized by the international community. For this reason, their financing needs to achieve economic, social and environmentally sustainable development are disproportionally large, both as a share of their GDP and as compared with other developing countries' needs. Mobilization of financing through various channels – private or public, and domestic or international – is no doubt required for sustainable development in SIDS. External finance includes ODA and private capital flows (both FDI and portfolio and other investment, such as bank loan flows) as well as remittances and other flows.

A third United Nations Conference on SIDS is to be held in September 2014 in Samoa. It seeks a renewed political commitment to SIDS' development through identifying new and emerging challenges and opportunities for their sustainable development and establishing priorities to be considered in the elaboration of the post-2015 UN development agenda. This section reviews a decade of FDI to the 29 SIDS countries – as listed by UNCTAD (box II.7) – in terms of their trends, patterns, determinants and impacts.

The global economic crisis halted strong FDI growth. FDI inflows into SIDS increased significantly over 2005–2008, reaching an annual average of $6.3 billion, more than twice the level over 2001–2004. However, the global financial crisis led to a severe reversal of this trend, with FDI plummeting by 47 per cent, from $8.7 billion in 2008 to $4.6 billion in 2009. Flows recovered in 2011 and 2012, before declining again in 2013, remaining below the annual average they had reached in 2005–2008 (figure II.27).

Although FDI flows to the SIDS are very small in relative terms, accounting for only 0.4 per cent of global FDI flows over 2001–2013, they are very high compared with the size of the SIDS' economies. The ratio of inflows to current GDP during 2001–2013 was almost three times the world average and more than twice the average of developing and transition economies. These relatively high inflows to the group are the result of fiscal advantages offered to foreign investors in a number of SIDS, and of a limited number of very large investments in extractive industries.

Caribbean SIDS have traditionally attracted the bulk of FDI into SIDS, accounting for 78 per cent of flows over the period 2001–2013. Their proximity to and economic dependence on the large North American market are the main factors

---

Box II.7. UNCTAD's list of SIDS

The United Nations has recognized the particular problems of SIDS without, however, establishing criteria for determining an official list of them. Fifty-two countries and territories are presently classified as SIDS by the United Nations Office of the High Representative for the Least Developed Countries, Landlocked Developing Countries and Small Island Developing States (UN-OHRLLS); 29 have been defined by UNCTAD and used for analytical purposes. This review regroups the 29 countries in three geographical regions:

• **Africa SIDS**: Cape Verde, São Tomé and Príncipe, the Comoros, Mauritius and Seychelles.

• **Asia and Oceania SIDS**: Maldives, Timor-Leste, Fiji, Kiribati, the Marshall Islands, the Federated States of Micronesia, Nauru, Palau, Papua New Guinea, Samoa, Solomon Islands, Tonga, Tuvalu and Vanuatu.

• **Caribbean SIDS**: Antigua and Barbuda, the Bahamas, Barbados, Dominica, Grenada, Jamaica, Saint Kitts and Nevis, Saint Lucia, Saint Vincent and the Grenadines, and Trinidad and Tobago.

Source: UNCTAD; UN OHRLLS, "Small Islands Developing States - Small Islands Big(ger) Stakes", United Nations, New York, 2011.

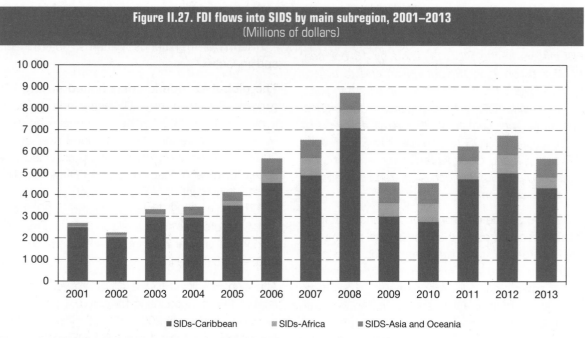

Figure II.27. FDI flows into SIDS by main subregion, 2001–2013
(Millions of dollars)

■ SIDs-Caribbean   ■ SIDs-Africa   ■ SIDS-Asia and Oceania

Source: UNCTAD FDI-TNC-GVC Information System, FDI/TNC database (www.unctad.org/fdistatistics).

explaining their higher attractiveness compared with other SIDS regions.

However, SIDS located in Africa and in Asia and Oceania experienced relatively stronger FDI growth during the 2000 (figure II.28). Their share in total FDI flows increased from 11 per cent in 2001–2004 to 20 per cent in 2005–2008, to 29 per cent in 2009–2013. The actual importance of Asia and Oceania as a SIDS recipient subregion is probably underestimated, because of the undervaluation of FDI flows to Papua New Guinea and Timor-Leste, two countries rich in natural resources that host significant FDI projects in the extractive industry (box II.8) but do not include those projects in official FDI statistics (Timor-Leste) or do not reflect them fully (Papua New Guinea).

Mineral extraction and downstream-related activities, tourism, business and finance are the main target industries for FDI. Sectoral FDI data are available for very few SIDS countries. Only Jamaica, Mauritius, Trinidad and Tobago, and Papua New Guinea make available official sectoral data on FDI. These data show a high concentration of FDI in the extractive industries in Papua New Guinea and in Trinidad and Tobago.[101] FDI flows to Mauritius are directed almost totally to the services

sector, with soaring investments in activities such as finance, hotels and restaurants, construction and business in the period 2007–2012. FDI to Jamaica, which used to be more diversified among the primary, manufacturing and services sectors, has increasingly targeted service industries during the period 2007–2012 (table II.12).

In the absence of FDI sectoral data for most SIDS countries, information on greenfield FDI projects announced by foreign investors in the SIDS

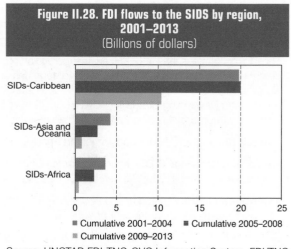

Figure II.28. FDI flows to the SIDS by region, 2001–2013
(Billions of dollars)

■ Cumulative 2001–2004   ■ Cumulative 2005–2008
■ Cumulative 2009–2013

Source: UNCTAD FDI-TNC-GVC Information System, FDI/TNC database (www.unctad.org/fdistatistics).

Box II.8. TNCs in the extractive industry in Papua New Guinea and Timor-Leste

Papua New Guinea has high prospects for oil and gas, with deposits of both found across its territory. The most developed of its projects is the liquefied natural gas (LNG) project led by ExxonMobil,[102] which is expected to begin production in 2014. It will produce 6.6 million tonnes of LNG per year for end users in Taiwan Province of China, Japan and China. The project cost is now estimated at $19 billion, significantly more than the initial cost ceiling of $15 billion. A potential second project is the Gulf LNG project initially driven by InterOil (United States) and now operated by Total (France), which took a majority share in 2013. Oil and gas drilling by foreign companies is continuing apace, with plenty of untapped potential and more gas and oil being discovered each year.

Papua New Guinea is also rich in metal mining, with copper and gold being the major mineral commodities produced. The country is estimated to be the 11th largest producer of gold, accounting for about 2.6 per cent of global production. It also has deposits of chromite, cobalt, nickel and molybdenum. Several international mining companies are majority owners or shareholders in metal-producing operations, including Newcrest Mining (Australia), Harmony Gold Mining (South Africa), Barrick Gold (Canada), New Guinea Gold (Canada) and MCC (China).

Timor-Leste has many oil and gas deposits both onshore and offshore, although most petroleum development has been far offshore. It also has significant untapped mineral potential in copper, gold, silver and chromite, but the mountainous terrain and poor infrastructure have impeded widespread exploration and development. Major oil and gas discoveries in the Timor Sea in 1994 have led to the development of a large-scale offshore oil industry. ConocoPhillips, Eni, Santos, INPEX Woodside, Shell and Osaka Gas are among the international oil companies operating there.

Source: United States Department of the Interior, *2011 Minerals Yearbook Papua New Guinea*, December 2012; Revenue Watch Institute, "Timor-Leste; Extractive Industries", www.revenuewatch.org.

between 2003 and 2013 is used as an alternative way to assess which countries and industries have attracted foreign investors' interest, if not actual investments. (M&As – another mode of FDI – are almost nonexistent in SIDS.) Upstream and downstream activities in the oil, gas and metal minerals industries[103] have been the focus of most capital expenditures in greenfield projects announced by foreign investors (57 per cent of the total), with Papua New Guinea, Trinidad and Tobago, Timor-Leste and Fiji hosting these projects. Hotels and restaurants are the next largest focus of foreign investors' pledges to invest (12 per cent of total announced investments), with Maldives being their favourite destination. Other services industries, such as construction, transport

Table II.12. SIDS: FDI flows and stock by sector, selected countries, various years
(Millions of dollars)

| Sector/industry | FDI flows (average per year) | | | | | | FDI stock | |
| | Jamaica | | Mauritius | | Trinidad and Tobago | | Papua New Guinea | |
	2001–2006	2007–2012	2001–2006	2007–2012	2001–2006	2007–2011	2006	2012
Primary	**141**	**71**	**3**	**4**	**768**	**796**	**1 115**	**4 189**
Mining, quarrying and petroleum	141	71	-	-	768	796	991	4 000
Manufacturing	**68**	**36**	**6**	**8**	**10**	**26**	**126**	**184**
Services	**169**	**238**	**78**	**363**	**43**	**487**	**61**	**149**
Business activities	67	133	18	146	..	..	..	..
Finance	..	..	37	114	..	..	43	64
Hotels and restaurants	99	106	10	46	..	..	3	5
Construction	..	..	2	31	..	..	..	..
Other services	3	-	11	26	..	..	14	80
Total	**663**	**587**	**87**	**375**	**876**	**1 344**	**1 350**	**4 576**
Unspecified	285	242	-	-	54	35	48	54

Source: UNCTAD·FDI-TNC-GVC Information System, FDI/TNC database (www.unctad.org/fdistatistics).

and communications, finance, public utilities and business activities, are among the other typical activities for which greenfield FDI projects have been announced in SIDS countries (table II.13).

Developed-country TNCs have announced the most capital spending in greenfield projects in SIDS countries (almost two thirds of total capital expenditures). Resource-rich countries such as Papua New Guinea, Trinidad and Tobago, and Timor-Leste represented 63 per cent of such TNCs' announced capital spending. TNCs from developing and transition economies have focused their interest mainly in four SIDS countries, namely Papua New Guinea, Maldives, Mauritius and Jamaica, which together represented the destinations of 89 per cent of those TNCs' total announced capital spending (table II.14).

Main location advantages of SIDS, and the opportunities and risks they represent for sustainable development. The endowments of SIDS, principally in natural resources and human capital, confer a number of location advantages. In addition, all of these countries qualify for at least one trade preference regime[104] that gives them, in principle, preferential access to developed-country markets. A number of industries have flourished based on these advantages:

- *Tourism and fishing industries* have been favoured because of the valuable natural resources, including oceans, sizeable exclusive economic zones, coastal environments and biodiversity. Tourism is often identified as a promising growth sector in SIDS, offering one of the few opportunities for economic diversification through the many linkages it can build with other economic sectors. If adequately integrated into national development plans, it can contribute to the growth of sectors such as agriculture, fishing and services. But if not properly planned and managed, tourism can have negative social and environmental impacts,

Table II.13. SIDS: announced value of greenfield FDI projects by sector, total and top 10 destination countries, 2003–2013
(Millions of dollars)

Sector/industry	Papua New Guinea	Trinidad and Tobago	Maldives	Timor-Leste	Mauritius	Jamaica	Fiji	Bahamas	Seychelles	São Tomé and Principe	Others	Total
Primary	**8 070**	**3 091**	**-**	**1 000**	**-**	**-**	**792**	**-**	**-**	**-**	**228**	**13 181**
Mining, quarrying and petroleum	8 070	3 091	-	1 000	-	-	792	-	-	-	228	13 181
Manufacturing	**7 155**	**3 865**	**78**	**4 010**	**203**	**687**	**59**	**142**	**102**	**351**	**248**	**16 900**
Coke, petroleum products and nuclear fuel	6 650	791	-	4 000	1	-	-	-	-	-	-	11 442
Metal and metal products	228	404	-	-	2	384	-	-	-	-	-	1 019
Chemicals and chemical products	-	2 435	-	-	3	10	-	-	-	-	80	2 527
Food, beverages and tobacco	214	92	-	10	-	258	46	-	59	-	129	808
Other manufacturing	63	143	78	-	197	35	13	142	43	351	39	1 104
Services	**1 113**	**301**	**5 683**	**116**	**4 344**	**3 147**	**551**	**1 079**	**695**	**161**	**2 337**	**19 527**
Hotels and restaurants	-	-	3 153	-	362	504	206	128	476	-	1 171	5 999
Construction	-	-	1 997	-	2 445	1 350	-	-	-	-	-	5 792
Transport, storage and communications	70	23	326	116	362	1 027	70	837	186	150	446	3 613
Finance	162	111	208	-	164	96	248	34	19	11	241	1 295
Electric, gas and water distribution	775	-	-	-	-	-	-	-	-	-	340	1 115
Business activities	48	55	-	-	774	43	27	55	14	-	77	1 094
Other services	59	111	-	-	237	126	-	24	-	-	63	619
Total	**16 338**	**7 256**	**5 762**	**5 126**	**4 547**	**3 834**	**1 403**	**1 220**	**797**	**512**	**2 813**	**49 608**

Source: UNCTAD, based on information from the Financial Times Ltd., fDi Markets (www.fdimarkets.com).

Home country	Papua New Guinea	Trinidad and Tobago	Maldives	Timor-Leste	Mauritius	Jamaica	Fiji	Bahamas	Seychelles	São Tomé and Principe	Other SIDS	Total SIDS
United States	3 005	3 094	206	-	569	1 207	554	252	-	-	1 161	10 046
Australia	3 535	316	-	4 000	5	-	456	-	-	-	290	8 601
China	3 528	-	-	-	-	1 350	8	-	-	-	98	4 983
South Africa	3 000	-	-	-	1 320	-	-	-	-	-	-	4 320
India	923	171	1 565	-	419	3	3	-	224	-	-	3 307
Canada	970	1 205	617	-	121	38	-	-	241	-	63	3 254
United Kingdom	139	1 412	42	-	119	367	13	328	7	351	367	3 145
France	-	-	13	-	1 732	103	41	550	-	-	-	2 439
Thailand	-	-	1 620	10	3	-	-	-	-	-	65	1 698
United Arab Emirates	-	23	715	-	72	-	42	-	265	-	64	1 180
Italy	8	-	-	1 000	-	-	-	-	-	-	-	1 008
Korea, Republic of	959	4	-	-	11	-	-	-	-	-	-	975
Others	272	1 032	985	116	178	766	288	90	60	161	707	4 653
World	**16 338**	**7 256**	**5 762**	**5 126**	**4 547**	**3 834**	**1 403**	**1 220**	**797**	**512**	**2 813**	**49 608**
Developed economies	7 705	6 967	1 302	5 108	2 686	2 441	1 115	1 131	298	501	2 072	31 325
Developing and transition economies	8 634	289	4 460	19	1 861	1 393	288	89	498	11	741	18 283

Table II.14. SIDS: announced value of greenfield FDI projects by top 10 home countries to top 10 destination countries, 2003–2013 (Millions of dollars)

Source: UNCTAD, based on information from the Financial Times Ltd., fDi Markets (www.fdimarkets.com).

significantly degrade the environment on which it is so dependent and lead to irreversible damage to ecosystems and to traditional activities such as agriculture and fishing (UN OHRLLS, 2011).

• *Mining and related activities* have been developed in some SIDS that have sizeable nonrenewable natural resources. If properly managed, mineral endowments can provide opportunities for economic development and poverty alleviation. However, exploitation of non-renewable resources poses serious challenges – economic, social and environmental – to prospects for long-term sustainable development. The economic challenges consist in defining how to create value from mineral resources, how to capture that value locally and how to make the best use of the revenues created. The social and environmental challenges derive from the strong environmental footprint and the profound social impacts that the extractive industry tends to have (see *WIR07*).

• *Business and offshore financial services* have prospered in a number of SIDS countries against the backdrop of strong incentives for non-resident companies and individuals to establish headquarters and financial and trading operations

in their jurisdictions. These include favourable tax regimes, efficient business registrations, secrecy rules and lax regulatory frameworks. Host countries see these services as a source of growth and economic diversification, with positive spillover effects on other activities, including tourism, hotels and restaurants, telecommunications and transport. However, they could bring some disadvantages, such as making small, open economies vulnerable to sharp changes in global financial flows and putting them under the scrutiny of the very countries affected by the activities facilitated by favourable tax regimes.[105]

• Exports such as textiles, apparel, garment assembly and processed fish have been developed in some SIDS – for example, Cabo Verde, Fiji, Jamaica and Mauritius – under the cover of preference trade regimes. However, trade liberalization on a most-favoured-nation basis and the dismantling of textile and clothing quotas under the Agreement on Textiles and Clothing of the World Trade Organization have resulted in preference erosion that has been particularly acute among garment-exporting SIDS.

These sectors have been the primary target of FDI and will continue to offer the greatest development opportunities. These activities also constitute the main sources of the foreign exchange earnings that are necessary to finance the energy and food imports on which these island countries are often highly dependent. Although FDI represents an important additional source of investment capital in industries that are critical to growth and development, very little is known about FDI impacts on SIDS – in particular, how these impacts interact with their structural vulnerabilities.

The small size of SIDS countries means that development and the environment are closely interrelated and interdependent. There is usually great competition for land and water resources among tourism, agriculture and other land uses (such as mining, in resource-rich countries), and the overdevelopment of any of these sectors could be detrimental to the others. The environmental consequences of ill-conceived development can threaten not only the livelihood of people but also the islands themselves and the cultures they nurture. The challenge for SIDS is to ensure that FDI and its use for economic development do not cause any permanent harm to sustainable use of land, water and marine resources.

Notes

[1] Estimates for Africa's middle class vary considerably among sources. The figure quoted is consistent with those of the African Development Bank (AfDB) and the Standard Chartered Bank regional head of research for Africa. It is based on a definition of middle class that includes people spending between $4 and $20 per day. This class of consumers represented in 2010 more than 13 per cent of the continent's population.

[2] "The MPLA sticks to its course", *Africa Confidential*, Vol. 55, No. 1, 10 January 2014.

[3] The African Union recognizes eight RECs as the building blocks of an eventual African Economic Community: the Arab Maghreb Union (UMA), the Common Market for East and Southern Africa (COMESA), the Community of Sahel-Saharan States (CENSAD), the Economic Community of Central African States (ECCAS), the East African Community (EAC), the Economic Community of West African States (ECOWAS), the Inter-Governmental Authority for Development (IGAD) and the Southern African Development Community (SADC). Other regional groups exist, but are not among these building blocks. Moreover, some of the RECs recognized by the African Union are not active. Thus, in this section, the analysis is limited to the major RECs: COMESA, SADC, ECOWAS, ECCAS, UMA and EAC.

[4] This involves the negotiation of seven main technical issues: (1) rules of origin; (2) non-tariff barriers; (3) standardization, metrology, conformity, assessment and accreditation (i.e. technical barriers to trade), and sanitary and phytosanitary measures; (4) customs cooperation, documentation, procedures and transit instruments; (5) trade remedies; (6) dispute settlement; and (7) tariff liberalization.

[5] Intra-African trade has increased fourfold since 2000, though its share in global trade has remained constant over the last decade at 11–14 per cent.

[6] Conclusive analysis of the impact of regional integration on FDI would require data on bilateral FDI flows and detailed sectoral data, which are not available for most African countries. There is also some degree of imprecision in FDI data for Africa related to the large scale of the informal economy. The analysis presented here relies on announced greenfield data.

[7] For example, 60 per cent of Japanese companies in Africa cite transport and energy service gaps as their biggest problems, according to a survey by the Japan External Trade Organization.

[8] Investment patterns as well as the establishment of special Chinese trade and investment zones in Africa lend some support to this hypothesis (Brautigam and Tang, 2011).

[9] By the middle of the century, Africa's working-age population will number 1.2 billion, from about 500 million today, meaning it will provide one in four of the world's workers, compared with one in eight from China.

[10] For instance, according to a policy document released in December 2013, overseas investment projects below $1 billion are not subject to government approval.

[11] "Sinopec will invest $20 billion in Africa in five years", China News Service, 17 December 2013.

[12] However, controversy and political turmoil related to the Cross-Strait Service Trade Agreement have cast doubt on the prospects for FDI in services. The agreement, signed in June 2013, aimed to substantially liberalize trade in services between mainland China and Taiwan Province of China. Under the terms of the treaty, service industries such as banking, health care, tourism, film, telecommunications and publishing will be opened to bilateral investment.

[13] Data released by the Shanghai Municipality.

[14] Board of Investment, Thailand (see: Michael Peel, "Thailand political turmoil imperils foreign and domestic investment", *Financial Times*, 9 March 2014).

[15] In the first three quarters of 2013, for example, 33 TNCs established headquarters in Shanghai, including 10 for the Asia Pacific region. In addition, some large storage and logistic projects are under construction in the zone. About 600 foreign affiliates have been established there.

[16] Each of the three East Asian economies has its own economic arrangement and relationship with ASEAN, and all three are currently negotiating their agreement on a free trade area.

[17] The East Asia Summit is an annual forum, initially held by leaders of the ASEAN+6 countries (ASEAN+3 and Australia, India and New Zealand). Membership has expanded to include the United States and the Russian Federation. The Summit has gradually moved towards a focus on economic cooperation and integration.

[18] Asia as a whole accounted for 58 per cent of Singapore's total outward FDI stock of $350 billion by the end of 2011, including ASEAN (which accounted for 22 percent of the total FDI stock of Singapore), China (18 per cent), Hong Kong (China) (9 per cent), Japan (4 per cent) and India (3 per cent). The largest recipients of Singaporean FDI within ASEAN are Malaysia (8 per cent), Indonesia (7 per cent) and Thailand (4 per cent). For many of these economies, Singapore ranks among the top investing countries. Detailed data on the breakdown of FDI stock of South-East Asian countries show that Singapore is among the leading investors for countries such as Malaysia and Thailand.

[19] In Viet Nam, for instance, a joint venture between China Southern Power Grid and a local firm is investing $2 billion in a power plant.

[20] According to the latest policy change approved in April 2014, harbour management may be 49 per cent foreign owned.

[21] China International Capital Corporation estimates.

[22] See, for instance, Saurabh Mukherjea, "Removing inflation distortions will bring back FDI", The Economic Times, 26 May 2014.

[23] See, for example, "Standard and Poor: Indian corporates divesting stake to improve cash flows", Singapore: Commodity Online, 19 March 2014.

[24] Saibal Dasgupta, "Plan for economic corridor linking India to China approved", *The Times of India*, 20 December 2013.

[25] In India, organized retailing refers to trading activities undertaken by licensed retailers, such as supermarkets and retail chains, while unorganized retailing refers to the traditional formats of low-cost retailing, such as local corner shops, convenience stores and pavement vendors. Currently supermarkets and similar organized retailing account for about 2–4 per cent of the whole retail market.

[26] In 2013, GCC countries began disbursing a $5 billion grant agreed in 2011, and the United States provided a 100 per cent guarantee for a seven-year, $1.25 billion Eurobond with interest set at 2.503 per cent. The International Finance Corporation (IFC) announced that it was heading a consortium of lenders that would provide $221 million for construction of a 117-megawatt wind farm in Jordan's southwest. The European Bank for Reconstruction and Development (EBRD) opened a permanent office in Amman and officially conferred "Recipient Nation" status on Jordan, which henceforth can benefit from more of EBRD's regular products and services, including financing tools, soft loans and technical assistance (EBRD has already provided a $100 million soft loan to finance a power plant near the capital). The United States Agency for International Development (USAID) launched two initiatives: the Jordan Competitiveness Program, a $45 million scheme aimed at attracting $700 million in FDI and creating 40,000 jobs over the next five years, and an agreement to provide $235 million for

education development over five years. And the EU announced about $54 million in new assistance to help Jordan cope with the costs of hosting Syrian refugees (Oxford Business Group, "Jordan attracts flurry of foreign funds", *Economic Update*, 19 December 2013).

[27] In 2012, GCC countries hosted 13 per cent of the world's primary petrochemicals production. Their production capacity grew by 5.6 per cent to 127.8 million tonnes in 2012, in contrast to that of the global industry, which grew by a mere 2.6 per cent. Among GCC countries, Saudi Arabia leads the industry with a production capacity of 86.4 million tonnes in 2012, or 68 per cent of total capacity in GCC countries. Forecasts are that the region's petrochemicals capacity will reach 191.2 million tonnes by 2020, with Saudi Arabia leading the expansion and adding 40.6 million tonnes, and Qatar and the United Arab Emirates adding 10 million tonnes and 8.3 million tonnes, respectively.

[28] Cheap natural gas has fed the industry's growth, but that advantage is slowly eroding as the opportunity cost of natural gas goes up. Despite huge reserves, natural gas is fast becoming a scarce commodity in the region owing to rising power consumption. The unrelenting drive towards industrialization and diversification in energy-intensive industries since the 2000s has placed significant demand pressure on gas production. Low regulated gas prices have resulted in physical shortages of gas in every GCC country except Qatar, as demand has outstripped local supply capacity. Consequently, the supply of ethane – a key by-product of natural gas used as a petrochemicals feedstock – is not expected to grow significantly, and most of the anticipated supply is already committed (Booz & Co., 2012).

[29] The price of natural gas in the United States was about $3.75 per million British thermal units at the end of 2012, down from more than $13 per million in 2008. United States ethane has fallen from about $0.90 a gallon in 2011 to about $0.30 a gallon at the end of 2012. ("Sabic looks to tap into US shale gas", *Financial Times*, 28 November 2012.)

[30] The United States produced nearly a third of the world's petrochemicals products in the 1980s, but that market share had shrunk to 10 per cent by 2010. ("GCC Petrochemicals Sector Under Threat From US", *Gulf Business*, 14 October 2013.)

[31] "Global shale revolution threatens Gulf petrochemicals expansion", *Financial Times*, 13 May 2013, www.ft.com.

[32] "Dow Chemical moving ahead with polyethylene investments", *Plastic News*, 19 March 2014; "Global Economic Weakness Pares Saudi Petchem Profits", MEES, 15 February 2013.

[33] To acquire upstream assets in North America, China's national oil companies have spent more than $34 billion since 2010, most of that on unconventional projects. The latest deal was the $15.1 billion acquisition by CNOOC of Nexen (Canada) in 2013, which gives CNOOC control over significant oil and shale gas operations in Canada. In the same vein, in 2010 Reliance Industries Limited (India) acquired shale gas assets in the United States for $3.45 billion, while State-owned GAIL India Limited acquired a 20 per cent stake in the Eagle Ford shale acreage from Carrizo Oil & Gas Inc. (United States) for $64 million.

[34] It is building a 454,000 tonne/year linear low-density polyethylene plant at its site in Alberta (Canada). ("NOVA weighs US Gulf, Canada ethylene to supply possible PE plant", Icis.com, 7 May 2013, www.icis.com.)

[35] The United States Energy Information authority is expected to publish new estimates that considerably downplay the country's recoverable shale reserves. ("U.S. officials cut estimate of recoverable Monterey Shale oil by 96%", Los Angeles Times,

20 May 2014; "Write-down of two-thirds of US shale oil explodes fracking myth", The Guardian, 22 May 2014.)

[36] "Sabic eyes investing in US petrochemicals", *Financial Times*, 8 October 2013.

[37] QP (70 per cent) and ExxonMobil (30 per cent) are partners in RasGas, an LNG-producing company in Qatar. In addition, ExxonMobil has a 7 per cent stake in QP's Barzan gas project, which is set to come online in 2014.

[38] Sectoral data for Brazil and Chile are from the Central Bank of Brazil and the Central Bank of Chile, respectively.

[39] Intracompany loans in both Brazil and Chile registered negative values in 2013, indicating that loan repayments to parent companies by foreign affiliates were higher than loans from the former to the latter. Net intracompany loans reached -$18 billion in Brazil (compared with -$10 billion in 2012), and -$2 billion in Chile (compared with $8 billion in 2012).

[40] The United States Energy Information Administration estimated Argentina's shale gas resources as the second largest in the world and its shale oil resources as the fourth largest (The Economist Intelligence Unit, "Industry Report, Energy, Argentina", April 2014).

[41] Under the agreement, Repsol will receive $5 billion in bonds. The dollar bond payment – which will mature between 2017 and 2033 – guarantees a minimum market value of $4.67 billion. If the market value of the bonds does not amount to the minimum, the Argentine government must pay Repsol an additional $1 billion in bonds. The agreement also stipulates the termination of all judicial and arbitration proceedings and the reciprocal waiver of future claims. (Repsol, "Argentina and Repsol reach a compensation agreement over the expropriation of YPF", press release, 25 February 2014, www.repsol.com).

[42] Brazil accounts for 57 per cent of South America's total manufactured exports, and Mexico accounts for 88 per cent of manufactured exports of Central America and the Caribbean (UNCTAD GlobalStat).

[43] The difference in market size between Brazil and Mexico has increased considerably in recent years. Vehicle sales amounted to 1.7 million and 1.2 million units, respectively, in Brazil and Mexico in 2005, and 3.8 million and 1.1 million units in 2013. This translated to a more than doubling of vehicle sales per capita in Brazil from 9.2 to 18.8 units per 1,000 inhabitants, and a decrease in Mexico from 10.6 to 9 per 1,000 inhabitants (Organisation Internationale des Constructeurs d'Automobiles, www.oica.net for vehicle sales data, and UNCTAD Globstat for population data).

[44] Including cars, light commercial vehicles, buses, trucks and agricultural machinery.

[45] Instituto Nacional de Estadística y Geografía (INEGI), 2013, "La industria automotriz en México", Serie Estadísticas Sectoriales; Associação Nacional dos Fabricantes de Veículos Automotores (ANFAVEA), www.anfavea.com.br; UNCTAD GlobalStat.

[46] Brazil and Argentina have been developing a common automotive policy since the creation of MERCOSUR. In 2002 they subscribed to the "Agreement on Common Automotive Policy between the Argentine Republic and the Federative Republic of Brazil", which establishes a bilateral regime of administered trade and was in force until 30 June 2014, before being extended in May 2014 for one year ("Brasil y Argentina prorrogarán su acuerdo automotriz por un año", *América Economía*, 5 mayo 2014).

[47] UNCTAD GlobalStat.

[48] On 1 November 2006, the Mexican government published the Decree for the Promotion of the Manufacturing, Maquila and Export Service Industry (the IMMEX Decree). This instrument integrates the programs for the Development and

Operation of the Maquila Export Industry and the Temporary Import Programs to Produce Export Goods. The companies supported by those programmes jointly represent 85 per cent of Mexico's manufactured exports.

[49] Mexico passed a tax reform law, which took effect on 1 January 2014, that includes certain provisions that reduce benefits for IMMEX companies. However, in order to reduce the impact of these reforms on IMMEX companies, a presidential decree and resolutions issued in late 2013 enabled IMMEX companies to retain some benefits taken away in the general provisions.

[50] In general, despite the higher technology content of its manufactured exports than the Latin American average (19 per cent versus 12 per cent), Mexico lags behind countries like Brazil and Argentina in terms of research intensity (R&D as a share of GDP). This share was 0.5 per cent in 2013 compared with 1.3 per cent for Brazil and 0.6 per cent for Argentina. The country's prospects for long-term growth based on innovation are perceived as limited, given its current resources, priorities and national aspirations. See "2014 global R&D funding forecast", *R&D Magazine*, December 2013; and Economist Intelligent Unit, "Intellectual-Property Environment in Mexico", 2010.

[51] For instance, anti-corrosion technologies related to the use of ethanol fuel have seen considerable development in research institutions in Brazil. In addition, national suppliers such as Arteb, Lupatech and Sabó have not only become more directly involved in co-design with assemblers' affiliates in Brazil, but have even become involved in innovation projects led by assemblers' headquarters or their European affiliates. Arteb and Lupatech provide innovation inputs directly from Brazil to General Motors. Sabó has worked with Volkswagen in Wolfsburg and through Sabó's European subsidiary (Quadros, 2009; Quadros et al., 2009).

[52] Economist Intelligence Unit, Industry Report, Automotive, Brazil, January 2014.

[53] See Economist Intelligence Unit, Industry Report, Automotive, Brazil, January 2014; "Brazil's growing taste for luxury", Economist Intelligence Unit, 14 January 2014.

[54] See Economist Intelligence Unit, Industry Report, Automotive, Mexico, April 2014.

[55] The pipeline will transport natural gas from the giant Shah Deniz II development in Azerbaijan through Greece and Albania to Italy, from which it can be transported farther into Western and Central Europe.

[56] The deal by Gazprom (Russian Federation) to take over one of Europe's largest gas storage facilities is attracting fresh scrutiny in Germany. The State-owned enterprise is finalizing an asset swap with BASF, its long-term German partner, under which it will increase its stake in Wingas, a German gas storage and distribution business, from less than 50 per cent to 100 per cent. In return, BASF will obtain stakes in western Siberian gas fields. When the deal was announced in 2012, it raised little concern in Germany, where Gazprom has been the biggest foreign supplier of energy for decades and an increasingly important investor in domestic energy. But the recent crisis has prompted some to question the transaction.

[57] Croatia is now counted as a developed country, as are all other EU member countries.

[58] "Companies flock to Europe to raise cash", *Financial Times*, 20 January 2014. The article reports data from Dealogic.

[59] See, for example, "Microsoft favors Europe for record bond sale: corporate finance", *Bloomberg*, 4 December 2013.

[60] Widely cited but also disputed research by the Centre for Economic Policy Research estimates that if the most ambitious comprehensive agreement is reached, the deal would add €120 billion and €95 billion, respectively, to the GDP of the

EU and the United States by 2027. The gains therefore would amount to about 0.5 per cent of projected GDP for 2027.

[61] The exception is 2005, when there was a net divestment of United States FDI in Europe caused by the repatriation tax holiday introduced by the United States Government.

[62] "Cross-border mergers and acquisitions deals soared in 2013", *Haaretz*, 9 January 2014.

[63] Moody's Investors Service, "US non-financial corporates' cash pile grows, led by technology", announcement, 31 March 2014.

[64] The takeover was approved by the New Zealand Overseas Investment Office in February 2014.

[65] If the plan is approved, ATMEA, the Paris-based joint venture between Mitsubishi Heavy Industries (Japan) and Areva (France), is to build reactors for the project worth $22 billion.

[66] The power plant will be built by Daewoo Engineering and Construction (Republic of Korea).

[67] The support is provided through the State-owned Japan Oil, Gas and Metals National Corporation.

[68] In Chad, Glencore acquired partial stakes in exclusive exploration authorizations owned by Griffiths Energy International (Canada). In the Democratic Republic of the Congo, Glencore raised its stake in a copper mining company to 69 per cent by acquiring a 14.5 per cent stake from High Grade Minerals (Panama).

[69] The number of projects in 2013 was 408, as compared with 357 in 2012.

[70] "Reykjavik plans to start $2 billion Ethiopian power project", *Bloomberg*, 12 March 2014, www.bloomberg.com.

[71] The largest was a $227 million project by the Mahindra Group in the automotive industry, followed by a $107 million telecommunication project by the Bharti Group and a $60 million project in the transport industry by Hero Cycles.

[72] Here, "infrastructure" refers to four sectors: energy and power, telecommunications, transportation, and water and sewerage.

[73] Based on the project data registered in the Thomson ONE database.

[74] The relevant project information for LDCs in the Thomson ONE database, however, is far from complete. For example, about 40 per cent of registered projects do not report announced or estimated project costs.

[75] The contributions by foreign sponsors could be greater because more than a quarter of foreign participating projects were registered without values.

[76] This project was reported with unspecified sponsors in the Thomson ONE database.

[77] All three were registered as build-own-operate projects with no information on sponsors.

[78] FDI inflows comprise capital provided by a foreign direct investor to an FDI enterprise (positive inflows) and capital received from an FDI enterprise by a foreign direct investor (negative inflows). Thus, external funding flows into LDCs under non-equity modes – without the involvement of direct investments – are beyond the scope of the FDI statistics.

[79] For example, in large-scale projects, investors' commitments are often divided in multiple phases, stretching into years or even decades. Delays in the execution of announced projects are also common, owing to changing political situations and to social or environmental concerns. These tendencies also apply to the value of announced greenfield FDI investments (table D), which are usually (but not always) much greater than annual FDI inflows in the corresponding years (figure B).

[80] "Agreement to investigate development of DRC aluminium smelter using power from Inga 3 hydropower scheme", 23 October 2007, www.bhpbilliton.com.

[81] "Africa's biggest electricity project, Inga 3 powers regional cooperation", 11 October 2013, www.theafricareport.com.

[82] "World Bank Group Supports DRC with Technical Assistance for Preparation of Inga 3 BC Hydropower Development", 20 March 2014, www.worldbank.org.

[83] "US and Chinese work together on Inga 3?", 22 January 2014, www.esi-africa.com.

[84] "Myanmar-Thai Dawei project likely to begin construction in April", 7 November 2012, www.4-traders.com.

[85] "Italian-Thai ditched as Thailand, Myanmar seize Dawei development zone", 21 November 2013, www.reuters.com; "Burma, Thailand push ahead with Dawei SEZ", *Bangkok Post*, 31 December 2013.

[86] To manage the Thilawa SEZ project, a Myanmar-Japan joint venture was established in October 2013. It comprises private and public entities from Myanmar (51 per cent), Japanese TNCs (about 40 per cent) and the Japan International Cooperation Agency (about 10 per cent).

[87] "Mitsubishi to build massive power plant in Myanmar", 22 November 2013, http://asia.nikkei.com.

[88] In this respect, UNCTAD's plan of action for investment in LDCs recommends strengthening public-private infrastructure development efforts (UNCTAD 2011c).

[89] In the OECD Creditor Reporting System, the corresponding sectors included here are "Energy" (excluding energy policy and administration management, and related education and training), "Transport & Storage" (excluding transport policy and administration management, and related education and training), "Telecommunications" and "Water Supply & Sanitation" (excluding water resources policy and administration management).

[90] Non-concessional financing, provided mainly by multilateral development banks to developing economies, is not ODA and is reported as "other official flows" (OOF) in the OECD Creditor Reporting System. Because of the significance of such financing for supporting infrastructure development, OECD (2014) argues that ODF, which includes both ODA and OOF, better represents the reality of infrastructure finance from DAC members to developing economies. In the case of LDCs, however, the scale of OOF (cumulative total of $1.1 billion in the selected four sectors) was insignificant, compared with that of ODA (cumulative total of $39.7 billion in the four sectors) for the period 2003–2012.

[91] This represents 10 per cent of cumulative gross ODF disbursements to all sectors in LDCs for the period 2003–2012.

[92] The OECD (2014) estimates that gross ODF disbursements account for only 5–8 per cent of all infrastructure finance in developing economies and that the rest comes from the domestic public sector and citizens (55–75 per cent) and the private sector (20–30 per cent). The majority of ODF has gone to upper-middle-income countries rather than low-income ones. The low level of support for low-income countries reflects the difficulty of maximizing returns on investment, reflecting their weak enabling environment (OECD 2014, p. 6).

[93] Estache (2010) estimated that the annual infrastructure investment needs (including both operating and capital expenditures for 2008–2015) in low-income countries were 12.5 per cent of their GDP. Because no estimates were available for LDCs as a group, the suggested ratio of 12.5 per cent was applied to LDCs' annual average GDP in 2003–2012 ($477 billion) to derive the estimate of $59.6 billion.

[94] Calculations were based on annex tables C–D in WHO (2012) by extracting total financial capital costs estimated for LDCs.

[95] For example, the Government of Japan not only supports PPPs in infrastructure "at the heart of its development co-

operation" but also encourages domestic companies to take part in infrastructure projects in its aid recipient countries through the Japan International Cooperation Agency's Private Sector Investment Finance (PSIF) component (OECD, 2014, p. 14).

[96] Blending grants with loans, equity or guarantees from public or private financiers reduces the financial risk of projects. Through regional EU blending facilities (e.g. the EU-Africa Infrastructure Trust Fund), grants from the European Commission and EU member States are combined with long-term loans or equity provided by development financial institutions or private financiers (OECD, 2014).

[97] See, for example, United Nations, "Review of progress made in implementing the Buenos Aires Plan of Action, the new directions strategy for South-South cooperation and the Nairobi outcome document of the High-level United Nations Conference on South-South Cooperation, taking into account the complementary role of South-South cooperation in the implementation of relevant major United Nations conferences in the social, economic and related fields", SSC/18/1, 31 March 2014.

[98] At the national level, this entails changes in fiscal policy and tax administration brought about by strengthening government capacity to manage revenues (UNCTAD 2013c).

[99] The Law on Foreign Investment in Strategic Sectors (SEFIL) established comprehensive permitting requirements on FDI entry and operation by private and State-owned enterprises in a number of sectors, including mining, in May 2012.

[100] Towards this end, UNCTAD will produce a comprehensive paper on investment in the LLDCs later in 2014.

[101] In Trinidad and Tobago, FDI to the services sector increased strongly in 2007–2011 as a consequence of one large acquisition undertaken in 2008 in the financial sector, namely the $2.2 billion purchase of RBTT Financial Group by the Royal Bank of Canada.

[102] Other partners in the project are Australian Oil Search Limited, Santos, Merlin Petroleum, local landowners and the State-owned Petromin.

[103] Petroleum, chemical and metal products are among the most relevant downstream activities of the oil, gas and metal minerals industries.

[104] SIDS status confers no special trade preference. However, all SIDS qualify for at least one preference scheme. Although SIDS that fall within the LDC category benefit from LDC-specific preferences, all other SIDS – a majority – are beneficiaries of preferences through special programmes such as the Caribbean Basin Initiative of the United States, Caribcan of Canada and SPARTECA of Australia and New Zealand. The EU grants special trade preferences to a large majority of SIDS by virtue of the Cotonou Partnership Agreement between African, Caribbean and Pacific countries on the one hand, and members of the EU on the other (UNCTAD, 2004).

[105] See "Bankers on the Beach", *Finance and Development*, vol. 48, no. 2, June 2011.

RECENT POLICY DEVELOPMENTS AND KEY ISSUES

CHAPTER III

A. NATIONAL INVESTMENT POLICIES

1. Overall trends

Most investment policy measures remain geared towards promotion and liberalization, but the share of regulatory or restrictive measures increased.

In 2013, according to UNCTAD's count, 59 countries and economies adopted 87 policy measures affecting foreign investment. Of these measures, 61 related to liberalization, promotion and facilitation of investment, while 23 introduced new restrictions or regulations on investment (table III.1). The share of new regulations and restrictions increased slightly, from 25 per cent in 2012 to 27 per cent in 2013 (figure III.1). Almost half of the policy measures applied across the board. Most of the industry-specific measures addressed the services sector (table III.2).

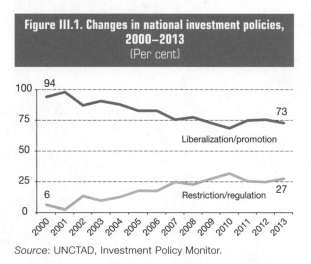

Figure III.1. Changes in national investment policies, 2000–2013
(Per cent)

Source: UNCTAD, Investment Policy Monitor.

a. FDI liberalization and promotion

New FDI liberalization measures were mainly reported for countries in Asia. Several of them pertained to the telecommunications industry. For instance, *India* removed the cap on foreign direct investment in telecommunications.[1] The *Republic of Korea* passed the amended Telecommunications Business Act, which allows foreign investors covered by a free trade agreement (FTA) with the Republic of Korea to acquire up to 100 per cent of Korea's facility-based telecommunications businesses with the exception of SK and KT Telecom.[2] *Mexico* increased the threshold for foreign investment in telecommunications to 100 per cent in all areas except radio and television broadcasting, where the limit is 49 per cent under certain conditions.[3]

In addition to liberalizing telecommunications investment, *India* raised the FDI cap in the defence sector beyond 26 per cent upon approval by the Cabinet Committee on Security and under specific conditions. In other sectors, including petroleum and natural gas, courier services, single-brand retail, commodity exchanges, credit information companies, infrastructure companies in the securities market and power exchanges, government approval requirements have been relaxed.[4] *Indonesia* amended the list of business fields open to foreign investors and increased the foreign investment ceiling in several industries, including pharmaceuticals, venture capital operations in financial services and power plant projects in energy generation.[5] *The Philippines*

Table III.1. Changes in national investment policies, 2000–2013
(Number of measures)

Item	2000	2001	2002	2003	2004	2005	2006	2007	2008	2009	2010	2011	2012	2013
Number of countries that introduced changes	46	52	44	60	80	78	71	50	41	47	55	49	54	59
Number of regulatory changes	**81**	**97**	**94**	**125**	**164**	**144**	**126**	**79**	**68**	**88**	**121**	**80**	**86**	**87**
Liberalization/promotion	75	85	79	113	142	118	104	58	51	61	80	59	61	61
Restriction/regulation	5	2	12	12	20	25	22	19	15	23	37	20	20	23
Neutral/indeterminate[a]	1	10	3	-	2	1	-	2	2	4	4	1	5	3

Source: UNCTAD, Investment Policy Monitor database.

[a] In some cases, the expected impact of the policy measure on the investment is undetermined.

Table III.2. Changes in national investment policies, by industry, 2013			
(Per cent and number of measures)			
Sector/industry	Liberalization/promotion (%)	Restriction/regulation (%)	Neutral/indeterminate (%)	Total number of measures
---	---	---	---	---
Total	72	25	3	93
Cross-industry	80	17	2	41
Agribusiness	80	20	-	5
Extractive industries	60	30	10	10
Manufacturing	75	25	-	4
Services	64	33	3	33

Source: UNCTAD, Investment Policy Monitor database.
Note: Overall totals differ from table III.1 because some of the measures can be classified under more than one type.

amended its Rural Bank Act to allow foreign individuals or entities to hold equity of up to 60 per cent in rural banks.[6]

Among the FDI promotion measures, the National Assembly of *Cuba* approved a new law on foreign investment which offers guarantees to investors and fiscal incentives.[7] The country also set up a new special economic zone (SEZ) for foreign investors in Mariel.[8] The *Republic of Korea* has introduced a new system lowering the minimum required area to designate an investment zone.[9] In *Pakistan*, the Commerce Ministry finalized an agreement with the National Insurance Company for comprehensive insurance coverage of foreign investors.[10]

b. Investment liberalization and promotion for domestic and foreign investors

General investment liberalization policies in 2013 were characterized mainly by new privatizations. Full or partial privatizations benefiting both domestic and foreign investors took place in at least 10 countries. For instance, in *Peru*, the Congress approved the privatization of up to 49 per cent of the State energy firm Petroperú – the first time that investment of private capital in Petroperú has been authorized.[11] In *Serbia*, Etihad Airways (United Arab Emirates) acquired a 49 per cent stake in JAT Airways, the Serbian national flag carrier (see also chapter II.A.4).[12] In *Slovenia*, the Parliament gave its support to the Government's plan to sell 15 State-owned firms, including the largest telecommunications operator, Telekom Slovenia.[13] Another important liberalization relates to recent energy reforms in *Mexico*. In December 2013, the Mexican Congress approved modifications to the Constitution, including the lifting of a restriction on private capital in the oil industry (see also chapter II.A.3). The reforms allow the Government to issue licenses and enter into contracts for production sharing, profit sharing and services.[14]

Investment incentives and facilitation measures applying to investors irrespective of their nationality were enacted most commonly in Africa and in Asia. Promotion measures, which mainly focused on fiscal incentive schemes, included a number of sector-specific programs. Some policies were adopted in early 2014. For instance, the *Dominican Republic* extended tax benefits for investors in its tourism development law.[15] *Malaysia* announced its National Automotive Policy 2014, which grants fiscal incentives with the objective to promote a competitive and sustainable domestic automotive industry.[16]

Facilitation measures concentrated on simplifying business registration. For instance, *Mongolia* passed a new Investment Law that reduces approval requirements, streamlines the registration process and provides certain legal guarantees and incentives.[17] *Mozambique* passed a decree that will facilitate the establishment of new companies through a single business registration form.[18] Dubai, in *the United Arab Emirates*, introduced a series of reforms making it easier to set up hotels.[19]

A number of countries introduced SEZs or revised policies related to existing SEZs. For instance, *China* launched the China (Shanghai) Pilot Free Trade Zone, introducing various new policy measures on trade, investment and finance (see also chapter II.A.2.a). With regard to inward FDI, this free trade zone adopts a new approach, providing for establishment rights, subject to exceptions. Specific segments in six service sectors – finance, transport, commerce and trade, professional services, cultural services and public services – were opened to foreign investors.[20] The Government of *South Sudan* officially launched the Juba SEZ, an industrial area for business and investment activities.[21]

c. New FDI restrictions and regulations

Newly introduced FDI restrictions and related policies included revision of entry regulations, rejection of investment projects after review and a nationalization. At least 13 countries introduced new restrictions specifically for foreign investors in 2013.

Among the revisions of entry regulations, *Indonesia* lowered the foreign ownership ceiling in several industries, including onshore oil production and data communications system services.[22] *Sri Lanka* restricted foreigners from owning land but still allows long-term leases of land.[23] *Canada* changed the Investment Canada Act to make it possible for the Minister of Industry to decide – in the context of "net benefit" reviews under the act – that an entity is controlled by one or more foreign State-owned enterprises even though it would qualify as Canadian-controlled under the criteria established by the act.[24] The Government of *France* issued a decree reinforcing its control mechanisms for foreign investments in the interests of public order, public security or national defence. The measure covers the following strategic sectors: energy, water, transportation, telecommunications, defence and health care.[25] The Government of *India* amended the definition of the term "control" for the purpose of calculating the total foreign investment in Indian companies.[26] Recently, the *Russian Federation* added three types of transport-related activities to its law on procedures for foreign investment in business entities of strategic importance for national defence and state security.[27]

Some governments blocked a number of foreign takeovers. For instance, under the national security provisions of the Investment Canada Act, *Canada* rejected the proposed acquisition

of the Allstream division of Manitoba Telecom Services by Accelero Capital Holdings (Egypt).[28] The Commission on Foreign Investment of the *Russian Federation* turned down the request by Abbott Laboratories (United States) to buy Russian vaccine maker Petrovax Pharm, citing protection of the country's national security interests, among other considerations.[29] In addition, the *European Commission* prohibited the proposed acquisition of TNT Express (the Netherlands) by UPS (United States). The Commission found that the takeover would have restricted competition in member States in the express delivery of small packages.[30]

The *Plurinational State of Bolivia* nationalized the Bolivian Airport Services (SABSA), a subsidiary of Abertis y Aena (Spain) for reasons of public interest.[31]

d. New regulations or restrictions for domestic and foreign investors

Some countries introduced restrictive or regulatory policies affecting both domestic and foreign investors. For instance, *the Plurinational State of Bolivia* introduced a new bank law that allows control by the State over the setting of interest rates by commercial banks. It also authorizes the Government to set quotas for lending to specific sectors or activities.[32] *Ecuador* issued rules for the return of radio and television frequencies in accordance with its media law, requiring that 66 per cent of radio frequencies be in the hands of private and public media (33 per cent each), with the remaining 34 per cent going to "community" media.[33] *The Bolivarian Republic of Venezuela* adopted a decree regulating the automotive sector regarding the production and sale of automobiles.[34]

e. Divestment prevention and reshoring promotion[35]

An interesting recent phenomenon entails government efforts to prevent divestments by foreign investors. In light of economic crises and persistently high domestic unemployment, some countries have introduced new approval requirements for dislocations and layoffs. In addition, some home countries have started to promote reshoring of overseas investment by their TNCs.

- In *France* the Parliament passed a bill imposing penalties on companies that shut down operations that are deemed economically viable. The law requires firms with more than 1,000 employees to prove that they have exhausted options for selling a plant before closing it.[36]

- *Greece* passed a law that makes it more difficult for companies listed on the Greek stock exchange to relocate their head offices abroad. The Greek capital markets law now requires approval of relocation by 90 per cent of shareholders, rather than the prior threshold of 67 per cent.[37]

- The *Republic of Korea* passed the Act on Supporting the Return of Overseas Korean Enterprises. Accordingly, the Government founded the Reshoring Support Centre and is planning to provide reshoring businesses with incentives that are similar to those provided to foreign-invested companies.[38]

- Since 2011, the Government of the *United States* has been operating the "Select USA" program, which, inter alia, has the objective of attracting and retaining investment in the United States economy.[39]

2. Recent trends in investment incentives

Incentives are widely used for attracting investment. Linking them to sustainable development goals and monitoring their impact could improve their effectiveness.

Policymakers use incentives to stimulate investments in specific industries, activities or disadvantaged regions. However, such schemes have been criticized for being economically inefficient and leading to misallocations of public funds.

a. *Investment incentives: types and objectives*

Although there is no uniform definition of what constitutes an investment incentive, such incentives can be described as non-market benefits that are used to influence the behaviour of investors. Incentives can be offered by national, regional and local governments, and they come in many forms. These forms can be classified in three main

categories on the basis of the types of benefits that are offered: financial benefits, fiscal benefits and regulatory benefits (see table III.3).

From January 2014 to April 2014, UNCTAD conducted a global survey of investment promotion agencies (IPAs) on their prospects for FDI and for the promotion of sustainable development through investment incentives for foreign investors.[40] According to the survey results, fiscal incentives are the most important type for attracting and benefiting from foreign investment (figure III.2).[41] This is particularly true in developing and transition economies. Financial and regulatory incentives are considered less important policy tools for attracting and benefiting from FDI. In addition to investment incentives, IPAs consider investment facilitation measures as particularly important for attracting investment.

Investment incentives can be used to attract or retain FDI in a particular host country (*locational incentives*). In such cases, they can be perceived as compensation for information asymmetries between the investor and the host government, as well as for deficiencies in the investment climate, such as weak infrastructure, underdeveloped human resources and administrative constraints. In this context, investment incentives can become a key policy instrument in the competition between countries and within countries to attract foreign investment.

Investment incentives can also be used as a tool to advance public policy objectives such as economic

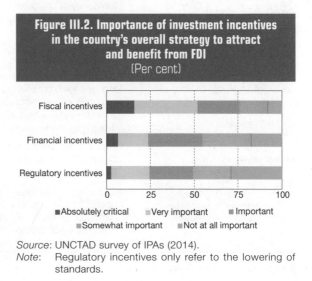

Figure III.2. Importance of investment incentives in the country's overall strategy to attract and benefit from FDI
(Per cent)

Source: UNCTAD survey of IPAs (2014).
Note: Regulatory incentives only refer to the lowering of standards.

Table III.3. Investment incentives by type and mechanism

Financial incentives

Investment grants	"Direct subsidies" to cover (part of) capital, production or marketing costs in relation to an investment project
Subsidized credits and credit guarantees	Subsidized loans Loan guarantees Guaranteed export credits
Government insurance at preferential rates, publicly funded venture capital participating in investments involving high commercial risks	Government insurance at preferential rates, usually available to cover certain types of risks (such as exchange rate volatility, currency devaluation and non-commercial risks such as expropriation and political turmoil), often provided through an international agency

Fiscal incentives

Profit-based	Reduction of the standard corporate income tax rate or profit tax rate, tax holiday
Capital-investment-based	Accelerated depreciation, investment and reinvestment allowances
Labour-based	Reduction in social security contribution Deductions from taxable earnings based on the number of employees or other labour-related expenditures
Sales-based	Corporate income tax reductions based on total sales
Import-based	Duty exemptions on capital goods, equipment or raw materials, parts and inputs related to the production process Tax credits for duties paid on imported materials or supplies
Export-based	Export tax exemptions, duty drawbacks and preferential tax treatment of income from exports Income tax reduction for special foreign-exchange-earning activities or for manufactured exports Tax credits on domestic sales in return for export performance, income tax credits on net local content of exports Deduction of overseas expenditures and capital allowance for export industries
Based on other particular expenses	Corporate income tax deduction based on, for example, expenditures relating to marketing and promotional activities
Value added based	Corporate income tax reductions or credits based on the net local content of outputs Income tax credits based on net value earned
Reduction of taxes for expatriates	Tax relief to help reduce personal tax liability and reduce income tax and social security contribution

Other incentives (including regulatory incentives)

Regulatory incentives	Lowering of environmental, health, safety or labour standards Temporary or permanent exemption from compliance with applicable standards Stabilization clauses guaranteeing that existing regulations will not be amended to the detriment of investors
Subsidized services (in kind)	Subsidized dedicated infrastructure: electricity, water, telecommunication, transportation or designated infrastructure at less than commercial price Subsidized services, including assistance in identifying sources of finance, implementing and managing projects and carrying out pre-investment studies; information on markets, availability of raw materials and supply of infrastructure; advice on production processes and marketing techniques; assistance with training and retraining; and technical facilities for developing know-how or improving quality control
Market privileges	Preferential government contracts Closing the market to further entry or the granting of monopoly rights Protection from import competition
Foreign exchange privileges	Special exchange rates Special foreign debt-to-equity conversion rates Elimination of exchange risks on foreign loans Concessions of foreign exchange credits for export earnings Special concessions on repatriation of earnings and capital

Source: Based on UNCTAD (2004).

growth through foreign investment or to make foreign affiliates in a country undertake activities regarded as desirable (*behavioural incentives*). For this purpose, incentives may focus on support for economic growth indicators, such as job creation, skill transfer, research and development (R&D), export generation and establishment of linkages with local firms.

For most countries, job creation is the most important objective of investment incentives. About 85 per cent of IPAs indicated that job creation ranks among their top five objectives (figure III.3), with almost 75 per cent ranking it their primary or secondary objective. In importance, job creation is followed by technology transfer, export promotion, local linkages and domestic value added, and skills development. Just over 40 per cent of respondents indicated that locational decisions and international competition rank among the top five objectives of their incentive policies. Interestingly, this is the case for more than half of IPAs from developed countries but less than one third of those from developing or transition economies. An explanation might be that other objectives, such as technological development, exports and skill development, are already relatively advanced in most developed countries. Finally, two potential objectives – environmental protection and promotion, and local development – do not rank as highly, confirming

that there is considerable room for improvement when it comes to connecting incentive strategies with sustainable development goals such as those being discussed for the United Nations post-2015 development agenda (see chapter IV for further details).

Investment incentives are usually conditioned on the fulfilment by the investor of certain performance requirements. The IPA survey shows that such requirements primarily relate to job creation and to technology and skill transfer, followed by minimum investment and locational and export requirements (figure III.4). Environmental protection, along with some other policy objectives, does not rank among the key concerns.

Investment incentives may target specific industries. According to IPAs, the most important target industry for investment incentives is the IT and business services industry. Over 40 per cent of the respondents indicate that this industry is among their top five target industries (figure III.5). Other key target industries include agriculture and hotels and restaurants. Even though renewable energy is among the top target industries, still less than one third of promotion agencies rank it among the top five industries.

The use of FDI-specific investment incentives differs from country to country. About 40 per cent

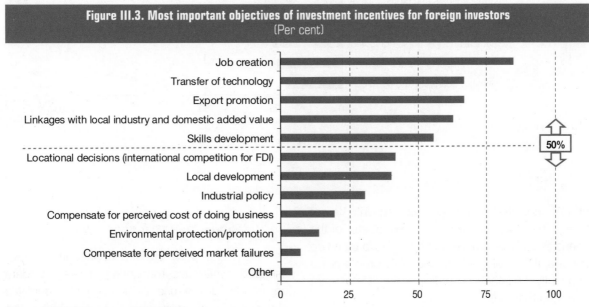

Figure III.3. Most important objectives of investment incentives for foreign investors
(Per cent)

Source: UNCTAD survey of IPAs (2014).
Note: Based on number of times mentioned as one of the top five objectives.

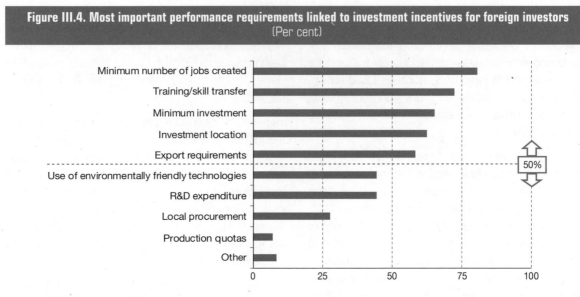

Figure III.4. Most important performance requirements linked to investment incentives for foreign investors
(Per cent)

Source: UNCTAD survey of IPAs (2014).
Note: Based on number of times mentioned as one of the top five performance requirements.

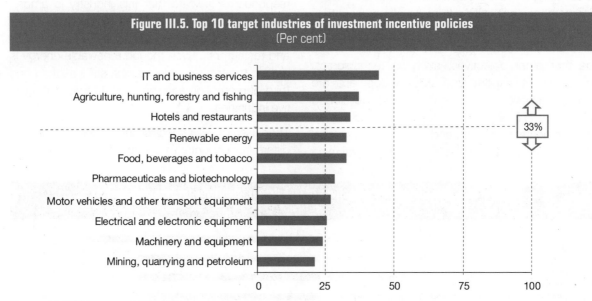

Figure III.5. Top 10 target industries of investment incentive policies
(Per cent)

Source: UNCTAD survey of IPAs (2014).
Note: Based on number of times mentioned as one of the top five target industries.

of IPAs indicated that incentives frequently target foreign investors specifically, while a quarter of the agencies say this is never the case. More than two thirds of IPAs indicated that incentive programmes frequently fulfil their purpose, while 11 per cent indicated that they always do so.

b. Developments related to investment incentives

For the most part, investment incentives have escaped systematic monitoring. Therefore, data on trends in the use of investment incentives and changes in policy objectives – including the promotion of sustainable development – are scarce.

Data from UNCTAD's Investment Policy Monitor suggest that investment incentives constitute a significant share of newly adopted investment policy measures that seek to create a more attractive investment climate for investors. Between 2004 and 2013, this share fluctuated between 26 per cent and 55 per cent, with their overall importance increasing during the period (figure III.6). In 2013, over half of new liberalization and promotion measures related to the provision of incentives to investors. More than half of these incentive measures are fiscal incentives.

Although sustainable development is not among the most prominent objectives of incentive policies, some recent measures cover areas such as health care, education, R&D and local development. For instance, in *Angola*, the Patrons Law of 2012 defines the tax and other incentives available to corporations that provide funding and support to projects related to social initiatives, education, culture, sports, science, health and information technology.[42] In 2010, *Bulgaria* adopted legislation that grants reimbursement of up to 50 per cent for spending on educational and R&D activities, and provides a subsidy of up to 10 per cent for investments in processing industries.[43] In 2011, *Poland* adopted the "Programme to support investments of high importance to the Polish economy for 2011–2020", with the aim of increasing innovation and the competitiveness of the economy by promoting FDI in high-tech sectors.[44] In 2011,

the *Russian Federation* exempted education and health-care services from the corporate profit tax under certain conditions.[45]

A number of countries introduced measures to promote local development. For instance in 2012, *Algeria* implemented an incentives regime that is applicable to the wilayas (provinces) of the South and the Highlands.[46] *China* has provided preferential taxation rates on imports of equipment, technologies and materials by foreigners investing in the central and western areas of the country.[47] *Japan* recently designated six SEZs in an attempt to boost local economies. These zones are located around the country and focus on different industries, including agriculture, tourism and R&D.[48]

Among regions, over the last decade Asia has introduced the most policy changes related to investment incentives, followed by Africa (figure III.7). China and the Republic of Korea took the lead in Asia, while Angola, Egypt, Libya and South Africa were the front-runners in Africa. Most of these incentives (75 per cent) do not target any industry in particular; of the industry-specific incentives, most target the services industries, followed by manufacturing.

c. Policy recommendations

Despite the fact that investment incentives have not been a major determinant of FDI and that their cost-effectiveness can be questioned, recent UNCTAD data show that policymakers continue to use incentives as an important policy instrument for attracting FDI. Linking investment incentives schemes to sustainable development goals could make them a more effective policy tool to remedy market failures and could offer a response to the criticism raised against the way investment incentives have traditionally been used (see also chapter IV).

Governments should also follow a number of good practices: (i) The rationale for investment incentives should derive explicitly from the country's development strategy, and their effectiveness should be fully assessed before adoption. (ii) Incentives for specific industries should aim to ensure self-sustained viability so as to avoid subsidizing non-viable industries at the expense of the economy

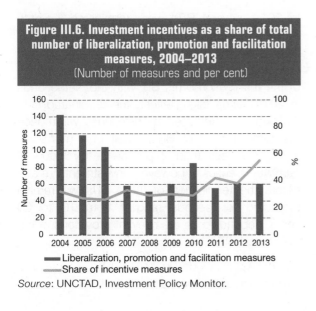

Figure III.6. Investment incentives as a share of total number of liberalization, promotion and facilitation measures, 2004–2013
(Number of measures and per cent)

Source: UNCTAD, Investment Policy Monitor.

as a whole. (iii) All incentives should be granted on the basis of pre-determined, objective, clear and transparent criteria, offered on a non-discriminatory basis and carefully assessed in terms of long-term costs and benefits prior to implementation. (iv) The costs and benefits of incentives should be periodically reviewed and their effectiveness in achieving the desired objectives thoroughly evaluated and monitored.[49]

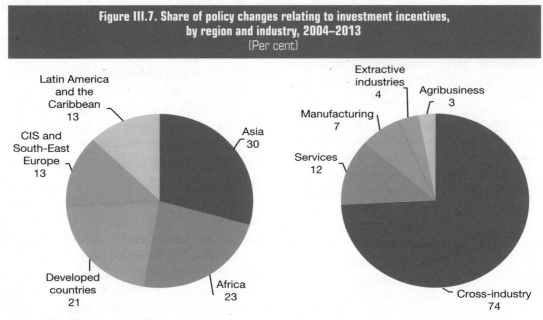

Figure III.7. Share of policy changes relating to investment incentives, by region and industry, 2004–2013
(Per cent)

Latin America and the Caribbean 13
CIS and South-East Europe 13
Asia 30
Developed countries 21
Africa 23

Extractive industries 4
Agribusiness 3
Manufacturing 7
Services 12
Cross-industry 74

Source: UNCTAD, Investment Policy Monitor.

B. INTERNATIONAL INVESTMENT POLICIES

1. Trends in the conclusion of international investment agreements

a. The IIA universe continues to grow

The past years brought an increasing dichotomy in investment treaty making: disengaging and "up-scaling."

The year 2013 saw the conclusion of 44 international investment agreements (IIAs) (30 bilateral investment treaties, or BITs, and 14 "other IIAs"[50]), bringing the total number of agreements to 3,236 (2,902 BITs and 334 "other IIAs") by year-end[51] (figure III.8). Countries that were particularly active in concluding BITs in 2013 include Kuwait (7); Turkey and the United Arab Emirates (4 each); and Japan, Mauritius and the United Republic of Tanzania (3 each). (See annex table III.7 for a list of each country's total number of BITs and "other IIAs".)

In 2013, several BITs were terminated.[52] South Africa, for example, gave notice of the termination of its BITs with Germany, the Netherlands, Spain and Switzerland in 2013;[53] and Indonesia gave notice of the termination of its BIT with the Netherlands in 2014. Once taking effect, the terminated BITs that were not replaced by new ones will reduce the total number of BITs, albeit only marginally (by 43, or less than 2 per cent). By virtue of "survival clauses", however, investments made before the termination of these BITs will remain protected for periods ranging from 10 to 20 years, depending on the relevant provisions of the terminated BITs.[54]

"Other IIAs" concluded in 2013 can be grouped into three broad categories, as identified in *WIR12*:

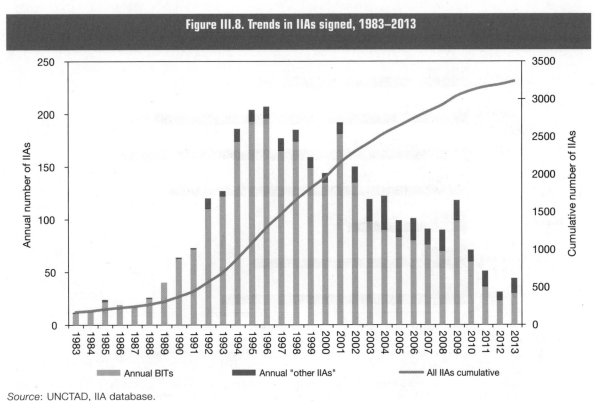

Figure III.8. Trends in IIAs signed, 1983–2013

Legend: Annual BITs | Annual "other IIAs" | All IIAs cumulative

Source: UNCTAD, IIA database.

- *Seven agreements with BIT-equivalent provisions.* The Canada–Honduras Free Trade Agreement (FTA); the China–Iceland FTA; Colombia's FTAs with Costa Rica, Israel, the Republic of Korea, and Panama; and New Zealand's FTA with Taiwan Province of China all fall in the category of IIAs that contain obligations commonly found in BITs, including substantive standards of investment protection and investor–State dispute settlement (ISDS).

- *Two agreements with limited investment provisions.* The China–Switzerland FTA and the EFTA–Costa Rica–Panama FTA fall in the category of agreements that provide limited investment-related provisions (e.g. national treatment with respect to commercial presence or free movement of capital relating to direct investments).

- *Five agreements with investment cooperation provisions and/or a future negotiating mandate.* The Chile–Thailand FTA and the EFTA–Bosnia and Herzegovina FTA, as well as the trade and investment framework agreements signed by the United States with the Caribbean Community (CARICOM), Myanmar and Libya, contain general provisions on cooperation in investment matters and/or a mandate for future negotiations on investment.

An important development occurred in early 2014, when Chile, Colombia, Mexico and Peru, the four countries that formed the Pacific Alliance in 2011, signed a comprehensive protocol that includes a chapter on investment protection with BITs-like substantive and procedural investment protection standards.

In addition, at least 40 countries and 4 regional integration organizations are currently or have been recently revising their model IIAs. In terms of ongoing negotiations of "other IIAs", the European Union (EU) is engaged in negotiating more than 20 agreements that are expected to include investment-related provisions (which may vary in their scope and depth).[55] Canada is engaged in negotiating 12 FTAs; the Republic of Korea is negotiating 10; Japan and Singapore are negotiating 9 agreements each; and Australia and the United States are negotiating 8 each (figure III.9). Some of these agreements are megaregional ones (see below).

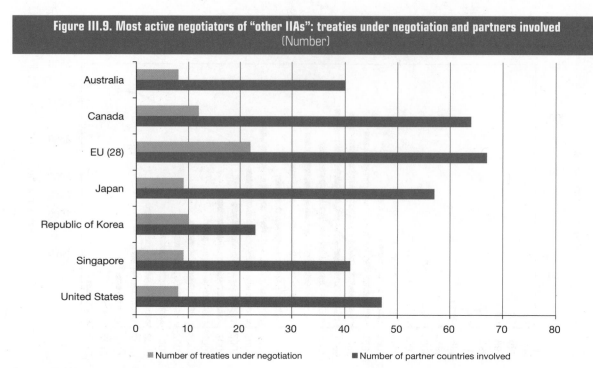

Figure III.9. Most active negotiators of "other IIAs": treaties under negotiation and partners involved
(Number)

■ Number of treaties under negotiation   ■ Number of partner countries involved

Source: UNCTAD, IIA database.
Note: The selection of countries represented in this chart is based on those that are the "most active" negotiators of "other IIAs". It has to be noted that the scope and depth of investment provisions under discussion varies considerably across negotiations.

The agreements concluded in past years and those currently under negotiation are contributing to an "up-scaling" of the global investment policy landscape. This effect can be seen in the participation rate (i.e. the large number of countries that have concluded or are negotiating treaties), the process (which exhibits an increasing dynamism) and the substance of agreements (the expansion of existing elements and inclusion of new ones). All of this contributes to a growing dichotomy in the directions of investment policies over the last few years, which has manifested itself in simultaneous moves by countries to expand the global IIA regime and to disengage from it.

In a general sense, the more countries engage in IIA negotiations, including megaregional ones, the more they create a spirit of action and engagement also for those countries that are not taking part. However, the successful creation of the numerous "other IIAs", BITs and megaregional agreements under negotiation is far from certain. A stagnation or breakdown of one or several of these negotiations could cause the climate for international investment policymaking to deteriorate and effectively hinder

the momentum and spirit of action at the bilateral, regional and multilateral levels.

b. Sustainable development elements increasingly feature in new IIAs

New IIAs illustrate the growing tendency to craft treaties that are in line with sustainable development objectives.

A review of the 18 IIAs concluded in 2013 for which texts are available (11 BITs and 7 FTAs with substantive investment provisions), shows that most of the treaties include sustainable-development-oriented features, such as those identified in UNCTAD's Investment Policy Framework for Sustainable Development (IPFSD) and in *WIR12* and *WIR13*.[56] Of these agreements, 15 have general exceptions – for example, for the protection of human, animal or plant life or health, or the conservation of exhaustible natural resources[57] – and 13 refer in their preambles to the protection of health and safety, labour rights, the environment or sustainable development. Twelve treaties under review contain a clause that explicitly

Table III.4. Selected aspects of IIAs signed in 2013

Select aspects of IIAs commonly found in IIAs, in order of appearance	Policy Objectives					Serbia-United Arab Emirates BIT	Russian Federation-Uzbekistan BIT	New Zealand-Taiwan Province of China FTA	Morocco-Serbia BIT	Japan-Saudi Arabia BIT	Japan-Myanmar BIT	Japan-Mozambique BIT	EFTA-Costa Rica-Panama FTA	Colombia-Singapore BIT	Colombia-Republic of Korea FTA	Colombia-Panama FTA	Colombia-Israel FTA	Colombia-Costa Rica FTA	Canada-United Republic of Tanzania BIT	Canada-Honduras FTA	Benin-Canada BIT	Belarus-Lao People's Democratic Republic BIT	Austria-Nigeria BIT
	Sustainable-development-enhancing features	Focus on investments conducive to development	Preserve the right to regulate in the public interest	Avoid overexposure to litigation	Stimulate responsible business practices																		
References to the protection of health and safety, labour rights, environment or sustainable development in the treaty preamble	X	X	X		X	X		X		X	X	X	X		X		X	X	X	X	X		X
Refined definition of investment (exclusion of portfolio investment, sovereign debt obligations or claims of money arising solely from commercial contracts)		X		X		X		X	X					X	X	X	X	X	X	X	X		
A carve-out for prudential measures in the financial services sector			X	X				X		X	X	X	X	X		X	X		X	X	X		
Fair and equitable standard equated to the minimum standard of treatment of aliens under customary international law			X	X				X						X	X	X		X	X	X	X		
Clarification of what does and does not constitute an indirect expropriation			X	X				X						X	X	X	X	X	X	X	X	X	
Detailed exceptions from the free-transfer-of-funds obligation, including balance-of-payments difficulties and/or enforcement of national laws			X	X		X		X	X	X	X	X	X	X	X	X	X	X	X	X	X	X	X
Omission of the so-called "umbrella" clause				X		X	X	X	X	X			X	X	X	X	X	X	X	X	X		
General exceptions, e.g. for the protection of human, animal or plant life or health; or the conservation of exhaustible natural resources	X		X	X				X	X	X	X	X	X	X	X	X	X	X	X	X	X	X	
Explicit recognition that parties should not relax health, safety or environmental standards to attract investment	X	X			X			X		X	X	X	X		X	X	X	X	X	X			X
Promotion of corporate and social responsibility standards by incorporating a separate provision into the IIA or as a general reference in the treaty preamble	X												X			X		X		X	X		
Limiting access to ISDS (e.g., limiting treaty provisions subject to ISDS, excluding policy areas from ISDS, limiting time period to submit claims, no ISDS mechanism)			X	X				X		X	X	X	X	X	X	X	X	X	X	X	X		X

Source: UNCTAD.

Note: This table is based on IIAs concluded in 2013 for which the text was available. It does not include "framework agreements", which do not include substantive investment provisions.

recognizes that parties should not relax health, safety or environmental standards in order to attract investment.

These sustainable development features are supplemented by treaty elements that aim more broadly at preserving regulatory space for public policies of host countries and/or at minimizing exposure to investment arbitration. Provisions found with differing frequency in the 18 IIAs include clauses that (i) limit treaty scope (for example, by excluding certain types of assets from the definition of investment); (ii) clarify obligations (by crafting detailed clauses on fair and equitable treatment (FET) and/ or indirect expropriation); (iii) set forth exceptions to the transfer-of-funds obligation or carve-outs for prudential measures; (iv) carefully regulate ISDS (for example, by limiting treaty provisions that are subject to ISDS, excluding certain policy areas from ISDS, setting out a special mechanism for taxation and prudential measures, and restricting the allotted time period within which claims can be submitted); or (v) omit the so-called umbrella clause (table III.4).

In addition to these two types of clauses (i.e. those strengthening the agreement's sustainable development dimension and those preserving policy space), a large number of the treaties concluded in 2013 also add elements that expand treaty standards. Such expansion can take the form of adding a liberalization dimension to the treaty and/or strengthening investment protections (e.g. by enlarging the scope of the treaty or prohibiting certain types of government conduct previously unregulated in investment treaties). Provisions on pre-establishment and rules that prohibit additional performance requirements or that require the publication of draft laws and regulations are examples (included in, e.g., the Benin–Canada BIT, the Canada–Tanzania FTA, the Japan–Mozambique BIT and the New Zealand–Taiwan Province of China FTA).

The ultimate protective and liberalizing strength of an agreement, as well as its impact on policy space and sustainable development, depends on the overall combination (i.e. the blend) of its provisions (IPFSD). Reconciling the two broad objectives – the pursuit of high standard investment protection and liberalization on the one hand and the preservation of the right to regulate in the public interest on the other – is the most important challenge facing IIA negotiators and investment policymakers today. Different combinations of treaty clauses represent each country's attempt to identify the "best fit" combination of treaty elements.

2. Megaregional agreements: emerging issues and systemic implications

Megaregional agreements are broad economic agreements among a group of countries that together have significant economic weight and in which investment is only one of several subjects addressed.[58] The last two years have seen an expansion of negotiations for such agreements. Work on the Trans-Pacific Partnership (TPP), the EU–United States Transatlantic Trade and Investment Partnership (TTIP) and the Canada–EU Comprehensive Economic and Trade Agreement (CETA) are cases in point. Once concluded, these are likely to have a major impact on global investment rule making and global investment patterns.

During the past months, negotiations for megaregional agreements have become increasingly prominent in the public debate, attracting considerable attention – support and criticism alike – from different stakeholders. Prime issues relate to the potential economic benefits of the agreements on the one hand, and their likely impact on Contracting Parties' regulatory space and sustainable development on the other. In this section, the focus is on the systemic implications of these agreements for the IIA regime.

a. The magnitude of megaregional agreements

Megaregional agreements merit attention because of their sheer size and potentially huge implications.

Megaregional agreements merit attention because of their sheer size, among other reasons (table III.5; see also table I.1 in chapter I). Together, the seven negotiations listed in table III.5 involve 88 countries.[59] In terms of population, the biggest is the Regional Comprehensive Economic

Table III.5. Overview of selected megaregional agreements under negotiation

Megaregional agreement	Negotiating parties	Number of countries	Selected indicators 2012			IIA impact	No.
			Items	Value ($ billion)	Share in global total (%)		
CETA	EU (28), Canada	29	GDP:	18 565	26.1	Overlap with current BITs:	7
			Exports:	2 588	17.5	Overlap with current "other IIAs":	0
			Intraregional exports:	81		New bilateral relationships created:[a]	21
			FDI inward stock:	2 691	17.6		
			Intraregional FDI inflows:	28			
Tripartite Agreement	COMESA, EAC and SADC	26[b]	GDP:	1 166	1.6	Overlap with current BITs:	43
			Exports:	355	2.4	Overlap with current "other IIAs":	8
			Intraregional exports:	68		New bilateral relationships created:[a]	67
			FDI inward stock:	372	2.4		
			Intraregional FDI inflows:	1.3			
EU-Japan FTA	EU (28), Japan	29	GDP:	22 729	32.0	Overlap with current BITs:	0
			Exports:	2 933	19.9	Overlap with current "other IIAs":	0
			Intraregional exports:	154		New bilateral relationships created:[a]	28
			FDI inward stock:	2 266	14.8		
			Intraregional FDI inflows:	3.6			
PACER Plus	Australia, New Zealand, Pacific Islands Forum developing countries	15	GDP:	1 756	2.5	Overlap with current BITs:	1
			Exports:	299	2.0	Overlap with current "other IIAs":	2
			Intraregional exports:	24		New bilateral relationships created:[a]	103
			FDI inward stock:	744	4.9		
			Intraregional FDI inflows:	1			
RCEP	ASEAN countries and Australia, China, Japan, India, Republic of Korea and New Zealand	16	GDP:	21 113	29.7	Overlap with current BITs:	68
			Exports:	5 226	35.4	Overlap with current "other IIAs":	28
			Intraregional exports:	2 195		New bilateral relationships created:[a]	5
			FDI inward stock:	3 618	23.7		
			Intraregional FDI inflows:	93			
TPP	Australia, Brunei Darussalam, Canada, Chile, Japan, Malaysia, Mexico, New Zealand, Peru, Singapore, United States and Viet Nam	12	GDP:	26 811	37.7	Overlap with current BITs:	14
			Exports:	4 345	29.4	Overlap with current "other IIAs":	26
			Intraregional exports:	2 012		New bilateral relationships created:[a]	22
			FDI inward stock:	7 140	46.7		
			Intraregional FDI inflows:	136.1			
TTIP	EU (28), United States	29	GDP:	31 784	44.7	Overlap with current BITs:	9
			Exports:	3 680	24.9	Overlap with current "other IIAs":	0
			Intraregional exports:	649		New bilateral relationships created:[a]	19
			FDI inward stock:	5 985	39.2		
			Intraregional FDI inflows:	152			

Source: UNCTAD.

[a] "New bilateral relationships" refers to the number of new bilateral IIA relationships created between countries upon signature of the megaregional agreement in question.

[b] Overlapping membership in COMESA, EAC and SADC have been taken into account.

Note: This table does not take into account the negotiations for the Trade in Services Agreement (TISA) which have sectoral focus.

ASEAN: Brunei Darussalam, Cambodia, Indonesia, Lao People's Democratic Republic, Malaysia, Myanmar, Philippines, Singapore, Thailand and Viet Nam.

COMESA: Burundi, the Comoros, the Democratic Republic of the Congo, Djibouti, Egypt, Eritrea, Ethiopia, Kenya, Libya, Madagascar, Malawi, Mauritius, Rwanda, Seychelles, Sudan, Swaziland, Uganda, Zambia and Zimbabwe.

EAC: Burundi, Kenya, Rwanda, Uganda, the United Republic of Tanzania.

EU (28): Austria, Belgium, Bulgaria, Croatia, Cyprus, the Czech Republic, Denmark, Estonia, Finland, France, Germany, Greece, Hungary, Ireland, Italy, Latvia, Lithuania, Luxembourg, Malta, the Netherlands, Poland, Portugal, Romania, the Slovak Republic, Slovenia, Spain, Sweden and the United Kingdom.

Pacific Island Forum countries: Australia, Cook Islands, Federated States of Micronesia, Kiribati, Nauru, New Zealand, Niue, Palau, Papua New Guinea, the Marshall Islands, Samoa, Solomon Islands, Tonga, Tuvalu and Vanuatu.

SADC: Angola, Botswana, the Democratic Republic of the Congo, Lesotho, Madagascar, Malawi, Mauritius, Mozambique, Namibia, Seychelles, South Africa, Swaziland, the United Republic of Tanzania, Zambia and Zimbabwe.

Partnership (RCEP), accounting for close to half of the global population. In terms of GDP, the biggest is TTIP, representing 45 per cent of global GDP. In terms of global FDI inward stock, TPP tops the list.

Megaregional agreements are also significant in terms of the new bilateral IIA relationships they can create. For example, when it is concluded, the Pacific Agreement on Closer Economic Relations (PACER) Plus may create 103 such new relationships.

b. Substantive issues at hand

Megaregional negotiations cover several of the issues typically addressed in negotiations for BITs or "other IIAs". For the investment chapter, negotiators need to devise key IIA provisions, including the clause setting out the treaty's coverage of investments and investors, the treaty's substantive standards of protection (e.g. national treatment,

most-favoured-nation (MFN) treatment, FET, expropriation, transfer of funds, performance requirements), its liberalization dimension and its procedural protections, notably ISDS.

Similar to what occurs in negotiations for "other IIAs", megaregional negotiators are also tasked with addressing treaty elements beyond the investment chapter that have important investment implications. The protection of intellectual property rights (IPRs), the liberalization of trade in services and the facilitation of employee work visas are examples in this regard.

In addition to issues that have been considered in numerous past agreements, some megaregional negotiators also face the challenge of dealing with new issues that have emerged only recently. How to address issues related to State-owned enterprises or sovereign wealth funds and how to pursue regulatory cooperation are cases in point.

Table III.6. Selected investment and investment-related issues under consideration in negotiations of megaregional agreements

Selected investment provisions	Selected investment-related provisions
Scope and coverage: the definition of public debt (i.e. whether or not debt instruments of a Party or of a State enterprise are considered covered investments), the type of sovereign wealth funds (SWF) investments that would be protected (e.g. only direct investments or also portfolio investments)	*Regulatory cooperation*: the requirement to provide information and to exchange data on regulatory initiatives (i.e. draft laws/regulations), the requirement to examine – where appropriate – regulations' impact on international trade and investment prior to their adoption, the use of mutual recognition arrangements in specific sectors, the establishment of a regulatory cooperation council
Performance requirements: the prohibition of performance requirements beyond those listed in TRIMs (e.g. prohibiting the use or purchase of a specific (domestic) technology)	*Intellectual property rights (IPRs)*: the property protected (e.g. undisclosed test data), the type of protection offered (e.g. exclusive rights) and the level of protection offered (e.g. extending the term of patent protection beyond what is required by TRIPS)
Standards of treatment: different techniques for clarifying the meaning of indirect expropriation and fair and equitable treatment (FET)	*Trade in services*: the nature of services investment covered ("trade in services" by means of commercial presence) and the relationship with the investment chapter
Investment liberalization: the depth of commitments, the possibility of applying ISDS to pre-establishment commitments	*Financial services*: the coverage of "commercial presence"-type investments in the sector and the promotion of more harmonized regulatory practices
Denial of benefit: a requirement for investors to conduct "substantial business operations" in the home country in order to benefit from treaty protection	*Government procurement*: the obligation to not discriminate against foreign companies bidding for State contracts and the opening of certain aspects of governments' procurement markets to foreign companies
Transfer of funds exceptions: the scope and depth of exceptions to free transfer obligations	*Competition*: provisions on competitive neutrality (e.g. to ensure that competition laws of Parties apply to SOEs)
ISDS: the inclusion of ISDS and its scope (e.g. only for post-establishment or also for pre-establishment commitments), potential carve-outs or special mechanisms applying to sensitive issues (e.g. public debt or financial issues), methods for effective dispute prevention and the inclusion of an appeals mechanism	*Corporate social responsibility (CSR)*: the inclusion of non-binding provisions on CSR
Key personnel: the inclusion of provisions facilitating the presence of (foreign) natural persons for business purposes	*General exceptions*: the inclusion of GATT- or GATS-type general exceptions for measures aimed at legitimate public policy objectives

Source: UNCTAD.

In all of this, negotiators have to carefully consider the possible interactions between megaregional agreements and other investment treaties; between the different chapters of the agreement; and between the clauses in the investment chapter of the agreement in question.

Table III.6 offers selected examples of key issues under discussion in various current megaregional negotiations. The table is not exhaustive, and the inclusion of an issue does not mean that it is being discussed in all megaregional agreements. Moreover, it should be noted that discussions on investment issues are at different stages (e.g. negotiations for the Tripartite agreement plan to address investment issues only in the second phase, which is yet to start). In sum, the table offers a snapshot of selected issues.

Negotiations of megaregional agreements may present opportunities for the formulation of a new generation of investment treaties that respond to the sustainable development imperative. Negotiators have to determine where on a spectrum between utmost investor protection and maximum policy flexibility a particular agreement should be located. This also offers space to apply lessons learned about how IIAs have been implemented and how they have been interpreted by arbitral tribunals.

c. Consolidation or further complexities

Depending on how they are implemented, megaregionals can either help consolidate the IIA regime or create further complexities and inconsistencies.

Once concluded, megaregional agreements may have important systemic implications for the IIA regime. They offer opportunities for consolidating today's multifaceted and multilayered treaty network. This is not automatic however. They could also create new inconsistencies resulting from overlaps with existing agreements.

Megaregional agreements present an opportunity to consolidate today's network of close to 3,240 IIAs. Overlapping with 140 agreements (45 bilateral and regional "other IIAs" and 95 BITs), the six megaregional agreements in which BITs-type provisions are on the agenda have the potential of transforming the fragmented IIA network into a more consolidated and manageable one of fewer, but more inclusive and more significant, IIAs. At the same time, the six agreements would create close to 200 new bilateral IIA relationships (figure III.10).

The extent of consolidation of the IIA regime that megaregional agreements may bring about

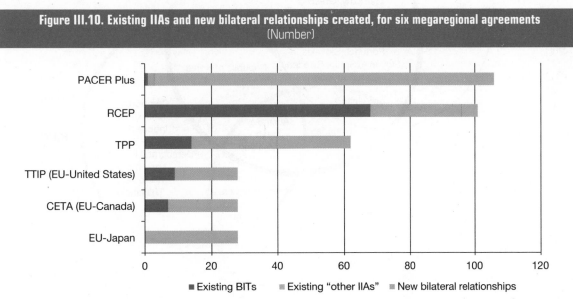

Figure III.10. Existing IIAs and new bilateral relationships created, for six megaregional agreements
(Number)

Source: UNCTAD, IIA database.
Note: "New bilateral relationships" refers to the number of new IIA relationships created between countries upon signature of a megaregional agreement.

depends crucially on whether the negotiating parties opt to replace existing bilateral IIAs with the pertinent megaregional agreement. The currently prevailing approach to regionalism has resulted in a degree of *parallelism* that adds complexities and inconsistencies to the system (*WIR13*). The coexistence of megaregional agreements and other investment treaties concluded between members of these agreements raises questions about which treaty should prevail.[60] This may change, however, with the increasing number of agreements involving the EU, where prior BITs between individual EU member States and megaregional partners will be replaced by the new EU-wide treaties.

In addition, megaregional agreements may create new investment standards on top of those that exist in the IIAs of the members of the megaregional agreement with third countries – be they bilateral or plurilateral. Insofar as these standards will differ, they increase the chance for "treaty shopping" by investors for the best clauses from different treaties

by using the MFN clause. This can work both ways, in terms of importing higher standards into megaregional agreements from other agreements ("cherry-picking") or benefiting from megaregionals' higher standards in other investment relationships ("free-riding").

Several arbitral decisions have interpreted the MFN clause as allowing investors to invoke more investor-friendly language from treaties between the respondent State and a third country, thereby effectively sidelining the "base" treaty (i.e. the treaty between the investor's home and host countries) on the basis of which the case was brought. Therefore, the issue of "cherry-picking" requires careful attention in the drafting of the MFN clause (UNCTAD, 2010; see also IPFSD).

Insofar as "free-riding" and excluding others from the megaregional agreement's benefits are concerned, treaty provisions that except investor treatment granted within a regional economic integration or-

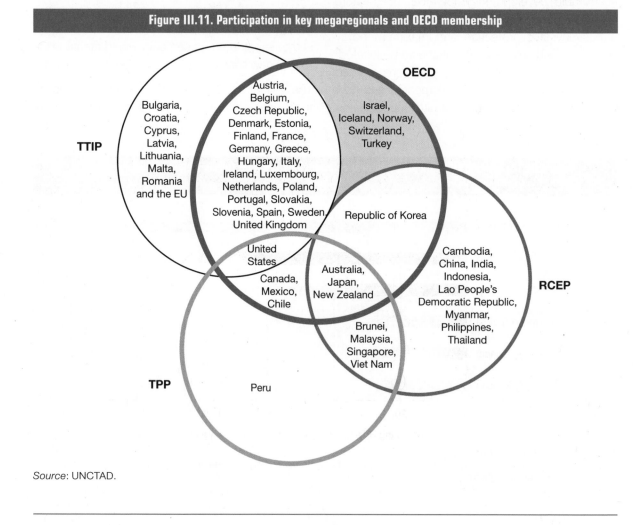

Figure III.11. Participation in key megaregionals and OECD membership

Source: UNCTAD.

ganization from the application of the MFN clause (the so-called regional economic integration organization, or REIO clause) can apply (UNCTAD, 2004).

d. Implications for existing plurilateral cooperation

Megaregional agreements can have implications for existing plurilateral cooperation.

At the plurilateral level, they raise questions about their future relationship with existing investment codes, such as the OECD instruments (i.e. the OECD Codes on Liberalization of Capital Movements and on Liberalization of Current Invisible Operations) and the Energy Charter Treaty (ECT).

Of the 34 OECD members, 22 would be bound by the TTIP's investment provisions, 7 participate in TPP and 4 in RCEP, resulting in a situation where all but 5 (Iceland, Israel, Norway, Switzerland and Turkey) would be party to one or more megaregional agreement (figure III.11). Similarly, 28 ECT members would be subject to the TTIP's provisions, and 2 ECT members are engaged in the TPP and 2 in RCEP negotiations.[61]

Once concluded, some megaregional agreements will therefore result in considerable overlap with existing plurilateral instruments and in possible inconsistencies that could give rise to "free-riding" problems.

Related to this are questions concerning the rationale for including an investment protection

chapter (including ISDS) in megaregional agreements between developed countries that have advanced regulatory and legal systems and generally open investment environments. To date, developed countries have been less active in concluding IIAs among themselves. The share of "North-North" BITs is only 9 per cent (259 of today's total of 2,902 BITs). Moreover, 200 of these BITs are intra-EU treaties – many of which were concluded by transition economies before they joined the EU (figure III.12).

e. Implications for non-participating third parties

In terms of systemic implications for the IIA regime, megaregional agreements may also affect countries that are not involved in the negotiations. These agreements can create risks but also offer opportunities for non-parties.

There is the risk of potential marginalization of third parties, which could further turn them from "rule makers" into "rule takers" (i.e. megaregional agreements make it even more difficult for non-parties to effectively contribute to the shaping of the global IIA regime). To the extent that megaregional agreements create new IIA rules, non-parties may be left behind in terms of the latest treaty practices.

At the same time, megaregional agreements may present opportunities. Apart from "free-riding" (see above), megaregional agreements can also have a demonstrating effect on other negotiations. This

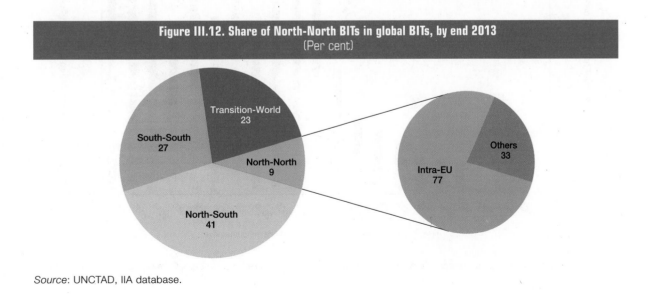

Figure III.12. Share of North-North BITs in global BITs, by end 2013
(Per cent)

Source: UNCTAD, IIA database.

applies to both the inclusion of new rules and the reformulation or revision or omission of existing standards.

Third parties may also have the option of acceding to megaregional agreements. This could, however, reinforce their role as "rule-takers" and expose them to the conditionalities that sometimes emanate from in accession procedures. This is particularly problematic, given that many non-participating third countries are poor developing countries.

* * *

Megaregional agreements are likely to have a major impact on global investment rule making in the coming years. This also includes the overall pursuit of sustainable development objectives. Transparency in rule making, with broader stakeholder engagement, can help in finding optimal solutions and ensuring buy-in from those affected by a treaty. It is similarly important that the interests of non-parties are adequately considered.

The challenge of marginalization that potentially arises from megaregional agreements can be overcome by "open regionalism". A multilateral platform for dialogue among regional groupings on key emerging issues would be helpful in this regard.

3. Trends in investor–State dispute settlement

With 44 new cases, the year saw the second largest number of known investment arbitrations filed in a single year, bringing the total number of known cases to 568.

In 2013, investors initiated at least 56 known ISDS cases pursuant to IIAs (UNCTAD 2014) (figure III.13). This comes close to the previous year's record-high number of new claims. In 2013 investors brought an unusually high number of cases against developed States (26); in the remaining cases, developing (19) and transition (11) economies are the respondents.

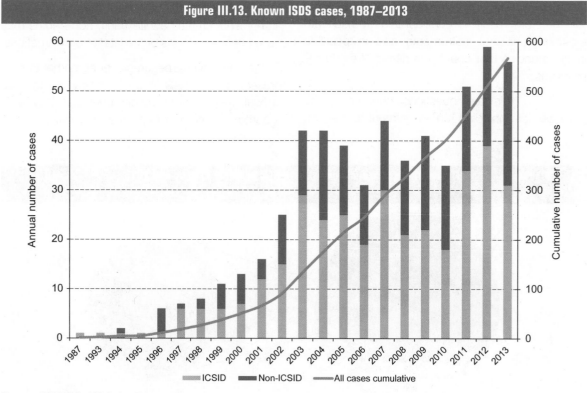

Figure III.13. Known ISDS cases, 1987–2013

Source: UNCTAD, ISDS database.
Note: Due to new information becoming available for 2012 and earlier years the number of known ISDS cases has been revised.

Forty-two per cent of cases initiated in 2013 were brought against member States of the EU. In all of these EU-related arbitrations, except for one, the claimants are EU nationals bringing the proceedings under either intra-EU BITs or the ECT (sometimes relying on both at the same time). In more than half of the cases against EU member States, the respondents are the Czech Republic or Spain.

In fact, nearly a quarter of all arbitrations initiated in 2013 involve challenges to regulatory actions by those two countries that affected the renewable energy sector. With respect to the Czech Republic, investors are challenging the 2011 amendments that placed a levy on electricity generated from solar power plants. They argue that these amendments undercut the viability of the investments and modified the incentive regime that had been originally put in place to stimulate the use of renewable energy in the country. The claims against Spain arise out of a 7 per cent tax on the revenues of power generators and a reduction of subsidies for renewable energy producers.

Investors also challenged the cancellation or alleged breaches of contracts by States, alleged direct or de facto expropriation, revocation of licenses or permits, regulation of energy tariffs, allegedly wrongful criminal prosecution and land zoning decisions. Investors also complained about

the creation of a State monopoly in a previously competitive sector, allegedly unfair tax assessments or penalties, invalidation of patents and legislation relating to sovereign bonds.

By the end of 2013, the number of known ISDS cases reached 568, and the number of countries that have been respondents in at least one dispute increased to 98. (For comparison, the World Trade Organization had registered 474 disputes by that time, involving 53 members as respondents.) About three quarters of these ISDS cases were brought against developing and transition economies, of which countries in Latin America and the Caribbean account for the largest share. EU countries ranked third as respondents, with 21 per cent of all cases (figure III.14). The majority of known disputes continued to accrue under the ICSID Convention and the ICSID Additional Facility Rules (62 per cent), and the UNCITRAL Rules (28 per cent). Other arbitral venues have been used only rarely.

The overwhelming majority (85 per cent) of all ISDS claims by end 2013 were brought by investors from developed countries, including the EU (53 per cent) and the United States (22 per cent).[62] Among the EU member States, claimants come most frequently from the Netherlands (61 cases), the United Kingdom (43) and Germany (39).

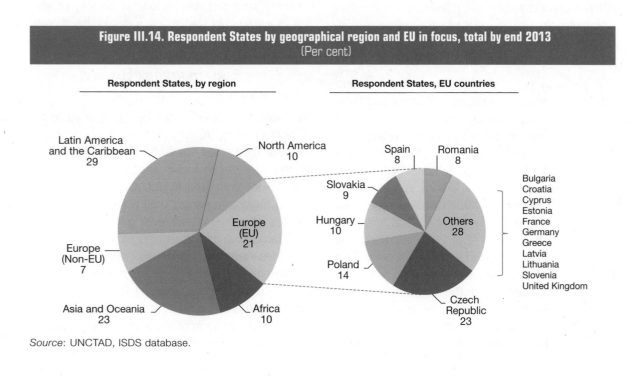

Figure III.14. Respondent States by geographical region and EU in focus, total by end 2013
(Per cent)

Respondent States, by region

Respondent States, EU countries

Latin America and the Caribbean 29

North America 10

Spain 8

Romania 8

Slovakia 9

Bulgaria
Croatia
Cyprus
Estonia
France
Germany
Greece
Latvia
Lithuania
Slovenia
United Kingdom

Hungary 10

Europe (EU) 21

Others 28

Europe (Non-EU) 7

Poland 14

Asia and Oceania 23

Africa 10

Czech Republic 23

Source: UNCTAD, ISDS database.

The three investment instruments most frequently used as a basis for all ISDS claims have been NAFTA (51 cases), the ECT (42) and the Argentina–United States BIT (17). At least 72 arbitrations have been brought pursuant to intra-EU BITs.

At least 37 arbitral decisions were issued in 2013, including decisions on objections to a tribunal's jurisdiction, on the substantive merits of the claims, on compensation and on applications for annulment of an arbitral award. For only 23 of these decisions are the texts in the public domain.

Known decisions on jurisdictional objections issued in 2013 show a 50/50 split – half of them rejecting the tribunal's jurisdiction over the dispute and half affirming it and thereby letting the claims proceed to their assessment on the merits. Of eight decisions on the merits that were rendered in 2013, seven accepted – at least in part – the claims of the investors, and one dismissed all of the claims; this represents a higher share of rulings in favour of investors than in previous years. At least five decisions rendered in 2013 awarded compensation to the investors, including an award of $935 million plus interest, the second highest known award in the history of ISDS.[63]

Arbitral developments in 2013 brought the overall number of concluded cases to 274.[64] Of these, approximately 43 per cent were decided in favour of the State and 31 per cent in favour of the investor. Approximately 26 per cent of cases were settled. In these cases, the specific terms of settlement typically remain confidential.

The growing number of cases and the broad range of policy issues raised in this context have turned ISDS into arguably the most controversial issue in international investment policymaking. Over the past year, the public discourse about the pros and cons of ISDS has continued to gain momentum. This has already spurred some action. For example, UNCITRAL adopted new Rules on Transparency in Treaty-based Investor–State Arbitration on 11 July 2013. Similarly, the Energy Charter Secretariat invited Contracting Parties to discuss measures to reform investment dispute settlement under the ECT. In all of this effort, UNCTAD's IPFSD table on policy options for IIAs (notably section 6) and the roadmap for five ways to reform the ISDS system identified in

WIR13 can help and guide policymakers and other stakeholders (figure III.15).

4. Reform of the IIA regime: four paths of action and a way forward

Four different paths of IIA regime reform emerge: status quo, disengagement, selective adjustments and systematic reform.

The IIA regime is undergoing a period of reflection, review and reform. While almost all countries are parties to one or several IIAs, few are satisfied with the current regime for several reasons: growing uneasiness about the actual effects of IIAs in terms of promoting FDI or reducing policy and regulatory space, increasing exposure to ISDS and the lack of specific pursuit of sustainable development objectives. Furthermore, views on IIAs are strongly diverse, even within countries. To this adds the complexity and multifaceted nature of the IIA regime and the absence of a multilateral institution (like the WTO for trade). All of this makes it difficult to take a systematic approach towards comprehensively reforming the IIA (and the ISDS) regime. Hence, IIA reform efforts have so far been relatively modest.

Many countries follow a "wait and see" approach. Hesitation in respect to more holistic and far-reaching reform reflects a government's dilemma: more substantive changes might undermine a country's attractiveness for foreign investment, and first movers could particularly suffer in this regard. In addition, there are questions about the concrete content of a "new" IIA model and fears that some approaches could aggravate the current complexity and uncertainty.

IIA reform has been occurring at different levels of policymaking. At the national level, countries have revised their model treaties, sometimes on the basis of inclusive and transparent multi-stakeholder processes. In fact, at least 40 countries (and 5 regional organizations) are currently in the process of reviewing and revising their approaches to international-investment-related rule making. Countries have also continued negotiating IIAs at the bilateral and regional levels, with novel provisions and reformulations (table III.4). Megaregional agreements are a case in point. A few countries have walked away from IIAs, terminating some of their BITs or denouncing international arbitration

Table III.7. Four paths of action: an overview		
Path	**Content of policy action**	**Level of policy action**
Systematic reform	**Designing investment-related international commitments that:** • create proactive sustainable-development-oriented IIAs (e.g. add SDG investment promotion) • effectively rebalance rights and obligations in IIAs (e.g. add investor responsibilities, preserve policy space) • comprehensively reform ISDS (i.e. follow five ways identified in *WIR 13*) • properly manage interactions and foster coherence between different levels of investment policies and investment and other public policies (e.g. multi-stakeholder review)	**Taking policy action at three levels of policymaking (simultaneously and/or sequentially):** • national (e.g. creating a new model IIA) • bilateral/regional (e.g. (re-)negotiating IIAs based on new model) • multilateral (e.g. multi-stakeholder consensus-building, including collective learning)
Selective adjustments	**Pursuing selective changes to:** • add a sustainable development dimension to IIAs (e.g. sustainable development in preamble) • move towards rebalancing rights and obligations (e.g. non-binding CSR provisions) • change specific aspects of ISDS (e.g. early discharge of frivolous claims) • selectively address policy interaction (e.g. not lowering standards clauses)	**Taking policy action at three levels of policymaking (selectively):** • national (e.g. modifying a new model IIA) • bilateral/regional (e.g. negotiating IIAs based on revised models or issuing joint interpretations) • multilateral (e.g. sharing of experiences)
Status quo	**Not pursuing any substantive change to IIA clauses or investment-related international commitments**	**Taking policy action at bilateral and regional levels:** • continue negotiating IIAs based on existing models • leave existing treaties untouched
Disengagement	**Eliminating investment-related commitments**	**Taking policy action regarding different aspects:** • national (e.g. eliminating consent to ISDS in domestic law and terminating investment contracts) • bilateral/regional (e.g. terminating existing IIAs)

Source: UNCTAD.

conventions. At the multilateral level, countries have come together to discuss specific aspects of IIA reform.

Bringing together these recent experiences allows the mapping of four broad paths that are emerging regarding actions for reforming the international investment regime (table III.7):

• Maintaining the status quo

• Disengaging from the regime

• Introducing selective adjustments

• Engaging in systematic reform

Each of the four paths of action comes with its own advantages and disadvantages, and responds to specific concerns in a distinctive way (table III.7).

Depending on the overall objective that is being pursued, what is considered an advantage by some stakeholders may be perceived as a challenge by others. In addition, the four paths of action, as pursued today, are not mutually exclusive; a country may adopt elements from one or several of them, and the content of a particular IIA may be influenced by one or several paths of action.

This section discusses each path from the perspective of strategic regime reform. The discussion begins with the two most opposed approaches to investment-related international commitments: at one end is the path that maintains the status quo; at the other is the path that disengages from the IIA regime. In between are the two paths of action that opt for reform of the regime, albeit to different degrees.

The underlying premise of the analysis here is that the case for reform has already been made (see above). UNCTAD's IPFSD, with its principle of "dynamic policymaking" – which calls for a continuing assessment of the effectiveness of policy instruments – is but one example. The questions are not about whether to reform the international investment regime but how to do so. Furthermore, today's questions are not only about the change to one aspect in a particular agreement but about the comprehensive reorientation of the global IIA regime to balance investor protection with sustainable development considerations.

a. Maintaining the status quo

At one end of the spectrum is a country's choice to maintain the status quo. Refraining from substantive changes to the way that investment-related international commitments are made sends an image of continuity and investor friendliness. This is particularly the case when maintaining the status quo involves the negotiation of new IIAs that are based on existing models. Above all, this path might be attractive for countries with a strong outward investment perspective and for countries that have not yet responded to numerous – and highly politicized – ISDS cases.

Intuitively, this path of action appears to be the easiest and most straightforward to implement. It requires limited resources (e.g. there is no need for assessments, domestic reviews and multi-stakeholder consultations) and avoids unintended, potentially far-reaching consequences arising from innovative approaches to IIA clauses.

At the same time, however, maintaining the status quo does not address any of the challenges arising from today's global IIA regime and might contribute to a further stakeholder backlash against IIAs. Moreover, as an increasing number of countries are beginning to reform IIAs, maintaining the status quo (i.e. maintaining BITs and negotiating new ones based on existing templates) may become increasingly difficult.

b. Disengaging from the IIA regime

At the other end of the spectrum is a country's choice to disengage from the international investment regime, be it from individual agreements, multilateral arbitration conventions or the regime as a whole. Unilaterally quitting IIAs sends a strong signal of dissatisfaction with the current regime. This path of action might be particularly attractive for countries in which IIA-related concerns feature prominently in the domestic policy debate.

Intuitively, disengaging from the IIA regime might be perceived as the strongest, or most far-reaching path of action. Ultimately, for inward and outward investors, it would result in the removal of international commitments on investment protection that are enshrined in international treaties. Moreover, this would result in the effective shielding from ISDS-related risks.

However, most of the desired implications will materialize only over time, and only for one treaty at a time. Quitting the system does not immediately protect the State against future ISDS cases, as IIA commitments usually endure for a period through survival clauses. In addition, there may be a need to review national laws and State contracts, as they may also provide for ISDS (including ICSID arbitration), even in the absence of an IIA. Moreover, unless termination is undertaken on a consensual basis, a government's ability to terminate an IIA is limited. Its ability to do so depends on the formulation of the treaty at issue (i.e. the "survival" clause) and may be available only at a particular, limited point in time *(WIR13)*.

Moreover, eliminating single international commitments at a time (treaty by treaty) does not contribute to the reform of the IIA regime as a whole, but only takes care of individual relationships. Only if such treaty termination is pursued with a view to renegotiation can it also constitute a move towards reforming the entire IIA regime.

c. *Introducing selective adjustments*

Limited, i.e. selective, adjustments that address specific concerns is the path of action that is gaining ground rapidly. It may be particularly attractive for those countries that wish to respond to the challenges posed by IIAs but wish to demonstrate their continued, constructive engagement with the investment regime. It can be directed towards sustainable development and other policy objectives.

This path of action has numerous advantages. The selective choice of modifications can permit the prioritization of "low-hanging fruit" or concerns that appear most relevant and pressing, while leaving the treaty core untouched (see for example, the option of "tailored modifications" in UNCTAD's five paths of reform for ISDS, figure III.15). It also allows the tailoring of the modification to a

particular negotiating counterpart so as to suit a particular economic relationship. Moreover, selective adjustment also allows the testing and piloting of different solutions; the focus on future treaties facilitates straightforward implementation (i.e. changes can be put in practice directly by the parties to individual negotiations); the use of "soft" (i.e. non-binding) modifications minimizes risk; and the incremental step-by-step approach avoids a "big bang" effect (and makes the change less prone to being perceived as reducing the agreement's protective value). Indeed, introducing selective adjustments in new agreements may appear as an appealing – if not the most realistic – option for reducing the mounting pressure on IIAs.

At the same time, however, selective adjustments in *future* IIAs cannot comprehensively address the challenges posed by the *existing* stock of treaties.[65] It cannot fully deal with the interaction of

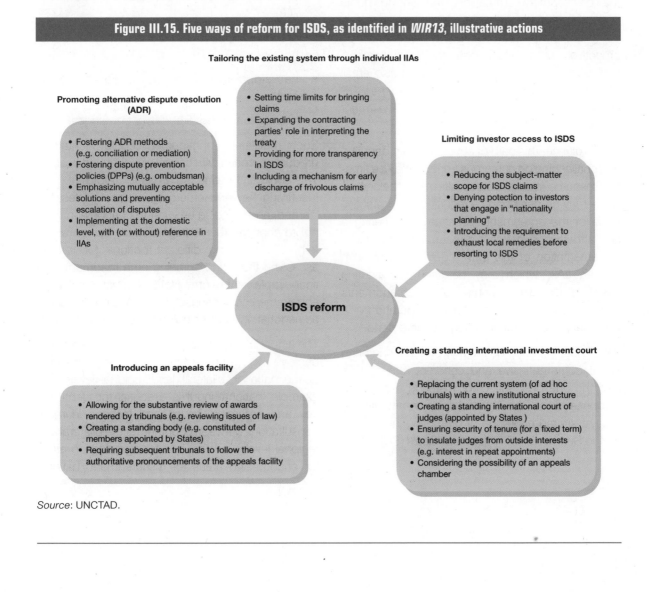

Figure III.15. Five ways of reform for ISDS, as identified in *WIR13*, illustrative actions

Tailoring the existing system through individual IIAs

Promoting alternative dispute resolution (ADR)

- Fostering ADR methods (e.g. conciliation or mediation)
- Fostering dispute prevention policies (DPPs) (e.g. ombudsman)
- Emphasizing mutually acceptable solutions and preventing escalation of disputes
- Implementing at the domestic level, with (or without) reference in IIAs

- Setting time limits for bringing claims
- Expanding the contracting parties' role in interpreting the treaty
- Providing for more transparency in ISDS
- Including a mechanism for early discharge of frivolous claims

Limiting investor access to ISDS

- Reducing the subject-matter scope for ISDS claims
- Denying potection to investors that engage in "nationality planning"
- Introducing the requirement to exhaust local remedies before resorting to ISDS

ISDS reform

Introducing an appeals facility

- Allowing for the substantive review of awards rendered by tribunals (e.g. reviewing issues of law)
- Creating a standing body (e.g. constituted of members appointed by States)
- Requiring subsequent tribunals to follow the authoritative pronouncements of the appeals facility

Creating a standing international investment court

- Replacing the current system (of ad hoc tribunals) with a new institutional structure
- Creating a standing international court of judges (appointed by States)
- Ensuring security of tenure (for a fixed term) to insulate judges from outside interests (e.g. interest in repeat appointments)
- Considering the possibility of an appeals chamber

Source: UNCTAD.

treaties with each other and, unless the selective adjustments address the MFN clause, it can allow for "treaty shopping" and "cherry-picking".[66] It may not satisfy all stakeholders. And, throughout all of this, it may lay the groundwork for further change, thus creating uncertainty instead of stability.

d. Pursuing systematic reform

Pursuing systematic reform means designing international commitments that promote sustainable development and that are in line with the investment and development paradigm shift (*WIR12*). With policy actions at all levels of governance, this is the most comprehensive approach to reforming the current IIA regime.

This path of action would entail the design of a new IIA treaty model that effectively addresses the three challenges mentioned above (increasing the development dimension, rebalancing rights and obligations, and managing the systemic complexity of the IIA regime), and that focuses on proactively promoting investment for sustainable development. Systematic reform would also entail comprehensively dealing with the reform of the ISDS system, as outlined in last year's *World Investment Report* (figure III.15).

At first glance, this path of action appears daunting and challenging on numerous fronts. It may be time- and resource-intensive. Its result – more "balanced" IIAs – may be perceived as reducing the protective value of the agreements at issue and offering a less attractive investment climate. Comprehensive implementation of this path requires dealing with existing IIAs, which may be seen as affecting investors' "acquired rights." And amendments or renegotiation may require the cooperation of a potentially large number of treaty counterparts.

Yet this path of action is the only one that can bring about comprehensive and coherent reform. It is also the one best suited for fostering a common response from the international community to today's shared challenge of promoting investment for the Sustainable Development Goals (SDGs).

* * *

A way forward: UNCTAD's perspective

Multilateral facilitation and a comprehensive gradual approach to reform could effectively address the systemic challenges of the IIA regime.

Whichever paths countries take, a multilateral process is helpful to bring all parties together. It also brings a number of other benefits to the reform process:

- facilitating a more holistic and more coordinated approach, in the interest of sustainable development (see chapter IV) and the interests of developing countries, particularly the LDCs;

- factoring in universally agreed principles related to business and development, including those adopted in the UN context and international standards;

- building on the 11 principles of investment policymaking set out in UNCTAD's IPFSD (table III.8);

- ensuring inclusiveness by involving all stakeholders;

- backstopping bilateral and regional actions; and

- helping to address first mover challenges.

Such multilateral engagement could facilitate a gradual approach with carefully sequenced actions. This could first define the areas for reform (e.g. by identifying key and emerging issues and lessons learned, and agreeing on what to change and what not to change), then design a roadmap for reform (e.g. by identifying different options for reform, assessing them and agreeing on a roadmap), and finally implement reform. Naturally, such multilateral engagement in consensus building is not the same as negotiating legally binding rules on investment.

The actual implementation of reform-oriented policy choices will be determined by and happening at the national, bilateral, and regional levels. For example, national input is essential for identifying key and emerging issues and lessons learned; consultations between countries (at the bilateral and regional levels) are required for agreeing on areas for change and areas for disagreement; national

Table III.8. Core Principles for investment policymaking for sustainable development

Area	Core Principles
1 **Investment for sustainable development**	• The overarching objective of investment policymaking is to promote investment for inclusive growth and sustainable development.
2 **Policy coherence**	• Investment policies should be grounded in a country's overall development strategy. All policies that impact on investment should be coherent and synergetic at both the national and international levels.
3 **Public governance and institutions**	• Investment policies should be developed involving all stakeholders, and embedded in an institutional framework based on the rule of law that adheres to high standards of public governance and ensures predictable, efficient and transparent procedures for investors.
4 **Dynamic policymaking**	• Investment policies should be regularly reviewed for effectiveness and relevance and adapted to changing development dynamics.
5 **Balanced rights and obligations**	• Investment policies should be balanced in setting out rights and obligations of States and investors in the interest of development for all.
6 **Right to regulate**	• Each country has the sovereign right to establish entry and operational conditions for foreign investment, subject to international commitments, in the interest of the public good and to minimize potential negative effects.
7 **Openness to investment**	• In line with each country's development strategy, investment policy should establish open, stable and predictable entry conditions for investment.
8 **Investment protection and treatment**	• Investment policies should provide adequate protection to established investors. The treatment of established investors should be non-discriminatory.
9 **Investment promotion and facilitation**	• Policies for investment promotion and facilitation should be aligned with sustainable development goals and designed to minimize the risk of harmful competition for investment.
10 **Corporate governance and responsibility**	• Investment policies should promote and facilitate the adoption of and compliance with best international practices of corporate social responsibility and good corporate governance.
11 **International cooperation**	• The international community should cooperate to address shared investment-for-development policy challenges, particularly in least developed countries. Collective efforts should also be made to avoid investment protectionism.

Source: IPFSD.

experiences are necessary for identifying different options for reform; and sharing such experiences at the multilateral level can help in assessing different options.

The successful pursuit of these steps requires effective support in four dimensions: consensus building, analytical support, technical assistance, and multi-stakeholder engagement.

• A multilateral focal point and platform could provide the infrastructure and institutional backstopping for *consensus building* activities that create a comfort zone for engagement, collective learning, sharing of experiences and identifyication of best practices and the way forward.

• A multilateral focal point could provide general backstopping and *analytical support*, with evidence-based policy analysis and system-wide information to provide a global picture and bridge the information gap.

• A multilateral focal point and platform could also offer effective *technical assistance*, particularly for low-income and vulnerable developing countries (including LDCs, LLDCs and SIDS) that face challenges when striving to engage effectively in IIA reform, be it at the bilateral or the regional level. Technical assistance is equally important when it comes to the implementation of policy choices at the national level.

• A multilateral platform can also help ensure the *inclusiveness and universality* of the process. International investment policymakers (e.g. IIA negotiators) would form the core of such an effort but be joined by a broad set of other investment-development stakeholders.

Through all of these means, a multilateral focal point and platform can effectively support national, bilateral and regional investment policymaking, facilitating efforts towards redesigning international commitments in line with today's sustainable development priorities. UNCTAD already offers some of these support functions. UNCTAD's 2014 World Investment Forum will offer a further opportunity in this regard.

Notes

1   Ministry of Commerce and Industry, Press Note No. 6, 22 August 2013.

2   Ministry of Science, ITC and Future Planning, Telecommunications Business Act Amendments, 14 August 2013.

3   Telecommunications Reform Decree, *Official Gazette*, 11 June 2013.

4   Ministry of Commerce and Industry, Press Note No. 6, 22 August 2013.

5   Indonesia Investment Coordinating Board, Presidential Decree No. 39/2014, 23 April 2014.

6   *Official Gazette*, 24 May 2013.

7   *Official Gazette*, No. 20 Extraordinary, Law 118, 16 April 2014.

8   Decree 313/2013, *Official Gazette* No. 026, 23 September 2013.

9   Ministry of Trade, Industry and Energy, "Korea Introduces Mini Foreign Investment Zones", 26 April 2013.

10 Ministry of Commerce, "Insurance Coverage to Foreign Buyers", 2 January 2013.

11 *Official Gazette*, 18 December 2013.

12 Etihad Airways, "Etihad Airways, Jat Airways and Government of Serbia unveil strategic partnership to secure future of Serbian National Airline", 1 August 2013.

13 Ministry of Finance, "The Parliament Gave a Green Light to the Privatization of 15 Companies", 30 June 2013.

14 *Official Gazette*, 20 December 2013.

15 Law No. 195-13, *Official Gazette*, 8 January 2014.

16 Ministry of International Trade and Industry, "National Automotive Policy (NAP) 2014", 20 January 2014.

17 Investment Mongolia Agency, "Mongolian Law on Investment", 3 October 2013.

18 Economist Intelligence Unit, "Government streamlines business registration procedures", 9 October 2013.

19 Government of Dubai Media Office, "Mohammed bin Rashid streamlines hotel investment and development in Dubai", 20 January 2014.

20 State Council, "Circular of the State Council on the Framework Plan for the China (Shanghai) Pilot Free Trade Zone", *Guo Fa* [2013] No. 38, 18 September 2013.

21 Embassy of South Sudan, "South Sudan launches modern business and investment city", 22 June 2013.

22 Indonesia Investment Coordinating Board, Presidential Decree No.39/2014, 23 April 2014.

23 Cabinet Decision, 21 February 2013.

24 Parliament of Canada, Bill C-60, Royal Assent (41-1), 26 June 2013.

25 *Official Gazette* No.112, Decree 2014-479, 15 May 2014; Ministry of the Economy, Industrial Renewal and the Digital Economy, Press Release No. 68, 15 May 2014.

26 Ministry of Commerce and Industry, Press Note No. 4, 22 August 2013.

27 Federal Law 15-FZ, "On introducing changes to some legislative acts of the Russian Federation on providing transport security", 3 February 2014.

28 Government of Canada, "Statement by the Honourable James Moore on the Proposed Acquisition of the Allstream Division of Manitoba Telecom Services Inc. by Accelero Capital Holdings", 7 October 2013.

29 "Abbott is denied permission to buy Petrovax", *Kommersant*, 22 April 2013.

30 European Commission, "Mergers: Commission blocks proposed acquisition of TNT Express by UPS", 30 January 2013.

31 Government of the Plurinational State of Bolivia, "Morales dispone nacionalización del paquete accionario de SABSA", press release, 18 February 2013.

32 National Assembly, Law 393 on Financial Services, 21 August 2013.

33 Ley Orgánica de Comunicación, *Official Gazette* No. 22, 25 June 2013.

34 Decree 625, *Official Gazette* No. 6.117 Extraordiary, 4 December 2013.

35 First published in UNCTAD Investment Policy Monitor No.11.

36 National Assembly, Text 1037, 1270, 1283 and adopted text 214, 1 October 2013.

37 *Official Gazette* No. 216, 11 October 2013.

38 National Assembly, Act on Supporting the Return of Overseas Korean Enterprises, 27 June 2013.

39 The White House, Office of the Press Secretary, "Executive Order: Establishment of the SelectUSA Initiative", 15 June 2011.

40 Of 257 IPAs contacted, 75 completed the questionnaire, representing an overall response rate of 29 per cent. Respondents included 62 national and 13 subnational agencies. Regarding the geographical breakdown, 24 per cent of respondents were from developed countries, 24 per cent from countries in Africa, 21 per cent from countries in Latin America and the Caribbean, 19 per cent from countries in Asia and 8 per cent from transition economies.

41 The survey also included investment facilitation as a policy instrument for attracting and benefiting from FDI. However, as that instrument falls outside the scope of this section, related results have been not been included here.

42 Deloitte, Tax News Flash No. 1/2012, 8 February 2012.

43 "Regulations for application of the Investment Promotion Act", *Official Gazette* No. 62, 10 August 2010.

44 "PLN727 million form the budget for the support of hi-tech investment projects", *Invest in Poland*, 5 July 2011.

45 Government Resolution No. 917 of 10 November 2011, *The Russian Gazette*, 18 November 2011.

46 National Agency for Investment Development, "The incentives regime applicable to the Wilayas of the South and the Highlands", 4 January 2012.

47 Ministry of Commerce, "Public Notice No. 4 [2009] of the General Administration of Customs", 9 January 2009.

48 "Okinawa, Tokyo designated as 'strategic special zone", *Nikkei Asian Review*, 28 March 2014.

49 For more details on policy recommendations, see the National Investment Policy Guidelines of UNCTAD's IPFSD.

50 "Other IIAs" refers to economic agreements other than BITs that include investment-related provisions (e.g., investment chapters in economic partnership agreements and FTAs, regional economic integration agreements and framework agreements on economic cooperation).

51 The total number of IIAs given in *WIR13* has been revised downward as a result of retroactive adjustments to UNCTAD's database on BITs and other IIAs. Readers are invited to visit UNCTAD's expanded and upgraded database on IIAs, which allows a number of new and more user-friendly search options (http://investmentpolicyhub.unctad.org).

52 Of 148 terminated BITs, 105 were replaced by a new treaty, 27 were unilaterally denounced, and 16 were terminated by consent.

53 South Africa gave notice of the termination of its BIT with Belgium and Luxembourg in 2012.

54 Investments made by investors in South Africa before the BITs' termination will remain protected for another 10 years in the case of Spanish investments (and vice versa), 15 years in the case of Dutch investments and 20 years in the cases of German and Swiss investments. Investments made by Dutch investors in Indonesia will remain protected for an additional 15 years after the end of the BIT.

55 This figure includes agreements for which negotiations have been finalized but which have not yet been signed.

56 See annex table III.3 of *WIR12* and annex table III.1 of *WIR13*. Note that in the case of "other IIAs", these exceptions are counted if they are included in the agreement's investment chapter or if they relate to the agreement as a whole.

58 This definition of "megaregional agreement" does not hinge on the requirement that the negotiating parties jointly meet a specific threshold in terms of share of global trade or global FDI.

59 The number avoids double counting by taking into account the overlap of negotiating countries, e.g. between TPP and RCEP or between TTIP and TPP, as well as between countries negotiating one agreement (Tripartite).

60 This is an issue governed by the Vienna Convention on the Law of Treaties.

61 "Membership in the Energy Charter Treaty", as counted here, includes States in which ratification of the treaty is still pending.

62 A State is counted if the claimant, or one of the co-claimants, is a national (physical person or company) of the respective State. This means that when a case is brought by claimants of different nationalities, it is counted for each nationality.

63 *Mohamed Abdulmohsen Al-Kharafi & Sons Co. v. Libya and others*, Final Arbitral Award, 22 March 2013.

64 A number of arbitral proceedings have been discontinued for reasons other than settlement (e.g., due to the failure to pay the required cost advances to the relevant arbitral institution). The status of some other proceedings is unknown. Such cases have not been counted as "concluded".

65 Unless the new treaty is a renegotiation of an old one (or otherwise supersedes the earlier treaty), modifications are applied only to newly concluded IIAs (leaving existing ones untouched).

66 Commitments made to some treaty partners in old IIAs may filter through to newer IIAs through an MFN clause (depending on its formulation), with possibly unintended consequences.

INVESTING IN THE SDGs: An Action Plan for promoting private sector contributions

CHAPTER IV

A. INTRODUCTION

1. The United Nations' Sustainable Development Goals and implied investment needs

The Sustainable Development Goals (SDGs) that are being formulated by the international community will have very significant implications for investment needs.

Faced with common global economic, social and environmental challenges, the international community is in the process of defining a set of Sustainable Development Goals (SDGs). The SDGs, to be adopted in 2015, are meant to galvanize action by governments, the private sector, international organizations, non-governmental organizations (NGOs) and other stakeholders worldwide by providing direction and setting concrete targets in areas ranging from poverty reduction to food security, health, education, employment, equality, climate change, ecosystems and biodiversity, among others (table IV.1).

The experience with the Millenium Development Goals (MDGs), which were agreed in 2000 at the UN Millennium Summit and will expire in 2015, has shown how achievable measurable targets can help provide direction in a world with many different priorities. They have brought focus to the work of the development community and helped mobilize investment to reduce poverty and achieve notable advances in human well-being in the world's poorest countries. However, the MDGs were not designed to create a dynamic process of investment in sustainable development and resilience to economic, social or environmental shocks. They were focused on a relatively narrow set of fundamental goals – for example, eradicating extreme poverty and hunger, reducing child mortality, improving maternal health – in order to trigger action and spending on targeted development programmes.

The SDGs are both a logical next step (from fundamental goals to broad-based sustainable development) and a more ambitious undertaking. They represent a concerted effort to shift the global economy – developed as well as developing – onto a more sustainable trajectory of long-term growth and development. The agenda is transformative, as for instance witnessed by the number of prospective SDGs that are not primarily oriented to specific economic, social or environmental issues but instead aim to put in place policies, institutions and systems necessary to generate sustained investment and growth.

Where the MDGs required significant financial resources for spending on focused development programmes, the SDGs will necessitate a major escalation in the financing effort for investment in broad-based economic transformation, in areas such as basic infrastructure, clean water and sanitation, renewable energy and agricultural production.

The formulation of the SDGs – and their associated investment needs – takes place against a seemingly unfavourable macroeconomic backdrop. Developed countries are only barely recovering from the financial crisis, and in many countries public sector finances are precarious. Emerging markets, where investment needs in economic infrastructure are greatest, but which also represent new potential

Table IV.1. Overview of prospective SDG focus areas		
• Poverty eradication, building shared prosperity and promoting equality	• Water and sanitation	• Climate change
• Sustainable agriculture, food security and nutrition	• Energy	• Conservation and sustainable use of marine resources, oceans and seas
• Health and population dynamics	• Economic growth, employment infrastructure	• Ecosystems and biodiversity
• Education and lifelong learning	• Industrialization and promotion of equality among nations	• Means of implementation; global partnership for sustainable development
• Gender equality and women's empowerment	• Sustainable cities and human settlements	• Peaceful and inclusive societies, rule of law and capable institutions
	• Sustainable consumption and production	

Source: UN Open Working Group on Sustainable Development Goals, working document, 5-9 May 2014 session.

sources of finance and investment, are showing signs of a slowdown in growth. And vulnerable economies, such as the least developed countries (LDCs), still rely to a significant extent on external sources of finance, including official development assistance (ODA) from donor countries with pressured budgets.

2. Private sector contributions to the SDGs

The role of the public sector is fundamental and pivotal. At the same time the contribution of the private sector is indispensable.

Given the broad scope of the prospective SDGs, private sector contributions can take many forms. Some will primarily place behavioural demands on firms and investors. Private sector good governance in relation to SDGs is key, this includes, e.g.:

- commitment of the business sector to sustainable development;
- commitment specifically to the SDGs;
- transparency and accountability in honoring sustainable development in economic, social and environmental practices;
- responsibility to avoid harm, e.g. environmental externalities, even if such harms are not strictly speaking prohibited;
- partnership with government on maximizing co-benefits of investment.

Beyond good governance aspects, a great deal of financial resources will be necessary.

The investment needs associated with the SDGs will require a step-change in the levels of both public and private investment in all countries, and especially in LDCs and other vulnerable economies. Public finances, though central and fundamental to investment in SDGs, cannot alone meet SDG-implied demands for financing. The combination of huge investment requirements and pressured public budgets – added to the economic transformation objective of the SDGs – means that the role of the private sector is even more important than before. The private sector cannot supplant the big public sector push needed to move investment in the SDGs in the right direction. But an associated

big push in private investment can build on the complementarity and potential synergies in the two sectors to accelerate the pace in realizing the SDGs and meeting crucial targets. In addition to domestic private investment, private investment flows from overseas will be needed in many developing countries, including foreign direct investment (FDI) and other external sources of finance.

At first glance, private investors (and other corporates, such as State-owned firms and sovereign wealth funds; see box IV.1), domestic and foreign, appear to have sufficient funds to potentially cover some of those investment needs. For instance, in terms of foreign sources, the cash holdings of transnational corporations (TNCs) are in the order of $5 trillion; sovereign wealth fund (SWF) assets today exceed $6 trillion; and the holdings of pension funds domiciled in developed countries alone have reached $20 trillion.

At the same time, there are instances of goodwill on the part of the private sector to invest in sustainable development; in consequence, the value of investments explicitly linked to sustainability objectives is growing. Many "innovative financing" initiatives have sprung up, many of which are collaborative efforts between the public and private sectors, as well as international organizations, foundations and NGOs. Signatories of the Principles for Responsible Investment (PRI) have assets under management of almost $35 trillion, an indication that sustainability principles do not necessarily impede the raising of private finance.

Thus there *appears* to be a paradox that has to be addressed. Enormous investment needs and opportunities are associated with sustainable development. Private investors worldwide appear to have sufficient funds available. Yet these funds are not finding their way to sustainable-development-oriented projects, especially in developing countries: e.g. only about 2 per cent of the assets of pension funds and insurers are invested in infrastructure, and FDI to LDCs stands at a meagre 2 per cent of global flows.

The macroeconomic backdrop of this situation is related to the processes which have led to large sums of financial capital being underutilized while parts of the real sector are starved of funds (TDR

2009; TDR 2011; UNCTAD 2011d; Wolf, M. 2010); this chapter deals with some of the microeconomic aspects of shifting such capital to productive investment in the SDGs.[1]

3. The need for a strategic framework for private investment in the SDGs

A strategic framework for private sector investment in SDGs can help structure efforts to mobilize funds, to channel them to SDG sectors, and to maximize impacts and mitigate drawbacks.

Since the formulation of the MDGs, many initiatives aimed at increasing private financial flows to sustainable development projects in developing countries have sprung up. They range from impact investing (investments with explicit social and environmental objectives) to numerous "innovative financing mechanisms" (which may entail partnerships between public and private actors). These private financing initiatives distinguish themselves either by the source of finance (e.g. institutional investors, private funds, corporations), their issue area (general funds, environmental investors, health-focused investors), the degree of recognition and public support, or many other

criteria, ranging from geographic focus to size to investment horizon. All face specific challenges, but broadly there are three common challenges:

- *Mobilizing funds for sustainable development* – raising resources in financial markets or through financial intermediaries that can be invested in sustainable development.

- *Channelling funds to sustainable development projects* – ensuring that available funds make their way to concrete sustainable-development-oriented investment projects on the ground in developing countries, and especially LDCs.

- *Maximizing impact and mitigating drawbacks* – creating an enabling environment and putting in place appropriate safeguards that need to accompany increased private sector engagement in what are often sensitive sectors.

The urgency of solving the problem, i.e. "resolving the paradox", to increase the private sector's contribution to SDG investment is the driving force behind this chapter. UNCTAD's objective is to show how the contribution of the private sector to investment in the SDGs can be increased through

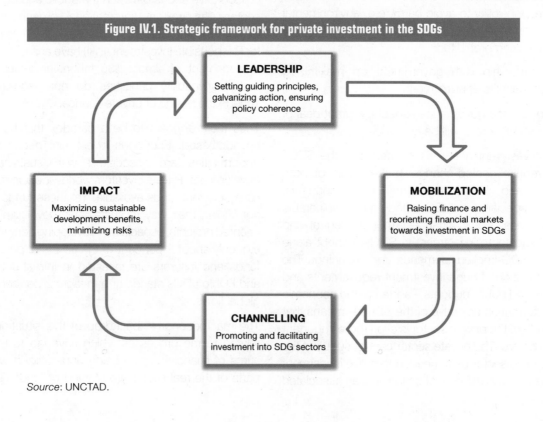

Figure IV.1. Strategic framework for private investment in the SDGs

LEADERSHIP
Setting guiding principles, galvanizing action, ensuring policy coherence

MOBILIZATION
Raising finance and reorienting financial markets towards investment in SDGs

CHANNELLING
Promoting and facilitating investment into SDG sectors

IMPACT
Maximizing sustainable development benefits, minimizing risks

Source: UNCTAD.

a *concerted push* by the international community, within a holistic strategic framework that addresses all key challenges in *mobilizing* funds, *channelling* them to sustainable development and maximizing beneficial *impact* (figure IV.1).

The chapter poses the following questions:

1. How large is the disparity between available financing and the investment required to achieve the SDGs? What is the potential for the private sector to fill this gap? What could be realistic targets for private investment in SDGs? (Section B.)

2. How can the basic policy dilemmas associated with increased private sector investment in SDG sectors be resolved through governments providing *leadership* in this respect? (Section C.)

3. What are the main constraints to *mobilizing* private sector financial resources for investment in sustainable development, and how can they be surmounted? (Section D.)

4. What are the main constraints for *channelling* investment into SDG sectors, and how can they be overcome? (Section E.)

5. What are the main challenges for investment in SDG sectors to have maximum *impact*, and what are the key risks involved with private investment in SDG sectors? How can these challenges be resolved and risks mitigated? (Section F.)

The concluding section (section G) of the chapter brings key findings together into an *Action Plan for Private Investment in the SDGs* that reflects the structure of the strategic framework.

Box IV.1. Investing in Sustainable Development: Scope and Definitions

The research for this chapter has benefited from a significant amount of existing work on financing for development, by many international and other stakeholder organizations. The scope of these efforts varies significantly along the dimensions of public and private sources of finance; domestic and international sources; global and developing-country financing needs; overall financing needs and capital investment; direct and portfolio investment; and overall development financing and specific SDG objectives. Within this context, the chapter focuses on five dimensions:

- *Private investment* by firms, including corporate investment. The term "corporate" is meant to include (semi-) public entities such as State-owned enterprises and SWFs. Private individuals, who mostly invest in sustainable development through funds or dedicated corporate-like vehicles are as such included. Other private sources of finance by individuals, such as remittances, are not addressed here. *As much of the data on investment distinguishes between public and private (rather than corporate) origin, and for ease of exposition, the term "private sector investment" will be used throughout the chapter.*

- *Domestic and foreign investors.* Unless specified differently, domestic firms are included in the scope of the analysis and recommendations. The respective roles of domestic and foreign investors in SDG projects will vary by country, sector and industry. A crucial aspect of sustainable development financing and investment will be linkages that foreign investors establish with the local economy.

- *Developing countries.* The focus of the chapter is on developing countries, with specific attention to weak and vulnerable economies (LDCs, landlocked developing countries and small island developing States). However, some of the data used are solely available as global estimates (indicated, where pertinent).

- *Capital investment.* "Investment" normally refers to "capital expenditures" (or "capex") in a project or facility. Financing needs also include operating expenditures (or "opex") – for example, on health care, education and social services – in addition to capital expenditures (or "capex"). While not regarded as investment, these expenditures are referred to where they are important from an SDG perspective. In keeping with this definition, the chapter does not examine corporate philanthropic initiatives, e.g. funds for emergency relief.

- *Broad-based sustainable development financing needs.* The chapter examines investment in all three broadly defined pillars of the SDGs: economic growth, social inclusion and environmental stewardship. In most cases, these are hard to separate in any given SDG investment. Infrastructure investments will have elements of all three objectives. The use of the terms "SDG sectors" or "SDG investments" in this chapter generally refers to social pillar investments (e.g. schools, hospitals, social housing); environmental pillar investments (e.g. climate change mitigation, conservation); and economic pillar investments (e.g. infrastructure, energy, industrial zones, agriculture).

Source: UNCTAD.

B. THE INVESTMENT GAP AND PRIVATE SECTOR POTENTIAL

This section explores the magnitude of total investment required to meet the SDGs in developing countries; examines how these investment needs compare to current investment in pertinent sectors (the investment gap); and establishes the degree to which the private sector can make a contribution, with specific attention to potential contributions in vulnerable economies.

Private sector contributions often depend on facilitating investments by the public sector. For instance, in some sectors – such as food security, health or energy sustainability – publicly supported R&D investments are needed as a prelude to large-scale SDG-related investments.

1. SDG investment gaps and the role of the private sector

The SDGs will have very significant resource implications worldwide. Total investment needs in developing countries alone could be about $3.9 trillion per year. Current investment levels leave a gap of some $2.5 trillion.

This section examines projected investment needs in key SDG sectors over the period 2015-2030, as well as the current levels of private sector participation in these sectors. It draws on a wide range of sources and studies conducted by specialized agencies, institutions and research entities (box IV.2).

At the global level, total investment needs are in the order of $5 to $7 trillion per year. Total investment needs in developing countries in key SDG sectors are estimated at $3.3 to $4.5 trillion per year over the proposed SDG delivery period, with a midpoint at $3.9 trillion (table IV.2).[2] Current investment in these sectors is around $1.4 trillion, implying an annual investment gap of between $1.9 and $3.1 trillion.

Economic infrastructure

Total investment in *economic infrastructure* in developing countries – power, transport (roads, rails and ports), telecommunications and water and sanitation – is currently under $1 trillion per year for all sectors, but will need to rise to between $1.6 and $2.5 trillion annually over the period 2015-2030.

Increases in investment of this scale are formidable, and much of the additional amount needs to come from the private sector. One basis for gauging the potential private sector contribution in meeting the investment gap in economic infrastructure is to compare the current level of this contribution in developing countries, with what could potentially be the case. For instance, the private sector share in infrastructure industries in developed countries (or more advanced developing countries) gives an indication of what is possible as countries climb the development ladder.

Apart from water and sanitation, the private share of investment in infrastructure in developing countries is already quite high (30-80 per cent depending on the industry); and if developed country participation levels are used as a benchmark, the private sector contribution could be much higher. Among developing countries, private sector participation ranges widely, implying that there is considerable leeway for governments to encourage more private sector involvement, depending on conditions and development strategies.

Recent trends in developing countries have, in fact, been towards greater private sector participation in power, telecommunications and transport (Indonesia, Ministry of National Development Planning 2011; Calderon and Serven 2010; OECD 2012; India, Planning Commission 2011). Even in water and sanitation, private sector participation can be as high as 20 per cent in some countries. At the same time, although the rate reaches 80 per cent in a number of developed countries, it can be as low as 20 per cent in others, indicating varying public policy preferences due to the social importance of water and sanitation in all countries. Given the sensitivity of water provision to the poor in developing countries, it is likely that the public sector there will retain its primacy in this industry, although a greater role for private sector in urban areas is likely.

Box IV.2. Data, methods and sources used in this section

As the contours of the future SDGs are becoming clearer, many organizations and stakeholders in the process have drawn up estimates of the additional financing requirements associated with the economic, social and environmental pillars of sustainable development. Such estimates take different forms. They may be lump-sum financing needs until 2030 or annual requirements. They may aggregate operational costs and capital expenditures. And they are often global estimates, as some of the SDGs are aimed at global commons (e.g. climate change mitigation).

This section uses data on SDG investment requirements as estimated and published by specialized agencies, institutions and research entities in their respective areas of competence, using a meta-analytic approach. As much as possible, the section aims to express all data in common terms: (i) as annual or annualized investment requirements and gaps; (ii) focusing on *investment* (capital expenditures only); and (iii) primarily narrowing the scope to investment in developing countries only. Any estimates by UNCTAD are as much as possible consistent with the work of other agencies and institutions. Figures are quoted on a constant price basis to allow comparisons between current investment, future investment needs and gaps. However agencies' estimates use different base years for the GDP deflator, and the GDP rate assumed also varies (usually between 4–5 per cent constant GDP growth).

This section has extensively reviewed many studies and analyses to establish consensus estimates on future investment requirements.[1] The principal sources drawn upon are:

- Infrastructure: McKinsey provided valuable support, including access to the MGI ISS database. McKinsey (2013), Bhattacharya et al. in collaboration with G-24 (2012), MDB Committee on Development Effectiveness (2011), Fay et al (2011), Airoldi et al. (2013), OECD (2006, 2007, 2012), WEF/PwC (2012).

- Climate Change: CPI and UNCTAD jointly determined the investment needs ranges provided in table IV.2, including unpublished CPI analysis. Buchner et al. (2013), World Bank (2010), McKinsey (2009), IEA (2009, 2012), UNFCCC (2007), WEF (2013).

- Food security and agriculture: FAO analysis, updated jointly by FAO-UNCTAD; context and methodology in Schmidhuber and Bruinsma (2011).

- Ecosystems/Biodiversity: HLP (2012) and Kettunen et al. (2013).

Further information and subsidiary sources used are provided in table IV.2. These sources were used to "sense check" the numbers in table IV.2 and estimate the private share of investment in each sector.

There are no available studies on social sectors (health and education) conducted on a basis comparable to the above sectors. UNCTAD estimated investment needs over 2015-2030 for social sectors using a methodology common to studies in other sectors, i.e. the sum of: the annualized investment required to shift low-income developing countries to the next level of middle income developing countries, the investment required to shift this latter group to the next level, and so on. The raw data required for the estimations were primarily derived from the World Bank, World Development Indicators Database.

The data presented in this chapter, while drawing on and consistent with other organizations, and based on recognized methodological principles, should nonetheless be treated only as a guide to likely investment. In addition to the many data and methodological difficulties that confront all agencies, projections many years into the future can never fully anticipate the dynamic nature of climate change, population growth and interest rates – all of which will have unknown impacts on investment and development needs.[2] Bearing in mind the above limitations, the estimates reported in this section provide orders of magnitude of investment requirements, gaps and private sector participation.

Source: UNCTAD.

[1] In a number of cases, this section draws on estimates for future investment requirements and gaps not made specifically with SDGs in mind. Nevertheless, the aims underlying these estimates are normally for sustainable development purposes consistent with the SDGs (e.g. estimates pertaining to climate change mitigation or infrastructure). This approach has also been taken by the UN System Task Team (UNTT 2013) and other United Nations bodies aiming to estimate the financing and investment implications of the SDGs.

[2] For instance, a spate of megaprojects in power and road transport in developing countries during the last few years has caused the proportion of infrastructure to GDP to rise for developing countries as a whole. A number of studies on projected investment requirements in infrastructure – which assume a baseline ratio of infrastructure, normally 3-4 per cent – do not fully factor this development in.

Table IV.2. Current investment, investment needs and gaps and private sector participation in key SDG sectors in developing countries[a]

Sector	Description	Estimated current investment	2015-2030 Total investment required	Investment Gap	Average private sector participation in current investment[b]	
		(latest available year) $ billion	Annualized $ billion (constant price)		Developing countries	Developed countries
		A	B	C = B - A	Per cent	
Power[c]	Investment in generation, transmission and distribution of electricity	~260	630–950	370–690	40–50	80–100
Transport[c]	Investment in roads, airports, ports and rail	~300	350–770	50–470	30–40	60–80
Telecommunications[c]	Investment in infrastructure (fixed lines, mobile and internet)	~160	230–400	70–240	40–80	60–100
Water and sanitation[c]	Provision of water and sanitation to industry and households	~150	~410	~260	0–20	20–80
Food security and agriculture	Investment in agriculture, research, rural development, safety nets, etc.	~220	~480	~260	~75	~90
Climate change mitigation	Investment in relevant infrastructure, renewable energy generation, research and deployment of climate-friendly technologies, etc.	170	550–850	380–680	~40	~90
Climate change adaptation	Investment to cope with impact of climate change in agriculture, infrastructure, water management, coastal zones, etc.	~20	80–120	60–100	0–20	0–20
Eco-systems/ biodiversity	Investment in conservation and safeguarding ecosystems, marine resource management, sustainable forestry, etc.		70–210[d]			
Health	Infrastructural investment, e.g. new hospitals	~70	~210	~140	~20	~40
Education	Infrastructural investment, e.g. new schools	~80	~330	~250	~15	0–20

Source: UNCTAD.

[a] Investment refers to capital expenditure. Operating expenditure, though sometimes referred to as 'investment' is not included. The main sources used, in addition to those in box IV.2, include, by sector:
   Infrastructure: ABDI (2009); Australia, Bureau of Infrastructure, Transport and Regional Economics (2012); Banerjee (2006); Bhattacharyay (2012); Australia, Reserve Bank (2013); Doshi et al. (2007); Calderon and Serven (2010); Cato Institute (2013); US Congress (2008); Copeland and Tiemann (2010); Edwards (2013); EPSU (2012); Estache (2010); ETNO (2013); Foster and Briceno-Garmendia (2010); Goldman Sachs (2013); G-30 (2013); Gunatilake and Carangal-San Jose (2008); Hall and Lobina (2010); UK H.M. Treasury (2011, 2013); Inderst (2013); Indonesia, Ministry of National Development Planning (2011); Izaguirre and Kulkarni (2011); Lloyd-Owen (2009); McKinsey (2011b); Perrotti and Sánchez (2011); Pezon (2009); Pisu (2010); India, Planning Commission (2011, 2012); Rhodes (2013); Rodriguez et al. (2012); Wagenvoort et al. (2010); World Bank (2013a) and Yepes (2008);
   Climate Change: AfDB et al. (2012); Buchner et al. (2011, 2012) and Helm et al.(2010).
   Social sectors: Baker (2010); High Level Task Force on Innovative International Financing for Health Systems (2009); Institute for Health Metrics and Evaluation (2010, 2012); Leading Group on Innovative Financing to Fund Development (2010); McCoy et al. (2009); The Lancet (2011, 2013); WHO (2012) and UNESCO (2012, 2013).
[b] The private sector share for each sector shows large variability between countries.
[c] Excluding investment required for climate change, which is included in the totals for climate change mitigation and adaptation.
[d] Investment requirements in ecosystems/biodiversity are not included in the totals used in the analysis in this section, as they overlap with other sectors.

Food security

Turning to investment in *food security and agriculture,* current relevant investment is around $220 billion per year. Investment needs in this area refer to the FAO's "zero hunger target" and primarily covers investment in relevant agriculture areas such as: agriculture-specific infrastructure, natural resource development, research, and food safety nets, which are all a part of the relevant SDG goals.

On this basis, total investment needs are around $480 billion per year, implying an annual gap of some $260 billion over and above the current level. The corporate sector contribution in the agricultural sector as a whole is already high at 75 per cent in developing countries, and is likely to be higher in the future (as in developed countries).

Social infrastructure

Investment in social infrastructure, such as education and health, is a prerequisite for effective sustainable development, and therefore an important component of the SDGs. Currently investment in *education* is about $80 billion per year in developing countries. In order to move towards sustainable development in this sector would require $330 billion to be invested per year, implying an annual gap of about $250 billion over and above the current level.

Investment in *health* is currently about $70 billion in developing countries. The SDGs would require investment of $210 billion per year, implying an investment gap of some $140 billion per year over and above the current level. The private sector investment contribution in healthcare in developing countries as a whole is already very high, and this is likely to continue, though perhaps less so in vulnerable economies. In contrast, the corporate contribution in both developed and developing countries in education is small to negligible and likely to remain that way. Generally, unlike in economic infrastructure, private sector contributions to investment in social infrastructure are not likely to see a marked increase.

For investment in social infrastructure it is also especially important to take into account additional operational expenditures as well as capital expenditures (i.e. investment per se). The relative weight of capital expenditures and operating expenditures varies considerably between sectors, depending on technology, capital intensity, the importance of the service component and many other factors. In meeting SDG objectives, operating expenditures cannot be ignored, especially in new facilities. In the case of health, for example, operating expenditures are high as a share of annual spending in the sector. After all, investing in new hospitals in a developing country is insufficient to deliver health services – that is to say doctors, nurses, administrators, etc. are essential. Consideration of operating cost is important in all sectors; not allowing for this aspect could see the gains of investment in the SDGs reversed.

Environmental sustainability

Investment requirements for *environmental sustainability* objectives are by nature hard to separate from investments in economic and social objectives. To avoid double counting, the figures for the investment gap for economic infrastructure in table IV.2 exclude estimates of additional investment required for climate change adaptation and mitigation. The figures for social infrastructure and agriculture are similarly adjusted (although some overlap remains). From a purely environmental point of view, including stewardship of global commons, the investment gap is largely captured through estimates for climate change, especially mitigation, and under ecosystems/biodiversity (including forests, oceans, etc.).

Current investments for climate change mitigation, i.e. to limit the rise in average global warming to 2° Celsius, are $170 billion in developing countries, but require a large increase over 2015-2030 (table IV.2). Only a minority share is presently contributed by the private sector – estimates range up to 40 per cent in developing countries. A bigger contribution is possible, inasmuch as the equivalent contribution in developed countries is roughly 90 per cent, though much of this is the result of legislation as well as incentives and specific initiatives.

The estimated additional investment required for climate change mitigation are not just for infrastructure, but for all sectors – although the specific areas for action depend very much on the types of policies and legislation that are enacted by governments (*WIR10*). In future these policies will be informed by the SDGs, including those related to areas such as growth, industrialization and sustainable cities/settlements. The size and pattern of future investment in climate change in developing countries (and developed ones) depends very much on which policies are adopted (e.g. feed-in tariffs for renewable energy, emissions from cars, the design of buildings, etc.), which is why the range of estimates is wide.

Investment in climate change adaptation in developing countries is currently very small, in the order of $20 billion per year, but also need to increase substantially, even if mitigation is successful (table IV.2). If it is not, with average temperatures rising further than anticipated, then adaptation needs will accelerate exponentially, especially with respect to infrastructure in coastal regions, water resource management and the viability of ecosystems.

The current private sector share of investment in climate change adaptation in developing countries appears to be no different, at up to 20 per cent, than in developed ones. In both cases considerable inventiveness is required to boost corporate contribution into territory which has traditionally been seen as the purview of the State, and in which – from a private sector perspective – the risks outweigh the returns.

Other investment needs: towards inclusiveness and universality

There are vulnerable communities in all economies. This is perhaps more so in structurally weak economies such as LDCs, but numerically greater pockets of poverty exist in better off developing countries (in terms of average incomes) such as in South Asia.

Thus, while the estimated investment needs discussed in this section are intended to meet the overall requirements for sustainable investment in all developing countries, they may not fully address the specific circumstance of many of the poorest communities or groups, especially those who are isolated (e.g. in rural areas or in forests) or excluded (e.g. people living in slums).

For this reason, a number of prospective SDGs (or specific elements of all SDGs) – such as those focusing on energy, water and sanitation, gender and equality – include elements addressing the prerequisites of the otherwise marginalized. Selected examples of potential types of targets

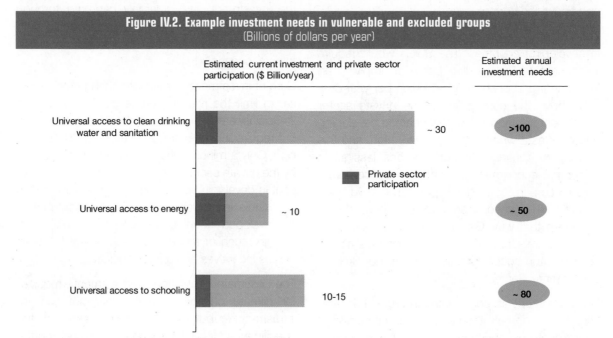

Figure IV.2. Example investment needs in vulnerable and excluded groups
(Billions of dollars per year)

Source: : UNCTAD, WHO (2012), IEA (2009, 2011), World Bank and IEA (2013), Bazilian et al. (2010) and UNESCO (2013).
Note: These needs are calculated on a different basis from table IV.2 and the numbers are not directly comparable.

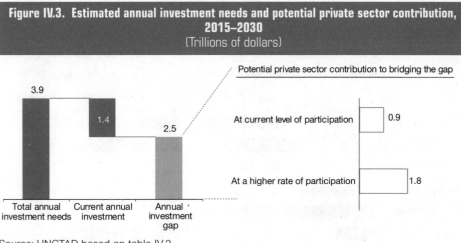

Figure IV.3. Estimated annual investment needs and potential private sector contribution, 2015–2030
(Trillions of dollars)

Potential private sector contribution to bridging the gap

At current level of participation   0.9

At a higher rate of participation   1.8

3.9

1.4

2.5

Total annual investment needs   Current annual investment   Annual investment gap

Source: UNCTAD based on table IV.2.
Note: Totals are the mid-points of range estimates.

are presented in figure IV.2, with estimates of the associated financing requirements.

In most such cases the private sector contribution in developing countries is low, although it should be possible to increase it (for instance, in electricity access). However, boosting this share will be easier in some places (e.g. in urban areas), but difficult in others (e.g. remote locations, among very low-income groups, and where the number of individuals or communities are relatively small or highly dispersed). The private sector contribution to goals aimed at vulnerable individuals and communities therefore needs to be considered carefully.

2. Exploring private sector potential

At today's level of private sector participation in SDG investments in developing countries, a funding shortfall of some $1.6 trillion would be left for the public sector (and ODA) to cover.

The previous section has established the order of magnitude of the investment gap that has to be bridged in order to meet the SDGs. Total annual SDG-related investment needs in developing countries until 2030 are in the range of $3.3 to $4.5 trillion, based on estimates for the most important SDG sectors from an investment point of view (figure IV.3). This entails a mid-point estimate of $3.9 trillion per year. Subtracting current annual investment of $1.4 trillion leaves a mid-point estimated investment gap of $2.5 trillion, over and above current levels. At the current private sector

share of investment in SDG areas, the private sector would cover only $900 billion of this gap, leaving $1.6 trillion to be covered by the public sector (including ODA). For developing countries as a group, including fast-growing emerging markets, this scenario corresponds approximately to a "business as usual" scenario; i.e. at current average growth rates of private investment, the current private sector share of total investment needs could be covered. However, increasing the participation of the private sector in SDG financing in developing countries could potentially cover a larger part of the gap, if the relative share of private sector investment increased to levels observed in developed countries. It is clear that in order to avoid what could be unrealistic demands on the public sector in many developing countries, the SDGs must be accompanied by strategic initiatives to increase private sector participation.

The potential for increasing private sector participation is greater in some sectors than in others (figure IV.4). Infrastructure sectors, such as power and renewable energy (under climate change mitigation), transport and water and sanitation, are natural candidates for greater private sector participation, under the right conditions and with appropriate safeguards. Other SDG sectors are less likely to generate significantly higher amounts of private sector interest, either because it is difficult to design risk-return models attractive to private investors (e.g. climate change adaptation), or

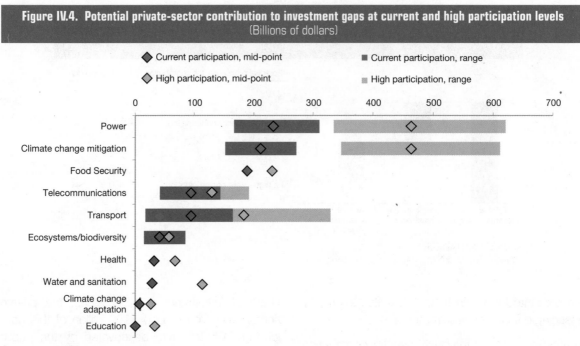

Figure IV.4. Potential private-sector contribution to investment gaps at current and high participation levels
(Billions of dollars)

Source: UNCTAD.
Note: Private-sector contribution to investment gaps calculated using mid-points of range estimates in table IV.2. The higher
           participation level is the average private-sector investment shares observed in developed countries. Some sectors do
           not have a range of estimates, hence the mid-point is the single estimated gap.

because they are more in the realm of public sector responsibilities and consequently highly sensitive to private sector involvement (e.g. education and healthcare).

3.   Realistic targets for private sector SDG investment in LDCs

The SDGs will necessitate a significant increase in public sector investment and ODA in LDCs. In order to reduce pressure on public funding requirements, a doubling of the growth rate of private investment is desirable.

Investment and private sector engagement across SDG sectors are highly variable across developing countries. The extent to which policy action to increase private sector investment is required therefore differs by country and country grouping. Emerging markets face entirely different conditions to vulnerable economies such as LDCs, LLDCs and small island developing States (SIDS), which are necessarily a focus of the post-2015 SDG agenda.

In LDCs, for instance, ODA remains the largest external capital flow, at $43 billion in 2012 (OECD 2013a), compared to FDI inflows of $28 billion and remittances of $31 billion in 2013. Moreover, a significant proportion of ODA is spent on government budget support and goes directly to SDG sectors like education and health. Given its importance to welfare systems and public services, ODA will continue to have an important role to play in the future ecology of development finance in LDCs and other vulnerable economies; and often it will be indispensable.

Nevertheless, precisely because the SDGs entail a large-scale increase in financing requirements in LDCs and other vulnerable economies (relative to their economic size and financing capacity), policy intervention to boost private investment will also be a priority. It is therefore useful to examine the degree to which private sector investment should be targeted by such policy actions.

Extrapolating from the earlier analysis of the total SDG investment need for developing countries as a whole (at about $3.9 trillion per year), the LDC share of investment in SDG sectors, based on the current size of their economies and on the specific needs related to vulnerable communities, amounts

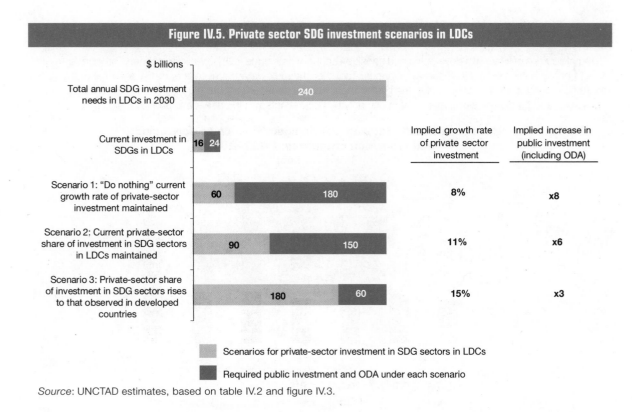

Figure IV.5. Private sector SDG investment scenarios in LDCs

Scenarios for private-sector investment in SDG sectors in LDCs

Required public investment and ODA under each scenario

Source: UNCTAD estimates, based on table IV.2 and figure IV.3.

to nearly $120 billion a year and a total for the 2015-2030 period of $1.8 trillion. Current investments in LDCs in SDG sectors are around $40 billion.[3] Figure IV.5 provides an example of a target-setting scenario for private investment in LDCs.

Total investment needs of $1.8 trillion would imply a target in 2030, the final year of the period, of $240 billion.[4] The current growth rate of private sector investment in LDCs, at around 8 per cent, would quadruple investment by 2030, but still fall short of the investment required (Scenario 1). This "doing nothing" scenario thus leaves a shortfall that would have to be filled by public sector funds, including ODA, requiring an eight-fold increase to 2030. This scenario, with the limited funding capabilities of LDC governments and the fact that much of ODA in LDCs is already used to support *current* (not investment) spending by LDC governments, is therefore not a viable option. Without higher levels of private sector investment, the financing requirements associated with the prospective SDGs in LDCs will be unrealistic for the public sector to bear.

One target for the promotion of private sector investment in SDGs could be to cover that part of the total investment needs that corresponds to its current share of investment in LDCs' SDG sectors (40 per cent), requiring a private sector investment growth rate of 11 per cent per year but still implying a six-fold increase in public sector investment and ODA by 2030 (Scenario 2). A "stretch" target for private investment (but one that would reduce public funding requirements to more realistic levels) could be to raise the share of the private sector in SDG investments to the 75 per cent observed in developed countries. This would obviously require the right policy setting both to attract such investment and to put in place appropriate public policy safeguards, and would imply the provision of relevant technical assistance. Such a stretch target would ease the pressure on public sector funds and ODA, but still imply almost trebling the current level.

Public sector funds, and especially ODA, will therefore remain important for SDG investments in LDCs, including for leveraging further private sector participation. At the same time, the private sector contribution must also rise in order to achieve the SDGs.

Box IV.3. External sources of finance and the role of FDI

External sources of finance to developing and transition economies include FDI, portfolio investment, other investment flows (mostly bank loans), ODA and remittances. Together these flows amount to around $2 trillion annually (box figure IV.3.1). After a sharp drop during the global financial crisis they returned to high levels in 2010, although they have seen a slight decline since then, driven primarily by fluctuating flows in bank loans and portfolio investment.

Box figure IV.3.1. External development finance to developing and transition economies, 2007–2013
(Billions of dollars)

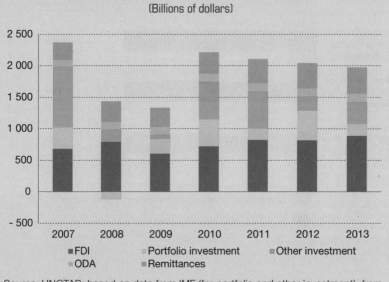

Source: UNCTAD, based on data from IMF (for portfolio and other investment), from the UNCTAD FDI-TNC-GVC Information System (for FDI inflows), from OECD (for ODA) and the World Bank (for remittances).

Note: Data are shown in the standard balance-of-payments presentation, thus on a net basis.

The composition of external sources of finance differs by countries' level of development (box figure IV.3.2). FDI is an important source for all groups of developing countries, including LDCs. ODA accounts for a relatively large share of external finance in LDCs, whereas these countries receive a low amount of portfolio investment, reflecting the lack of developed financial markets.

Box figure IV.3.2. Composition of external sources of development finance, 2012

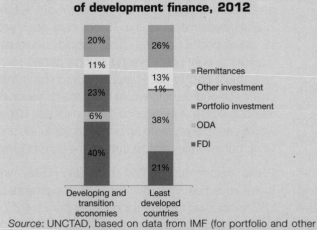

Source: UNCTAD, based on data from IMF (for portfolio and other investment), from the UNCTAD FDI-TNC-GVC Information System (for FDI inflows), from OECD (for ODA) and the World Bank (for remittances).

The components of external finance show different degrees of volatility. FDI has been the largest and most stable component over the past decade, and the most resilient to financial and economic crises. It now accounts for just under half of all net capital flows to developing and transition economies. The relative stability and steady growth of FDI arises primarily because it is associated with the build-up of productive capacity in host countries. Direct investors tend to take a long-term interest in assets located in host countries, leading to longer gestation periods for investment decisions, and making existing investments more difficult to unwind. FDI thus tends to be less sensitive to short-term macroeconomic, exchange rate or interest rate fluctuations.

/...

Box IV.3. External sources of finance and the role of FDI (concluded)

The nature of FDI as a relatively stable and long-term investment in productive assets thus brings it close to the type of investment required in SDG sectors. A number of caveats are warranted, including:

- The relative importance of FDI is lower in the poorest countries; on its own, FDI (like all types of private sector investment) will first flow to lower risk/higher return opportunities, both in terms of location and in terms of sector. This is an important consideration in balancing public and private investment policy priorities.

- FDI flows do not always translate into equivalent capital expenditures, especially where they are driven by retained earnings or by transactions (such as mergers and acquisitions (M&As), although some M&A transactions, such as brownfield investment in agriculture do results in significant capital expenditure).

- FDI can contain short-term, relatively volatile components, such as "hot money" or investments in real estate.

Nevertheless, a comparison with other external sources of finance shows that FDI will have a key role to play in investing in the SDGs. For example, ODA is partly used for direct budgetary support in the poorest countries and on current spending in SDG sectors, rather than for capital expenditures. Remittances are predominantly spent on household consumption (although a small but growing share is used for investment entrepreneurial ventures). Portfolio investment is typically in more liquid financial assets rather than in fixed capital and tends to be more volatile. And with portfolio investment, bank loans have been the most volatile external source of finance for developing economies over the last decade.

Source: UNCTAD.

Reaching the "stretch" target over a period of 15 years requires a doubling in the current growth rate of private investment. Such an increase has implications for the components of private investment. For instance, foreign investment, especially FDI, is relatively important in private sector capital formation in LDCs (box IV.3). While FDI amounts to less than 10 per cent of the value of gross fixed capital formation in developing countries, in LDCs it reaches around 15 per cent, with higher peaks in particular groups of structurally weak economies (for example, more than 23 per cent in landlocked developing countries). As private capital formation is around half of the total in LDCs on average, foreign investment could therefore constitute close to 30 per cent of private investment, potentially with higher growth potential. Pursuing a "stretch" target for private investment in LDCs may thus require a particular focus on the attraction of external sources of private finance.

C. INVESTING IN THE SDGs: A CALL FOR LEADERSHIP

1. Leadership challenges in raising private sector investment in the SDGs

Increasing the involvement of private investors in SDG sectors, many of which are sensitive or involve public services, leads to a number of policy dilemmas. Public and private sector investment are no substitutes, but they can be complementary.

Measures to increase private sector involvement in investment in sustainable development lead to a number of policy dilemmas which require careful consideration.

- *Increasing private investment is necessary. But the role of public investment remains fundamental.* Increases in private sector investment to help achieve the prospective SDGs are necessary, but public sector investment remains vital and central. The two sectors are not substitutes, they are complementary. Moreover, the role of the public sector goes beyond investment per se, and includes all the conditions necessary to meet the SDG challenge.

- *Attracting private investment into SDG sectors entails a conducive investment climate. At the same time, there are risks involved.* Private sector engagement in a number of SDG sectors where a strong public sector responsibility exists has traditionally been a sensitive issue. Private sector service provision in healthcare and education, for instance, can have negative effects on standards unless strong governance and oversight is in place, which in turn requires capable institutions and technical competencies. Private sector involvement in essential infrastructure industries, such as power or telecommunications can be sensitive in countries where this implies the transfer of public sector assets to the private sector, requiring appropriate safeguards against anti-competitive behaviour and for consumer protection. Private sector operations in infrastructure such as water and sanitation are particularly sensitive because of the basic-needs nature of these sectors.

- *Private sector investors require attractive risk-return rates. At the same time, basic-needs services must be accessible and affordable to all.* The fundamental hurdle for increased private sector contributions to investment in SDG sectors is the inadequate risk-return profile of many such investments. Perceived risks can be high at all levels, including country and political risks, risks related to the market and operating environment, down to project and financial risks. Projects in the poorest countries, in particular, can be easily dismissed by the private sector as "poor investments". Many mechanisms exist to share risks or otherwise improve the risk-return profile for private sector investors. Increasing investment returns, however, cannot lead to the services provided by private investors ultimately becoming inaccessible or unaffordable for the poorest in society. Allowing energy or water suppliers to cover only economically attractive urban areas while ignoring rural needs, or to raise prices of essential services, are not a sustainable outcome.

- *The scope of the SDGs is global. But LDCs need a special effort to attract more private investment.* From the perspective of policymakers at the international level, the problems that the SDGs aim to address are global issues, although specific targets may focus on particularly acute problems in poor countries. While overall financing for development needs may be defined globally, with respect to private sector financing contribution, special efforts are required for LDCs and other vulnerable economies. Without targeted policy intervention these countries will not be able to attract resources from investors which often regard operating conditions and risks in those economies as prohibitive.

2. Meeting the leadership challenge: key elements

The process of increasing private investment in SDGs requires leadership at the global level, as well as from national policymakers, to provide guiding principles, set targets, galvanize action, foster dialogue, and guarantee inclusiveness.

Given the massive financing needs concomitant to the achievement of the SDGs, what is needed is a *concerted push*, which in turn requires strong global leadership, (i) providing clear direction and basic principles of action, (ii) setting objectives and targets, (iii) building strong and lasting consensus among many stakeholders worldwide and (iv) ensuring that the process is inclusive, keeping on board countries that require support along the way (figure IV.6).

Guiding principles for private sector investment in the SDGs

The many stakeholders involved in stimulating private investment in SDGs will have varying perspectives on how to resolve the policy dilemmas inherent in seeking greater private sector participation in SDG sectors. A common set of principles for investment in SDGs can help establish a collective sense of direction and purpose.

The following broad principles could provide a framework.

- *Balancing liberalization and regulation.* Greater private sector involvement in SDG sectors is a must where public sector resources are insufficient (although selective, gradual or sequenced approaches are possible); at the same time, such increased involvement must be accompanied by appropriate regulations and government oversight.

- *Balancing the need for attractive risk-return rates with the need for accessible and affordable services for all.* This requires governments to proactively address market failures in both respects. It means placing clear obligations on investors and extracting firm commitments, while providing incentives to improve the risk-return profile of investment. And it implies making incentives or subsidies conditional on social inclusiveness.

- *Balancing a push for private investment funds with the push for public investment.* Synergies between public and private funds should be found both at the level of financial resources – e.g. raising private sector funds with public sector funds as base capital – and at the policy level, where governments can seek to engage

---

Figure IV.6. Providing leadership to the process of raising private-sector investment in the SDGs: key challenges and policy options

Key challenges	Policy options
▪ Need for a clear sense of direction and common policy design criteria	**Agree a set of guiding principles for SDG investment policymaking** • Increasing private-sector involvement in SDG sectors can lead to policy dilemmas (e.g. public vs private responsibilities, liberalization vs regulation, investment returns vs accessibility and affordability of services); an agreed set of broad policy principles can help provide direction
▪ Need for clear objectives to galvanize global action	**Set SDG investment targets** • Focus targets on areas where private investment is most needed and where increasing such investment is most dependent on action by policymakers and other stakeholders: LDCs
▪ Need to manage investment policy interactions	**Ensure policy coherence and synergies** • Manage national and international, investment and related policies, micro- and macro-economic policies
▪ Need for global consensus and an inclusive process, keeping on board countries that need support	**Multi-stakeholder platform and multi-agency technical assistance facility** • International discussion on private-sector investment in sustainable development is dispersed among many organizations, institutions and forums, each addressing specific areas of interest. There is a need for a common platform to discuss goals, approaches and mechanisms for mobilizing of finance and channelling investment into sustainable development • Financing solutions and private-sector partnership arrangements are complex, requiring significant technical capabilities and strong institutions. Technical assistance will be needed to avoid leaving behind the most vulnerable countries, where investment in SDGs is most important.

Source: UNCTAD.

private investors to support programmes of economic or public service reform. Private and public sector investment should thus be complementary and mutually supporting.

- *Balancing the global scope of the SDGs with the need to make a special effort in LDCs.* Special targets and special measures should be adopted for private investment in LDCs. ODA and public funds should be used where possible to leverage further private sector financing. And targeted technical assistance and capacity-building should be aimed at LDCs to help attract and manage investment.

Beyond such broad principles, in its Investment Policy Framework for Sustainable Development (*IPFSD*), an open-source tool for investment policymakers, UNCTAD has included a set of principles specifically focused on investment policies that could inform wider debate on guiding principles for investment in the SDGs. The *IPFSD* Principles are the design criteria for sound investment policies, at the national and international levels, that can support SDG investment promotion and facilitation objectives while safeguarding public interests. UNCTAD has already provided the infrastructure for further discussion of the Principles through its *Investment Policy Hub*, which allows stakeholders to discuss and provide feedback on an ongoing basis.

SDG investment targets

The rationale behind the SDGs, and the experience with the MDGs, is that targets help provide direction and purpose. Ambitious investment targets are implied by the prospective SDGs. The international community would do well to make targets explicit and spell out the consequences for investment policies and investment promotion at national and international levels. Achievable but ambitious targets, including for increasing public and private sector investment in LDCs, are thus a must. Meeting targets to increase private sector investment in the SDGs will require action at many levels by policymakers in developed and developing countries; internationally in international policymaking bodies and by the development community; and by the private sector itself. Such broad engagement needs coordination and strong consensus on a common direction.

Policy coherence and synergies

Policymaking for investment in SDG sectors, and setting investment targets, needs to take into account the broader context that affects the sustainable development outcome of such investment. Ensuring coherence and creating synergies with a range of other policy areas is a key element of the leadership challenge, at both national and global levels. Policy interaction and coherence are important principally at three levels:

- *National and international investment policies.* Success in attracting and benefiting from foreign investment for SDG purposes depends on the interaction between national investment policies and international investment rulemaking. National rules on investor rights and obligations need to be consistent with countries' commitments in international investment agreements, and these treaties must not unduly undermine regulatory space required for sustainable development policies. In addition, it is important to ensure coherence between different IIAs to which a country is a party.

- *Investment and other sustainable-development-related policies.* Accomplishing SDGs through private investment depends not only on investment policy per se (i.e., entry and establishment rules, treatment and protection, promotion and facilitation) but on a host of investment-related policy areas including tax, trade, competition, technology, and environmental, social and labour market policies. These policy areas interact, and an overall coherent approach is needed to make them conducive to investment in the SDGs and to achieve synergies (*WIR12*, p. 108; *IPFSD*).

- *Micro- and macroeconomic policies.* Sound macro-economic policies are a key determinant for investment, and financial systems conducive to converting financial capital into productive capital are important facilitators, if not prerequisites, for promoting investment in the SDGs. A key part of the leadership challenge is to push for and support coordinated efforts towards creating an overall macro-economic climate that provides a stable environment for investors, and towards re-orienting the global financial architecture to focus on mobilizing and channelling funds into real, productive assets, especially in SDG sectors (TDR 2009; TDR 2011; UNCTAD 2011b, Wolf, M. 2010).[5]

Global multi-stakeholder platform on investing in the SDGs

At present international discussions on private sector investment in sustainable development are dispersed among many organizations, institutions and forums, each addressing specific areas of interest. There is a need for a regular body that provides a platform for discussion on overall investment goals and targets, shared mechanisms for mobilization of finance and channelling of investment into sustainable development projects, and ways and means of measuring and maximizing positive impact while minimizing negative effects.

A *global multi-stakeholder platform on investing in the SDGs* could fill that gap, galvanizing promising initiatives to mobilize finance and spreading good practices, supporting actions on the ground channelling investment to priority areas, and ensuring a common approach to impact measurement. Such a multi-stakeholder platform could have subgroups by sector, e.g. on energy, agriculture, urban infrastructure, because the cross-sector span of investments is so great.

Multi-agency technical assistance facility

Finally, many of the solutions discussed in this chapter are complex, requiring significant technical capabilities and strong institutions. Since this is seldom the case in some of the poorest countries, which often have relatively weak governance systems, technical assistance will be required in order to avoid leaving behind vulnerable countries where progress on the SDGs is most essential. A *multi-agency consortia* (a "one-stop shop" for SDG investment solutions) could help to support LDCs, advising on, for example, investment guarantee and insurance schemes, the set-up of SDG project development agencies that can plan, package and promote pipelines of bankable projects, design of SDG-oriented incentive schemes, regulatory frameworks, etc. Coordinated efforts to enhance synergies are imperative.

D. MOBILIZING FUNDS FOR INVESTMENT IN THE SDGs

The mobilization of funds for SDG investment occurs within a global financial system with numerous and diverse participants. Efforts to direct more financial flows to SDG sectors need to take into account the different challenges and constraints faced by all actors.

1. Prospective sources of finance

The global financial system, its institutions and actors, can mobilize capital for investment in the SDGs. The flow of funds from sources to users of capital is mediated along an investment chain with many actors (figure IV.7), including owners of capital, financial intermediaries, markets, and advisors. Constraints to mobilizing funds for SDG financing can be found both at the systemic level and at the level of individual actors in the system and their interactions. Policy responses will therefore need to address each of these levels.

Policy measures are also needed more widely to stimulate economic growth in order to create supportive conditions for investment and capital mobilization. This requires a coherent economic and development strategy, addressing macroeconomic and systemic issues at the global and national levels, feeding into a conducive investment climate. In return, if global and national leaders get their policies right, the resulting investment will boost growth and macroeconomic conditions, creating a virtuous cycle.

Prospective sources of investment finance range widely from large institutional investors, such as pension funds, to the private wealth industry. They include private sector sources as well as publicly owned and backed funds and companies; domestic and international sources; and direct and indirect investors (figure IV.8 illustrates some potential

---

Figure IV.7. SDG investment chain and key actors involved

Principal institutions	**Sources of capital**	**Asset pools** (or primary intermediaries)	**Markets**

	• Governments (e.g. ODA)
	• Households/individuals, e.g.:
	  – Retail investors
	  – High-net-worth individuals
	  – Pensions
	  – Insurance premia
	• Firms (e.g. reserves/retained earnings
	• Philanthropic institutions or foundations
	• Other institutions with capital reserves (e.g. universities)
		• Banks
		• Pension funds
		• Insurance companies
		• Mutual funds
		• Sovereign wealth funds
		• Endowment funds
		• Private Equity
		• Venture capital
		• Impact investors
		• ...
			• Equity
			• Corporate debt
			• Sovereign debt
			• Other markets and financial instruments

Intermediaries	• Investment banks and brokerage firms	• Institutional asset managers	
Advisors	• Financial advisors • Wealth managers • Investment consultants	• Rating agencies	

Users of capital for SDG investment
• Governments
• International organizations and development banks
• Public and semi-public institutions
• Multinational and local firms entrepreneurs
• NGOs
• Impact investors
• ...

Source: UNCTAD.

---

corporate sources of finance; others, including some non-traditional sources, are discussed in box IV.4).

The overall gap of about $2.5 trillion is daunting, but not impossible to bridge; domestic and international sources of capital are notionally far in excess of SDG requirements. However, existing savings and assets of private sector actors are not sitting idle; they are already deployed to generate financial returns. Nevertheless, the relative sizes of private sector sources of finance can help set priorities for action.

All the sources indicated in figure IV.8 are invested globally, of which a proportion is in developing countries (including by domestic companies). In the case of TNCs, for example, a third of global inward FDI stock in 2013 was invested in developing countries (and a bigger share of FDI flows). Pension funds, insurance companies, mutual funds and sovereign wealth funds, on the other hand, currently have much less involvement in developing markets. The majority of bank lending also goes to developed markets.

Each group of investor has a different propensity for investment in the SDGs.

• *Banks.* Flows of cross-border bank lending to developing countries were roughly $325 billion in 2013, making international bank lending the third most important source of foreign capital after FDI and remittances. The stock of international cross-border bank claims on all countries stood at $31.1 trillion at the end of

Figure IV.8. Relative sizes of selected potential sources of investment, 2012
(Value of assets, stocks and loans in trillions of dollars)

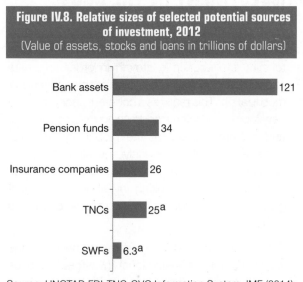

Source: UNCTAD FDI-TNC-GVC Information System, IMF (2014); SWF Institute, fund rankings; TheCityUK (2013).

Note: This figure is not exhaustive but seeks to list some key players and sources of finance. The amounts for assets, stocks and loans indicated are not equivalent, in some cases, overlap, and cannot be added.

[a] 2014 figure.

2014, of which $8.8 trillion, or 28 per cent of the total, was in developing countries.[6]

As well as an important source of project debt finance, banks are in a powerful position to contribute to the SDGs through, for instance, the implementation of the Equator Principles (EPs), a risk management framework that helps determine, assess and manage environmental and social risk specifically in infrastructure and other industrial projects. Currently 78 financial institutions in 34 countries have officially adopted the EPs, a third of which are in developing countries. These institutions cover over 70 per cent of international project finance debt in emerging markets.[7]

State-owned banks (including development banks), regional development banks and local banking institutions (Marois, 2013) all have particular and significant relevance for investment in SDGs. State-owned banks and other financial institutions have always played an important role in development, targeting specific sectors, for example, infrastructure and public services, often at preferential rates. Today State-owned financial institutions (SOFI) account for 25 per cent of total assets in banking systems around the world; and the capital available in SOFIs in developing countries can be used both for investment in SDGs directly and to leverage funds and investment from the private sector (sections D.3 and E).

- *Pension funds.* UNCTAD estimates that pension funds have at least $1.4 trillion of assets invested in developing markets; and the value of developed-country assets invested in the South is growing in addition to the value of pension funds based in developing countries (and which are predominantly invested in their own domestic markets). By 2020, it is estimated that global pension fund assets will have grown to more than $56 trillion (PwC 2014a). Pension funds are investors with long-term liabilities able to take on less liquid investment products. In the past two decades, they have begun to recognize infrastructure investment as a distinct asset class and

there is the potential for future investment by them in more illiquid forms of infrastructure investment. Current engagement of pension funds in infrastructure investment is still small, at an estimated average of 2 per cent of assets (OECD 2013b). However, lessons can be drawn from some countries, including Australia and Canada, which have been successful in packaging infrastructure projects specifically to increase investment by pension funds (in both cases infrastructure investment makes up some 5 per cent of pension fund portfolios).

- *Insurance companies.* Insurance companies are comparable in size to pension and mutual funds. With similar long-term liabilities as pension funds (in the life insurance industry), insurance companies are also less concerned about liquidity and have been increasingly prepared to invest in infrastructure, albeit predominantly in developed markets. One study suggests that insurance companies currently allocate an average of 2 per cent of their portfolio to infrastructure, although this increases to more than 5 per cent in some countries (Preqin 2013). While insurance companies could provide a source of finance for investment in SDG sectors, their greater contribution may come from off-setting investments in areas such as climate change adaptation against savings from fewer insurance claims and lower insurance premiums.[8]

The growth of parts of the insurance industry is therefore intimately tied to investment in sustainable development sectors, e.g. investment in agricultural technologies to resist climate change, or flood defences to protect homes and businesses, can have a positive impact on the sustainability of the insurance fund industry. There is a virtuous cycle to be explored whereby insurance funds can finance the type of investment that will reduce future liabilities to events such as natural disasters. Already, the insurance industry is committed to mainstreaming ESG goals into its activities and raising awareness of the impact of new risks on the industry, for example through the UN-backed Principles for Sustainable Insurance.

- *Transnational corporations (TNCs).* With $7.7 trillion currently invested by TNCs in developing economies, and with some $5 trillion in cash holdings, TNCs offer a significant potential source of finance for investment in SDG sectors in developing countries. FDI already represents the largest source of external finance for developing countries as a whole, and an important source (with ODA and remittances) even in the poorest countries. It is an important source of relatively stable development capital, partly because investors typically seek a long-term controlling interest in a project making their participation less volatile than other sources. In addition, FDI has the advantage of bringing with it a package of technology, managerial and technical know-how that may be required for the successful set-up and running of SDG investment projects.

- *Sovereign wealth funds (SWFs).* With 80 per cent of SWF assets owned by developing countries, there is significant potential for SWFs to make a contribution to investment in SDG sectors in the global South. However, more than 70 per cent of direct investments by SWFs are currently made in developed markets (chapter I), and a high proportion of their total assets under management may also be invested in developed markets. SWFs share many similarities with institutional investors such as pension funds – several SWFs are constituted for this purpose, or also have that function, such as CalPERS and SPU (Truman 2008; Monk 2008). Other SWFs are established as strategic investment vehicles (Qatar holdings of the Qatar Investment Authority); as stabilization funds displaying the characteristics of a central bank (SAMA); or as development funds (Temasek).

Box IV.4. Selected examples of other sources of capital for investment in the SDGs

Foundations, endowments and family offices. Some estimates put total private wealth at $46 trillion (TheCityUK 2013), albeit a third of this figure is estimated to be incorporated in other investment vehicles, such as mutual funds. The private wealth management of family offices stands at $1.2 trillion and foundations/endowment funds at $1.3 trillion in 2011 (WEF 2011). From this source of wealth it may be possible to mobilize greater philanthropic contributions to long-term investment, as well as investments for sustainable development through the fund management industry. In 2011 the United States alone were home to more than 80,000 foundations with $662 billion in assets, representing over 20 per cent of estimated global foundations and endowments by assets, although much of this was allocated domestically.

Venture capital. The venture capital industry is estimated at $42 billion (E&Y 2013) which is relatively small compared to some of the sums invested by institutional investors but which differs in several important respects. Investors seeking to allocate finance through venture capital often take an active and direct interest in their investment. In addition, they might provide finance from the start or early stages of a commercial venture and have a long-term investment horizon for the realization of a return on their initial capital. This makes venture capital more characteristic of a direct investor than a short-term portfolio investor.

Impact investment. Sources for impact investment include individuals, foundations, NGOs and capital markets. Impact investments funded through capital markets are valued at more than $36 billion (Martin 2013). The impact investment industry has grown in size and scope over the past decade (from the Acumen fund in 2001 to an estimated 125 funds supporting impact investment in 2010 (Simon and Barmeier 2010)). Again, while relatively small in comparison to the potential of large institutional investors, impact investments are directly targeted at SDG sectors, such as farming and education. Moreover, their promotion of social and economic development outcomes in exchange for lower risk-adjusted returns makes impact investment funds a potentially useful source of development finance.

Microfinance. Some studies show that microfinance has had some impact on consumption smoothing during periods of economic stress and on consumption patterns. However, other studies also indicate that there has been limited impact on health care, education and female empowerment (Bauchet et al 2011; Bateman and Chang 2012). Nevertheless, as the microfinance industry has matured, initiatives such as credit unions have had more success; the encouragement of responsible financial behaviour through prior saving and affordable loans has made valuable contributions to consumption, health and education.

Source: UNCTAD, based on sources in text.

Despite several reported concerns about SWF governance (Bagnall and Truman 2013), SWFs can offer a number of advantages for investment in SDG sectors in poor countries, not least because their finance is unleveraged, and their investment outlook is often long term. For example, 60 per cent of SWFs already actively invest in infrastructure (Preqin 2013); moreover in sectors such as water and energy, SWFs may honour the inherent public nature of these services in a way that private investors may not. This is because some SWFs (and public pension funds) have non-profit driven obligations, such as social protection or intergenerational equity; they also represent a form of "public capital" that could be used for the provision of essential services in low-income communities (Lipschutz and Romano 2012).

All the institutions and markets described above face obstacles and incentives, internal and external, that shape investment decisions and determine whether their choices contribute to or hinder

attainment of the SDGs. Policy interventions can thus target specific links in the investment chain and/or specific types of institutions to ensure that financial markets and end users are better geared towards sustainable outcomes than is presently the case.

2. Challenges to mobilizing funds for SDG investments

Constraints in financial markets hindering the flow of funds to SDG investments include start-up and scaling problems for innovative solutions market failures, lack of transparency on ESG performance and misaligned rewards for market participants.

There are a number of impediments or constraints to mobilizing funds for investment in SDG-related projects (figure IV.9).

An important constraint lies in *start-up and scaling issues for innovative financing solutions.* Tapping the pool of available global financial resources for SDG investments requires greater provision

---

Figure IV.9. Mobilizing funds for SDG investment: key challenges and policy options

Key challenges	Policy options
• Start-up and scaling issues for new financing solutions	**Create fertile soil for innovative SDG-financing approaches and corporate initiatives** • Facilitation and support for SDG dedicated financial instruments and impact investing initiatives through incentives and other mechanisms • Expansion or creation of funding mechanisms that use public-sector resources to catalyze mobilization of private-sector resources • "Go-to-market" channels for SDG investment projects in financial markets: channels for SDG investment projects to reach fund managers, savers and investors in mature financial markets, ranging from securitization to crowd funding
• Failures in global capital markets	**Build or improve pricing mechanisms for externalities** • Internalization in investment decisions of externalities e.g. carbon emissions, water use, social impacts
• Lack of transparency on sustainable corporate performance	**Promote Sustainable Stock Exchanges** • SDG listing requirements, indices for performance measurement and reporting for investors
• Misaligned investor incentive/pay structures	**Introduce financial market reforms** • Reform of pay, performance and reporting structures to favor long-term investment conducive to SDG realization • Rating methodologies that reward long-term real investment in SDG sectors

Source: UNCTAD.

of financial instruments and mechanisms that are attractive for institutions to own or manage. A range of innovative solutions has begun to emerge, including new financial instruments (e.g. green bonds) and financing approaches (e.g. future income securitization for development finance); new investor classes are also becoming important (e.g. funds pursuing impact investing). To date, however, these solutions remain relatively small in scale and limited in scope, or operate on the margins of capital markets (figure IV.9, section D.3).

Over time, changing the mindset of investors towards SDG investment is of fundamental importance, and a number of further constraints hinder this. First, *market failures* in global capital markets contribute to a misallocation of capital in favour of non-sustainable projects/firms and against those that could contribute positively to the SDGs. Failure by markets and holders of capital to price negative externalities into their capital allocation decisions means that the cost of capital for investors reflects solely the private cost. Thus, profit-maximizing investors do not take sufficient account of environmental and other social costs when evaluating potential investments because these costs do not materially affect their cost of capital, earnings or profitability. For instance, the absence of a material price for carbon implies social costs associated with emissions are virtually irrelevant for capital allocation decisions.

Second, a *lack of transparency on ESG performance* further precludes consideration of such factors in the investment decisions of investors, financial intermediaries and their advisors (and the ultimate sources of capital, such as households). The fragmentation of capital markets, while facilitating the allocation of capital, has disconnected the sources of capital from end users. For example, households do not have sufficient information about where and how their pensions are invested in order to evaluate whether it is being invested responsibly and, for example, whether it is in line with the SDGs. Similarly, asset managers and institutional investors do not have sufficient information to make better informed investment decisions that might align firms with the SDGs.

Third, the *rewards that individuals and firms receive in terms of pay, performance and reporting* also influence investment allocations decisions. This includes not only incentive structures at TNCs and other direct investors in SDG-relevant sectors, but also incentive structures at financial intermediaries (and their advisors) who fund these investors. The broad effects of these incentive structures are three-fold: (i) an excessive short-term focus within investment and portfolio allocation decisions; (ii) a tendency towards passive investment strategies and herding behaviour in financial markets; and (iii) an emphasis on financial returns rather than a consideration of broader social or environment risk-return trade-offs. These market incentives and their effects have knock-on consequences for real economic activity.

3. Creating fertile soil for innovative financing approaches

Innovative financial instruments and funding mechanisms to raise resources for investment in SDGs deserve support to achieve scale and scope.

A range of innovative financing solutions to support sustainable development have emerged in recent years, including new financial instruments, investment funds and financing approaches. These have the potential to contribute significantly to the realization of the SDGs, but need to be supported, adapted to purpose and scaled up as appropriate. It is important to note that many of these solutions are led by the private sector, reflecting an increasing alignment between UN and international community priorities and those of the business community (box IV.5).

Facilitate and support SDG-dedicated financial instruments and impact investment

Financial instruments which raise funds for investment in social or environmental programs are proliferating, and include green bonds[9] and the proposed development impact bonds. They target investors that are keen to integrate social and environmental concerns into their investment decisions. They are appealing because they ensure a safer return to investors (many are backed by

Box IV.5. Convergence between UN priorities and those of the international business community

In a globe-spanning series of consultations, UN Global Compact participants offered their views on global development priorities they consider central to any future development agenda. The results of these consultations reflect a growing understanding of the convergence between the priorities of the United Nations and those of the international business community on a wide range of global issues and challenges.

Box Figure IV.5.1. Global Development Priorities Identified by Businesses

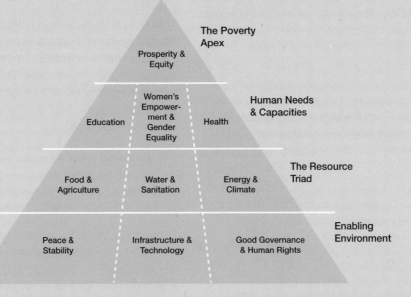

Private Sustainability Finance: from managing risks to embracing new opportunities that create value for business and society. Over the past decade, a number of principles-based initiatives have been adopted throughout the finance-production value chain, from portfolio investors, banks and insurance companies, to foundations and TNCs in the real economy. For instance, led by private actors *Responsible Private Finance* has already reached a significant critical mass across the private sector. There is now a broad consensus that incorporating social, environmental and governance concerns in decision-making improves risk management, avoids harmful investments and makes business sense. Examples of this trend include initiatives such as the Principles for Responsible Investment, the Equator Principles, the Principles for Sustainable Insurance, the Sustainable Stock Exchanges initiative and innovative approaches to sustainable foreign direct investment by multinationals.

Private sustainability finance holds enormous potential to contribute to the broad implementation efforts in the post-2015 future. However, public action through good governance, conducive policies, regulations and incentives is required to drive the inclusion of sustainability considerations in private investment decisions. And it requires private action to significantly enhance the scale and intensity of private sustainability finance.

Source: UN Global Compact.

donors or multilateral banks), but also because they are clearly defined sustainable projects or products.[10] The proceeds are often credited to special accounts that support loan disbursements for SDG projects (e.g. development or climate change adaptation and mitigation projects).

These instruments were often initially the domain of multilateral development banks (MDBs) because this lent credibility with investors in terms of

classifying which investments were socially and environmentally friendly. More recently, however, a number of TNCs have issued green bonds. For instance, EDF Energy undertook a €1.4 billion issue to finance investment in solar and wind energy;[11] Toyota raised $1.75 billion for the development of hybrid vehicles;[12] and Unilever raised £250 million for projects that would reduce greenhouse gas emissions, water usage or waste within its supply chain.[13] While the development of this market by corporate issuers is positive, its continued advance may give rise to the need for labelling or certification of investments, so investors have assurance about which are genuinely "green" or have "social impact".

Impact investing is a phenomenon that reflects investors' desire to generate societal value (social, environmental, cultural) as well as achieve financial return. Impact investment can be a valuable source of capital, especially to finance the needs of low-income developing countries or for products and services aimed at vulnerable communities. The types of projects targeted can include basic infrastructure development, social and health services provision and education – all of which are being considered as SDGs. Impact investors include aid agencies, NGOs, philanthropic foundations and wealthy individuals, as well as banks, institutional investors and other types of firms and funds. Impact investing is defined not by the type of investor, but by their motives and objectives.[14]

A number of financial vehicles have emerged to facilitate impact investing by some such groups (others invest directly). Estimated impact investments through these funds presently range from $30 to $100 billion, depending on which sectors and types of activity are defined as constituting "impact investing"; and similarly the estimated future global potential of impact investing varies from the relatively modest to up to $1 trillion in total (J.P. Morgan 2010). A joint study of impact investment by UNCTAD and the United States Department of State observed in 2012 that over 90 per cent of impact investment funds are still invested in the developed world, mostly in social impact and renewable energy projects. Among developing countries, the largest recipient of impact investing is Latin America and the Caribbean, followed by Africa and South Asia (Addis et al. 2013). A key objective should be to direct more impact investment to developing countries, and especially LDCs.

A number of constraints hold back the expansion of impact investing in developing countries. Key constraints related to the mobilization of impact investment funds include lack of capital across the risk-return spectrum; lack of a common understanding of what impact investment entails; inadequate ways to measure "impact"; lack of research and data on products and performance; and a lack of investment professionals with the relevant skills. Key demand-related constraints in developing countries are: shortage of high-quality investment opportunities with a track record; and a lack of innovative deal structures to accommodate portfolio investors' needs. A number of initiatives are underway to address these constraints and expand impact investment, including the Global Impact Investing Network (GIIN), the United States State Department Global Impact Economy Forum, Impact Reporting and Investment Standards, Global Impact Investment Ratings System, the United Kingdom Impact Program for sub-Saharan Africa and South Asia and the G8 Social Impact Investing Taskforce.

Expand and create funding mechanisms that use public sector resources to catalyze mobilization of private sector resources

A range of initiatives exist to use the capacity of the public sector to mobilize private finance. Often these operate at the project level (Section E), but initiatives also exist at a macro level to raise funds from the private sector, including through financial markets.

Vertical funds (or financial intermediary funds) are dedicated mechanisms which allow multiple stakeholders (government, civil society, individuals and the private sector) to provide funding for pre-specified purposes, often to underfunded sectors such as disease eradication or climate change. Funds such as the Global Fund to Fight AIDS, Tuberculosis and Malaria[15] or the Global Environment Fund[16] have now reached a significant size. Similar funds could be created in alignment with other specific SDG focus areas of the SDGs in general. The Africa Enterprise Challenge Fund[17] is another prominent example of a fund that has been used as a vehicle to provide preferential loans for the purpose of developing inclusive business.

Matching funds have been used to incentivize private sector contributions to development initiatives by making a commitment that the public sector will contribute an equal or proportionate amount. For example, under the GAVI Matching Fund, the United Kingdom Department for International Development and the Bill and Melinda Gates Foundation have pledged about $130 million combined to match contributions from corporations, foundations, their customers, members, employees and business partners.[18]

Front-loading of aid. In addition to catalyzing additional contributions, the public sector can induce private sector actors to use financing mechanisms that change the time profile of development financing, through front-loading of aid disbursements. The International Finance Facility for Immunization (IFFIm) issues AAA-rated bonds in capital markets which are backed by long-term donor government pledges. As such, aid flows to developing countries which would normally occur over a period of 20 years are converted to cash immediately upon issuance. For investors, the bonds are attractive due to the credit rating, a market-comparable interest rate and the perceived "socially responsible return" on investment. IFFIm has raised more than $4.5 billion to date through bond issuances purchased by institutional and retail investors in a range of different mature financial markets.[19]

Future-flow securitization. Front-loading of aid is a subset of a broader range of initiatives under the umbrella of future-flow securitization which allows developing countries to issue marketable financial instruments whose repayments are secured against a relatively stable revenue stream. These can be used to attract a broader class of investors than would otherwise be the case. Other prominent examples are diaspora bonds whose issuance is secured against migrant remittance flows, and bonds backed by the revenue stream from, e.g. natural resources. These instruments allow developing countries to access funding immediately that would normally be received over a protracted period.

Build and support "go-to-market" channels for SDG investment projects in financial markets

A range of options is available, and can be expanded, to help bring concrete SDG investment projects of sufficient scale directly to financial markets and investors in mature economies,

reducing dependence on donors and increasing the engagement of the private sector.

Project aggregation and securitization. SDG investment projects and SDG sectors are often not well aligned with the needs of institutional investors in mature financial markets because projects are too small and sectors fragmented. For example, renewable energy markets are more disaggregated than traditional energy markets. Institutional investors prefer to invest in assets which have more scale and marketability than investment in individual projects provide. As such, aggregating individual projects in a pooled portfolio can create investment products more in line with the appetite of large investors. This can be achieved through securitization of loans to many individual projects to create tradable, rated asset backed securities. For instance, a group of insurers and reinsurers with $3 trillion of assets under management have recently called for more scale and standardization of products in low-carbon investments.[20]

Crowd funding. Crowd funding is an internet-based method for raising money, either through donations or investments, from a large number of individuals or organizations. Globally it is estimated that crowd funding platforms raised $2.7 billion in 2012 and were forecast to increase 81 per cent in 2013, to $5.1 billion (Massolution 2013). While currently more prevalent in developed countries, it has the potential to fund SDG-related projects in developing countries. Crowd funding has been an effective means for entrepreneurs or businesses in developed countries that do not have access to more formal financial markets. In a similar way, crowd funding could help dormant entrepreneurial talent and activity to circumvent traditional capital markets and obtain finance. For example, since 2005 the crowd funding platform Kiva Microfunds has facilitated over $560 million in internet-based loans to entrepreneurs and students in 70 countries.[21]

4. Building an SDG-supportive financial system

A financial system supportive of SDG investment ensures that actors in the SDG investment chain (i) receive the right stimuli through prices for investment instruments that internalize social costs and benefits; (ii) have access to information on the sustainability performance of investments so that they can make informed decisions; and (iii) are rewarded through mechanisms that take into account responsible investment behavior. These elements are part of a wider context of systemic issues in the global financial architecture,[22] which is not functioning optimally for the purposes of channeling funds to productive, real assets (rather than financial assets).[23]

a. Build or improve pricing mechanisms to curb externalities

Effective pricing mechanisms to internalize social and environmental costs are necessary to align market signals with sustainable development goals.

The most effective and yet most challenging way to ensure that global capital allocation decisions are aligned with the needs of sustainable development would be to "get the prices right". That is, to ensure that negative (and positive) social and environmental externalities are factored into the price signals that financial market participants and direct investors receive.

A long-term influence is adherence to responsible investment principles which helps firms to recognize and price-in both the financial costs associated with compliance, but also the rewards: i.e. less risk, potential efficiency gains, and the positive externalities arising from a good reputation.

A number of environmental externalities have been traditionally addressed using tools such as fines or technical standards, but more recently pricing and tax methods have become more common. In the area of climate change, for carbon emissions, a number of countries have experimented with innovative approaches over the past two decades. Two principle methods have been explored for establishing a price for carbon emissions: a cap and trade "carbon market" characterized by the trading of emissions permits; and "carbon taxes" characterized by a special tax on fossil fuels and other carbon-intensive activities. The EU Emissions Trading Scheme (ETS) was the first major carbon market and remains the largest. Carbon markets exist in a handful of other developed countries,

and regional markets exist in a few US states and Canadian provinces. Carbon trading schemes are rarer in developing countries, although there are pilot schemes, such as one covering six Chinese cities and provinces.

Complexities associated with carbon markets, and the failure so far of such markets to establish prices in line with the social costs of emissions, have increased experimentation with taxation. For instance, Ireland, Sweden and the United Kingdom are examples of countries that have implemented some form of carbon tax or "climate levy". Carbon taxes have also been implemented in the Canadian provinces of British Columbia and Quebec, and in 2013 a Climate Protection Act was introduced in the United States Senate proposing a federal carbon tax. The experience with carbon pricing is applicable to other sectors, appropriately adapted to context.

b. Promote Sustainable Stock Exchanges

Sustainable stock exchanges provide listed entities with the incentives and tools to improve transparency on ESG performance, and allow investors to make informed decisions on responsible allocation of capital.

Sustainability reporting initiatives are important because they help to align capital market signals with sustainable development and thereby to mobilize responsible investment in the SDGs. Sustainability reporting should be a requirement not only for TNCs on their global activities, but also for asset owners and asset managers and other financial intermediaries outlined in figure IV.8 on their investment practices.

Many pension funds around the world do not report on if and how they incorporate sustainability issues into their investment decisions (UNCTAD 2011c). Given their direct and indirect influence over a large share of the global pool of available financial resources, all institutional investors should be required to formally articulate their stance on sustainable development issues to all stakeholders. Such disclosure would be in line with best practices and the current disclosure practices of funds in other areas.

Greater accountability and transparency of the entire investment chain is essential, including investment allocation decisions, proxy voting practices and advice of asset owners, asset managers, pension funds, insurance companies, investment consultants and investment banks. Without proper measurement, verification and reporting of financial, social and environmental sustainability information, ultimate sources of capital (especially households and governments) cannot determine how the funds that have been entrusted to these institutions have been deployed.

Stock exchanges and capital market regulators play an important role in this respect, because of their position at the intersection of investors, companies and government policy. The United Nations Sustainable Stock Exchanges (SSE) initiative is a peer-to-peer learning platform for exploring how exchanges can work together with investors, regulators, and companies to enhance corporate transparency, and ultimately performance, on ESG (environmental, social and corporate governance) issues and encourage responsible long-term approaches to investment. Launched by the UN Secretary-General in 2009, the SSE is co-organized by UNCTAD, the UN Global Compact, the UN-supported Principles for Responsible Investment, and the UNEP Finance Initiative.[24]

An increasing number of stock exchanges and regulators have introduced, or are in the process of developing, initiatives to help companies meet the evolving information needs of investors; navigate increasingly complex disclosure requirements and expectations; manage sustainability performance; and understand and address social and environmental risks and opportunities. UNCTAD has provided guidance to help policymakers and stock exchanges in this effort.

c. Introduce financial market reforms

Realigning rewards in financial markets to favour investment in SDGs will require action, including reform of pay and performance structures, and innovative rating methodologies.

Reforms at both the regulatory and institutional levels may lead to more effective alignment of the system of rewards to help ensure that global capital markets serve the needs of sustainable development. This would require policy action and corporate-led initiatives affecting a wide range of different institutions, markets as well as financial behaviour.

Reform pay, performance and reporting structures to favour long-term investment conducive to SDG realization

The performance evaluation and reward structures of both institutions and individuals operating in financial markets are not conducive to investment in SDGs. Areas of action may include:

* *Pay and performance structures.* Pay and performance structures should be aligned with long-term sustainable performance objectives rather than short-term relative performance. For instance, compensation schemes for asset managers, corporate executives and a range of financial market participants could be paid out over the period during which results are realized, and compensation linked to sustainable, fundamental drivers of long-term value. Companies need to take action to minimize the impact of short-termism on the part of financial intermediaries on their businesses and, more positively, create the conditions that enable these capital sources to support and reward action and behaviour by direct investors that contribute to the realization of the SDGs.

* *Reporting requirements.* Reporting requirements could be revised to reduce pressure to make decisions based on short-term financial or investment performance. Reporting structures such as quarterly earnings guidance can over emphasise the significance of short-term measures at the expense of the longer-term sustainable value creation.

Promote rating methodologies that reward long-term investment in SDG sectors

Ratings that incorporate ESG performance help investors make informed decisions for capital allocation towards SDGs. Existing initiatives and potential areas for development include:

- *Non-financial ratings.* Rating agencies have a critical influence on asset allocation decisions by providing an independent assessment of the credit risk associated with marketable debt instruments. Rating agencies' traditional models are based on an estimation of the relative probability of default only, and hence do not incorporate social or environmental risks and benefits associated with particular investments. In order to invest in SDG-beneficial firms and projects, investors need access to ratings which assess the relative ESG performance of firms. Dow Jones, MSCI and Standard and Poor's have for several years been incorporating ESG criteria into specialized sustainability indices and ratings for securities. Standard and Poor's also announced in 2013 that risks from climate change will be an increasingly important factor in its ratings of sovereign debt. Greater effort could be taken to further integrate sustainability issues into both debt and equity ratings. An important dimension of sustainability ratings for equity is that ratings are typically paid for by investors, the users of the rating. This helps address the conflict of interest inherent within the "issuer pays" model that has plagued financial ratings agencies in the wake of the global financial crisis and remains common for debt ratings.

- *Connecting reporting, ratings, integration and capacity-building.* Maximizing the contribution of corporate sustainability reporting to sustainable development is a multi-stage process (figure IV.10). Corporate sustainability information should feed into systems of analysis that can produce actionable information in the form of corporate sustainability ratings. Such ratings

on corporate debt and equities should be integrated into the decision-making processes of key investment stakeholders including policymakers and regulators, portfolio investors, TNCs, media and civil society. These investment stakeholders can seek to implement a range of incentives and sanctions to provide market signals that help to better align the outcomes of market mechanisms with the sustainable development policies of countries. To be truly transformative, this integration process needs to align itself with the policy objectives of the SDGs and to create material implications for poor sustainability performance. Finally, sustainability ratings and standards can also be used as a basis for capacity-building programmes to assist developing-country TNCs and small and medium-sized enterprises to adopt best practices in the area of sustainability reporting and management systems. This will provide new information to guide investors and promote investment.

Figure IV.10. The reporting and ratings chain of action

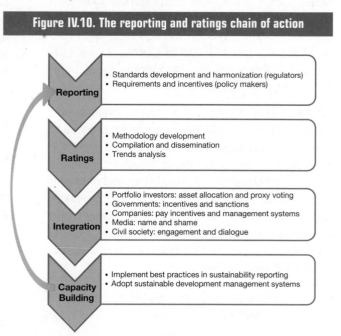

Reporting
- Standards development and harmonization (regulators)
- Requirements and incentives (policy makers)

Ratings
- Methodology development
- Compilation and dissemination
- Trends analysis

Integration
- Portfolio investors: asset allocation and proxy voting
- Governments: incentives and sanctions
- Companies: pay incentives and management systems
- Media: name and shame
- Civil society: engagement and dialogue

Capacity Building
- Implement best practices in sustainability reporting
- Adopt sustainable development management systems

Source: UNCTAD.

E. CHANNELLING INVESTMENT INTO THE SDGs

1. Challenges to channelling funds into the SDGs

Key constraints to channelling funds into SDGs include entry barriers, inadequate risk-return ratios for SDG investments, a lack of information, effective packaging and promotion of projects, and a lack of investor expertise.

Investment in SDG sectors is not solely a question of availability and mobilization of capital, but also of the allocation of capital to sustainable development projects. Macroeconomic policies improving overall conditions for investment and growth, industrial policies establishing or refining a development strategy, and similar policies, can encourage investment, public or private, domestic or foreign, into SDG sectors or others. However, while they are necessary conditions for investment, they are not necessarily enough.

Investors face a number of constraints and challenges in channelling funds to SDG projects:

Entry barriers to SDG investments. Investment for sustainable development can be discouraged by an unwelcoming investment climate. Investors may face administrative or policy-related hurdles in some sectors related to SDGs which are often sensitive as many constitute a public service responsibility. These sectors may even be closed either to private investors in general, or to foreign investors in particular.

Inadequate risk-return ratios for SDG investment. Risks related to SDG investment projects can occur at the country and policy level (e.g. legal protection for investment); at the market or sector level (e.g. uncertain demand); and at the project (financial) level. For example, investments in agriculture or infrastructure are subject to uncertainty and concerns about local demand and spending power of the local population; ownership or access to sensitive resources (e.g. land); and the very long payback periods involved. As a result, investors, especially those not accustomed to investing in SDG sectors in developing countries, demand higher rates of return for investment in countries with greater (perceived or real) risks.

Lack of information, effective packaging and promotion of bankable investment projects in SDG sectors. Investment opportunities in commercial activities are usually clearly delineated; location options may be pre-defined in industrial zones; the investment process and associated rules are clearly framed; and investors are familiar with the process of appraising risks and assessing potential financial returns on investment in their own business. SDG sectors are usually more complex. Investment projects such as in infrastructure, energy or health, may require a process where political priorities need to be defined, regulatory preparation is needed (e.g. planning permissions and licenses, market rules) and feasibility studies carried out. In addition, smaller projects may not easily provide the scale that large investors, such as pension funds, require. Therefore, aggregation and packaging can be necessary. While commercial investments are often more of a "push" nature, where investors are looking for opportunities, SDG projects may be more of a "pull" nature, where local needs drive the shaping of investment opportunities. Effective promotion and information provision is therefore even more important because investors face greater difficulty in appraising potential investment risks and returns, due to a lack of historical data and investment benchmarks to make meaningful comparisons of performance.

Lack of investor expertise in SDG sectors. Some of the private sector investors that developing countries are aiming to attract to large-scale projects, such as infrastructure or agriculture, are relatively inexperienced, including private equity funds and SWFs. These investors have not traditionally been engaged in direct investment in these countries (particularly low-income economies) nor in SDG sectors, and they may not have the necessary expertise in-house to evaluate investments, to manage the investment process (and, where applicable, to manage operations).

These constraints can be addressed through public policy responses, as well as by actions and behavioural change by corporations themselves (see figure IV.11).

Figure IV.11. Channelling investment into SDG sectors: key challenges and policy options

Key challenges	Policy options
• Entry barriers to SDG investments	**Alleviate entry barriers, while safeguarding legitimate public interests** • Creation of an enabling policy environment for investment in sustainable development (e.g. UNCTAD's IPFSD), and formulation of national strategies for attracting investment in SDG sectors.
• Inadequate risk-return ratios for SDG investments	**Expand use of risk-sharing and mitigation mechanisms for SDG investments** • Wider use of PPPs for SDG projects to improve risk-return profiles and address market failures. • Wider availability of investment guarantee and risk insurance facilities to specifically support and protect SDG investments. • Public sector and ODA leveraging and blended financing: public and donor funds as base capital or junior debt, to share risks or improve risk-return profile for private-sector funders. • Advance market commitments and other mechanisms to provide more stable and/or reliable markets for investors.
• Lack of information and effective packaging and promotion of SDG investment projects	**Establish new incentives schemes and a new generation of investment promotion institutions** • Transforming IPAs into SDG investment development agencies, focusing on the preparation and marketing of pipelines of bankable projects in the SDGs. • Redesign of investment incentives, facilitating SDG investment projects, and supporting impact objectives of all investments. • Regional SDG investment compacts: regional cooperation mechanisms to promote investment in SDGs, e.g. regional cross-border infrastructure, regional SDG clusters
• Lack of investor expertise in SDG sectors	**Build SDG investment partnerships** • Partnerships between home and host-country investment promotion agencies: home country partner to act as business development agency for investment in the SDGs in developing countries. • SVE-TNC-MDB triangular partnerships: global companies and MDBs partner with LDCs and small vulnerable economies, focusing on a key SDG sector or a product key for economic development.

Source: UNCTAD.

2. Alleviating entry barriers, while safeguarding public interests

A basic prerequisite for successful promotion of SDG investment is a sound overall policy climate, conducive to attracting investment while safeguarding public interests, especially in sensitive sectors.

A development strategy for attracting and guiding private investment into priority areas for sustainable development requires the creation of an enabling policy environment. Key determinants for a host country's attractiveness, such as political, economic and social stability; clear, coherent and transparent rules on the entry and operational conditions for investment; and effective business facilitation are all relevant for encouraging investment in SDG sectors. The rule of law needs to be respected, together with a credible commitment to transparency, participation and sound institutions that are capable,

efficient and immune to corruption (Sachs 2012). At the same time, alleviating policy constraints for private investment in SDG sectors must not come at the price of compromising legitimate public interests concerning the ownership structure and the regulatory framework for activities related to sustainable development. This calls for a gradual approach towards liberalization of SDG sectors and proper sequencing.

The enabling policy framework should clearly stipulate in what SDG areas private investment is permitted and under what conditions. While many SDG sectors are open to private investment in numerous countries, important country-specific limitations persist. One case in point is infrastructure, where public monopolies are common.[25] Reducing investment barriers can open up new investment opportunities, but may require a gradual approach, starting with those SDG sectors where private involvement faces fewer political concerns. Host countries may first allow service and management contracts and move to PPPs once contractual partners have gained more experience.

Private investment may also be hindered by exclusive rights that governments grant to single service providers (e.g. in water or energy supply) to ensure sufficient revenue for the operator through economies of scale. Such policies should not entirely impede market access for small-scale providers, since the latter can be essential to fill the gap of service provision where the main operator fails to reach the poorest or isolated segments of the population (OECD 2009).

If concerns exist particularly in respect of *foreign* participation in SDG sectors, host countries can opt for foreign ownership limitations instead of complete prohibitions. They can also subject foreign investment to a national benefit test on a case-by-case basis, for instance as regards investment in critical infrastructure. Investment contracts (such as PPPs) between the host country and foreign investors, as well as business concessions offer the possibility to admit foreign investment under the condition that the investor actively contributes to SDGs. For instance, foreign investors have received the right to exploit natural resources in exchange for a commitment to build certain infrastructure or social institutions, such as hospitals or schools.

With respect to foreign participation in agriculture, unambiguous land tenure rights, including a land registry system, are critical not only for attracting investors, but also for protecting smallholders from dispossession and for increasing their bargaining power vis-à-vis foreign investors. Political opposition against foreign investment in agriculture can be alleviated by promoting outgrower schemes (*WIR09*, UNCTAD and World Bank 2014).

In infrastructure sectors, which are often monopolies, a crucial prerequisite for liberalization or opening up to private or foreign investors is the establishment of effective competition policies and authorities. In such cases, the establishment of an independent regulator can help ensure a level playing field. A similar case can be made in other sectors, where policy action can help avoid a crowding out of local micro- and small and medium-sized firms (such as

agricultural smallholders) who form the backbone of the economy in most developing countries.

Other regulatory and policy areas are relevant for the creation of a conducive investment climate and for safeguarding public policy interest. UNCTAD's Investment Policy Framework for Sustainable Development (IPFSD) has been successful in moving discussion and policy in this direction since its publication in 2012.

3. Expanding the use of risk-sharing tools for SDG investments

A number of tools, including PPPs, investment insurance, blended financing and advance market commitments, can help improve the risk-return profile of SDG investment projects.

A key means to improve the risk-return profile for private sector actors is the ability of relevant stakeholders (the public sector, typically home-country governments, development banks or international organizations) to share, minimize or offer alternatives to the risks associated with investment in sustainable development.

Innovative risk management tools can help channel finance and private investment in SDGs depending on the specific requirements of sustainable development projects.

Widen the use of public-private partnerships

The use of PPPs can be critical in channelling investment to SDG sectors because they involve the public and private sectors working together, combining skills and resources (financial, managerial and technical), and sharing risks. Many governments turn to PPPs when the scale and the level of resources required for projects mean they cannot be undertaken solely through conventional public expenditures or procurement. PPPs are typically used for infrastructure projects, especially for water and transportation projects (such as roads, rail and subway networks), but also in social infrastructure, health care and education.[26] PPPs may also involve international sustainable development programmes and donor funds; for instance, the International Finance Facility for Immunization is a PPP, which uses the long-term borrowing capacity of donor governments, with support of the international capital markets to collect funds and finance the GAVI immunization programmes.

PPPs can offer various means for improving the risk-return profile of sustainable development projects. They offer the possibility for tailor-made risk sharing in respect of individual sustainable development investments. PPPs also allow for cost sharing concerning the preparation of feasibility studies; risk sharing of the investment operations through co-investment, guarantees and insurances; and an increase of investor returns through, for example, tax credits and industry support by providing capacity for research and innovation. Direct financial support agreed upon in PPPs can help to overcome start-up barriers for sustainable-development-related investments.

Caution is needed when developing PPPs as they can prove relatively expensive methods of financing and may increase the cost to the public sector if up-front investment costs and subsequent revenue streams (investment returns) are not adequately assessed. This is especially relevant for LDCs and small vulnerable economies (SVEs) with weaker technical, institutional and negotiation capacities (Griffiths et al. 2014). Examples of risks associated with PPPs for governments include high fiscal commitments and difficulty in the estimation of the cost of guarantees (e.g. when governments provide guarantees on demand, exchange rates or other costs). Governments should carefully design contractual arrangements, ensure fair risk sharing between the public and the private sector, develop the capacities to monitor and evaluate partnerships, and promote good governance in PPP projects.[27]

Given the technical complexity of PPP projects and the institutional and governance capabilities required on the part of developing countries, widening the use of PPPs will require:

- the creation of dedicated units and expertise in public institutions, e.g. in SDG investment development agencies or relevant investment authorities, or in the context of regional SDG investment development compacts where costs and know-how can be shared.

- technical assistance from the international development community, e.g. through dedicated units in international organizations (or in a multi-agency context) advising on PPP project set-up and management.

An option that can alleviate risks associated with PPPs, further leverage of public funds to increase private sector contributions, and bring in technical expertise, are three- or four-way PPP schemes with the involvement not only of local governments and private sector investors, but also with donor countries and MDBs as partners.

Link the availability of guarantee and risk insurance facilities to SDGs

Numerous countries promote outward investment by providing investment guarantees that protect investors against certain political risks in host countries (such as the risk of discrimination, expropriation, transfer restrictions or breach of contract). Granting such guarantees can be conditional on the investment complying with sustainability criteria. A number of countries, such as Australia, Austria, Belgium, Japan, the Netherlands, the United Kingdom and the United States require environmental and social impact assessments be done for projects with potentially significant adverse impacts.[28]

In addition to mechanisms providing insurance against political risks at the country level, mechanisms providing guarantees and risk insurance offered by multilateral development institutions also take into account sustainable development objectives. For instance, in determining whether to issue a guarantee, the Multilateral Investment Guarantee Agency evaluates all projects in accordance with its Policy on Environmental and Social Sustainability, adopted in October 2013. [29]

Public sector and ODA-leveraging and blended financing

National, regional and multilateral development banks, as well as ODA, can represent critical sources of finance that can be used as leveraging mechanisms. In a similar vein, development banks can play a crowding-in role, enabling private investment, or providing support for the private sector in periods of crisis when firms cannot receive financing from private banks. In addition development banks have played, and continue to play, a role in socially oriented projects where private investment is lacking.

ODA can play similar roles, especially in vulnerable economies. For instance, the 2002 Monterrey Consensus already pointed out the need to intensify efforts to promote the use of ODA to leverage additional financing for development. ODA continues to be of critical importance, particularly for LDCs, because financial flows to these countries are small and the capacity to raise sufficient resources domestically is lacking. Aid can act as a catalyst for private investment, and there is growing consensus on the potential complementarity of public aid and private investment to foster development (UNECOSOC 2013). To date, the share of ODA supporting private investment is small, but interest in this mechanism is rising among donor countries and development finance institutions; for example, blended ODA from EU institutions rose from 0.2 per cent in 2007 to almost 4 per cent in 2012 (EURODAD 2014). The amount of ODA directed to private sector blending mechanisms is expected to increase.

Public sector and ODA-leveraged and blended financing involves using public and donor funds as base capital, to share risks or improve risk-return profiles for private sector funders. Blending can reduce costs as it involves the complementary use of grants and non-grant sources such as loans or risk capital to finance investment projects in developing countries. It can be an effective tool for investment with long gestation periods and with economic and social rates of return exceeding the pure financial rate of return (e.g. in the renewable energy sector).

Caution must be exercised in the use of blending, as it involves risks. Where the private funding component exclusively pursues financial returns, development impact objectives may be blurred. ODA can also crowd out non-grant finance (Griffiths et al. 2014). Evaluating blended projects is not easy and it can be difficult to demonstrate key success factors, such as additionality, transparency and accountability and to provide evidence of development impact.

Advance market commitments and other market creation mechanisms

In several SDG sectors, private investment is severely constrained by the absence of a sufficient market. For instance, private basic health and education services, but also infrastructure services, such as private water and electricity supply, may not be affordable to large parts of the population. Examples of policy options to help create markets in SDG sectors that can attract private sector investment include:

- Policies aimed at enhancing *social inclusiveness and accessibility* of basic services – such as subsidy schemes for the poor in the form of education vouchers or cash grants for energy and water distribution.

- *Public procurement policies,* through which governments at the central and local level can give preference to the purchase of goods that have been produced in an environmentally and socially-friendly manner. Cities, for example, increasingly have programs relating to the purchase of hybrid fleets or renewable power, the upgrading of mass transportation systems, green city buildings or recycling systems (*WIR10*).

- *Feed-in tariffs* for green electricity produced by households or other private sector entities that are not utilities but that can supply excess energy to the grid (*WIR10*).

- *Regional cooperation* can help create markets, especially for cross-border infrastructure projects, such as roads, electricity or water supply, by overcoming market fragmentation.

Other concrete mechanisms may include so-called advance market commitments. These are binding contracts typically offered by governments or financing entities which can be used (i) to guarantee a viable market, e.g. for goods that embody socially beneficial technologies for which private demand is inadequate, such as in pharmaceuticals and renewable energy technologies (UNDESA 2012); (ii) to provide assured funding for the innovation of socially beneficial technologies, e.g. through rewards, payments, patent buyouts, even if the private demand for the resulting goods is insufficient; and/or (iii) to act as a consumption subsidy when the R&D costs are high and the returns uncertain, with a result of lowering the price for consumers, often allowing the private sector to remain in charge of the production, marketing and distribution strategies. Donors guarantee a viable market for a known period, which reduces the risks for producers associated with R&D spending (i.e. commitments act as incentives for producers to invest in research, staff training and production facilities). Advance market commitments (United Nations I-8 Group 2009) have been used to raise finance for development of vaccine production for developing countries, for instance by successfully accelerating the availability of the pneumococcal vaccine in low-income countries.

4. Establishing new incentives schemes and a new generation of investment promotion institutions

Alleviating constraints in the policy framework of host countries may not be sufficient to trigger private investment in SDGs. Potential investors may still hesitate to invest because they consider the overall risk-return ratio as unfavourable. Investment promotion and facilitation efforts can help overcome investor reluctance.

a. Transform IPAs into SDG investment development agencies

A new generation of investment promotion requires agencies to target SDG investors and to develop and market pipelines of bankable projects.

Through their investment promotion and facilitation policies, and especially in the priorities given to investment promotion agencies (IPAs), host countries pursue a variety of mostly economic objectives, above all job creation, export promotion, technology dissemination and diffusion, linkages with local industry and domestic value added as well as skills development (see figure III.4 in chapter III). Most IPAs, therefore, do not focus specifically on SDG investment objectives or SDG sectors, although the existing strategic priorities do

contribute to sustainable development through the generation of income and poverty alleviation.

Pursuing investments in SDGs implies, (i) targeting investors in sectors or activities that are particularly conducive to SDGs and (ii) creating and bringing to market a pipeline of pre-packaged bankable projects.

In pursuing SDG-related investment projects, IPAs face a number of challenges beyond those experienced in the promotion of conventional FDI. In particular:

- A broadening of the IPA network of in-country *partnerships*. Currently, typical partners of IPAs include trade promotion organizations, economic development agencies, export processing zones and industrial estates, business development organizations, research institutions and universities. While these relationships can help promote investment in SDG projects, the network needs to expand to include public sector institutions dealing with policies and services related to infrastructure, health, education, energy and rural development, as well as local governments, rural extension services, non-profit organizations, donors and other development stakeholders.

- Broadening of contacts with wider groups of *targets* and potential investors, including not only TNCs but also new potential sources of finance, such as sovereign wealth funds, pension funds, asset managers, non-profit organizations, and others.

- Development of *in-house expertise* on sustainable development-related investment projects, new sectors and possible support measures. IPAs, which traditionally focus on attracting investments in manufacturing and commercial services, need to become familiar with the concept of SDG-related investment projects, including PPPs. Training in international best practice and investment promotion techniques could be acquired from international organizations and private sector groups. For example, in 2013, UNCTAD started a program that assists IPAs from developing countries in the promotion of green FDI.

To channel investment into SDG sectors that may be less visible or attractive to investors, governments – alone or in the context of regional cooperation – should develop a *pipeline of bankable SDG investment projects*.

Key characteristics of bankable projects are prioritization, preparation and packaging:

- *Political prioritization* involves the identification of priority projects and the determination of priority sectors, based on national development objectives and strategies. The projects should be politically feasible within the economic development strategy of the country, with a clear political consensus at all levels (national, state and provincial as applicable) and public support. Thus projects should be selected on the basis of a consensus among government entities on their priorities. At this inception stage, policymakers should identify scalable business models and develop strategies for large-scale roll-out over the long term.

- *Regulatory preparation* involves the pre-clearing of regulatory aspects and facilitation of administrative procedures that might otherwise deter investors. Examples include pre-approval of market-support mechanisms or targeted financial incentives (such as fiscal incentives aiming to reduce the cost of capital); advance processing of required licenses and permits (e.g. planning permissions); or carrying out environmental impact studies prior to inviting bids from investors.

- *Packaging* relates to the preparation of concrete project proposals that show viability from the standpoint of all relevant stakeholders, e.g. technical feasibility studies for investors, financial feasibility assessments for banks or environmental impact studies for wider stakeholders. Governments can call upon service providers (e.g. technical auditors, test and certification organizations) to assist in packaging projects. Packaging may also include break up or aggregation/bundling of projects into suitable investment sizes for relevant target groups. And it will include the production of the "prospectus" that can be marketed to investors.

Public funding needs for feasibility studies and other project preparation costs can be significant. They typically average 5–10 per cent of total project costs, which can add up to hundreds of millions of dollars for large infrastructure projects (World Bank 2013b). To accelerate and increase the supply of bankable projects at the national and regional levels, particularly in LDCs, international support programmes could be established with the financial support of ODA and technical assistance of MDBs.

b. Redesign of investment incentives for SDGs

Reorienting investment incentives towards SDGs implies targeting investments in SDG sectors and making incentives conditional on social and environmental performance.

Designing investment incentives schemes for SDGs implies putting emphasis on the quality of investments in terms of their mid- and long-term social and environmental effects (table IV.3). Essentially, incentives would move from purely *"location-focused"* (a tool to increase the competitiveness of a location) to more *"SDG-focused"* (a tool to promote investment in sustainable development).

SDG-oriented investment incentives can be of two types:

- Incentives targeted specifically at SDG sectors (e.g. those provided for investment in renewable energy, infrastructure or health).

- Incentives conditional upon social and environmental performance of investors (including, for instance, related to policies on social inclusion). Examples include performance requirements relating to employment, training, local sourcing of inputs, R&D, energy efficiency or location of facilities in disadvantaged regions.

Table IV.4 contains some examples of investment incentives related to environmental sustainability.

In UNCTAD's most recent survey of IPAs, these agencies noted that among SDG sectors investment incentive schemes are mostly provided for energy, R&D and infrastructure development projects. In addition to these sectors, incentives are sometimes

Table IV.3. Traditional and sustainable development oriented investment incentives

Traditional economic growth oriented investment incentives	Investment incentives that take into account sustainable development considerations
Focus on sectors important for economic growth, job creation and export generation	Additional focus on SDG sectors
Focus on short- and medium-term economic gains	Long-term implications of investment for sustainable development considered
Cost-benefit analysis in favour of economic gains	Cost-benefit analysis with adequate weight to long-term social and environmental costs of investment
Lowering of regulatory standards considered as a policy option	Lowering of regulatory standards as part of the incentives package excluded
Monitoring primarily of economic impacts of the investment	Monitoring of the overall impact of the investment on sustainable development

Source: UNCTAD.

provided for projects across numerous SDG areas, or linked to SDG objectives through performance criteria.

In addition to financial, fiscal or regulatory incentives, governments can facilitate investors by building surrounding enabling infrastructure or by letting them use such infrastructure at low or zero cost. For instance, investments in agricultural production require good storage and transportation facilities. Investments in renewable energy (e.g. wind or solar parks) necessitate the building of a grid to transport the energy to consumers. The construction of schools and hospitals in rural areas calls for adequate roads, and public transportation to make education and health services easily reachable. There is an important role for domestic, regional and multilateral development banks in realizing such enabling projects.

A reorientation of investment incentives policies (especially regulatory incentives) towards sustainable development could also necessitate a phasing out of incentives that may have negative social or ecological side effects, in particular where such incentives result in a "race-to-the-bottom" with regard to social or environmental standards or in a financially unsustainable "race to the top".

A stronger focus on sustainable development may call for a review of existing subsidy programs for entire industries. For example, the World Bank estimates that $1 trillion to $1.2 trillion per year are currently being spent on environmentally harmful subsidies for fossil fuels, agriculture, water and fisheries (World Bank 2012). More generally,

investment incentives are costly. Opportunity costs must be carefully considered. Public financial outlays in case of financial incentives, or missed revenues in case of fiscal incentives, could be used directly for SDG investment projects.

Investment incentives should also not become permanent; the supported project must have the potential to become self-sustainable over time – something that may be difficult to achieve in some SDG sectors. This underlines the importance of monitoring the actual effects of investment incentives on sustainable development, including the possibility of their withdrawal if the impact proves unsatisfactory.

c. Establish regional SDG investment compacts

Regional SDG investment compacts can help spur private investment in cross-border infrastructure projects and build regional clusters of firms in SDG sectors.

Regional cooperation can foster SDG investment. A key area for such SDG-related cross-border cooperation is infrastructure development.

Existing regional economic cooperation initiatives could evolve towards *regional SDG investment compacts*. Such compacts could focus on liberalization and facilitation of investment and establish joint investment promotion mechanisms and institutions. Regional industrial development compacts could include in their scope all policy areas important for enabling regional development, such as the harmonization, mutual recognition or

Table IV.4. Examples of investment incentives linked to environmental sustainability	
Country	**Environmental incentives**
Brazil	• Initiative and incentive programs for wind, power, biomass and small hydro-subsectors
Canada	• Special tax credits for development of new technologies that address issues of climate change, clean air, and water and soil quality
	• Nova Scotia provides up to 20 per cent of the development cost of ocean tech and non-traditional energy sources
Germany	• Grant programs for projects related to energy efficiency, CO_2 reduction and renewable energy
Indonesia	• 5- to 10-year tax break in renewable energy
Japan	• Investments in smart communities that unite information networks, energy systems and traffic systems as well as improve comfort and reduce CO_2 emissions
South Africa	• Accelerated depreciation for investments in renewable energy and biofuel production
	• Tax break for entities that become more energy-efficient
	• Allowance for expenditure on green technology and improved resource efficiency
Turkey	• Interest-free loans for renewable energy production and for projects to improve energy efficiency and reduce environmental impact
United Kingdom	• Funding schemes for off-shore wind farms
United States	• Guaranteed loans to eligible clean energy projects and direct loans to manufacturers of advanced technology vehicles and components
	• Tax incentives to improve energy efficiency in the industrial sector
	• Incentives at the state level

Source: UNCTAD based on desk research.[30]

approximation of regulatory standards and the consolidation of private standards on environmental, social and governance issues.

Regional SDG investment compacts could aim to create cross-border clusters through the build-up of relevant infrastructure and absorptive capacity. Establishing such compacts implies working in partnership, between governments of the region to identify joint investment projects, between investment promotion agencies for joint promotion efforts, between governments and international organizations for technical assistance and capacity-building, and between the public and private sector for investment in infrastructure and absorptive capacity (figure IV.12) (see also *WIR13*).

5.   Building SDG investment partnerships

Partnerships between home countries of investors, host countries, TNCs and MDBs can help overcome knowledge gaps as well as generate joint investments in SDG sectors.

Private investors' lack of awareness of suitable sustainable development projects, and a shortfall in expertise, can be overcome through *knowledge-*

sharing mechanisms, networks and multi-stakeholder partnerships.

Multi-stakeholder partnerships can support investment in SDG sectors because they enhance cooperation, understanding and trust between key partners. Partnerships can facilitate and strengthen expertise, for instance by supporting the development of innovative and synergistic ways to pool resources and talents, and by involving relevant stakeholders that can make a contribution to sustainable development. Partnerships can have a number of goals, such as joint analysis and research, information sharing to identify problems and solutions, development of guidelines for best practices, capacity-building, progress monitoring and implementation, or promotion of understanding and trust between stakeholders. The following are two examples of potential partnerships that can raise investor expertise in SDGs.

Partnerships between home- and host-country investment promotion agencies.

Cooperation between outward investment agencies in home countries and IPAs in host

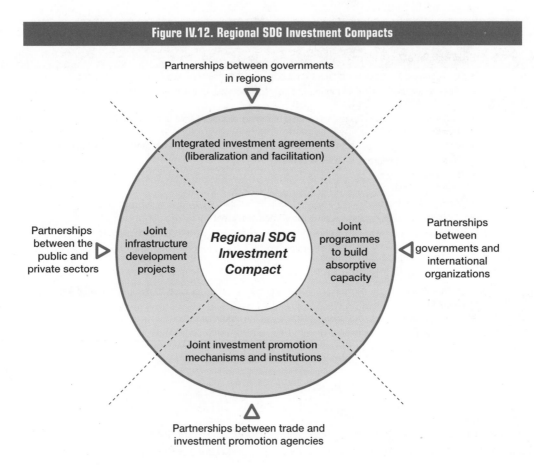

Figure IV.12. Regional SDG Investment Compacts

Partnerships between governments
in regions

Integrated investment agreements
(liberalization and facilitation)

Partnerships
between the
public and
private sectors

Joint
infrastructure
development
projects

*Regional SDG
Investment
Compact*

Joint
programmes
to build
absorptive
capacity

Partnerships
between
governments and
international
organizations

Joint investment promotion
mechanisms and institutions

Partnerships between trade and
investment promotion agencies

Source: UNCTAD.

countries could be ad hoc or systematic, and potentially institutionalized. IPAs that target projects related to sustainable development could partner with outward investment agencies for three broad purposes:

- Information dissemination and marketing of SDG investment opportunities in home countries. Outward investment agencies could provide matching services, helping IPAs identify potential investors to approach.

- Where outward investment agencies provide investment incentives and facilitation services to their investors for SDG projects, the partnership could increase chances of realizing the investment.

- Outward investment agencies incentives for SDG investments could be conditional on the ESG performance of investors, ensuring continued involvement of both parties in

the partnership for monitoring and impact assessment.

Through such partnerships outward investment agencies could evolve into genuine business development agencies for investments in SDGs in developing countries, raising awareness of investment opportunities, helping investors bridge knowledge gaps and gain expertise, and practically facilitating the investment process.

SVE-TNC-MDB triangular partnerships

Partnerships between governments of SVEs, private investors (TNCs), and MDBs could be fostered with the aim of promoting investments in SDG sectors which are of strategic interest to SVEs. Depending on the economy, the strategic sector may be infrastructure, a manufacturing industry or even a value chain segment. Crucially, in such "triangular" partnerships, stakeholders would work together to identify the bottlenecks for private investment, and jointly develop public-private solutions to develop the strategic sector, bearing in mind wider socioeconomic and long-term ramifications. In particular, the partnership would work towards raising long-term, sound and sustainable investment in SDGs, but also promote investment in surrounding economic and social infrastructure, giving support to governments towards a sound management of resources through collaborative stakeholder engagement. In all cases, the SVE government has to be in the "driver's seat".

Participating TNCs will typically be players in the sector, with consequent reputational risks if the partnership fails. In some case the SVE may make up (or become) an important part of the TNCs' operations in a sector – e.g. as a supply base for a commodity – leading to the firm having a stake in a well-run economy and local development. TNCs may also enter the partnership to demonstrate good corporate citizenship. The participation of MDBs – or equivalent entities – is required to monitor progress and impact, safeguard against unwarranted economic dominance, provide policy advice, and run contiguous development projects (e.g. linkages created with local firms).

Beyond formal partnerships, broad knowledge-sharing platforms can also help. Governments, private and public research institutions, market intermediaries and development agencies all play a role in producing and disseminating information on investment experience and future project opportunities. This can be done through platforms for knowledge sharing and dissemination. Examples include the Green Growth Knowledge Platform (GGKP), launched by the Global Green Growth Institute, the OECD, UNEP and the World Bank. Investors themselves also establish networks that foster relationships, propose tools, support advocacy, allow sharing of experiences, and can lead to new investment opportunities.

F. ENSURING SUSTAINABLE DEVELOPMENT IMPACT OF INVESTMENT IN THE SDGs

1. Challenges in managing the impact of private investment in SDG sectors

Key challenges in managing the impact of private investment in SDG sectors include weak absorptive capacity in some developing countries, social and environmental impact risks, the need for stakeholder engagement and effective impact monitoring.

Once investment has been mobilized and channelled towards SDG sectors, there remain challenges to overcome in order to ensure that the resultant benefits for sustainable development are maximized, and the potential associated drawbacks mitigated (figure IV.13). Key challenges include the following.

Weak absorptive capacity in developing economies. Developing countries, LDCs in particular, often suffer from a lack of capacity to absorb the benefits of investment. There is a risk that the gains from investment accrue primarily to the investor and are not shared through spillovers and improvement in local productive capacity. A lack of managerial or technical capabilities among local firms and workers hinders the extent to which they can form business linkages with foreign investors, integrate new technologies, and develop local skills and capacity.

Risks associated with private investment in SDG sectors. There are challenges associated with greater private sector engagement in often sensitive SDG sectors in developing countries. At a general level, the social and environmental impacts of private sector operations need to be addressed across the board. But opening basic-needs sectors such as water and sanitation, health care or education to private investors requires careful preparation and the establishment of appropriate regulatory frameworks within which firms will operate.

In addition, where efforts are made specifically to attract private investment from international investors, there are risks that part of the positive impact of such investment for local economies does

---

Figure IV.13. Maximizing the sustainable development impact of investment and minimizing risks

Key challenges

- Weak absorptive capacity in developing countries

- Need to minimize risks associated with private investment in SDG sectors

- Need to engage stakeholders and manage impact trade-offs

- Inadequate investment impact measurement and reporting tools

Policy options

Build productive capacity, entrepreneurship, technology, skills, linkages
- Entrepreneurship development, inclusive finance initiatives, technology dissemination, business linkages.
- New economic zones for SDG investment, or conversion of existing SEZs and technology zones.

Establish effective regulatory frameworks and standards
- Environmental, labour, social regulations; effective taxation; mainstreaming of SDGs into IIAs; coordination of SDG investment policies at national and international levels.

Good governance, capable institutions, stakeholders engagement
- Stakeholder engagement for private investment in sensitive SDG sectors; institutions with the power to act in the interest of stakeholders.

Implement SDG impact assessment systems
- Indicators for measuring (and reporting to stakeholders) the economic, social and environmental performance of SDG investments.
- Corporates to add ESG and SDG dimensions to financial reporting to influence their behaviour on the ground.

Source: UNCTAD.

---

not materialize or leaks away as a result of relatively low taxes paid by investors (in cases where they are attracted with the help of fiscal incentives) or profits being shifted out of the country within the international networks of TNCs. The tax collection capabilities of developing countries, and especially LDCs, may not be sufficient to safeguard against such practices.

Finally, regulatory options for governments to mitigate risks and safeguard against negative effects when attracting private investment into SDG sectors can be affected by international commitments that reduce policy space.

Need to engage stakeholders and manage trade-offs effectively. Attracting needed investment in agriculture to increase food production may have consequences for smallholders or displace local populations. Investments in infrastructure can affect local communities in a variety of ways. Investments in water supply can involve making trade-offs between availability and affordability in urban areas versus wider accessibility. Health and education investments, especially by private sector

operators, are generally sensitive areas that require engagement with stakeholders and buy-in from local communities. Managing such engagement in the investment process, and managing the consequences or negative side effects of investments requires adequate consultation processes and strong institutions.

Inadequate investment impact measurement and reporting tools. Ensuring the on-the-ground impact of investment in SDG sectors is fundamental to justifying continued efforts to attract private investment in them and to enhance governance of such investment. Many initiatives to mobilize and channel funds to SDGs are hampered by a lack of accurate impact indicators. Even where measurement tools exist at the project level (e.g. for direct impacts of individual investments on their immediate environment), they may be available at the macro level (e.g. long-term aggregate impacts of investments across a sector). Adequate measurement of impact is a prerequisite for many upstream initiatives.

2. Increasing absorptive capacity

The development of local enterprise and local technological capabilities that will enhance the ability of domestic firms to engage in and benefit from technology and skills dissemination is referred to in this chapter as domestic absorptive capacity. Domestic absorptive capacity is crucial not only to increase chances of attracting private investment, but also in order to maximize the benefits of private investment in SDG sectors. Policy can help create an operating environment that allows local firms, entrepreneurs and workers to realize the benefits of investment in SDG sectors. The key elements that enhance absorptive capacity differ by SDG sector (table IV.5). The development of these absorptive capacity elements also builds productive capacity in host countries which in turn encourages further investment, creating a virtuous circle.

a. Key policy areas: entrepreneurship, technology, skills, linkages

A range of policy tools is available to increase absorptive capacity, including the promotion and facilitation of entrepreneurship, support to technology development, human resource and skills development, business development services and promotion of business linkages.

A wide range of policy options exist for governments to improve the absorptive capacity of local economies, in order to maximize the benefits of private investment entering SDG sectors. Firstly, this revolves around increasing involvement of local entrepreneurs; micro, small and medium-sized firms; and smallholders, in the case of agricultural investment. Secondly, governments can increase the domestic skills base not only as an enabler for private investment, but also to increase the transfer of benefits to local economies. Thirdly, local enterprise development and upgrading can be further encouraged through the widening and deepening of SDG-oriented linkages programmes. Technology dissemination and knowledge sharing between firms is key to technological development, for instance of new technologies that would result in green growth. Fostering linkages between firms, within and across borders, can facilitate the process of technology dissemination and diffusion, which

in turn can be instrumental in helping developing countries catch up with developed countries and shift towards more sustainable growth paths.

Promote entrepreneurship

- *Stimulating entrepreneurship, including social entrepreneurship, for sustainable development.* Domestic entrepreneurial development can strengthen participation of local entrepreneurs within or related to SDG sectors, and foster inclusiveness (see UNCTAD's Entrepreneurship Policy Framework[31]). In particular, through social entrepreneurship, governments can create special business incubators for social enterprises. The criteria for ventures to be hosted in such "social business incubators" are that they should have a social impact, be sustainable and show potential for growth. These kinds of initiatives are proliferating worldwide, as social entrepreneurs are identified as critical change agents who will use economic and technological innovation to achieve social development goals.[32]

Table IV.5. Selected ways to raise absorptive capacity in SDG sectors

SDG sector	Examples
Infrastructure (50%)	Construction and engineering capabilities of local firms and workforce
	Project management expertise of local workforce
	Presence of local suppliers and contractors
Climate change and environment (27%)	Entrepreneurship skills, clusters of renewable energy firms
	R&D, science and technology parks for low carbon technology
	Presence of laboratories, research institutes, universities
Food security (12%)	Clusters of agribusiness processing firms
	Local suppliers of inputs, crops, fertilizers, replacement machinery
	Local workforce skilled in crop production and processing
Social sectors (11%)	Local skills in provision of services e.g. teaching, nursing
	Managerial capabilities to run schools, hospitals
	Local (social) entrepreneurship skills

Source: UNCTAD.

Note: Percentages represent the average share of investment needs identified for each sector in section B.

- *Encourage financial inclusiveness.* Initiatives and programmes can be encouraged to facilitate access to finance for entrepreneurs in micro, small and medium-sized firms or women-owned firms (or firms owned by under-represented groups). In order to improve access to credit by local small and medium-sized enterprises and smallholders, loans can be provided by public bodies when no other reasonable option exists. They enable local actors to make investments of a size and kind that the domestic private banking sector may not support. Financial guarantees by governments put commercial banks in a position to grant credits to small customers without a financial history or collateral. Policies can also relax some regulatory requirements for providing credits, for instance the "know your customer" requirement in financial services (Tewes-Gradl et al. 2013).

Boost technology and skills development

- *Support science and technology development.* Technical support organizations in standards, metrology, quality, testing, R&D, productivity and extension for small and medium-sized enterprises are necessary to complete and improve the technology systems with which firms operate and grow. Appropriate levels of intellectual property (IP) protection and an effective IP rights framework can help give firms confidence in employing advanced technologies and provide incentives for local firms to develop or adapt their own technologies.

- *Develop human resources and skills.* Focus on training and education to raise availability of relevant local skills in SDG sectors is a crucial determinant to maximize long-term benefits from investment in SDG sectors. Countries can also adopt a degree of openness in granting work permits to skilled foreign workers, to allow for a lack of domestic skills and/or to avail themselves of foreign skills which complement and fertilize local knowledge and expertise.

- *Provide business development services.* A range of services can facilitate business activity and investment, and generate spillover effects. Such services might include business development services centres and capacity-building facilities to help local firms meet technical standards and improve their understanding of international trade rules and practices. Increased access could be granted for social enterprises, including through social business incubators, clusters and green technology parks.

- *Establish enterprise clustering and networking.* Enterprise agglomeration may determine "collective efficiency" that in turn enhances the productivity and overall performance of clustered firms. Both offer opportunities to foster competitiveness via learning and upgrading. Other initiatives include the creation of social entrepreneurship networks and networks of innovative institutions and enterprises to support inclusive innovation initiatives.

Widen and deepen SDG-oriented linkages programmes

- *Stimulate business linkages.* Domestic and international inter-firm and inter-institution linkages can provide local firms with the necessary externalities to cope with the dual challenge of knowledge creation and upgrading. Policies should be focused on promoting more inclusive business linkages models, including support for the development of local processing units; fostering inclusive rural markets including through pro-poor public-private sector partnerships; integrating inclusive business linkages promotion into national development strategies; and encouraging domestic and foreign investors to develop inclusive business linkages.

- *Create pro-poor business linkages opportunities.* Private investment in SDGs can create new pro-poor opportunities for local suppliers – small farmers, small service providers and local vendors. Potential policy actions to foster pro-poor linkages include disseminating information about bottom of the pyramid consumers' needs; creating shared supplier databases; leveraging local logistics networks; introduce market diversification services for local suppliers; addressing constraints related to inadequate physical infrastructure through supply collection centres, shared premises and internet-based solutions; and promoting micro-franchising schemes, for instance in the health-care sector, in order to promote access (to health services), awareness, availability and affordability.

b. SDG incubators and special economic zones

Development of linkages and clusters in incubators or economic zones specifically aimed at stimulating businesses in SDG sectors may be particularly effective.

The aforementioned range of initiatives to maximize absorptive capacity of SDG investment could be made more (cost-) effective if they are conducted in one place through the creation of special economic zones (SEZs) or technology zones, or the conversion of existing ones into SDG-focused clusters. These can be used to promote, attract, and retain investment in specific and interrelated SDG sectors with a positive impact arising from:

- *Clusters and networks* of closely associated firms and activities supporting the development of inclusive spillovers and linkages within zones, and beyond. As local firms' capabilities rise, demonstration effects become increasingly important.

- *Incubator facilities and processes* designed into zones' sustainable development support services and infrastructure to nurture local business and social firms/entrepreneurs (and assist them in benefitting from the local cluster).

- Zones acting as mechanisms to *diffuse responsible practices*, including in terms of labour practices, environmental sustainability,[33] health and safety, and good governance.

An SDG-focused zone could be *rural-based*, linked to specific agricultural products, and designed to support and nurture smallholder farmers, social

entrepreneurs from the informal sector and ensure social inclusion of disadvantaged groups.

In the context of SDG-focused SEZs, policymakers should consider broadening the availability of sustainable-development-related policies, services and infrastructure to assist companies in meeting stakeholder demands – for instance, improved corporate social responsibility policies and practices. This would strengthen the State's ability to promote environmental best practices and meet its obligation to protect the human rights of workers. Finally, SEZs should improve their reporting to better communicate the sustainable development services.

3. Establishing effective regulatory frameworks and standards

Increased private sector engagement in often sensitive SDG sectors needs to be accompanied by effective regulation. Particular areas of attention include human health and safety, environmental and social protection, quality and inclusiveness of public services, taxation, and national and international policy coherence.

Reaping the development benefits from investment in SDG sectors requires not only an enabling policy framework, but also adequate regulation to minimize any risks associated with investment (see table IV.6 for examples of regulatory tools). Moreover, investment policy and regulations must be adequately enforced by impartial, capable and efficient public institutions, which is as important for policy effectiveness as policy design itself.

In regulating investment in SDG sectors, and in investment regulations geared towards sustainable development in general, protection of human rights, health and safety standards, social and environmental protection and respect of core labour rights are essential. A number of further considerations are especially important:

- *Safeguarding quality and inclusiveness of public services.* Easing constraints for private investors in SDGs must not come at the price of poor quality of services (e.g. in electricity or water supply, education and health services). This calls for appropriate standard setting by

Table IV.6. Examples of policy tools to ensure the sustainability of investment

SDG	Regulations
Environmental sustainability	Pollution emission rules (e.g. carbon taxes)
	Environmental protection zones
	Risk-sensitive land zoning
	Environmental impact assessments of investments
	Reporting requirements on environmental performance of investment
	Good corporate citizenship
Social sustainability	Labour policies and contract law
	Human rights
	Land tenure rights
	Migration policies
	Safety regulations
	Provisions on safe land and housing for low-income communities
	Prohibition of discrimination
	Reporting requirements on social performance of investment
	Social impact assessments of investments

Source: UNCTAD.

host countries concerning the content, quality, inclusiveness and reliability of the services (e.g. programs for school education, hygienic standards in hospitals, provision of clean water, uninterrupted electricity supply, compulsory contracting for essential infrastructure services), and for monitoring compliance. Laws on consumer protection further reinforce the position of service recipients.

• Contractual arrangements between host countries and private investors can play a significant role. Through the terms of concession agreements, joint ventures or PPPs, host countries can ensure that private service providers respect certain quality standards in respect of human health, environmental protection, inclusiveness and reliability of supply. This includes a sanction mechanism if the contractual partners fail to live up to their commitments.

• *Balancing the need for fair tax revenues with investment attractiveness.* Effective tax policies are crucial to ensure that tax revenues are sufficient and that they can be used for SDGs, such as the financing of public

services, infrastructure development or health and education services. Taxation is also an important policy tool to correct market failures in respect of the SDG impact of investment, e.g. through imposing carbon taxes or providing tax relief for renewable energies. Introducing an efficient and fair tax system is, however, far from straightforward, especially in developing countries. A recent report on tax compliance puts many developing countries at the bottom in the ranking on tax efficiency (PwC 2014b). Countries should consider how to broaden the tax base, (i) by reviewing incentive schemes for effectiveness, and (ii) by improving tax collection capabilities and combating tax avoidance. An example of a successful recent tax reform is Ecuador, which significantly increased its tax collection rate. These additional revenues were spent for infrastructure development and other social purposes. The country now has the highest proportion of public investment as a share of GDP in the region.[34] To combat tax avoidance and tax evasion, it is necessary to close existing loopholes in taxation laws. In addition to efforts at the domestic level, this requires more international cooperation, as demonstrated by recent undertakings in the G-20, the OECD and the EU, among others. Developing countries, especially LDCs, will require technical assistance to improve tax collection capabilities and to deal with new and complex rules that will emerge from ongoing international initiatives.

• *Ensuring coherence in national and international policymaking.* Regulations need to cover a broad range of policy areas beyond investment policies per se, such as taxation, competition, labour market regulation, environmental policies and access to land. The coverage of such a multitude of different policy areas confirms the need for consistency and coherence in policymaking across government institutions. At the domestic level, this means, e.g. coordination at the interministerial level and between central, regional and local governments.

Coherence is also an issue for the relationship between domestic legislation and international agreements in the areas of investment, environmental protection and social rights, among others. Numerous international conventions and non-binding principles provide important policy guidance on how to design and improve domestic regulatory frameworks, including UNCTAD's IPFSD.

- *Making international investment agreements (IIAs) proactive in mobilizing and channelling investment into SDGs.* Most IIAs still remain silent on environmental and social issues. Only recent agreements start dealing with sustainability issues, but primarily from the perspective of maintaining regulatory space for environmental and social purposes. IIAs could do more and also promote investment in SDGs in a proactive manner. This includes, for example, emphasising the importance of SDGs as an overarching objective of the agreement or a commitment of contracting parties to particularly encourage and facilitate investment in SDGs. These are issues both for the negotiation of new IIAs and the renegotiation of existing agreements. Systematic reform, as outlined in chapter III of this report, can help.

Finally, while laws and regulations are the basis of investor responsibility, voluntary CSR initiatives and standards have proliferated in recent years, and they are increasingly influencing corporate practices, behaviour and investment decisions. Governments can build on them to complement the regulatory framework and maximize the development benefits of investment. A number of areas can benefit from the encouragement of CSR initiatives and the voluntary dissemination of standards; for example, they can be used to promote responsible investment and business behaviour (including the avoidance of corrupt business practices), and they can play an important role in promoting low-carbon and environmentally sound investment.

4. Good governance, capable institutions, stakeholder engagement

Good governance and capable institutions are key enablers for the attraction of private investment in general, and in SDG sectors in particular. They are also needed for effective stakeholder engagement and management of impact trade-offs.

Good governance and capable institutions are essential to promoting investment in SDGs and maximizing positive impact in a number of ways: (i) to attract investment, (ii) to guarantee inclusive policymaking and impacts, (iii) to manage synergies and trade-offs.

Attracting investment. Good governance is a prerequisite for attracting investment in general, and in SDG sectors in particular. Investments in infrastructure, with their long gestation period, are particularly contingent on a stable policy environment and capable local institutions. Institutional capabilities are also important in dealing or negotiating with investors, and for the effective implementation of investment regulation.

Stakeholder engagement. Additionally, investment in SDG areas affects many stakeholders in different ways. Managing differential impacts and "side effects" of SDG investments requires giving a say to affected populations through effective consultative processes. It also requires strong capabilities on the part of governments to deal with consequences, for example to mitigate negative impacts on local communities where necessary, while still progressing on investment in targeted SDG objectives.

Adequate participation of multiple stakeholders at various levels is needed, as governance of investment in SDGs is important not just at the national level but also at the regional and local levels. In fact, SDG investments are subject to governance at different levels, e.g. from local metropolitan areas to national investments to regional infrastructure (such as highways, intercity rail, port-related services for many countries, transnational power systems).

Synergies and trade-offs. A holistic, cross-sectoral approach that creates synergies between the different SDG pillars and deals with trade-offs is important to promote sustainable development. Objectives such as economic growth, poverty reduction, social development, equity, and sustainability should be considered together with a long-term outlook to ensure coherence. To do this, governments can make strategic choices about which sectors to build on, and all relevant ministries can be involved in developing a focused development agenda grounded on assessments of emerging challenges. Integration of budgets and allocating resources to strategic goals rather than individual ministries can encourage coherence across governments. Integrated decision-making for SDGs is also important at sub-national levels (Clark 2012).

Promoting SDGs through investment-related policies may also result in trade-offs between potentially conflicting policy objectives. For example, excessive regulation of investor activity can deter investment; fiscal or financial investment incentives for the development of one SDG pillar can reduce the budget available for the promotion of other pillars. Also, within regions or among social groups, choices may have to be made when it comes to prioritizing individual investment projects.

At the international policymaking level, synergies are equally important. International macroeconomic policy setting, and reforms of the international financial architecture, have a direct bearing on national and international investment policies, and on the chances of success in attracting investment in SDGs.

5. Implementing SDG impact assessment systems

a. Develop a common set of SDG impact indicators

Monitoring of the impact of investment, especially along social and environmental dimensions, is key to effective policy implementation. A set of core quantifiable impact indicators can help.

Monitoring. SDG-related governance requires monitoring the impact of investments, including measuring progress against goals. UNCTAD has suggested a number of guiding principles that are relevant in this context (IPFSD, *WIR12*). Investment policies should be based on a set of explicitly formulated objectives related to SDGs and ideally include a number of quantifiable goals for both the attraction of investment and the impact of investment on SDGs. The objectives should set

clear priorities, a time frame for achieving them, and the principal measures intended to support the objectives.

To measure policy effectiveness for the attraction of investment, policymakers should use a focused set of key indicators that are the most direct expression of the core sustainable development contributions of private investments, including direct contributions to GDP growth through additional value added, capital formation and export generation; entrepreneurial development and development of the formal sector and tax base; and job creation. Central to this should be indicators addressing labour, social, environmental and sustainability development aspects.

The impact indicator methodology developed for the G-20 Development Working Group by UNCTAD, in collaboration with other agencies, may provide guidance to policymakers on the choice of indicators of investment impact and, by extension, of investment policy effectiveness (see table IV.7). The indicator framework, which has been tested in a number of developing countries, is meant to serve as a tool that countries can adapt and adopt in accordance with their national sustainable development priorities and strategies (see also IPFSD, *WIR12*).

Sustainable development impacts of investment in SDGs can be cross-cutting. For instance, clusters promoting green technology entrepreneurship can serve as economic growth poles, with employment generation and creation of value added as positive side effects. Investments in environmental protection schemes can have positive effects on human health and indirectly on economic growth. Such cross-cutting effects should be reflected in impact measurement methodologies.

At the micro level (i.e. the sustainable development impact of individual investments), the choice of indicators can be further detailed and sophisticated, as data availability is greater. Additional indicators might include qualitative measures such as new management practices or techniques transferred, social benefits generated for workers (health care, pensions, insurance), or ancillary benefits not directly related to the investment project objectives

Table IV.7. Possible indicators for the definition of investment impact objectives and the measurement of policy effectiveness		
Area	**Indicators**	**Details and examples**
Economic value added	1. Total value added	• Gross output (GDP contribution) of the new/additional economic activity resulting from the investment (direct and induced)
	2. Value of capital formation	• Contribution to gross fixed capital formation
	3. Total and net export generation	• Total export generation; net export generation (net of imports) is also captured by the value added indicator
	4. Number of formal business entities	• Number of businesses in the value chain supported by the investment; this is a proxy for entrepreneurial development and expansion of the formal (tax-paying) economy .
	5. Total fiscal revenues	• Total fiscal take from the economic activity resulting from the investment, through all forms of taxation
Job creation	6. Employment (number)	• Total number of jobs generated by the investment, both direct and induced (value chain view), dependent and self-employed
	7. Wages	• Total household income generated, direct and induced
	8. Typologies of employee skill levels	• Number of jobs generated, by ILO job type, as a proxy for job quality and technology levels (including technology dissemination)
Sustainable development	9. Labour impact indicators	• Employment of women (and comparable pay) and of disadvantaged groups • Skills upgrading, training provided • Health and safety effects, occupational injuries
	10. Social impact indicators	• Number of families lifted out of poverty, wages above subsistence level • Expansion of goods and services offered, access to and affordability of basic goods and services
	11. Environmental impact indicators	• GHG emissions, carbon offset/credits, carbon credit revenues • Energy and water consumption/efficiency hazardous materials • Enterprise development in eco-sectors
	12. Development impact indicators	• Development of local resources • Technology dissemination

Source: IAWG (2011).

Note: The report was produced by an inter-agency working group coordinated by UNCTAD.

(recreational facilities, schools and clinics for workers, families or local communities).

b. Require integrated corporate reporting for SDGs

Impact measurement and reporting by private investors on their social and environmental performance promotes corporate responsibility on the ground and supports mobilization and channelling of investment.

Corporate sustainability reporting is an important enabler of policies to promote the SDGs. High-quality sustainability reporting involves the generation of internal company data on sustainability related activities and control systems, facilitating proactive management, target setting and benchmarking. Publicly reported data can play an important role in enabling governments to monitor the effectiveness

of policies and incentive structures, and often serve as a prerequisite for resource mobilization for SDG investment.

The importance of sustainability reporting has been recognized throughout the process leading up to the formation of the SDGs. In 2013, the High-Level Panel of Eminent Persons on the Post-2015 Development Agenda proposed that "in future – at latest by 2030 – all large businesses should be reporting on their environmental and social impact – or explain why if they are not doing so". (United Nations 2013). In 2014, the European Parliament adopted a directive which will require the disclosure of environmental and social information by large public-interest companies (500+ employees). Individual UN Member States around the world have also taken steps to promote sustainability reporting.[35] Apart from regulatory initiatives, some stock exchanges have implemented mandatory listing requirements in the area of sustainability reporting.[36]

The content and approach to the preparation of sustainability reports is influenced by a number of international initiatives actively promoting reporting practices, standards and frameworks.

Recent examples of such initiatives and entities include the Global Reporting Initiative (GRI),[37] the Carbon Disclosure Project (CDP),[38] the International Integrated Reporting Council (IIRC),[39] the Accounting for Sustainability (A4S)[40] and the Sustainability Accounting Standards Board (SASB).[41] UNCTAD has also been active in this area (box IV.6)

Box IV.6. UNCTAD's initiative on sustainability reporting

UNCTAD has provided guidance on sustainability rule making via its Intergovernmental Working Group of Experts on International Standards of Accounting and Reporting (ISAR) (UNCTAD 2014). Member States at ISAR endorsed the following recommendations:

- Introducing voluntary sustainability reporting initiatives can be a practical option to allow companies time to develop the capacity to prepare high-quality sustainability reports.

- Sustainability reporting initiatives can also be introduced on a comply or explain basis, to establish a clear set of disclosure expectations while allowing for flexibility and avoiding an undue burden on enterprises.

- Stock exchanges and/or regulators may consider advising the market on the future direction of sustainability reporting rules. Companies should be allotted sufficient time to adapt, especially if stock exchanges or regulators are considering moving from a voluntary approach to a mandatory approach.

- Sustainability reporting initiatives should avoid creating reporting obligations for companies that may not have the capacity to meet them. Particularly in the case of mandatory disclosure initiatives, one option is to require only a subset of companies (e.g. large companies or State-owned companies) to disclose on sustainability issues.

- Stock exchanges and regulators may wish to consider highlighting sustainability issues in their existing definitions of what constitutes material information for the purposes of corporate reporting.

- With a view to promoting an internationally harmonized approach, stock exchanges and regulators may wish to consider basing sustainability reporting initiatives on an international reporting framework.

Considerations for the design and implementation of sustainability reporting initiatives include using a multi-stakeholder consultation approach in the development process for creating widespread adoption and buy-in and creating incentives for compliance, including public recognition and investor engagement.

Source: UNCTAD.

G. AN ACTION PLAN FOR PRIVATE SECTOR INVESTMENT IN THE SDGs

The range of challenges discussed in previous sections, as well as the wide array of existing and potential policy solutions available to overcome those challenges, demonstrate above all that there is no single all-encompassing solution or "magic bullet" for increasing the engagement of the private sector in raising finance for, and investing in, sustainable development. The potential sources and destinations of financial resources are varied, and so are the constraints they face. This chapter has attempted to highlight some of the paths that financial flows can follow towards useful investment in sustainable development projects, indicating a number of policy solutions to encourage such flows, to remove hurdles, to maximize the positive impacts and to minimize the potential risks involved.

Many of the more concrete solutions have been tried and tested over a significant period of time already

– such as risk-sharing mechanisms including PPPs and investment guarantees. Others have emerged more recently, such as various ways to raise finance for and stimulate impact investment. And yet others require broader change in markets themselves, in the mindset of participants in the market, in the way sustainable development projects are packaged and marketed, or in the broader policy setting for investment.

Given the massive financing needs that will be associated with the achievement of the SDGs, all of these solutions are worth exploring. What they need is a *concerted push* to address the main challenges they face in raising finance and in channelling it to sustainable development objectives. Figure IV.14 summarizes the key challenges and solutions discussed in this chapter in the context of the proposed Strategic Framework for Private Investment in the SDGs.

Figure IV.14. Key challenges and possible policy responses

	Key challenges	Policy responses
LEADERSHIP *Setting guiding principles, galvanizing action, ensuring policy coherence*	• Need for a clear sense of direction and common policy design criteria • Need for clear objectives to galvanize global action • Need to manage investment policy interactions • Need for global consensus and an inclusive process	• Agree a set of guiding principles for SDG investment policymaking • Set SDG investment targets • Ensure policy coherence and synergies • Multi-stakeholder platform and multi-agency technical assistance facility
MOBILIZATION *Raising finance and re-orienting financial markets towards investment in SDGs*	• Start-up and scaling issues for new financing solutions • Failures in global capital markets • Lack of transparency on sustainable corporate performance • Misaligned investor rewards/pay structures	• Create fertile soil for innovative SDG-financing approaches and corporate initiatives • Build or improve pricing mechanisms for externalities • Promote Sustainable Stock Exchanges • Introduce financial market reforms
CHANNELLING *Promoting and facilitating investment into SDG sectors*	• Entry barriers • Lack of information and effective packaging and promotion of SDG investment projects • Inadequate risk-return ratios for SDG investments • Lack of investor expertise in SDG sectors	• Build an investment policy climate conducive to investing in SDGs, while safeguarding public interests • Expand use of risk sharing mechanisms for SDG investments • Establish new incentives schemes and a new generation of investment promotion institutions • Build SDG investment partnerships
IMPACT *Maximizing sustainable development benefits, minimizing risks*	• Weak absorptive capacity in developing countries • Need to minimize risks associated with private investment in SDG sectors • Need to engage stakeholders and manage impact trade-offs • Inadequate investment impact measurement and reporting tools	• Build productive capacity, entrepreneurship, technology, skills, linkages • Establish effective regulatory frameworks and standards • Good governance, capable institutions, stakeholder engagements • Implement a common set of SDG investment impact indicators and push Integrated Corporate Reporting

Source: UNCTAD.

1. A Big Push for private investment in the SDGs

While there is a range of policy ideas and options available to policymakers, a focused set of priority packages can help shape a big push for SDG investment.

There are many solutions, mechanisms and policy initiatives that can work in raising private sector investment in sustainable development. However, a concerted push by the international community, and by policymakers at national levels, needs to focus on few priority actions – or packages. Six priority packages that address specific segments of the "SDG investment chain" and relatively homogenous groups of stakeholders, could constitute a significant "Big Push" for investment in the SDGs (figure IV.15). Such actions must be in line with the guiding principles for private sector investment in SDGs (section C.2), namely balancing liberalization and regulation, attractive risk return with accessible and affordable services, the push for private funds with the fundamental role of the State, and the global scope of the SDGs with special efforts for LDCs and other vulnerable economies.

1. *A new generation of investment promotion strategies and institutions.* Sustainable development projects, whether in infrastructure, social housing or renewable energy, require intensified efforts for investment promotion and facilitation. Such projects should become a priority of the work of investment promotion agencies and business development organizations, taking into account their peculiarities compared to other sectors. For example, some categories of investors in such projects may be less experienced in business operations in challenging host economies and require more intensive business development support.

The most frequent constraint faced by potential investors in sustainable development projects is the lack of concrete proposals of sizeable, impactful, and bankable projects. Promotion and facilitation of investment in sustainable development should include the marketing of pre-packaged and structured projects with priority consideration and sponsorship at the highest political level. This requires specialist expertise and dedicated units, e.g. government-sponsored "brokers" of sustainable development investment projects.

Putting in place such specialist expertise (ranging from project and structured finance expertise to engineering and project design skills) can be supported by technical assistance from international organizations and MDBs. Units could also be set up at the regional level (see also the regional compacts) to share costs and achieve economies of scale.

At the *international investment policy level*, promotion and facilitation objectives should be supported by ensuring that IIAs pursue the same objectives. Current agreements focus on the protection of investment. Mainstreaming sustainable development in IIAs requires, among others, proactive promotion of SDG investment, with commitments in areas such as technical assistance. Other measures include linking investment promotion institutions, facilitating SDG investments through investment insurance and guarantees, and regular impact monitoring.

2. *SDG-oriented investment incentives.* Investment incentive schemes can be restructured specifically to facilitate sustainable development projects, e.g. as part of risk-sharing solutions. In addition, investment incentives in general – independent of the economic sector for which they are granted – can incorporate sustainable development considerations by encouraging corporate behaviour in line with SDGs. A transformation is needed to move incentives from purely "*location-focused*" (aiming to increase the attractiveness of a location) towards increasingly "*SDG-focused*", aiming to promote investment for sustainable development.

Regional economic cooperation organizations, with national investment authorities in their region could adopt common incentive design criteria with the objective of reorienting investment incentive schemes towards sustainable development.

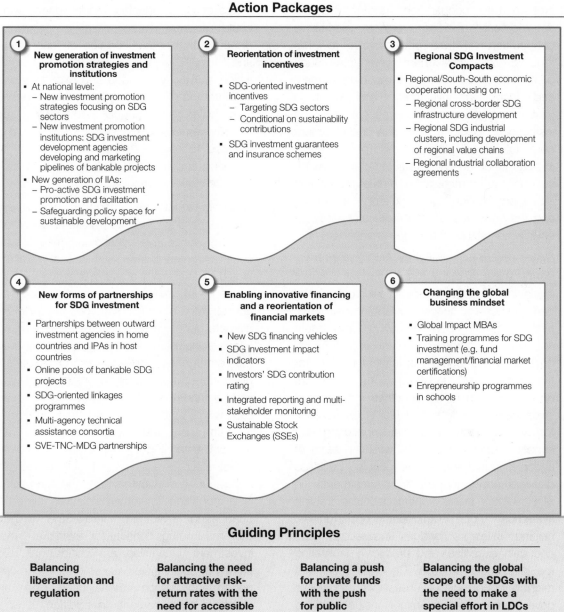

Figure IV.15. A Big Push for private investment in the SDGs: action packages

Source: UNCTAD.

3. *Regional SDG Investment Compacts*. Regional South-South cooperation can foster SDG investment. A key area for such SDG-related cross-border cooperation is infrastructure development. Existing regional economic cooperation initiatives could evolve towards regional SDG investment compacts. Such compacts could focus on reducing barriers and facilitating investment and establish joint investment promotion mechanisms and institutions. Regional industrial development compacts could include all policy areas important for enabling regional development, such as the harmonization, mutual recognition or approximation of regulatory standards and the consolidation of private standards on environmental, social and governance issues.

4. *New forms of partnership for SDG investments*. Partnerships in many forms, and at different levels, including South-South, are crucial to the performance and success of SDG investments. First, cooperation between outward investment agencies in home countries and IPAs in host countries could be institutionalized for the purpose of marketing SDG investment opportunities in home countries, provision of investment incentives and facilitation services for SDG projects; and joint monitoring and impact assessment. Outward investment agencies could evolve into genuine business development agencies for investments in SDG sectors in developing countries, raising awareness of investment opportunities, helping investors bridge knowledge gaps and gain expertise, and practically facilitating the investment process. Concrete tools that might support SDG investment business development services might include on-line tools with pipelines of bankable projects, and opportunities for linkages programmes in developing countries. **Multi-agency consortia** (a "one-stop shop" for SDG investment solutions) could help to support LDCs in establishing appropriate institutions and schemes to encourage, channel and maximize the impact from private sector investment.

Other forms of partnership might lead to SDG incubators and special economic zones based on close collaboration between the public and private sectors (domestic and foreign), such as SDG-focused rural-based agriculture zones or SDG industrial model towns, which could support more effective generation, dissemination and absorption of technologies and skills. They would represent hubs from which activity, knowledge and expertise could spill into and diffuse across the wider economy. In a similar vein, triangular partnerships, such as between SVEs, TNCs and MDBs could be fostered to engage the private sector in the nurturing and expansion of sectors, industries or value chain segments.

5. *Enabling innovative financing mechanisms and reorienting financial markets*. New and existing innovative financing mechanisms, such as green bonds and impact investing, would benefit from a more effective enabling environment, allowing them to be scaled up and targeted at relevant sources of capital and ultimate beneficiaries. Systematic support and effective inclusion would especially encourage the emergence, take-up and/or expansion of under-utilized catalytic instruments (e.g. vertical funds) or go-to-market channels such as crowd funding. Beyond this, integrated reporting on the economic, social and environmental impact of private investors is a first step towards encouraging responsible behaviour by investors on the ground. It is a condition for other initiatives aimed at channelling investment into SDG projects and maximizing impact; for example, where investment incentives are conditional upon criteria of social inclusiveness or environmental performance, such criteria need clear and objective measurement. In addition, it is an enabler for responsible investment behaviour in financial markets and a prerequisite for initiatives aimed at mobilizing funds for investment in SDGs.

6. *Changing the business mindset and developing SDG investment expertise*. The majority of managers in the world's financial institutions and large multinational enterprises – the main sources of global investment – as well as most successful entrepreneurs

tend to be strongly influenced by models of business, management and investment that are commonly taught in business schools. Such models tend to focus on business and investment opportunities in mature or emerging markets, with the risk-return profiles associated with those markets, while they tend to ignore opportunities outside the parameters of these models. Conventional models also tend to be driven exclusively by calculations of economic risks and returns, often ignoring broader social and environmental impacts, both positive and negative. Moreover, a lack of consideration in standard business school teachings of the challenges associated with operating in poor countries, and the resulting need for innovative problem solving, tend to leave managers ill-prepared for pro-poor investments.

The majority of students interested in social entrepreneurship end up starting projects in middle- to high-income countries, and most impact investments – investments with objectives that explicitly include social or environmental returns – are located in mature markets. A curriculum for business schools that generates awareness of investment opportunities in poor countries and that instils in students the problem solving skills needed in developing-country operating environments will have an important long-term impact.

UNCTAD, in partnership with business school networks, teachers, students as well as corporates, is currently running an initiative to develop an "impact curriculum" for MBA programmes and management schools, and a platform for knowledge sharing, exchange of teaching materials and pooling of "pro-poor" internship opportunities in LDCs. UNCTAD invites all stakeholders who can contribute to join the partnership.

2. Stakeholder engagement and a platform for new ideas

The Strategic Framework for Private Investment in the SDGs provides a basis for stakeholder engagement and development of further ideas. UNCTAD's World Investment Forum and its Investment Policy Hub provide the infrastructure.

The Plan of Action for Private Investment in the SDGs (figure IV.16) proposed in this chapter is not an all-encompassing or exhaustive list of solutions and initiatives. Primarily it provides a structured framework for thinking about future ideas. Within each broad solution area, a range of further options may be available or may be developed, by stakeholders in governments, international organizations, NGOs, or corporate networks.

UNCTAD is keen to learn about such ideas and to engage in discussion on how to operationalize them, principally through two channels: first, through UNCTAD's intergovernmental and expert group meetings on investment, and in particular the biennial World Investment Forum (WIF); and, second, through an open process for collecting inputs and feedback on the Plan of Action, and through an on-line discussion forum on UNCTAD's Investment Policy Hub.

(i) The World Investment Forum: Investing in Sustainable Development

The World Investment Forum 2014 will be held in October 2014 in Geneva, and will have as its theme "Investing in Sustainable Development". High-level participants including Heads of State, parliamentarians, ministers, heads of international organizations, CEOs, stock exchange executives, SWF managers, impact investors, business leaders, academics, and many other stakeholders will consider how to raise financing by the private sector, how to channel investment to sustainable development projects, and how to maximize the impact of such investment while minimizing potential risks involved. They will explore existing and new solutions and discuss questions such as:

- which financing mechanisms provide the best return, i.e. which mechanisms can mobilize more resources, more rapidly and at the lowest opportunity cost for sustainable development;

- which types of investments will yield the most progress on the SDGs and are natural candidates for involvement of the private sector;

- which types of investment in which a significant role is envisaged for the private sector require the most policy attention.

As suggested in the Plan of Action, the biennial WIF could become a permanent "Global Stakeholder Review Mechanism" for investment in the SDGs, reporting to ECOSOC and the UN General Assembly.

(ii) UNCTAD's Investment Policy Hub

In its current form, the Plan of Action for Investment in the SDGs has gone through numerous consultations with experts and practitioners. It is UNCTAD's intention to provide a platform for further consultation and discussion with all investment and sustainable development stakeholders, including policymakers, the international development community, investors, business associations, and relevant NGOs and interest groups. To allow for further improvements resulting from such consultations, the Plan of Action has been designed as a "living document". The fact that the SDGs are still under discussion, as wells as the dynamic nature of the investment policy environment add to the rationale for such an approach.

The Plan of Action provides a point of reference and a common structure for debate and cooperation on national and international policies to mobilize private sector funds, channel them to SDGs, and maximize impact. UNCTAD will add the infrastructure for such cooperation, not only through its policy forums on investment, but also by providing a platform for "open sourcing" of best practice investment policies through its website, as a basis for the inclusive development of further options with the participation of all.

Figure IV.16. Detailed plan of action for private investment in the SDGs

	Recommended Actions	Description
Leadership Setting guiding principles, galvanizing action, ensuring policy coherence	▪ Agree a set of guiding principles for SDG investment policymaking	▪ Internationally agreed principles, including definition of SDGs, policy-setting parameters, and operating, monitoring and impact assessment mechanisms.
	▪ Set SDG investment targets	▪ Quantitative and time-bound targets for investment in SDG sectors and LDCs, committed to by the international community.
	▪ Establish a global multi-stakeholder platform on investing in the SDGs	▪ A regular forum bringing together all stakeholders, such as a regular segment in UNCTAD's World Investment Forum or an expert committee on SDG investment reporting to ECOSOC and the General Assembly.
	▪ Create a multi-agency technical assistance facility	▪ A multi-agency institutional arrangement to support LDCs, advising on e.g. guarantees, bankable project set-up, incentive scheme design and regulatory frameworks.
Further policy options	▪ Change business/investor mindsets – "Global Impact MBA"	▪ Dedicated MBA programme or modules to teach mindset and skills required for investing and operating in SDG sectors in low-income countries (e.g. pro-poor business models).
	– Other educational initiatives	▪ Changes in other educational programmes, e.g. specialized financial markets/advisors training, accounting training, SDG entrepreneurship training.
Mobilization Raising finance and reorienting financial markets towards investment in SDGs	▪ Create fertile soil for innovative SDG-financing approaches and corporate initiatives	
	– Facilitate and support SDG-dedicated financial instruments and impact Investing initiatives	▪ Incentives for and facilitation of financial instruments that link investor returns to impact, e.g. green bonds.
	– Expand initiatives that use the capacity of a public sector to mobilize private finance	▪ Use of government-development funds as seed capital or guarantee to raise further private sector resources in financial markets
	– Build and support go-to-market channels for SDG investment projects in financial markets	▪ Channels for SDG investment projects to reach fund managers, savers and investors in mature financial markets, ranging from securitization to crowd funding.
	▪ Build or improve pricing mechanisms for externalities	▪ Modalities to internalize in investment decisions the cots of externalities, e.g. carbon emissions, water use.
	▪ Promote Sustainable Stock Exchanges	▪ SDG listing requirements, indices for performance measurement and reporting for investors and broader stakeholders.
	▪ Introduce financial market reforms	
	– Realign incentives in capital markets	▪ Reform of pay, performance and reporting structures to favor long-term investment conducive to SDG achievement
	– Develop new rating methodologies for SDG investments	▪ Rating methodologies that reward long-term real investment in SDG sectors.
Further policy options	▪ Debt swaps and write-offs	▪ Mechanisms to redirect debt repayment to SDG sectors.
	▪ Voluntary contributions/product labelling/certification	▪ Contributions collected by firms (e.g. through product sales) and passed on to development funds.

Figure IV.16. Detailed plan of action for private investment in the SDGs (concluded)

	Recommended Actions	Description
Chanelling Promoting and facilitating investment in SDG sectors	▪ Build an investment policy climate conducive to investing in SDGs, while safeguarding public interests	▪ National and international investment policy elements geared towards promoting sustainable development (e.g. UNCTAD's IPFSD); formulating national strategies for attracting investment in SDG sectors.
	▪ Establish new incentives schemes and a new generation of investment promotion institution – Transform IPAs into SDG investment development agencies – Make investment incentives fit-for-purpose for the promotion of SDG investment – Establish regional SDG investment compacts	▪ Transformation of IPAs towards a new generation of investment promotion, focusing on the preparation and marketing of pipelines of bankable projects and impact assessment ▪ Re-design of investment incentives, facilitating SDG investment projects, and supporting impact objectives of all investment. ▪ Regional cooperation mechanisms to promote investment in SDGs, e.g. regional cross-border infrastructure, regional SDG clusters.
	▪ Expand use of risk-sharing tools for SDG investments – Improve and expand use of PPPs – Provide SDG investment guarantees and risk insurance facilities – Expand use of ODA-leveraged and blended financing – Create markets for SDG investment outputs	▪ Wider use of PPPs for SDG projects to improve risk-return profiles and address market failures. ▪ Wider availability of investment guarantee and risk insurance facilities to specifically support and protect SDG investments. ▪ Use of ODA funds as base capital or junior debt, to share risks or improve risk-return profile for private sector funders. ▪ Advance market commitments and other mechanisms to provide more stable and more reliable markets for SDG investors.
	▪ Build SDG investment partnerships – Partner home- and host-country investment promotion agencies for investment in the SDGs – Develop SVE-TNC-MDB triangular partnerships	 ▪ Home-country partner to act as business development agency to facilitate investment in SDG sectors in developing countries. ▪ Global companies and MDBs to partner with LDCs and small vulnerable economies, focusing on a key SDG sector or a product key to economic development.
Further policy options	▪ Create a global SDG Wiki platform and investor networks	▪ Knowledge-sharing platforms and networks to share expertise on SDG investments and signal opportunities
Impact Maximizing sustainable development benefits, minimizing risks	▪ Increase absorptive capacity – Build productive capacities, linkages and spillovers – Create SDG incubators and clusters	 ▪ Entrepreneurship development, technology dissemination, business linkages, inclusive finance initiatives, etc. ▪ New economic zones for SDG investment, or conversion of existing SEZs and technology zones.
	▪ Establish effective regulatory frameworks and standards	▪ Environmental, labour and social regulations; effective taxation; mainstreaming of SDGs into IIAs; coordination of SDG investment policies at national and international levels, etc.
	▪ Good governance, capable institutions, stake-holder engagement	▪ Stakeholder engagement for private investment in sensitive SDG sectors; institutions with the power to act in the interest of stakeholders, etc.
	▪ Implement SDG impact assessment systems – Develop a common set of SDG investment impact indicators – Require integrated corporate reporting for SDGs	 ▪ Indicators for measuring (and reporting to stakeholders) the economic, social and environmental performance of SDG investments. ▪ Addition of ESG and SDG dimensions to financial reporting to influence corporate behavior on the ground.
Further policy options		

Source: UNCTAD.

Notes

[1] For the macroeconomic aspects of investment, see TDR 2008, TDR 2013, UNDESA 2009.

[2] Estimates for ecosystems/biodiversity are excluded from totals because these overlap with estimates for other sectors, such as climate change and agriculture.

[3] Both figures are annualized averages over the period 2015-2030.

[4] The final year target results from a standard exponential growth projection, to avoid an unrealistic increase in investment in the first year.

[5] See also Summers, L. (2010). "The over-financialization of the US economy", www.cambridgeforecast.wordpress.com.

[6] BIS International Banking Statistics (2014), www.bis.org.

[7] Equator Principles, www.equator-principles.com.

[8] Joint statement by Climatewise, MunichRe Climate Insurance Initiative and the UNPRI, November 2013 www.climatewise.org.uk.

[9] Green bonds were designed in partnership with the financial group Skandinaviska Enskilda Banken so that they could ensure a triple A rated fixed-income product to support projects related to climate change. They can be linked to carbon credits, so that investors can simultaneously fight global warming, support SDG projects and hedge their exposure to carbon credits. According to the WEF (2013 - Box 2.2) "The size of the green bond market has been estimated at $174 billion by HSBC and the Climate Bonds Initiative, under a definition that looks beyond explicitly labeled 'green/climate bonds'. Other estimates, including those from the OECD, place the market nearer to $86 billion."

[10] In the case of green bonds, these were mainly the preserve of international financial institutions until recently. In 2013 and 2014, EDF and Toyota became issuers of green bonds and in 2014 Unilever went beyond projects such as renewable energy and electric vehicles, aiming to reduce the environmental footprint of its ordinary activities ("Green Bonds: Spring in the air", The Economist, 22 March 2014).

[11] "EDF: Successful launch of EDF's first Green Bond", Reuters, 20 November 2013.

[12] "Toyota Said to Issue $1.75 Billion of Green Asset-Backed Bonds", Bloomberg News, 11 March 2014.

[13] "Unilever issues first ever green sustainability bond", www.unilever.com.

[14] Some typologies differentiate between social and impact investment, with the former stressing the generation of societal value and the latter profit, but the distinction is not clear (a mix of impact and profit prevails in both types); many organisations and institutions use the terms interchangeably.

[15] The Global Fund to fight AIDS, Tuberculosis and Malaria has secured pledges of about $30 billion since its creation in 2002, and over 60 per cent of pledges have been paid to date (World Bank 2013b).

[16] The Global Environment Fund GEF – a partnership between 182 countries, international agencies, civil society and private sector – has provided $11.5 billion in grants since its creation in 1991 and leveraged $57 billion in co-financing for over 3,215 projects in over 165 countries (World Bank 2013b).

[17] Africa Enterprise Challenge Fund, www.aecfafrica.org.

[18] GAVI Matching Fund, www.gavialliance.org.

[19] The International Finance Facility for Immunisation Bonds, www.iffim.org.

[20] "Call to increase opportunities to make low carbon fixed income investments", www.climatewise.org.uk.

[21] Kiva, www.kiva.org.

[22] A wide range of institutions has made proposals in this area, for example, UNCTAD (2009a), Council of the EU (2009), FSB (2008), G-20 (2009), IMF (2009), UK Financial Services Authority (2009), UK H.M. Treasury (2009), US Treasury (2009), among others.

[23] For an update on global financial architecture see FSB (2014).

[24] The SSE has a number of Partner Exchanges from around the world, including the Bombay Stock Exchange, Borsa Istanbul, BM&FBOVESPA (Brazil), the Egyptian Exchange, the Johannesburg Stock Exchange, the London Stock Exchange, the Nigerian Stock Exchange, the New York Stock Exchange, NASDAX OMX, and the Warsaw Stock Exchange. Collectively these exchanges list over 10,000 companies with a market capitalization of over $32 trillion.

[25] However, certain SDG sectors, such as water supply or energy distribution, may form a natural monopoly, thereby de-facto impeding the entry of new market participants even in the absence of formal entry barriers.

[26] Examples and case studies can be found in UNDP (2008), World Bank (2009a), IFC (2011), UNECE (2012).

[27] There exist a number of useful guides, for instance, World Bank (2009b) and UNECE (2008).

[28] Australia, Export Finance and Insurance Commission, http://stpf.efic.gov.au; Austrian Environmental and Social Assessment Procedure, www.oekb.at; Delcredere | Ducroire (2014); Nippon Export and Investment Insurance "Guidelines on Environmental and Social Considerations in Trade Insurance", http://nexi.go.jp; Atradius Dutch State Business, "Environmental and Social Aspects", www.atradiusdutchstatebusiness.nl; UK Export Finance, "Guidance to Applicants: Processes and Factors in UK Export Finance Consideration of Applications", www.gov.uk; Overseas Private Investment Corporation (2010).

[29] Multilateral Investment Guarantee Agency, "Policy on Environmental and Social Sustainability", www.miga.org.

[30] ApexBrasil - Renewable Energy, www2.apexbrasil.com.br; Deloitte (2013b); "Environmental financial incentives in South Africa", Green Business Guide, 14 January 2013, www.greenbusinessguide.co.za; Japan External Trade Organization - Attractive Sectors: Future Energy Systems, http://jetro.org; Nova Scotia – Capital Investment Incentive, www.novascotia.ca; Regulation of the Minister of Finance of Indonesia Number 130/PMK.011/2011, "Provision of Corporate Income Tax Relief or Reduction Facility"; South Africa Department of Trade and Industry, "A Guide to Incentive Schemes 2012/13", www.thedti.gov.za; Turkey Investment Support and Promotion Agency – Turkey's Investment Incentives System, www.invest.gov.tr; United Kingdom of Great Britain and Northern Ireland. Department for Business, Innovation & Skills – Grant for Business Investment: Guidelines, www.gov.uk; U.S. Department of Energy – About the Loan Programs Office (LPO): Our Mission, www.energy.gov/lpo/mission; U.S. Department of Energy – State Energy Efficiency Tax Incentives for Industry, www.energy.gov.

[31] UNCTAD Entrepreneurship Policy Framework, www.unctad-org/diae/epf.

[32] For example, RLabs Innovation Incubator in South Africa provides entrepreneurs with a space to develop social businesses ideas aimed at impacting, reconstructing and empowering local communities through innovation. The

Asian Social Enterprise Incubator (ASEI) in the Philippines provides comprehensive services and state of the art technology for social enterprises engaged at the base of the pyramid. The GSBI Accelerator program, from Santa Clara University, California, pairs selected social entrepreneurs with two Silicon Valley executive mentors, to enable them to achieve scale, sustainability and impact. At the global level, the Yunus Social Business Incubator Fund operates in several developing countries to create and empower local social businesses and entrepreneurs to help their own communities by providing pro-poor healthcare, housing, financial services, nutrition, safe drinking water and renewable energy.

[33] For instance, the zones may have well developed environmental reporting requirements under which companies are required to report their anticipated amounts of wastes, pollutants, and even the decibel level of noise that is expected to be produced (see also WIR 2013). Several zones around the world have been certified to the ISO 14001 environmental management system standard.

[34] World Bank – Ecuador Overview, www.worldbank.org.

[35] India, for example, requires the largest 100 listed companies on its major stock exchanges to report on environmental and social impacts.

[36] For example, the Johannesburg Stock Exchange in South Africa. Many other exchanges, such as BM&FBovespa in Brazil, have actively promoted voluntary mechanisms such as reporting standards and indices to incentivize corporate sustainability reporting.

[37] Producer of the most widely used sustainability reporting guidelines. According to a 2013 KPMG study, 93 per cent of the world's largest 250 companies issue a CR report, of which 82 per cent refer to the GRI Guidelines. Three-quarters of the largest 100 companies in 41 countries produce CR reports, with 78 per cent of these referring to the GRI Guidelines (KPMG 2013).

[38] A global system for companies and cities to measure, disclose, manage and share environmental information and host to the Climate Disclosure Standards Board. Over 4,000 companies worldwide use the CDP reporting system.

[39] Producer of the International Integrated Reporting Framework, recognizes sustainability as a contributor to value creation.

[40] Works to catalyze action by the finance, accounting and investor community to support a fundamental shift towards resilient business models and a sustainable economy.

[41] Provides standards for use by publicly listed corporations in the United States in disclosing material sustainability issues for the benefit of investors and the public.

REFERENCES

ADBI (2009). Demand for Infrastructure Financing in Asia 2010–2020. *ADBI Internal Report*. Tokyo: ADBI.

Addis, R., J. McLeod and A. Raine (2013). "IMPACT – Australia: Investment for social and economic benefit", March. Canberra: Department of Education, Government of Australia.

AfD, ADB, EBRD, EIB, IDB, IFC and WB (2012). Joint Report on MDB Climate Finance 2012. November.

Airoldi, M., J. Chua, P. Gerbert, J. Justus and R. Rilo (2013). "Bridging the Gap: Meeting the Infrastructure Challenge with Public-Private Partnership", The Boston Consulting Group. www.bcg.de

Aizenman, J. and R. Glick (2008). "Sovereign wealth funds: Stylized facts about their determinants and governance", *NBER Working Papers*, No. 14562, Cambridge, MA: NBER.

Argondona A. and H.W. Hoivik (2009). "Corporate social responsibility: One size does not fit all", *Journal of Business Ethics*, 89: 221-234.

Australia, Bureau of Infrastructure, Transport and Regional Economics (2012*). Australian Infrastructure Statistics: Yearbook 2012*. July. Canberra: Commonwealth of Australia.

Australia, Reserve Bank (2013). "Financing infrastructure: A spectrum of country approaches", Bulletin: September Quarter.

Bagnall, A.E. and E.M. Truman (2013). "Progress on Sovereign Wealth Fund Transparency and Accountability: an Updated SWF Scoreboard". *Policy Brief*, 13-19. Peterson Institute for International Economics.

Baker, B.K. (2010). "CTL-for-Health/FTT-with-Health: Resource-Needs Estimates and an Assessment of Funding Modalities", paper commissioned by the Action Global Health, July.

Banerjee, Sudeshna Ghosh (2006). "Private provision of infrastructure in emerging markets: Do institutions matters?", *Development Policy Review*, 24(2).

Bateman, M. and H.-J. Chang (2012). "Microfinance and the Illusion of Development: from Hubris to Nemesis in Thirty Years", *World Economic Review*, 1: 13–36.

Bauchet, J., C. Marshall, L. Starita, J. Thomas and A. Yalouris (2011). "Latest Findings from Randomized Evaluations of Microfinance". Access to Finance Forum, Report Number 2, December. Washington, D.C.: Consultative Group to Assist the Poor/World Bank.

Bazilian, M., P. Nussbaumer, E. Haites, M. Levi, M. Howells and K. Yumk (2010). "Understanding the Scale of Investment for Universal Energy Acces", *Geopolitics of Energy*, 32(10/11).

Bhattacharya, A. , M. Romani and N. Stern (2012). "Infrastructure for development: meeting the challenge", *Policy Paper*, June. Centre for Climate Change Economics and Policy, Grantham Research Institute on Climate Change and the Environment in collaboration with G-24.

Bhattacharyay, B.N. (2012). "Estimating demand for infrastructure, 2010-2020" in B.N. Bhattacharyay et al. (eds.), *Infrastructure for Asian Connectivity*. Cheltenham, United Kingdom and Northampton, MA: Edward Elgar.

Bhattacharyya, Rajib (2012). "The opportunities and challenges of FDI in retail in India", *Journal of Humanities and Social Science*, 5(5): 99-109.

Blomström, M. and A. Kokko (1997). "Regional integration and foreign direct investment: a conceptual framework and three cases", *Policy Research Working Paper Series*, No. 1750. Washington, D.C.: World Bank.

Booz&Co. (2012). Future of Chemicals Rebalancing Global Feedstock Disruptions with "On-Purpose" Technologies. Available from www.booz.com

Brautigam, D. (2010). "Looking East: Africa's Newest Investment Partners", *Global Journal of Emerging Market Economies*, 2(2): 173–188.

Brautigam, D. and X. Tang (2011). "China's Investment in Special Economic Zones in Africa: Overview and Initial Lessons", in Thomas Farole and Gokhan Akinci (eds.), Special Economic Zones: Progress, Emerging Challenges, and Future Directions. Washington, D.C.: World Bank.

Buchner, B., A. Falconer, M. Hervé-Mignucci, C. Trabacchi (2012). "The Global Landscape of Climate Finance 2012", Climate Policy Initiative (CPI) Report, December.

Buchner, B., A. Falconer, M. Hervé-Mignucci, C. Trabacchi, m. Brinkman (2011). "The Global Landscape of Climate Finance 2011", Climate Policy Initiative (CPI) Report, October.

Buchner, B., M. Herve-Mignucci, C. Trabacchi, J. Wilkinson, M. Stadelmann, R. Boyd, F. Mazza, A. Falconer, V. Micale (2013). "The Global Landscape of Climate Finance", Climate Policy Initiative (CPI) Report, October.

Calderon, C. and L. Serven (2010). "Infrastructure in Latin America", *Policy Research Working Paper*, No. 5317. Washington, D.C.: World Bank.

Cato Institute (2013). "Infrastructure investment: A State, Local and Private Responsibility", Tax and Budget Bulletin, No. 67, January.

Clark, H. (2012). The Importance of Governance for Sustainable Development. Singapore: Institute of Southeast Asian Studies.

Clarke, V. (2014). "Investment governance in the Tripartite Free Trade Area", in *Cape to Cairo: Exploring the Tripartite FTA agenda*. Stellenbosch, South Africa: Tralac.

Copeland, C. and M. Tiemann (2010). "Water infrastructure needs and investment: review and analysis of key issues", Congressional Research Service Report 7-5700, December.

Council of the European Union (2009). "Brussels European Council – the Presidency Conclusions, 18–19 June", 10 July, Brussels. https://www.consilium.europa.eu

De La Cruz, J., R.B. Koopman, Z. Wang and S. Wei (2011). "Estimating foreign value-added in Mexico's manufacturing exports", *Office of Economics Working Paper*, No. 2011-04. Washington, D.C.: U.S. International Trade Commission.

Delcredere | Ducroire (2014). "Delcredere | Ducroire's Environmental and Social Policy", www.delcredereducroire.be

Deloitte (2013a). Global Powers of Retailing 2013: Retail Beyond. Deloitte, January 2013.

Deloitte (2013b). "Global Survey of R&D Tax Incentives". March. www.deloitte.com

Doshi, V., G. Schulman and D. Gabaldon (2007). "Lights! Water! Motion!", *Strategy & Business*. No. 46. February. Buzz Allen Hamilton.

E&Y (Ernst and Young) (2013). "Turning the Corner: Global Venture Capital Insights and Trends 2013", April. www.ey.com

Edwards, Chris (2013). "Encouraging private infrastructure investment", Testimony at Joint Economic Committee, 24 July. www.cato.org

EPSU (2012). "Why water is a public service: exposing the myths of privatisation". Report commissioned by EPSU to Public Services International Research Unit (PSIRU). April www.right2water.eu

Estache, A. (2010). "Infrastructure finance in developing countries: an overview", *EIB Papers*, 15(2): 60–88.

ETNO (European Telecommunications Network Operators' Association) (2013). *Annual Economic Report 2013*. November.

EURODAD (2014). "A dangerous blend? The EU's agenda to 'blend' public development finance with private finance". www.eurodad.org

European Chamber (2011). *European Business in China: Asia-Pacific Headquarters Study*. Beijing: European Union Chamber of Commerce in China.

Fay, M., M. Toman, D. Benitez and S. Csordas (2011). "Infrastruture and Sustainable Development" in S. Fardoust, Y.-B. Kim, C. Sepúlveda (eds.), *Postcrisis Growth and Development: a Development Agenda for the G-20*. Washinton, D.C.: World Bank .

Foster, V. and C. Briceno-Garmendia (2010). *Africa's Infrastructure: A Time for Transformation*. Washington, D.C.: World Bank.

FSB (Financial Stability Board) (2008). "Enhancing Market and Institutional Resilience", 7 April. www.financialstabilityboard.org

G-20 (Group of Twenty) (2009). "Declaration on Strengthening the Financial System", 2 April.

G-30 (Group of Thirty) (2013). "Long term finance and economic growth". www.group30.org

Goldman Sachs (2013). "ASEAN's half a trillion dollar infrastructure opportunity", Asia Economics Analyst, Issue No: 13/18, 30 May.

GPFG (2010). GPFG Responsible Investment. Government Pension Fund Global. Oslo: Norway Ministry of Finance.

Griffiths, J., M. Martin, J. Pereira, T. Strawson (2014). "Financing for development post-2015: Improving the contribution of private finance". Study requested by the European Parliament's Committee on Development. Brussels: European Union.

Gunatilake, H. and M.J. Carangal-San Jose (2008). "Privatisation Revisited: Lessons from Private Sector Participation in Water Supply and Sanitation in Developing Countries", *ERD Working Paper*, No. 115, Manila: Asian Development Bank.

Hall, D. and E. Lobina (2010). "The past, present and future of finance for investment in water systems". Paper for keynote presentation at IRC conference: Pumps, Pipes and Promises, Den Haag, November.

Helm, D., J. Stewart, M. Fay, A. Iimi, B. Perrissin-Fabert, A. Estache (2010). "Public and private financing of infrastructure: Policy challenges in mobilizing finance", Vol. 15, No. 2. European Investment Bank: Economic and Financial Studies Division.

High Level Task Force on Innovative International Financing for Health Systems (2009). "More money for health, and more health for the money".

HLP (High-Level Panel on Global Assessment of Resources for Implementing the Strategic Plan for Biodiversity 2011-2020) (2012). "Resourcing the Aichi Biodiversity Targets: A First Assessment of the Resources Required for Implementing the Strategic Plan for Biodiversity 2011-2020", www.cbd.int

IAWG (Inter-Agency Working Group on the Private Investment and Job Creation Pillar of the G20 Multi-Year Action Plan on Development) (2011). " Indicators for measuring and maximizing economic value added and job creation arising from private sector investment in value chains", Report to the G-20 High-Level Development Working Group, September.

IEA (2009). *World Energy Outlook 2009*. Paris: OECD/IEA.

IEA (2011). *World Energy Outlook 2011*. Paris: OECD/IEA.

IEA (2012). *Energy Technology Perspectives 2012: Pathways to a Clean Energy System*. Paris: OECD/IEA.

IFC (2011). IFC support to Health Public-Private Partnerships. www.ifc.org

ILO (2010). *Qualifications Frameworks: Implementation and Impact, Background Case Study on Bangladesh*. Geneva: ILO.

IMF (2009). "Lessons of the Financial Crisis for Future Regulation of Financial Institutions and Markets and for Liquidity Management", 4 February. Washington, D.C: IMF.

IMF (2014a). World Economic Outlook April 2014, Recovery Strengthens, Remains Uneven, World Economic and Financial Surveys. Washington, D.C.: IMF

IMF (2014b). Global Financial Stability Report, Statistical Appendix, April. Washington, D.C.: IMF.

Inderst, G. (2013). "Private infrastructure finance and investment in Europe", *EIB Working Paper*, 2013/02. Luxembourg: European Investment Bank.

India, Planning Commission (2011). Mid-term appraisal: Eleventh Five Year Plan 2007–2012. New Delhi: Oxford University Press.

India, Planning Commission (2012). "Interim report of High level Committee", August 2012.

Indonesia, Ministry of National Development Planning/ National Development Planning Agency (2011). "Infrastructure development strategy in Indonesia", www.oecd.org

Institute for Health Metrics and Evaluation (2010). "Financing Global Health 2010: Development assistance and country spending in economic uncertainty", Seattle, WA: IHME.

Institute for Health Metrics and Evaluation (2012). "Financing Global Health 2012: The end of the golden age?", Seattle, WA: IHME

IWG (2008). Generally Accepted Principles and Practices (GAPP) - Santiago Principles. Washington D.C: The International Working Group of Sovereign Wealth Funds.

Izaguirre, A.K. and S.P. Kulkarni (2011). "Identifying main sources of funding for infrastructure projects with private participation in developing countries: a pilot study", *World Bank Working Paper*, No. 9. Washington, D.C.: World Bank.

J.P. Morgan (2010). "Impact Investments: An emerging asset class", Global Research, 29 November. www.morgan-markets.com

Kettunen, M., D. D'Amato, P.ten Brink, L. Mazza, A. Malou, S. Withana (2013). "Potential of sectoral resource mobilization to implement the Aichi targets in developing countries: A scoping study", Brussels: Institute for European Environmental Policy (IEEP).

KPMG (2013). "The KPMG Survey of Corporate Responsibility Reporting 2013", December.

Leading Group on Innovative Financing to Fund Development (2010). "Globalizing Solidarity: The Case for Financial Levies", Report of the Committee of Experts to the Taskforce on International Financial Transactions and Development, June.

Lin, J.Y. (2011). "From Flying Geese to Leading Dragons. New Opportunities and Strategies for Structural Transformation in Developing Countries", Policy Research Working Paper Series, No. 5702. Washington, D.C.: World Bank.

Lipschutz, R.D. and S.T. Romano (2012). "The Cupboard is Full: Public Finance for Public Services in the Global South". Municipal Services Project, *Occasional Paper*, No. 16, May.

Lloyd-Owen, D. (2009). "Tapping liquidity: financing water and wastewater to 2029". Report for PFI market intelligence. London: Thomson Reuters.

Marois, T. (2013). "State-owned banks and development: dispelling mainstream myths". Municipal services Project, *Occasional Paper*, No. 21 – December.

Martin, M. (2013). "Making impact investible", *Impact Economy Working Papers*, Vol. 4, www.impacteconomy.com

Massolution (2013). "2013CF Crowdfunding Industry Report", http://research.crowdsourcing.org

McCoy, D., S. Chang, and D. Sridhar (2009). "Global Health funding: how much, where it comes from and where it goes", *Health Policy and Planning*, 24(6): 407–417.

McKinsey (2009). "Pathways to a Low-Carbon Economy: Version 2 of the Global Greenhouse Gas Abatement Cost Curve", www.mckinsey.com

McKinsey (2011a). Bangladesh's ready-made garments landscape: The challenge of growth. McKinsey & Company, November 2011.

McKinsey (2011b). "Asia's $1 trilllion infrastructure opportunity", www.mckinsey.com

McKinsey (2013). "Infrastructure productivity: How to save $1 trillion a year", www.mckinsey.com

MDB Committee on Development Effectiveness (2011). "Supporting Infrastructure in Developing Countries". Paper submitted to the G20, 30 November. www.boell.org

Monk, A. (2008). "Is CalPERS a Sovereign Wealth Fund?", Number 8-21. Center for Retirement Research, Boston College.

OECD (2006). *Infrastructure to 2030: Telecom, Land Transport, Water and Electricity*. Paris: OECD.

OECD (2007). *Infrastructure to 2030: Mapping Policy for Electricity, Water and Transport*. Paris: OECD.

OECD (2009). *Private Sector Participation in Water Infrastructure*. Paris: OECD

OECD (2012). *Strategic Transport Infrastructure Needs to 2030*. Paris: OECD.

OECD (2013a). *Development Co-operation Report 2013: Ending Poverty*. Paris: OECD..

OECD (2013b). *Annual Survey of Large Pension Funds and Public Reserve Funds: Report on Pension Funds' Long-term Investments*. Paris: OECD.

OECD (2014). "Official support for Pirvate Investment in Developing Country Infrastructure", 21 March, DCD/WKP(2014)2/PROV, www.oecd.org.

Overseas Private Investment Corporation (2010). "OPIC – Environmental and Social Policy Statement", October. www.opic.gov

Perrotti, D.E. and R.J. Sánchez (2011). "La brecha de infraestructura en América Latina y el Caribe", Serie recursos naturales e infraestructura, 153. Santiago de Chile: CEPAL

Petri, P.A., M.G. Plummer and F. Zhai (2011). "The Trans-Pacific Partnership and Asia Pacific integration: a quantitative assessment", *East-West Center Working Papers*, Economics Series No. 119. Honolulu, HI: East-West Center.

Pezon, C. (2009). "Decentralization and Delegation of Water and Sanitation Services in France" in J.E. Castro and L. Heller (eds.), *Water and Sanitation Services: Public Policy and Management*. Londond: Earthscan.

Pisu, M. (2010). "Tackling the Infrastructure Challenge in Indonesia", *OECD Economics Department Working Papers*, No. 809. Paris: OECD.

Preqin (2013). "The 2014 Preqin Sovereign Wealth Fund Review", October. www.prequin.com

PwC (2014a). "Asset Management 2020: A Brave New World", www.pwc.com

PwC (2014b). " Paying Taxes 2014: The global picture ", www.pwc.com

Quadros, Ruy (2009). Brazilian innovation in the global automotive value chain: Implications of the organisational decomposition of the innovation process. Research Report prepared for Institute of Development Studies under the Project "The Changing knowledge Divide in the Global Economy", Campinas, Brazil

Quadros, Ruy, and Flavia Consoni (2009). "Innovation capabilities in the Brazilian automobile industry: a study of vehicle assemblers' technological strategies and policy recommendations", *International Journal of Technological Learning, Innovation and Development*, 2(1/2): 53–75.

Rhodes, Chris (2013). "Infrastructure Policy". House of Common Library, Standard Note SN/EP/6594, 23 December.

Rodriguez, D.J., C. van den Berg and A. McMahon (2012). "Investing in water infrastructure: Capital, operations and maintenance", *World Bank Water Papers*, November. Washington, D.C.: World Bank.

Sachs, J.D. (2012). "From Millenium Development Goals to Sustainable Development Goals", *Lancet*, 379: 2206–2211.

Sauvant K., L. Sachs and S.W. Jongbloed (eds.) (2012). *Sovereign Investment: Concerns and Policy Reactions*. Oxford: Oxford University Press.

Schmidhuber, J.and J. Bruinsma (2011). "Investing towards a world free of hunger: lowering vulnerability and enhancing resilience" in A. Prakash (ed.), *Safeguarding Food Security in Volatile Global Markets*. Rome: FAO.

Simon, J. and J. Barmeier (2010). "More than Money: Impact Investing for Development. Centre for Global Development". www.cgdev.org

Sovereign Wealth Fund Institute (2013a). *The Linaburg-Maduell Transparency Index*. Las Vegas, NV: Sovereign Wealth Fund Institute

Sovereign Wealth Fund Institute (2013b). *Sovereign Wealth Fund Asset Allocation 2013*. Las Vegas, NV: Sovereign Wealth Fund Institute.

Sturgeon, Timothy J., and Johannes Van Biesebroeck (2010). "Effects of the crisis on the automotive industry in developing countries a global value chain perspective", *Policy Research Working Paper*, No. 5330. Washington, D.C.: World Bank.

TDR08. Trade and Development Report 2008: Commodity Prices, Capital Flows and the Financing of Investment. New York and Geneva: United Nations.

TDR09. Trade and Development Report 2009: Responding to the global crisis – Climate Change Mitigation and Development. New York and Geneva: United Nations.

TDR11. Trade and Development Report 2011: Post-crisis Policy Challenges in the World Economy. New York and Geneva: United Nations.

TDR13. Trade and Development Report 2013: Adjusting to the Changing Dynamics of the World Economy. New York and Geneva: United Nations.

Tewes-Gradl, C., A. Peters, K. Vohla, L. Lütjens-Schilling (2013). "Inclusive Business Policies", BMZ/ENDEVA, www.enterprise-development.org

The Economist (2012). State Capitalism: Special Report, January 21st.

The Lancet (2011). "The Commission on Macroeconomics and Health: 10 years on", 378(9807), December.

The Lancet (2013). "Advancing social and economic development by investing in women's and children's health: a new Global Investment Framework", 19 November. www.thelancet.com

TheCityUK (2013). "Financial Markets Series: Fund Management". September. www.thecityuk.com

Truman, E.M. (2008). "A Blueprint for Sovereign Wealth Fund Best Practices", *Policy Brief*, 08-3. Peterson Institute for International Economics. www.iie.com

UN Open Working Group on Sustainable Development Goals (2014), "Working Document for 5-9 May Session of Open Working Group", http://sustainabledevelopment.un.org

UNCTAD (2004a). *Is a Special Treatment of Small Island Developing States possible?* New York and Geneva: United Nations.

UNCTAD (2004b). *The REIO Exception in MFN Treatment Clauses.* UNCTAD Series on International Investment Policies for Development. New York and Geneva: United Nations.

UNCTAD (2009). *The Role of International Investment Agreements in Attracting Foreign Direct Investment to Developing Countries*. UNCTAD Series on International Investment Policies for Development. New York and Geneva: United Nations.

UNCTAD (2010). *Most-Favoured-Nation Treatment*. UNCTAD Series on Issues in International Investment Agreements II. New York and Geneva: United Nations.

UNCTAD (2011a). Local Production of Pharmaceuticals and Related Technology Transfer: A Series of Case Studies by the UNCTAD Secretariat. New York and Geneva: United Nations.

UNCTAD (2011b). *Foreign Direct Investment in LDCs: Lessons Learned from the Decade 2001–2010 and the Way Forward*. New York and Geneva: United Nations.

UNCTAD (2011c). *Investment and Enterprise Responsibility Review*. New York and Geneva: United Nations.

UNCTAD (2011d). "Development-led globalization: Towards sustainable and inclusive development paths", Report of the Secretary-General of UNCTAD to UNCTAD XIII

UNCTAD (2012). *Investment Policy Framework for Sustainable Development: Towards a New Generation of Investment Policies* (IPFSD). Geneva and New York: United Nations.

UNCTAD (2013a). *Investment Policy Review: Bangladesh*. New York and Geneva: United Nations.

UNCTAD (2013b). *Economic Development in Africa Report 2013: Intra-African Trade – Unlocking Private Sector Dynamism*. New York and Geneva: United Nations.

UNCTAD (2013c). *The Least Development Countries Report 2013: Growth with Employment for Inclusive and Sustainable Development*. New York and Geneva: United Nations.

UNCTAD (2014a). *Skill Development in the Bangladesh Garments Industry: the Role of TNCs*. New York and Geneva: United Nations.

UNCTAD (2014b). *Investment Policy Review of Mongolia*. New York and Geneva: United Nations.

UNCTAD (2014c). "Latest Developments in Investor–State Dispute Settlement." *IIA Issues Note*, No. 1. New York and Geneva: United Nations.

UNCTAD (2014d). *Best Practice Guidance for Policymakers and Stock Exchanges on Sustainability Reporting Initiatives*. New York and Geneva: United Nations.

UNCTAD and World Bank (2014). "The Practice of Responsible Investment Principles in Larger-Scale Agricultural Investments - Implications for corporate performance and impact on local communities", World Bank Report Number 86175-GLB. Washington D.C.: World Bank

UNDESA (2009). *World Economic and Social Survey 2009: Promoting Development, Saving the Planet* New York: United Nations.

UNDESA (2012). *World Economic and Social Survey 2012: In Search of New Development Finance*. New York: United Nations.

UNDP (2008). "Sharing Innovative Experiences: Examples of Successful Public-Private Partnerships". New York: UNDP.

UNDP (2014). "Governance for Sustainable Development: Integrating Governance in the Post-2015 Development Framework", March 2014, www.undp.org

UNECE (2008). *Guidebook on Promoting Good Governance in PPPs*. Geneva: United Nations.

UNECE (2012). "A preliminary reflection on the best practice in PPP in Healthcare sector", Discussion Paper prepared for the conference PPPs in Health Manila 2012: Developing Models, Ensuring Sustainability: Perspectives from Asia and Europe. www.unece.org

UNECOSOC (2013). "Public aid as a driver for private investment, Preparing for the 2014 Development Cooperation Forum". Background Study for the DCF Switzerland High-level Symposium, 24-25 October.

UNESCO (2012). EFA Global Monitoring Report 2012: Youth and skills: Putting Education to Work. Paris: UNESCO.

UNESCO (2013). "Education for All is affordable – by 2015 and beyond", Policy Paper 06, 13 February, UNESCO.

UNFCCC (2007). "Investment and Financial Flows to Address Climate Change". Bonn: UNFCC.

United Kingdom Financial Services Authority (2009). "The Turner Review: A regulatory response to the global banking crisis", March. www.fsa.gov.uk

United Kingdom H.M. Treasury (2009). "Reforming financial markets", July. www.gov.uk

United Kingdom H.M. Treasury (2011). National infrastructure plan 2011. United Kingdom. www.gov.uk

United Kingdom H.M. Treasury (2013). National Infrastructure Plan 2013. United Kingdom. www.gov.uk

United Nations (2013). *Report of the High-Level Panel of Eminent Persons on the Post-2015 Development Agenda*. New York: United Nations.

United Nations I-8 (L.I.F.E.) Group (2009). *Innovative Financing for Development*. New York: United Nations.

United States Congress (2008). "Issues and options in infrastructure investment", www.cbo.gov

United States Treasury (2009). Financial Regulatory Reform: A New Foundation. www.financialstability.gov.

UN-OHRLLS (2011). The SIDS Tourism, Biodiversity and Culture Nexus in Context of the Green Economy, Special event, October, New York.

UNTT Working Group on Sustainable Development Financing (2013). "Financing for sustainable development: review of global investment requirement estimates" http://sustainabledevelopment.un.org

Vale Columbia Centre on Sustainable International Investment (VCC), World Bank and ICA (2013). "Investment incentives: scoping paper, cost-benefits, and regulatory mechanism". Draft available from: www.vcc.columbia.edu

Vasudeva, G. (2013). "Weaving together the normative and regulative roles of government: How the Norwegian Sovereign Wealth Fund's responsible conduct is shaping firms' cross-border investments", *Organization Science*, 24(6): 1662-1682.

Wagenvoort, R., C. de Nicola and A. Kappeler (2010). "Infrastructure finance in Europe: Composition, evolution and crisis impact", *EIB Papers*, Vol.15, No. 1. Luxembourg: European Investment Bank.

WEF (2011). *The Future of Long-term Investing*. Geneva: WEF.

WEF (2013). *The Green Investment Report: the Ways and Means to Unlock Private Finance for Green Growth*. Geneva: WEF.

WEF and PwC (2012). "Strategic Infrastructure: Steps to Prioritize and Deliver Infrastructure Effectively and Efficiently", September. Geneva: WEF.

WHO (2012). "Global costs and benefits of drinking-water supply and sanitation intervantions to reach the MDG target and universal coverage", Geneva.

WIR07. World Investment Report 2007: Transnational Corporations, Extractive Industries and Development. New York and Geneva: United Nations.

WIR08. World Investment Report 2008: Transnational Corporations and Infrastructure Challenge. New York and Geneva: United Nations.

WIR09. World Investment Report 2009: Transnational Corporations, Agricultural Production and Development. New York and Geneva: United Nations.

WIR10. World Investment Report 2010: Investing in a Low-Carbon Economy. New York and Geneva: United Nations.

WIR11. World Investment Report 2011: Non-Equity Modes of International Production and Development. New York and Geneva: United Nations

WIR12. World Investment Report 2012: Towards a New Generation of Investment Policies. New York and Geneva: United Nations.

WIR13. World Investment Report 2013: Global Value Chains: Investment and Trade for Development. New York and Geneva: United Nations.

Wolf, M. (2010). *Fixing Global Finance*. New Haven, CT: Yale University Press.

Wong, A. (2009). "Sovereign Wealth Funds and the problem of asymmetric information: the Santiago Principles and International Regulations", *Brooklyn Journal of International Law* 1081: 1098-1102.

World Bank (2009a). *The Role and Impact of Public-Private Partnerships in Education*. Washington, D.C.: World Bank.

World Bank (2009b). *Public-Private Partnerships: Reference Guide*. Washington, D.C.: World Bank.

World Bank (2010). The Economics of Adaptation to Climate Change", A Synthesis Report - Final Consultation Draft, August. Washinton D.C.: World Bank.

World Bank (2012). *Inclusive Green Growth: The Pathway to Sustainable Development*. Washington, D.C.: World Bank.

World Bank (2013a). "Long term investment financing for growth and development", Umbrella Paper, February. Washington, D.C.: World Bank.

World Bank (2013b). *Financing for Development Post-2015*. Washington, D.C.: World Bank.

World Bank and IEA (2013). "Sustainable Energy for All 2013-2014: Global Tracking Framework", Washington D.C: World Bank

Wrigley, N. and M. Lowe (2010). The Globalization of Trade in Retail Services. Report commissioned by the OECD Trade Policy Linkages and Services Division for the OECD Experts Meeting on Distribution Services, Paris, November 2010.

Yepes, T. (2008). "Investment needs in infrastructure in developing countries: 2008–2015". World Bank, mimeo.

ANNEX TABLES

List of annex tables available on the UNCTAD site, www.unctad.org/wir, and on the CD-ROM

1. FDI inflows, by region and economy, 1990–2013
2. FDI outflows, by region and economy, 1990–2013
3. FDI inward stock, by region and economy, 1990–2013
4. FDI outward stock, by region and economy, 1990–2013
5. FDI inflows as a percentage of gross fixed capital formation, 1990–2013
6. FDI outflows as a percentage of gross fixed capital formation, 1990–2013
7. FDI inward stock as percentage of gross domestic products, by region and economy, 1990–2013
8. FDI outward stock as percentage of gross domestic products, by region and economy, 1990–2013
9. Value of cross-border M&A sales, by region/economy of seller, 1990–2013
10. Value of cross-border M&A purchases, by region/economy of purchaser, 1990–2013
11. Number of cross-border M&A sales, by region/economy of seller, 1990–2013
12. Number of cross-border M&A purchases, by region/economy of purchaser, 1990–2013
13. Value of cross-border M&A sales, by sector/industry, 1990–2013
14. Value of cross-border M&A purchases, by sector/industry, 1990–2013
15. Number of cross-border M&A sales, by sector/industry, 1990–2013
16. Number of cross-border M&A purchases, by sector/industry, 1990–2013
17. Cross-border M&A deals worth over $1 billion completed in 2013
18. Value of greenfield FDI projects, by source, 2003–2013
19. Value of greenfield FDI projects, by destination, 2003–2013
20. Value of greenfield FDI projects, by sector/industry, 2003–2013
21. Number of greenfield FDI projects, by source, 2003–2013
22. Number of greenfield FDI projects, by destination, 2003–2013
23. Number of greenfield FDI projects, by sector/industry, 2003–2013
24. Estimated world inward FDI stock, by sector and industry, 1990 and 2012
25. Estimated world outward FDI stock, by sector and industry, 1990 and 2012
26. Estimated world inward FDI flows, by sector and industry, 1990–1992 and 2010–2012
27. Estimated world outward FDI flows, by sector and industry, 1990–1992 and 2010–2012
28. The world's top 100 non-financial TNCs, ranked by foreign assets, 2013
29. The top 100 non-financial TNCs from developing and transition economies, ranked by foreign assets, 2012

Annex table 1. FDI flows, by region and economy, 2008–2013
(Millions of dollars)

Region/economy	FDI inflows						FDI outflows					
	2008	2009	2010	2011	2012	2013	2008	2009	2010	2011	2012	2013
World	1 818 834	1 221 840	1 422 255	1 700 082	1 330 273	1 451 965	1 999 326	1 171 240	1 467 580	1 711 652	1 346 671	1 410 696
Developed economies	1 032 385	618 596	703 474	880 406	516 664	565 626	1 599 317	846 305	988 769	1 215 690	852 708	857 454
Europe	577 952	408 924	436 303	538 877	244 090	250 799	1 045 129	431 433	591 326	653 000	299 478	328 729
European Union	551 413	363 133	383 703	490 427	216 012	246 207	983 601	383 598	483 002	585 275	237 865	250 460
Austria	6 858	9 303	840	10 618	3 939	11 083	29 452	10 006	9 994	21 878	17 059	13 940
Belgium	193 950	60 963	77 014	119 022	- 30 261	- 2 406	221 023	7 525	24 535	96 785	- 17 443	- 26 372
Bulgaria	9 855	3 385	1 525	1 849	1 375	1 450	765	- 95	230	163	345	179
Croatia	5 938	3 346	490	1 517	1 356	580	1 405	1 273	- 152	53	- 36	- 187
Cyprus	1 414	3 472	766	2 384	1 257	533	2 717	383	679	2 201	- 281	308
Czech Republic	6 451	2 927	6 141	2 318	7 984	4 990	4 323	949	1 167	- 327	1 790	3 294
Denmark	1 824	3 917	- 11 522	13 094	2 831	2 083	13 240	6 305	- 124	12 610	7 976	9 170
Estonia	1 731	1 840	1 598	340	1 517	950	1 114	1 547	142	- 1 452	952	357
Finland	- 1 144	718	7 359	2 550	4 153	- 1 065	9 297	5 681	10 167	5 011	7 543	4 035
France	64 184	24 215	33 628	38 547	25 086	4 875	155 047	107 136	64 575	59 552	37 195	- 2 555
Germany	8 109	23 789	65 620	59 317	13 203	26 721	72 758	69 639	126 310	80 971	79 607	57 550
Greece	4 499	2 436	330	1 143	1 740	2 567	2 418	2 055	1 558	1 772	677	- 627
Hungary	6 325	1 995	2 202	6 290	13 983	3 091	2 234	1 883	1 148	4 663	11 337	2 269
Ireland	- 16 453	25 715	42 804	23 545	38 315	35 520	18 949	26 616	22 348	- 1 165	18 519	22 852
Italy	- 10 835	20 077	9 178	34 324	93	16 508	67 000	21 275	32 655	53 629	7 980	31 663
Latvia	1 261	94	380	1 466	1 109	808	243	- 62	19	62	192	345
Lithuania	1 965	- 14	800	1 448	700	531	336	198	- 6	55	392	101
Luxembourg	16 853	19 314	39 731	18 116	9 527	30 075	14 809	1 522	21 226	7 750	3 063	21 626
Malta	943	412	924	276	4	- 2 100	457	136	130	4	- 42	- 7
Netherlands	4 549	38 610	- 7 324	21 047	9 706	24 389	68 334	34 471	68 341	39 502	267	37 432
Poland	14 839	12 932	13 876	20 616	6 059	- 6 038	4 414	4 699	7 226	8 155	727	- 4 852
Portugal	4 665	2 706	2 646	11 150	8 995	3 114	2 741	816	- 7 493	14 905	579	1 427
Romania	13 909	4 844	2 940	2 522	2 748	3 617	274	- 88	- 21	- 33	- 112	119
Slovakia	4 868	- 6	1 770	3 491	2 826	591	550	904	946	713	- 73	- 422
Slovenia	1 947	- 659	360	998	- 59	- 679	1 468	262	- 207	118	- 272	58
Spain	76 993	10 407	39 873	28 379	25 696	39 167	74 717	13 070	37 844	41 164	- 3 982	26 035
Sweden	36 888	10 093	140	12 924	16 334	8 150	30 363	26 202	20 349	29 861	28 951	33 281
United Kingdom	89 026	76 301	49 617	51 137	45 796	37 101	183 153	39 287	39 416	106 673	34 955	19 440
Other developed Europe	26 539	45 791	52 600	48 450	28 079	4 592	61 528	47 835	108 323	67 725	61 613	78 269
Gibraltar	159[a]	172[a]	165[a]	166[a]	168[a]	166[a]	-	-	-	-	-	-
Iceland	917	86	246	1 108	1 025	348	- 4 209	2 292	- 2 357	23	- 3 206	395
Norway	10 251	16 641	17 044	20 586	16 648	9 330	20 404	19 165	23 239	19 880	19 782	17 913
Switzerland	15 212	28 891	35 145	26 590	10 238	- 5 252	45 333	26 378	87 442	47 822	45 037	59 961
North America	367 919	166 304	226 449	263 428	203 594	249 853	387 573	327 502	312 502	438 872	422 386	380 938
Canada	61 553	22 700	28 400	39 669	43 025	62 325	79 277	39 601	34 723	52 148	55 446	42 636
United States	306 366	143 604	198 049	223 759	160 569	187 528	308 296	287 901	277 779	386 724	366 940	338 302
Other developed countries	86 514	43 368	40 722	78 101	68 980	64 975	166 615	87 371	84 942	123 818	130 844	147 786
Australia	47 162	27 192	35 799	65 209	55 518	49 826	30 661	11 933	19 607	8 702	6 212	6 364
Bermuda	78	- 70	231	- 258	48	55	323	21	- 33	- 337	241	50
Israel	10 875	4 607	5 510	10 766	9 481	11 804	7 210	1 751	8 656	5 329	2 352	4 932
Japan	24 425	11 938	- 1 252	- 1 758	1 732	2 304	128 020	74 699	56 263	107 599	122 549	135 749
New Zealand	3 974	- 299	434	4 142	2 202	987	401	- 1 034	448	2 525	- 510	691
Developing economies	668 758	532 580	648 208	724 840	729 449	778 372	338 354	276 664	420 919	422 582	440 164	454 067
Africa	59 276	56 043	47 034	48 021	55 180	57 239	4 947	6 278	6 659	6 773	12 000	12 418
North Africa	23 153	18 980	16 576	8 506	16 624	15 494	8 752	2 588	4 847	1 575	3 273	1 481
Algeria	2 632	2 746	2 301	2 581	1 499	1 691	318	215	220	534	- 41	- 268
Egypt	9 495	6 712	6 386	- 483	6 881	5 553	1 920	571	1 176	626	211	301
Libya	3 180	3 310	1 909	.	1 425	702	5 888	1 165	2 722	131	2 509	180
Morocco	2 487	1 952	1 574	2 568	2 728	3 358	485	470	589	179	406	331
Sudan	2 600	2 572	2 894	2 692	2 488	3 094	98	89	66	84	175	915
Tunisia	2 759	1 688	1 513	1 148	1 603	1 096	42	77	74	21	13	22
Other Africa	36 124	37 063	30 458	39 515	38 556	41 744	- 3 805	3 690	1 813	5 198	8 726	10 937
West Africa	12 538	14 764	12 024	18 649	16 575	14 203	1 709	2 120	1 292	2 731	3 155	2 185
Benin	170	134	177	161	282	320	- 4	31	- 18	60	40	46
Burkina Faso	106	101	35	144	329	374	- 0	8	- 4	102	73	83
Cabo Verde	264	174	158	153	57	19	0	- 0	0	1	- 1	2[a]
Côte d'Ivoire	446	377	339	302	322	371	-	- 9	25	15	29	33
Gambia	70	40	37	36	25	25[a]	-	-	-	-	-	-
Ghana	1 220	2 897	2 527	3 222	3 293	3 226[a]	8	7	-	25	1	9[a]
Guinea	382	141	101	956	606	25	126	-	-	1	3	1
Guinea-Bissau	5	17	33	25	7	15	- 1	- 0	6	1	- 0	0
Liberia	284	218	450	508	985	1 061	382	364	369	372	1 354	698[a]
Mali	180	748	406	556	398	410	1	- 1	7	4	16	9
Mauritania	343[a]	- 3[a]	131[a]	589[a]	1 383[a]	1 154[a]	4[a]	4[a]	4[a]	4[a]	4[a]	4[a]
Niger	340	791	940	1 066	841	631	24	59	- 60	9	2	- 7

/...

Annex table 1. FDI flows, by region and economy, 2008-2013 (continued)
(Millions of dollars)

Region/economy	FDI inflows						FDI outflows					
	2008	2009	2010	2011	2012	2013	2008	2009	2010	2011	2012	2013
Nigeria	8 249	8 650	6 099	8 915	7 127	5 609	1 058	1 542	923	824	1 543	1 237
Senegal	398	320	266	338	276	298	126	77	2	47	56	32
Sierra Leone	58	111	238	950	548	579ᵃ	-	-	-	-	-	-
Togo	24	49	86	728	94	84	- 16	37	37	1 264	35	37
Central Africa	5 021	6 027	9 389	8 527	9 904	8 165	149	53	590	366	222	634
Burundi	4	0	1	3	1	7	1	-	-	.	-	-
Cameroon	21	740	538	652	526	572ᵃ	- 2	- 69	503	187	- 284	135ᵃ
Central African Republic	117	42	62	37	71	1	-	-	-	-	-	-
Chad	466ᵃ	376ᵃ	313ᵃ	282ᵃ	343ᵃ	538ᵃ	-	-	-	-	-	-
Congo	2 526ᵃ	1 862ᵃ	2 211ᵃ	3 056ᵃ	2 758ᵃ	2 038ᵃ	-	-	-	-	-	-
Congo, Democratic Republic of the	1 727	664	2 939	1 687	3 312	2 098	54	35	7	91	421	401
Equatorial Guinea	- 794	1 636	2 734ᵃ	1 975ᵃ	2 015ᵃ	1 914ᵃ	-	-	-	-	-	-
Gabon	773ᵃ	573ᵃ	499ᵃ	696ᵃ	696ᵃ	856ᵃ	96ᵃ	87ᵃ	81ᵃ	88ᵃ	85ᵃ	85ᵃ
Rwanda	102	119	42	106	160	111	-	-	-	-	-	14
São Tomé and Príncipe	79	16	51	32	23	30	0	0	0	0	0	0
East Africa	4 358	3 928	4 511	4 778	5 378	6 210	109	89	141	174	205	148
Comoros	5	14	8	23	10	14ᵃ	-	-	-	-	-	-
Djibouti	229	100	27	78	110	286	-	-	-	-	-	-
Eritrea	39ᵃ	91ᵃ	91ᵃ	39ᵃ	41ᵃ	44ᵃ	-	-	-	-	-	-
Ethiopia	109	221	288	627	279	953ᵃ	-	-	-	-	-	-
Kenya	96	115	178	335	259	514	44	46	2	9	16	6
Madagascar	1 169	1 066	808	810	812	838ᵃ	-	-	-	-	-	-
Mauritius	383	248	430	433	589	259	52	37	129	158	180	135
Seychelles	130	171	211	207	166	178	13	5	6	8	9	8
Somalia	87ᵃ	108ᵃ	112ᵃ	102ᵃ	107ᵃ	107ᵃ	-	-	-	-	-	-
Uganda	729	842	544	894	1 205	1 146	-	-	4	- 1	- 0	- 1
United Republic of Tanzania	1 383	953	1 813	1 229	1 800	1 872	-	-	-	-	-	-
Southern Africa	14 206	12 343	4 534	7 561	6 699	13 166	- 5 771	1 429	- 210	1 927	5 144	7 970
Angola	1 679	2 205	- 3 227	- 3 024	- 6 898	- 4 285	- 2 570	- 7	- 1 340	2 093	2 741	2 087
Botswana	521	129	136	1 093	147	188	- 91	6	1	- 10	9	- 0
Lesotho	194	178	51	53	50	44	- 0	3	21	22	20	17
Malawi	195	49	97	129	129	118ᵃ	19	- 1	42	50	50	47ᵃ
Mozambique	592	893	1 018	2 663	5 629	5 935	0	3	- 1	3	3	- 0
Namibia	720	522	793	816	861	699	5	- 3	5	5	- 6	- 8
South Africa	9 209	7 502	3 636	4 243	4 559	8 188	- 3 134	1 151	- 76	- 257	2 988	5 620
Swaziland	106	66	136	93	90	67ᵃ	- 8	7	- 1	9	- 6	1ᵃ
Zambia	939	695	1 729	1 108	1 732	1 811	-	270	1 095	- 2	- 702	181
Zimbabwe	52	105	166	387	400	400	8	-	43	14	49	27
Asia	396 025	323 683	409 021	430 622	415 106	426 355	236 380	215 294	296 186	304 293	302 130	326 013
East and South-East Asia	245 786	209 371	313 115	333 036	334 206	346 513	176 810	180 897	264 271	269 605	274 039	292 516
East Asia	195 446	162 578	213 991	233 423	216 679	221 058	142 852	137 826	206 699	213 225	220 192	236 141
China	108 312	95 000	114 734	123 985	121 080	123 911	55 910	56 530	68 811	74 654	87 804	101 000
Hong Kong, China	67 035	54 274	82 708	96 125	74 888	76 633	57 099	57 940	98 414	95 885	88 118	91 530
Korea, Democratic People's Republic of	44ᵃ	2ᵃ	38ᵃ	56ᵃ	120ᵃ	227ᵃ	-	-	-	-	-	-
Korea, Republic of	11 188	9 022	9 497	9 773	9 496	12 221	19 633	17 436	28 280	29 705	30 632	29 172
Macao, China	2 591	852	2 831	726	3 437	2 331ᵃ	- 83	- 11	- 441	120	456	45ᵃ
Mongolia	845	624	1 691	4 715	4 452	2 047	6	54	62	94	44	50
Taiwan Province of China	5 432	2 805	2 492	- 1 957	3 207	3 688	10 287	5 877	11 574	12 766	13 137	14 344
South-East Asia	50 340	46 793	99 124	99 613	117 527	125 455	33 958	43 071	57 572	56 380	53 847	56 374
Brunei Darussalam	330	371	626	1 208	865	895ᵃ	16	9	6	10	- 422ᵃ	- 135ᵃ
Cambodia	815	539	783	815	1 447	1 396ᵃ	20	19	21	29	36	42ᵃ
Indonesia	9 318	4 877	13 771	19 241	19 138	18 444ᵃ	5 900	2 249	2 664	7 713	5 422	3 676ᵃ
Lao People's Democratic Republic	228	190	279	301	294	296ᵃ	- 75ᵃ	1ᵃ	- 1ᵃ	0ᵃ	- 21ᵃ	- 7ᵃ
Malaysia	7 172	1 453	9 060	12 198	10 074	12 306ᵃ	14 965ᵃ	7 784ᵃ	13 399ᵃ	15 249ᵃ	17 115ᵃ	13 600ᵃ
Myanmar	863	973	1 285	2 200	2 243	2 621	-	-	-	-	-	-
Philippines	1 340	2 065	1 070	2 007	3 215	3 860	1 970	1 897	2 712	2 350	4 173	3 642
Singapore	12 201	23 821	55 076	50 368	61 159	63 772	6 806	26 239	33 377	23 492	13 462	26 967
Thailand	8 455	4 854	9 147	3 710	10 705	12 946	4 057	4 172	4 467	6 620	12 869	6 620
Timor-Leste	40	50	29	47	18	20ᵃ	-	-	26	- 33	13	13ᵃ
Viet Nam	9 579	7 600	8 000	7 519	8 368	8 900	300	700	900	950	1 200	1 956
South Asia	56 692	42 427	35 038	44 372	32 442	35 561	21 647	16 507	16 383	12 952	9 114	2 393
Afghanistan	94	76	211	83	94	69	-	-	-	-	-	-
Bangladesh	1 086	700	913	1 136	1 293	1 599	9	29	15	13	53	32
Bhutan	20	72	31	26	22	21	-	-	-	-	-	-
India	47 139	35 657	27 431	36 190	24 196	28 199	21 147	16 031	15 933	12 456	8 486	1 679
Iran, Islamic Republic of	1 980	2 983	3 649	4 277	4 662	3 050	380ᵃ	356ᵃ	346ᵃ	360ᵃ	430ᵃ	380ᵃ
Maldives	181	158	216	256	284	325ᵃ	-	-	-	-	-	-
Nepal	1	39	87	95	92	74	-	-	-	-	-	-
Pakistan	5 438	2 338	2 022	1 326	859	1 307	49	71	47	62	82	237

/...

Annex table 1. FDI flows, by region and economy, 2008-2013 (continued)
(Millions of dollars)

Region/economy	FDI inflows						FDI outflows					
	2008	2009	2010	2011	2012	2013	2008	2009	2010	2011	2012	2013
Sri Lanka	752	404	478	981	941	916	62	20	43	60	64	65
West Asia	93 547	71 885	60 868	53 215	48 458	44 282	37 922	17 890	15 532	21 736	18 977	31 104
Bahrain	1 794	257	156	781	891	989	1 620	- 1 791	334	894	922	1 052
Iraq	1 856	1 598	1 396	2 082	2 376	2 852[a]	34	72	125	366	448	538[a]
Jordan	2 826	2 413	1 651	1 474	1 497	1 798	13	72	28	31	5	16
Kuwait	- 6	1 114	1 304	3 260	3 931	2 329[a]	9 100	8 584	3 663	4 434	3 231	8 377[a]
Lebanon	4 333	4 804	4 280	3 485	3 674	2 833[a]	987	1 126	487	755	572	690[a]
Oman	2 952	1 485	1 782	1 563	1 040	1 626	585	109	1 498	1 233	877	1 384
Qatar	3 779	8 125	4 670	- 87	327	- 840	3 658	3 215	1 863	6 027	1 840	8 021
Saudi Arabia	39 456	36 458	29 233	16 308	12 182	9 298	3 498	2 177	3 907	3 430	4 402	4 943
State of Palestine	52	301	180	214	244	177	- 8	- 15	77	- 37	- 2	- 9
Syrian Arab Republic	1 466	2 570	1 469	804	.	.	2[a]	.	.	.	.	.
Turkey	19 762	8 629	9 058	16 171	13 224	12 866	2 549	1 553	1 464	2 349	4 074	3 114
United Arab Emirates	13 724	4 003	5 500	7 679	9 602	10 488	15 820	2 723	2 015	2 178	2 536	2 905
Yemen	1 555	129	189	- 518	- 531	- 134	66[a]	66[a]	70[a]	77[a]	71[a]	73[a]
Latin America and the Caribbean	211 138	150 913	189 513	243 914	255 864	292 081	95 931	55 026	117 420	110 598	124 382	114 590
South and Central America	129 440	78 631	125 567	163 106	168 695	182 389	37 237	13 358	46 423	40 939	45 100	32 258
South America	93 394	56 677	95 875	131 120	142 063	133 354	35 869	3 920	30 996	28 042	22 339	18 638
Argentina	9 726	4 017	11 333	10 720	12 116	9 082	1 391	712	965	1 488	1 052	1 225
Bolivia, Plurinational State of	513	423	643	859	1 060	1 750	5	- 3	- 29	.	.	.
Brazil	45 058	25 949	48 506	66 660	65 272	64 045	20 457	- 10 084	11 588	- 1 029	- 2 821	- 3 496
Chile	15 518	12 887	15 725	23 444	28 542	20 258	9 151	7 233	9 461	20 252	22 330	10 923
Colombia	10 596	7 137	6 746	13 405	15 529	16 772	2 486	3 348	6 893	8 304	- 606	7 652
Ecuador	1 058	308	163	644	585	703	48[a]	51[a]	136[a]	65[a]	- 14[a]	62[a]
Guyana	178	164	198	247	276	240[a]	.	.	.	.	.	.
Paraguay	209	95	216	557	480	382	8	.	.	.	.	.
Peru	6 924	6 431	8 455	8 233	12 240	10 172	736	411	266	113	- 57	136
Suriname	- 231	- 93	- 248	70	62	113	.	.	.	- 3	1	- 0
Uruguay	2 106	1 529	2 289	2 504	2 687	2 796	- 11	16	- 60	- 7	- 5	- 16
Venezuela, Bolivarian Republic of	1 741	- 2 169	1 849	3 778	3 216	7 040	1 598	2 236	1 776	- 1 141	2 460	2 152
Central America	36 046	21 954	29 692	31 985	26 632	49 036	1 368	9 439	15 427	12 897	22 761	13 620
Belize	170	109	97	95	194	89	3	0	1	1	1	1
Costa Rica	2 078	1 347	1 466	2 176	2 332	2 652	6	7	25	58	428	273
El Salvador	903	366	- 230	219	482	140	- 80	.	- 5	0	- 2	3
Guatemala	754	600	806	1 026	1 245	1 309	16	26	24	17	39	34
Honduras	1 006	509	969	1 014	1 059	1 060	- 1	4	- 1	2	55	26
Mexico	28 313	17 331	23 353	23 354	17 628	38 286	1 157	9 604	15 050	12 636	22 470	12 938
Nicaragua	626	434	508	968	805	849	19	- 29	18	7	44	64
Panama	2 196	1 259	2 723	3 132	2 887	4 651	248	- 174	317	176	- 274	281
Caribbean	81 698	72 282	63 946	80 808	87 169	109 692	58 693	41 668	70 998	69 658	79 282	82 332
Anguilla	101	44	11	39	44	56	2	0	0	0	0	.
Antigua and Barbuda	161	85	101	68	134	138	2	4	5	3	4	4
Aruba	15	- 11	187	488	- 326	163	3	1	3	3	3	4
Bahamas	1 512	873	1 148	1 533	1 073	1 111	410	216	150	524	132	277
Barbados	464	247	290	725	516	376[a]	- 6	- 56	- 54	- 25	89	3[a]
British Virgin Islands	51 722[a]	46 503[a]	50 142[a]	58 429[a]	72 259[a]	92 300[a]	44 118[a]	35 143[a]	53 883[a]	56 414[a]	64 118[a]	68 628[a]
Cayman Islands	19 634[a]	20 426[a]	8 659[a]	14 702[a]	6 808[a]	10 577[a]	13 377[a]	6 311[a]	16 946[a]	11 649[a]	13 262[a]	12 704[a]
Curaçao	147	55	89	69	57	27	- 1	5	15	- 30	12	- 20
Dominica	57	43	25	14	23	18	0	1	1	0	0	0
Dominican Republic	2 870	2 165	1 896	2 275	3 142	1 991	- 19	- 32	- 23	- 25	- 27[a]	- 21[a]
Grenada	141	104	64	45	34	78	6	1	3	3	3	3
Haiti	29	56	178	119	156	190	.	.	.	.	.	.
Jamaica	1 437	541	228	218	490	567	76	61	58	75	3	- 2
Montserrat	13	3	4	2	3	2	0	0	0	0	0	0
Saint Kitts and Nevis	184	136	119	112	94	112	6	5	3	2	2	2
Saint Lucia	166	152	127	100	80	88	5	6	5	4	4	4
Saint Vincent and the Grenadines	159	111	97	86	115	127	0	1	0	0	0	0
Sint Maarten	86	40	33	- 48	14	58	16	1	3	1	- 4	2
Trinidad and Tobago	2 801	709	549	1 831	2 453	1 713	700	.	.	1 060	1 681	742
Oceania	2 318	1 942	2 640	2 283	3 299	2 698	1 097	66	654	918	1 652	1 047
Cook Islands	.	- 6[a]	.	.	.	.	963[a]	13[a]	540[a]	814[a]	1 307[a]	887[a]
Fiji	341	164	350	403	376	272	- 8	3	6	1	2	4
French Polynesia	14	22	64	136	156	119[a]	30	8	38	27	43	36[a]
Kiribati	3	3	- 0[a]	0[a]	1[a]	9[a]	1	- 1	- 0	.	- 0[a]	- 0[a]
Marshall Islands	40[a]	- 11[a]	27[a]	34[a]	27[a]	23[a]	35[a]	- 25[a]	- 11[a]	29[a]	24[a]	19[a]
Micronesia, Federated States of	- 5[a]	1[a]	1[a]	1[a]	1[a]	1[a]	.	.	.	.	.	.
Nauru	1[a]	1[a]	.	.	.	.	.	.	.	.	.	.
New Caledonia	1 746	1 182	1 863	1 768	2 564	2 065[a]	64	58	76	41	175	97[a]
Niue	.	.	.	.	.	.	4[a]	- 0[a]	.	- 1[a]	.	.

Annex table 1.　FDI flows, by region and economy, 2008-2013 (concluded)
(Millions of dollars)

Region/economy	FDI inflows						FDI outflows					
	2008	2009	2010	2011	2012	2013	2008	2009	2010	2011	2012	2013
Palau	6[a]	1[a]	5[a]	5[a]	5[a]	6[a]	0[a]	-	-	-	-	-
Papua New Guinea	- 30	423	29	- 310	25	18	0	4	0	1	89	-
Samoa	49	10	1	15	24	28	-	1	-	1	9	0
Solomon Islands	95	120	238	146	68	105	4	3	2	4	3	2
Tonga	4	- 0	7	28	8	12[a]	2	0	2	1	1[a]	1[a]
Vanuatu	44	32	41	58	38	35	1	1	1	1	1	0
Transition economies	117 692	70 664	70 573	94 836	84 159	107 967	61 655	48 270	57 891	73 380	53 799	99 175
South-East Europe	7 014	5 333	4 242	5 653	2 593	3 716	511	168	318	256	132	80
Albania	974	996	1 051	876	855	1 225	81	39	6	30	23	40
Bosnia and Herzegovina	1 002	250	406	493	366	332	17	6	46	18	15	- 13
Serbia	2 955	1 959	1 329	2 709	365	1 034	283	52	189	170	54	13
Montenegro	960	1 527	760	558	620	447	108	46	29	17	27	17
The former Yugoslav Republic of Macedonia	586	201	212	468	93	334	- 14	11	2	- 0	- 8	- 2
CIS	109 113	64 673	65 517	88 135	80 655	103 241	60 998	48 120	57 437	72 977	53 371	98 982
Armenia	944	760	529	515	489	370	19	50	8	78	16	16
Azerbaijan	14	473	563	1 465	2 005	2 632	556	326	232	533	1 192	1 490
Belarus	2 188	1 877	1 393	4 002	1 464	2 233	31	102	51	126	156	173
Kazakhstan	16 819	14 276	7 456	13 760	13 785	9 739	3 704	4 193	3 791	5 178	1 959	1 948
Kyrgyzstan	377	189	438	694	293	758	- 0	- 0	0	0	- 0	- 0
Moldova, Republic of	711	208	208	288	175	231	16	7	4	21	20	28
Russian Federation	74 783	36 583	43 168	55 084	50 588	79 262	55 663	43 281	52 616	66 851	48 822	94 907
Tajikistan	376	95	8	70	233	108	-	-	-	-	-	-
Turkmenistan	1 277[a]	4 553[a]	3 631[a]	3 399[a]	3 117[a]	3 061[a]	-	-	-	-	-	-
Ukraine	10 913	4 816	6 495	7 207	7 833	3 771	1 010	162.	736	192	1 206	420
Uzbekistan	711[a]	842[a]	1 628[a]	1 651[a]	674[a]	1 077[a]	-	-	-	-	-	-
Georgia	1 564	659	814	1 048	911	1 010	147	- 19	135	147	297	113
Memorandum												
Least developed countries (LDCs)[b]	18 931	18 491	19 559	22 126	24 452	27 984	- 1 728	1 092	375	4 297	4 454	4 719
Landlocked developing countries (LLDCs)[c]	27 884	27 576	22 776	35 524	33 530	29 748	4 178	4 990	5 219	6 101	2 712	3 895
Small island developing States (SIDS)[d]	8 711	4 575	4 548	6 266	6 733	5 680	1 299	269	331	1 818	2 246	1 217

Source: UNCTAD FDI-TNC-GVC Information System, FDI database (www.unctad.org/fdistatistics).

[a]　Estimates.

[b]　Least developed countries include Afghanistan, Angola, Bangladesh, Benin, Bhutan, Burkina Faso, Burundi, Cambodia, the Central African Republic, Chad, the Comoros, the Democratic Republic of the Congo, Djibouti, Equatorial Guinea, Eritrea, Ethiopia, the Gambia, Guinea, Guinea-Bissau, Haiti, Kiribati, the Lao People's Democratic Republic, Lesotho, Liberia, Madagascar, Malawi, Mali, Mauritania, Mozambique, Myanmar, Nepal, Niger, Rwanda, Samoa (which, however, graduated from LDC status effective 1 January 2014), São Tomé and Príncipe, Senegal, Sierra Leone, Solomon Islands, Somalia, South Sudan, Sudan, Timor-Leste, Togo, Tuvalu, Uganda, the United Republic of Tanzania, Vanuatu, Yemen and Zambia.

[c]　Landlocked developing countries include Afghanistan, Armenia, Azerbaijan, Bhutan, the Plurinational State of Bolivia, Botswana, Burkina Faso, Burundi, the Central African Republic, Chad, Ethiopia, Kazakhstan, Kyrgyzstan, the Lao People's Democratic Republic, Lesotho, the former Yugoslav Republic of Macedonia, Malawi, Mali, the Republic of Moldova, Mongolia, Nepal, Niger, Paraguay, Rwanda, South Sudan, Swaziland, Tajikistan, Turkmenistan, Uganda, Uzbekistan, Zambia and Zimbabwe.

[d]　Small island developing States include Antigua and Barbuda, the Bahamas, Barbados, Cabo Verde, the Comoros, Dominica, Fiji, Grenada, Jamaica, Kiribati, Maldives, the Marshall Islands, Mauritius, the Federated States of Micronesia, Nauru, Palau, Papua New Guinea, Saint Kitts and Nevis, Saint Lucia, Saint Vincent and the Grenadines, Samoa, São Tomé and Príncipe, Seychelles, Solomon Islands, Timor-Leste, Tonga, Trinidad and Tobago, Tuvalu and Vanuatu.

Annex table 2. FDI stock, by region and economy, 1990, 2000, 2013
(Millions of dollars)

Region/economy	FDI inward stock			FDI outward stock		
	1990	2000	2013	1990	2000	2013
World	2 078 267	7 511 300	25 464 173	2 087 908	8 008 434	26 312 635
Developed economies	1 563 939	5 681 797	16 053 149	1 946 832	7 100 064	20 764 527
Europe	808 866	2 471 019	9 535 639	885 707	3 776 300	12 119 889
European Union	761 821	2 352 810	8 582 673	808 660	3 509 450	10 616 765
Austria	10 972	31 165	183 558	4 747	24 821	238 033
Belgium	-	-	924 020	-	-	1 009 000
Belgium and Luxembourg	58 388	195 219	-	40 636	179 773	-
Bulgaria	112	2 704	52 623	124	67	2 280
Croatia	..	2 796	32 484	..	824	4 361
Cyprus	..[a,b]	2 846[a]	21 182	8	557[a]	8 300
Czech Republic	1 363	21 644	135 976	..	738	21 384
Denmark	9 192	73 574	158 996[a]	7 342	73 100	256 120[a]
Estonia	-	2 645	21 451	-	259	6 650
Finland	5 132	24 273	101 307	11 227	52 109	162 360
France	97 814	390 953	1 081 497[a]	112 441	925 925	1 637 143[a]
Germany	111 231	271 613	851 512[a]	151 581	541 866	1 710 298[a]
Greece	5 681	14 113	27 741	2 882	6 094	46 352
Hungary	570	22 870	111 015	159	1 280	39 613
Ireland	37 989	127 089	377 696	14 942	27 925	502 880
Italy	59 998	122 533	403 747	60 184	169 957	598 357
Latvia	-	2 084	15 654	-	23	1 466
Lithuania	-	2 334	17 049	-	29	2 852
Luxembourg	-	-	141 381	-	-	181 607
Malta	465	2 263	14 859[a]	..	193	1 521[a]
Netherlands	68 701	243 733	670 115	105 088	305 461	1 071 819
Poland	109	34 227	252 037	95	1 018	54 974
Portugal	10 571	32 043	128 488	900	19 794	81 889
Romania	0	6 953	84 596	66	136	1 465
Slovakia	282	6 970	58 832	..	555	4 292
Slovenia	1 643	2 893	15 235	560	768	7 739
Spain	65 916	156 348	715 994	15 652	129 194	643 226
Sweden	12 636	93 791	378 107	50 720	123 618	435 964
United Kingdom	203 905	463 134	1 605 522	229 307	923 367	1 884 819
Other developed Europe	47 045	118 209	952 966	77 047	266 850	1 503 124
Gibraltar	263[a]	642[a]	2 403[a]	-	-	-
Iceland	147	497	10 719	75	663	12 646
Norway	12 391	30 265	192 409[a]	10 884	34 026	231 109[a]
Switzerland	34 245	86 804	747 436	66 087	232 161	1 259 369
North America	652 444	2 995 951	5 580 144	816 569	2 931 653	7 081 929
Canada	112 843	212 716	644 977	84 807	237 639	732 417
United States	539 601	2 783 235	4 935 167	731 762	2 694 014	6 349 512
Other developed countries	102 629	214 827	937 365	244 556	392 111	1 562 710
Australia	80 364	118 858	591 568	37 505	95 979	471 804
Bermuda	-	265[a]	2 664	-	108[a]	835
Israel	4 476	20 426	88 179	1 188	9 091	78 704
Japan	9 850	50 322	170 929[a]	201 441	278 442	992 901[a]
New Zealand	7 938	24 957	84 026	4 422	8 491	18 465
Developing economies	514 319	1 771 479	8 483 009	141 076	887 829	4 993 339
Africa	60 675	153 742	686 962	20 229	38 858	162 396
North Africa	23 962	45 590	241 789	1 836	3 199	30 635
Algeria	1 561[a]	3 379[a]	25 298[a]	183[a]	205[a]	1 737[a]
Egypt	11 043[a]	19 955	85 046	163[a]	655	6 586
Libya	678[a]	471	18 461	1 321[a]	1 903	19 435
Morocco	3 011[a]	8 842[a]	50 280[a]	155[a]	402[a]	2 573[a]
Sudan	55[a]	1 398[a]	29 148	-	-	-
Tunisia	7 615	11 545	33 557	15	33	304
Other Africa	36 712	108 153	445 173	18 393	35 660	131 761
West Africa	14 013	33 010	145 233	2 202	6 381	15 840
Benin	- 173[a]	213	1 354	2[a]	11	149
Burkina Faso	39[a]	28	1 432	4[a]	0	277
Cabo Verde	4[a]	192[a]	1 576	-	-	- 0[a]
Côte d'Ivoire	975[a]	2 483	8 233	6[a]	9	177
Gambia	157	216	754[a]	-	-	-
Ghana	319[a]	1 554[a]	19 848[a]	-	-	118[a]
Guinea	69[a]	263[a]	3 303[a]	..	12[a]	144[a]
Guinea-Bissau	8[a]	38	112	-	-	6
Liberia	2 732[a]	3 247	6 267	846[a]	2 188	4 345
Mali	229[a]	132	3 432	22[a]	1	49
Mauritania	59[a]	146[a]	5 499[a]	3[a]	4[a]	43[a]

/...

Annex table 2. FDI stock, by region and economy, 1990, 2000, 2013 (continued)
(Millions of dollars)

Region/economy	FDI inward stock			FDI outward stock		
	1990	2000	2013	1990	2000	2013
Niger	286[a]	45	4 940	54[a]	1	14
Nigeria	8 539[a]	23 786	81 977	1 219[a]	4 144	8 645
Senegal	258[a]	295	2 696	47[a]	22	412
Sierra Leone	243[a]	284[a]	2 319[a]	-	-	-
Togo	268[a]	87	1 494	-	- 10	1 460
Central Africa	3 808	5 732	61 946	372	681	2 903
Burundi	30[a]	47[a]	16[a]	0[a]	2[a]	1[a]
Cameroon	1 044[a]	1 600[a]	6 239[a]	150[a]	254[a]	717[a]
Central African Republic	95[a]	104[a]	620[a]	18[a]	43[a]	43[a]
Chad	250[a]	576[a]	4 758[a]	37[a]	70[a]	70[a]
Congo	575[a]	1 889[a]	23 050[a]	-	-	-
Congo, Democratic Republic of the	546	617	5 631[a]	-	34[a]	1 136[a]
Equatorial Guinea	25[a]	1 060[a]	15 317[a]	0[a]	- 2[a]	3[a]
Gabon	1 208[a]	- 227[a]	5 119[a]	167[a]	280[a]	920[a]
Rwanda	33[a]	55	854	-	-	13
São Tomé and Principe	0[a]	11[a]	345[a]	-	-	-
East Africa	1 701	7 202	46 397	165	387	2 160
Comoros	17[a]	21[a]	107[a]	-	-	-
Djibouti	13[a]	40	1 352	-	-	-
Eritrea	..	337[a]	791[a]	-	-	-
Ethiopia	124[a]	941[a]	6 064[a]	-	-	-
Kenya	668[a]	932[a]	3 390[a]	99[a]	115[a]	321[a]
Madagascar	107[a]	141	6 488[a]	1[a]	10[a]	6[a]
Mauritius	168[a]	683[a]	3 530[a]	1[a]	132[a]	1 559[a]
Seychelles	213	515	2 256	64	130	271
Somalia	..[a,b]	4[a]	883[a]	-	-	-
Uganda	6[a]	807	8 821	-	-	2
United Republic of Tanzania	388[a]	2 781	12 715	-	-	-
Southern Africa	17 191	62 209	191 597	15 653	28 210	110 858
Angola	1 024[a]	7 978[a]	2 348	1[a]	2[a]	11 964
Botswana	1 309	1 827	3 337	447	517	750
Lesotho	83[a]	330	1 237	0[a]	2	205
Malawi	228[a]	358	1 285[a]	-	..[a,b]	119[a]
Mozambique	25	1 249	20 967	2[a]	1	24
Namibia	2 047	1 276	4 277	80	45	32
South Africa	9 207	43 451	140 047[a]	15 004	27 328	95 760[a]
Swaziland	336	536	838[a]	38	87	76[a]
Zambia	2 655[a]	3 966[a]	14 260	-	-	1 590
Zimbabwe	277[a]	1 238[a]	3 001	80[a]	234[a]	337
Asia	340 270	1 108 173	5 202 188	67 010	653 364	3 512 719
East and South-East Asia	302 281	1 009 804	4 223 370	58 504	636 451	3 153 048
East Asia	240 645	752 559	2 670 165	49 032	551 714	2 432 635
China	20 691[a]	193 348	956 793[a]	4 455[a]	27 768[a]	613 585[a]
Hong Kong, China	201 653	491 923	1 443 947	11 920	435 791	1 352 353
Korea, Democratic People's Republic of	572[a]	1 044[a]	1 878[a]	-	-	-
Korea, Republic of	5 186	43 740	167 350	2 301	21 500	219 050
Macao, China	2 809[a]	2 801[a]	21 279[a]	-	-	1 213[a]
Mongolia	0[a]	182[a]	15 471	-	-	552
Taiwan Province of China	9 735[a]	19 521	63 448[a]	30 356[a]	66 655	245 882[a]
South-East Asia	61 636	257 244	1 553 205	9 471	84 736	720 413
Brunei Darussalam	33[a]	3 868	14 212[a]	0[a]	512	134[a]
Cambodia	38[a]	1 580	9 399[a]	..	193	465[a]
Indonesia	8 732[a]	25 060[a]	230 344[a]	86[a]	6 940[a]	16 070[a]
Lao People's Democratic Republic	13[a]	588[a]	2 779[a]	1[a]	20[a]	- 16[a]
Malaysia	10 318	52 747[a]	144 705[a]	753	15 878[a]	133 996[a]
Myanmar	281	3 211	14 171	-	-	-
Philippines	3 268[a]	13 762[a]	32 547[a]	405[a]	1 032[a]	13 191[a]
Singapore	30 468	110 570	837 652	7 808	56 755	497 880
Thailand	8 242	31 118	185 463[a]	418	3 406	58 610[a]
Timor-Leste	-	-	230	-	-	83
Viet Nam	243[a]	14 739[a]	81 702	-	-	-
South Asia	6 795	29 834	316 015	422	2 949	125 993
Afghanistan	12[a]	17[a]	1 638[a]	-	-	-
Bangladesh	477[a]	2 162	8 596[a]	45[a]	69	130[a]
Bhutan	2[a]	4[a]	163[a]	-	-	-
India	1 657[a]	16 339	226 748	124[a]	1 733	119 838
Iran, Islamic Republic of	2 039[a]	2 597[a]	40 941	..	572[a]	3 725[a]
Maldives	25[a]	128[a]	1 980[a]	-	-	-
Nepal	12[a]	72[a]	514[a]	-	-	-

/...

Annex table 2. FDI stock, by region and economy, 1990, 2000, 2013 (continued)
(Millions of dollars)

Region/economy	FDI inward stock			FDI outward stock		
	1990	2000	2013	1990	2000	2013
Pakistan	1 892	6 919	27 589	245	489	1 731
Sri Lanka	679ᵃ	1 596	7 846ᵃ	8ᵃ	86	569ᵃ
West Asia	31 194	68 535	662 803	8 084	13 964	233 678
Bahrain	552	5 906	17 815	719	1 752	10 751
Iraq	..ᵃ,ᵇ	..ᵃ,ᵇ	15 295ᵃ	-	-	1 984ᵃ
Jordan	1 368ᵃ	3 135	26 668	158ᵃ	44	525
Kuwait	37ᵃ	608ᵃ	21 242ᵃ	3 662ᵃ	1 428ᵃ	40 247ᵃ
Lebanon	53ᵃ	14 233	55 604ᵃ	43ᵃ	352	8 849ᵃ
Oman	1 723ᵃ	2 577ᵃ	19 756	-	-	6 289
Qatar	63ᵃ	1 912	29 964ᵃ	-	74	28 434ᵃ
Saudi Arabia	15 193ᵃ	17 577	208 330ᵃ	2 328ᵃ	5 285ᵃ	39 303ᵃ
State of Palestine	-	647ᵃ	2 750ᵃ	-	..ᵃ,ᵇ	181ᵃ
Syrian Arab Republic	154ᵃ	1 244	10 743ᵃ	4ᵃ	107ᵃ	421ᵃ
Turkey	11 150ᵃ	18 812	145 467	1 150ᵃ	3 668	32 782
United Arab Emirates	751ᵃ	1 069ᵃ	105 496	14ᵃ	1 938ᵃ	63 179ᵃ
Yemen	180ᵃ	843	3 675ᵃ	5ᵃ	12ᵃ	733ᵃ
Latin America and the Caribbean	111 373	507 344	2 568 596	53 768	195 339	1 312 258
South and Central America	103 311	428 929	1 842 626	52 138	104 646	647 088
South America	74 815	308 949	1 362 832	49 346	96 046	496 692
Argentina	9 085ᵃ	67 601	112 349	6 057ᵃ	21 141	34 080
Bolivia, Plurinational State of	1 026	5 188	10 558	7ᵃ	29	8
Brazil	37 143	122 250	724 644	41 044ᵃ	51 946	293 277
Chile	16 107ᵃ	45 753	215 452	154ᵃ	11 154	101 933
Colombia	3 500	11 157	127 895	402	2 989	39 003
Ecuador	1 626	6 337	13 785	18ᵃ	252ᵃ	687ᵃ
Falkland Islands (Malvinas)	0ᵃ	58ᵃ	75ᵃ	-	-	-
Guyana	45ᵃ	756ᵃ	2 547ᵃ	-	1ᵃ	2ᵃ
Paraguay	418ᵃ	1 219	4 886	134ᵃ	214	238ᵃ
Peru	1 330	11 062	73 620ᵃ	122	505	4 122ᵃ
Suriname	-	-	910	-	-	-
Uruguay	671ᵃ	2 088	20 344ᵃ	186ᵃ	138	428ᵃ
Venezuela, Bolivarian Republic of	3 865	35 480	55 766	1 221	7 676	22 915
Central America	28 496	119 980	479 793	2 793	8 600	150 396
Belize	89ᵃ	301	1 621	20ᵃ	43	53
Costa Rica	1 324ᵃ	2 709	21 792	44ᵃ	86	1 822
El Salvador	212	1 973	8 225	56ᵃ	104	2
Guatemala	1 734	3 420	10 256	..	93	472
Honduras	293	1 392	10 084	-	-	353
Mexico	22 424	101 996	389 083	2 672ᵃ	8 273	143 907
Nicaragua	145ᵃ	1 414	7 319	-	-	230
Panama	2 275	6 775	31 413	-	-	3 556
Caribbean	8 062	78 415	725 971	1 630	90 693	665 170
Anguilla	11ᵃ	231ᵃ	1 107ᵃ	-	5ᵃ	31ᵃ
Antigua and Barbuda	290ᵃ	619ᵃ	2 712ᵃ	-	5ᵃ	104ᵃ
Aruba	145ᵃ	1 161	3 634	-	675	689
Bahamas	586ᵃ	3 278ᵃ	17 155ᵃ	-	452ᵃ	3 471ᵃ
Barbados	171	308	4 635ᵃ	23	41	1 025ᵃ
British Virgin Islands	126ᵃ	32 093ᵃ	459 342ᵃ	875ᵃ	67 132ᵃ	523 287ᵃ
Cayman Islands	1 749ᵃ	25 585ᵃ	165 500ᵃ	648ᵃ	20 788ᵃ	129 360ᵃ
Curaçao	-	-	717ᵃ	-	-	56ᵃ
Dominica	66ᵃ	275ᵃ	665ᵃ	-	3ᵃ	33ᵃ
Dominican Republic	572	1 673	25 411	-	572ᵃ	921ᵃ
Grenada	70ᵃ	348ᵃ	1 430ᵃ	-	2ᵃ	53ᵃ
Haiti	149ᵃ	95	1 114	..	2ᵃ	2ᵃ
Jamaica	790ᵃ	3 317	12 730ᵃ	42ᵃ	709ᵃ	401
Montserrat	40ᵃ	83ᵃ	132ᵃ	-	0ᵃ	1ᵃ
Netherlands Antillesᶜ	408ᵃ	277	-	21ᵃ	6ᵃ	-
Saint Kitts and Nevis	160ᵃ	487ᵃ	1 916ᵃ	-	3ᵃ	56ᵃ
Saint Lucia	316ᵃ	807ᵃ	2 430ᵃ	-	4ᵃ	65ᵃ
Saint Vincent and the Grenadines	48ᵃ	499ᵃ	1 643ᵃ	-	0ᵃ	5ᵃ
Sint Maarten	-	-	278ᵃ	-	-	8ᵃ
Trinidad and Tobago	2 365ᵃ	7 280ᵃ	23 421ᵃ	21ᵃ	293ᵃ	5 602ᵃ
Oceania	2 001	2 220	25 262	68	267	5 965
Cook Islands	1ᵃ	218ᵃ	836ᵃ	-	- 1ᵃ	5 037ᵃ
Fiji	284	356	3 612	25ᵃ	39	52
French Polynesia	69ᵃ	139ᵃ	803ᵃ	-	-	251ᵃ
Kiribati	-	-	14ᵃ	-	-	1ᵃ
Marshall Islands	1ᵃ	218ᵃ	1 029ᵃ	-	..ᵃ,ᵇ	181ᵃ

/...

Annex table 2. FDI stock, by region and economy, 1990, 2000, 2013 (concluded)
(Millions of dollars)

Region/economy	FDI inward stock			FDI outward stock		
	1990	2000	2013	1990	2000	2013
Nauru	..[a,b]	..[a,b]	..[a,b]	18[a]	22[a]	22[a]
New Caledonia	70[a]	67[a]	12 720[a]	-	-	-
Niue	-	6[a]	..[a,b]	-	10[a]	22[a]
Palau	2[a]	4[a]	37[a]	-	-	-
Papua New Guinea	1 582[a]	935	4 082[a]	26[a]	210[a]	315[a]
Samoa	9[a]	77	282	-	-	21
Solomon Islands	-	106[a]	1 040	-	-	38
Tonga	1[a]	15[a]	132[a]	-	-	-
Vanuatu	-	61[a]	578	-	-	23
Transition economies	9	58 023	928 015	..	20 541	554 769
South-East Europe	..	2 886	58 186	..	16	3 336
Albania	-	247	6 104[a]	..	-	244[a]
Bosnia and Herzegovina	-	1 083[a]	8 070[a]	-	-	199[a]
Montenegro	-	-	5 384[a]	-	-	47[a]
Serbia	-	1 017[a]	29 269	-	-	2 557
The former Yugoslav Republic of Macedonia	..	540	5 534	-	16	102
CIS	9	54 375	858 153	..	20 408	550 068
Armenia	9[a]	513	5 448	-	0	186
Azerbaijan	-	3 735	13 750	-	1	9 005
Belarus	..	1 306	16 729	..	24	677
Kazakhstan	-	10 078	129 554	-	16	29 122
Kyrgyzstan	-	432	3 473	-	33	1
Moldova, Republic of	-	449	3 668	-	23	136
Russian Federation	-	32 204	575 658[a]	-	20 141	501 202[a]
Tajikistan	..	136	1 625	-	-	-
Turkmenistan	..	949[a]	23 018[a]	-	-	-
Ukraine	..	3 875	76 719	..	170	9 739
Uzbekistan	-	698[a]	8 512[a]	-	-	-
Georgia	..	762	11 676	-	118	1 365
Memorandum						
Least developed countries (LDCs)[d]	11 051	36 631	211 797	1 089	2 683	23 557
Landlocked developing countries (LLDCs)[e]	7 471	35 790	285 482	844	1 305	42 883
Small island developing States (SIDS)[f]	7 136	20 511	89 548	220	2 033	13 383

Source: UNCTAD FDI-TNC-GVC Information System, FDI database (www.unctad.org/fdistatistics).

[a]   Estimates.

[b]   Negative stock value. However, this value is included in the regional and global total.

[c]   This economy dissolved on 10 October 2010.

[d]   Least developed countries include Afghanistan, Angola, Bangladesh, Benin, Bhutan, Burkina Faso, Burundi, Cambodia, the Central African Republic, Chad, the Comoros, the Democratic Republic of the Congo, Djibouti, Equatorial Guinea, Eritrea, Ethiopia, the Gambia, Guinea, Guinea-Bissau, Haiti, Kiribati, the Lao People's Democratic Republic, Lesotho, Liberia, Madagascar, Malawi, Mali, Mauritania, Mozambique, Myanmar, Nepal, Niger, Rwanda, Samoa (which, however, graduated from LDC status effective 1 January 2014), São Tomé and Príncipe, Senegal, Sierra Leone, Solomon Islands, Somalia, South Sudan, Sudan, Timor-Leste, Togo, Tuvalu, Uganda, the United Republic of Tanzania, Vanuatu, Yemen and Zambia.

[d]   Landlocked developing countries include Afghanistan, Armenia, Azerbaijan, Bhutan, the Plurinational State of Bolivia, Botswana, Burkina Faso, Burundi, the Central African Republic, Chad, Ethiopia, Kazakhstan, Kyrgyzstan, the Lao People's Democratic Republic, Lesotho, the former Yugoslav Republic of Macedonia, Malawi, Mali, the Republic of Moldova, Mongolia, Nepal, Niger, Paraguay, Rwanda, South Sudan, Swaziland, Tajikistan, Turkmenistan, Uganda, Uzbekistan, Zambia and Zimbabwe.

[f]   Small island developing States include Antigua and Barbuda, the Bahamas, Barbados, Cabo Verde, the Comoros, Dominica, Fiji, Grenada, Jamaica, Kiribati, Maldives, the Marshall Islands, Mauritius, the Federated States of Micronesia, Nauru, Palau, Papua New Guinea, Saint Kitts and Nevis, Saint Lucia, Saint Vincent and the Grenadines, Samoa, São Tomé and Príncipe, Seychelles, Solomon Islands, Timor-Leste, Tonga, Trinidad and Tobago, Tuvalu and Vanuatu.

Annex table 3. Value of cross-border M&As, by region/economy of seller/purchaser, 2007–2013
(Millions of dollars)

Region / economy	Net sales^a							Net purchases^b						
	2007	2008	2009	2010	2011	2012	2013	2007	2008	2009	2010	2011	2012	2013
World	1 045 085	626 235	285 396	349 399	556 051	331 651	348 755	1 045 085	626 235	285 396	349 399	556 051	331 651	348 755
Developed economies	915 675	479 687	236 505	260 391	438 645	268 652	239 606	870 435	486 166	191 637	225 830	430 134	183 914	151 752
Europe	565 152	175 645	139 356	127 606	214 420	144 651	132 963	593 585	382 058	133 024	44 682	171 902	38 504	6 798
European Union	533 185	260 664	119 344	118 328	185 332	128 630	120 813	538 138	322 169	120 722	23 489	140 634	15 660	- 786
Austria	9 661	1 327	2 067	354	7 002	1 687	148	5 923	3 243	3 309	1 525	3 733	1 835	8 813
Belgium	733	3 995	12 375	9 449	3 946	1 786	6 429	9 269	30 775	- 9 804	477	7 841	- 1 354	13 251
Bulgaria	959	227	191	24	- 96	31	- 52	20	39	2	17			- 0
Croatia	674	274	-	201	92	81	100		12	8	325			5
Cyprus	1 301	853	47	693	782	51	1 417	5 879	8 875	647	- 562	3 738	8 060	652
Czech Republic	246	276	2 473	- 530	725	37	1 617	572	72	1 573	14	26	474	4 012
Denmark	7 158	5 962	1 270	1 319	7 958	4 759	1 341	3 339	2 841	3 337	- 3 601	- 133	553	214
Estonia	- 59	110	28	3	239	58	- 39		7	- 0	4	- 1	1	- 36
Finland	8 571	1 163	382	336	1 028	1 929	- 35	- 1 054	12 951	641	1 015	2 353	4 116	1 754
France	30 145	6 609	609	3 573	23 161	12 013	8 953	73 312	66 893	42 175	6 180	37 090	- 3 051	2 177
Germany	37 551	34 081	12 753	10 577	13 440	7 793	16 739	59 904	63 785	26 985	7 025	5 656	15 674	6 829
Greece	1 379	7 387	2 074	283	1 204	35	2 488	1 502	3 484	387	553	- 148	- 1 561	- 1 015
Hungary	2 068	1 728	1 853	223	1 714	96	- 1 108	1	- 41	0	799	17	- 7	-
Ireland	811	3 025	1 712	2 127	1 934	12 096	11 147	7 340	3 505	- 664	5 143	- 5 648	2 629	- 4 091
Italy	27 211	- 5 116	2 341	6 329	15 095	5 286	5 910	62 173	20 976	17 165	- 5 190	3 902	- 1 633	2 440
Latvia	47	195	109	72	1	1	4	4		- 30	40	- 3		
Lithuania	35	172	23	470	386	39	30		31	-	- 0	4	- 3	10
Luxembourg	7 379	- 3 510	444	2 138	9 495	6 461	177	16	5 906	54	1 558	1 110	- 4 247	3 794
Malta	- 86	-	13	315	-	96	7		- 25		235	- 16	25	22
Netherlands	162 533	- 9 443	18 114	4 162	14 076	17 637	22 896	4 291	48 521	- 3 222	16 418	- 3 841	- 1 092	- 3 243
Poland	680	1 507	666	1 195	9 963	824	434	189	1 090	229	201	511	3 399	243
Portugal	1 574	- 1 312	504	2 772	911	8 225	7 465	4 071	1 330	723	- 8 965	1 642	- 4 735	- 603
Romania	1 926	1 010	331	148	88	151	- 45		4	7	24			
Slovakia	66	136	21	-	0	126	541				10	- 18	- 30	
Slovenia	57	418	-	332	51	330	30	74	320	251	- 50	- 10		
Spain	57 440	37 041	31 849	10 348	17 716	4 978	5 185	40 015	- 12 160	- 507	2 898	15 505	- 1 621	- 7 348
Sweden	3 151	17 930	2 175	527	7 647	5 086	- 76	30 983	6 883	9 819	918	- 2 381	151	- 4 994
United Kingdom	169 974	154 619	24 920	60 886	46 774	36 936	29 110	230 314	52 768	27 639	- 3 521	69 704	- 1 926	- 23 671
Other developed Europe	31 967	- 85 019	20 011	9 278	29 088	16 021	12 150	55 448	59 889	12 302	21 193	31 268	22 845	7 584
Andorra						12						166		
Faeroe Islands	-	0		85									13	35
Gibraltar		212				19	50	116	- 13	253	8	1 757	- 527	- 48
Guernsey	31	36	2 011	175	25	1 294	17	7 383	890	4 171	10 338	- 1 183	1 968	- 768
Iceland	- 227			14		11		4 770	744	- 806	- 221	- 437	- 2 559	126
Isle of Man	221	35	114	157	- 217	55	1	535	324	137	852	- 736	- 162	- 850
Jersey	816	251	414	81	88	133		537	- 686	401	1 054	5 192	3 564	2 015
Liechtenstein								270		12				
Monaco	437				30			1		100	16			2
Norway	7 659	15 025	1 867	7 445	9 517	5 862	7 874	9 162	7 556	391	- 3 905	5 661	4 191	87
Switzerland	23 032	- 100 578	15 606	1 321	19 647	8 635	4 208	32 675	51 074	7 742	12 967	20 832	16 357	6 984
North America	281 057	257 478	78 270	97 766	180 302	95 656	82 910	230 393	18 280	41 856	121 461	173 157	113 486	89 106
Canada	99 682	35 147	12 431	13 307	33 344	29 484	23 342	46 864	44 247	17 538	35 744	36 049	37 580	30 180
United States	181 375	222 331	65 838	84 459	146 958	66 172	59 567	183 529	- 25 967	24 317	85 717	137 107	75 907	58 926
Other developed countries	69 466	46 564	18 879	35 019	43 923	28 345	23 733	46 457	85 828	16 757	59 687	85 076	31 924	55 848
Australia	44 751	33 730	22 534	27 192	34 671	23 959	11 923	43 309	18 823	- 3 471	15 623	6 453	- 7 023	- 5 260
Bermuda	480	1 006	883	- 405	121	905	3 273	- 38 408	2 064	2 981	1 935	2 468	3 249	4 412
Israel	1 064	1 443	1 351	1 207	3 663	1 026	3 339	8 166	11 054	183	5 929	8 720	- 2 210	676
Japan	19 132	9 909	- 5 833	7 261	4 671	1 791	4 271	29 607	49 826	17 307	31 268	62 372	37 795	55 122
New Zealand	4 039	476	- 55	- 235	797	664	928	3 782	4 061	- 243	4 933	5 063	113	899
Developing economies	97 023	120 669	41 999	84 913	84 645	56 147	112 969	146 269	116 419	77 800	101 605	105 381	127 547	129 491
Africa	5 325	24 540	5 903	7 410	8 634	- 1 254	3 848	10 356	8 266	2 577	3 792	4 393	629	3 019
North Africa	2 267	19 495	2 520	1 066	1 353	- 388	2 969	1 401	4 729	1 004	1 471	17	85	459
Algeria		82					10	- 47						312
Egypt	1 798	18 903	1 680	120	609	- 705	1 836	1 448	4 678	76	1 092		- 16	
Libya	200	307	145	91	20				51	601	377			
Morocco	269	80	691	846	274	296	1 092			324		17	101	147
Sudan					450									
Tunisia		122	4	9		21	31			3	2			
Other Africa	3 058	5 045	3 383	6 343	7 281	- 865	879	8 955	3 537	1 573	2 322	4 376	543	2 560
Angola		- 475	- 471	1 300				- 60					69	
Botswana	1		50		6	7			3			- 14	10	3
Burkina Faso		20				1	0							
Cameroon		1	1		0									
Congo		435				7								
Congo, Democratic Republic of the			5	175			- 51	- 45					19	
Côte d'Ivoire			10			0								
Equatorial Guinea		- 2 200												
Eritrea				12	- 254	- 54								
Ethiopia					146	366								
Gabon	82							- 16						
Ghana	122	900	0		- 3		15				1			
Guinea														
Kenya	396				19	86	103		18			- 3		
Liberia				587										
Madagascar							12							

/...

Annex table 3. Value of cross-border M&As, by region/economy of seller/purchaser, 2007–2013 (continued)
(Millions of dollars)

Region / economy	Net sales[a]							Net purchases[b]						
	2007	2008	2009	2010	2011	2012	2013	2007	2008	2009	2010	2011	2012	2013
Malawi	5	-	0	0	-	-	20	-	-	-	-	-	-	-
Mali	-	-	-	-	-	-	-	-	-	-	-	-	-	2
Mauritania	375	-	-	-	-	-	-	-	-	-	-	-	-	-
Mauritius	8	26	37	176	6	13	-	253	136	16	433	- 173	- 418	65
Mozambique	2	-	-	35	27	3	2	-	-	-	-	-	-	-
Namibia	2	15	59	104	40	15	6	-	-	-	-	-	-	-
Niger	-	-	-	-	-	-	- 1	-	-	-	-	-	- 185	-
Nigeria	485	- 597	- 197	476	539	- 159	537	196	418	25	-	1	40	241
Rwanda	-	6	9	-	-	69	- 2	-	-	-	-	-	-	-
Senegal	80	-	-	- 457	-	-	-	-	-	-	-	-	-	-
Seychelles	89	49	-	19	-	-	-	0	66	13	5	- 78	189	1
Sierra Leone	31	40	-	13	52	-	-	-	-	-	-	-	-	-
South Africa	1 374	6 815	3 860	3 570	6 673	- 968	214	8 646	2 873	1 504	1 619	4 291	825	2 246
Swaziland	-	-	-	-	-	-	-	-	-	-	-	6	-	-
Togo	-	-	-	-	-	-	-	-	20	-	-	353	- 5	-
Uganda	-	1	-	-	-	-	15	-	-	-	257	-	-	-
United Republic of Tanzania	-	-	2	60	0	36	-	-	-	-	-	-	-	-
Zambia	8	1	11	272	-	8	-	25	-	16	2	-	-	-
Zimbabwe	0	7	6	-	27	- 296	5	- 44	1	- 1	-	-	-	-
Asia	68 930	85 903	38 993	38 667	56 732	33 418	47 504	98 606	103 539	70 088	80 332	83 013	93 230	107 915
East and South-East Asia	41 374	55 421	29 287	27 972	32 476	22 377	40 655	25 795	60 664	41 456	67 896	70 122	78 736	98 217
East Asia	24 049	30 358	16 437	18 641	14 699	11 987	27 423	1 774	41 318	36 836	53 444	52 057	62 005	70 587
China	8 272	17 768	11 362	7 092	12 083	9 531	26 866	1 559	35 834	23 444	30 524	37 111	37 930	50 195
Hong Kong, China	7 778	8 661	3 185	13 113	2 157	2 948	459	- 9 077	1 074	6 462	13 255	10 125	16 076	16 784
Korea, Republic of	101	1 219	1 962	- 2 063	2 550	- 1 528	- 615	8 377	5 247	6 601	9 952	4 574	5 754	3 765
Macao, China	157	593	- 57	33	34	30	213	-	0	- 580	52	-	10	-
Mongolia	7	-	344	57	88	82	- 77	-	106	- 24	-	-	-	-
Taiwan Province of China	7 735	2 117	- 360	409	- 2 212	925	578	915	- 943	932	- 339	247	2 235	- 157
South-East Asia	17 325	25 063	12 850	9 331	17 776	10 390	13 232	24 021	19 346	4 620	14 452	18 065	16 731	27 630
Brunei Darussalam	0	-	3	-	-	-	0	-	-	10	-	-	-	-
Cambodia	3	30	- 336	5	50	- 100	12	-	-	-	-	0	-	-
Indonesia	753	2 879	817	1 416	6 826	477	844	474	757	- 2 381	197	409	315	2 923
Lao People's Democratic Republic	-	-	-	110	6	-	-	-	-	-	-	-	-	-
Malaysia	5 260	2 990	354	2 837	4 450	721	- 749	4 010	9 457	3 293	2 416	4 137	9 251	1 862
Myanmar	- 1	-	- 0	-	-	-	-	-	-	-	-	-	-	-
Philippines	1 175	3 988	1 476	329	2 586	411	890	- 2 514	- 150	57	19	479	682	71
Singapore	7 700	14 106	9 893	3 884	1 730	8 037	10 950	21 762	7 919	2 775	8 953	8 044	802	6 269
Thailand	1 991	150	351	461	954	- 65	40	42	1 339	865	2 810	4 996	5 659	16 498
Viet Nam	445	921	293	289	1 175	908	1 245	247	25	-	57	-	21	7
South Asia	6 027	12 884	5 931	5 634	13 093	2 821	4 784	28 786	13 376	347	26 870	6 288	3 104	1 621
Bangladesh	4	-	10	13	-	-	13	-	-	-	1	-	-	-
Iran, Islamic Republic of	-	765	-	-	-	16	-	-	-	-	-	-	-	-
India	4 805	10 317	5 877	5 613	12 798	2 805	4 763	28 774	13 370	347	26 886	6 282	3 103	1 619
Maldives	-	3	-	-	-	-	-	-	-	-	- 3	-	-	-
Nepal	-	13	-	-	4	-	-	-	-	-	-	-	-	-
Pakistan	1 213	1 377	-	- 0	247	- 153	8	-	-	-	- 13	-	-	2
Sri Lanka	6	409	44	9	44	153	- 0	12	6	-	-	6	1	-
West Asia	21 529	17 598	3 775	5 061	11 163	8 219	2 065	44 025	29 499	28 285	- 14 434	6 604	11 390	8 077
Bahrain	63	335	-	452	30	-	- 111	1 545	3 451	155	- 3 662	- 2 691	527	317
Iraq	-	34	-	11	717	1 727	324	33	-	-	-	-	- 14	8
Jordan	760	877	30	- 99	183	22	- 5	45	322	-	- 29	37	- 2	-
Kuwait	3 963	506	- 55	460	16	2 230	414	2 003	3 688	441	- 10 793	2 078	376	258
Lebanon	- 153	108	-	642	46	317	-	210	- 233	253	26	836	80	-
Oman	621	10	-	388	-	- 774	-	79	601	893	- 530	222	354	- 20
Qatar	-	124	298	12	28	169	-	6 797	6 028	10 276	626	- 790	7 971	3 078
Saudi Arabia	125	330	42	297	657	1 429	291	16 010	1 518	121	1 698	107	294	520
Syrian Arab Republic	-	-	2	66	-	-	-	-	-	-	-	-	-	-
Turkey	15 150	13 982	3 159	2 058	8 930	2 690	867	767	1 495	-	- 38	908	2 012	590
United Arab Emirates	856	1 292	299	755	556	366	286	16 536	12 629	16 145	- 1 732	5 896	- 207	3 326
Yemen	144	-	-	20	-	44	-	-	-	-	-	-	-	-
Latin America and the Caribbean	22 534	10 969	- 2 901	29 992	19 256	24 050	61 613	37 032	3 708	4 961	17 485	18 010	33 673	18 479
South America	15 940	4 205	- 3 879	18 659	14 833	20 259	17 063	12 020	5 068	4 771	13 719	10 312	23 719	12 516
Argentina	989	- 1 757	97	3 457	- 295	360	- 76	587	259	- 80	514	102	2 754	99
Bolivia, Plurinational State of	- 77	24	- 4	- 16	-	1	74	-	-	-	-	-	2	-
Brazil	7 642	1 900	84	10 115	15 112	18 087	9 996	10 794	5 480	2 518	9 030	5 541	7 401	2 971
Chile	1 998	3 252	1 301	826	- 197	- 78	2 299	466	47	1 707	882	628	10 248	2 771
Colombia	4 813	- 46	- 1 633	- 1 296	- 1 216	1 974	3 881	1 177	16	211	3 210	5 085	3 007	6 406
Ecuador	29	0	6	357	167	140	108	-	0	-	-	40	-	-
Falkland Islands (Malvinas)	-	48	-	-	-	-	-	-	-	-	-	-	-	-
Guyana	3	1	1	-	3	-	-	-	-	-	-	0	3	-
Paraguay	10	4	- 60	- 1	0	-	-	-	-	-	-	-	-	-
Peru	1 135	430	38	612	512	- 67	618	-	623	417	77	171	319	225
Suriname	-	-	-	-	-	3	-	-	-	-	-	-	-	-
Uruguay	158	20	2	448	747	89	162	-	-	-	7	13	0	8
Venezuela, Bolivarian Republic of	- 760	329	- 3 710	4 158	-	- 249	-	- 1 003	- 1 358	- 2	-	- 1 268	- 16	35
Central America	4 317	2 900	182	8 853	1 222	1 841	16 845	16 863	- 780	3 354	2 949	4 736	6 887	3 585
Belize	-	0	-	1	-	60	-	- 43	-	2	-	-	-	-
Costa Rica	- 34	405	-	5	17	120	191	- 16	-	-	-	-	354	50
El Salvador	835	-	30	43	103	- 1	-	550	-	-	-	-	12	-
Guatemala	5	145	-	650	100	- 213	411	140	-	-	-	-	-	-

Annex table 3. Value of cross-border M&As, by region/economy of seller/purchaser, 2007–2013 (concluded)
(Millions of dollars)

Region / economy	Net sales[a]							Net purchases[b]						
	2007	2008	2009	2010	2011	2012	2013	2007	2008	2009	2010	2011	2012	2013
Honduras	140	-	-	1	23	-	-	-	-	-	-	-	-	104
Mexico	3 144	2 306	129	7 989	1 143	1 116	15 896	17 629	- 190	3 187	2 896	4 274	6 504	3 845
Nicaragua	-	-	- 1	-	71	0	130	-	-	-	-	-	-	-
Panama	226	44	23	164	- 235	758	216	- 1 397	- 590	165	53	462	18	- 414
Caribbean	2 277	3 864	796	2 480	3 201	1 950	27 706	8 149	- 579	- 3 164	817	2 962	3 067	2 378
Anguilla	-	-	-	-	-	-	-	-	30	-	- 10	3	-	-
Antigua and Barbuda	1	-	-	-	-	-	-	-	-	-	-	-	-	-
Bahamas	-	41	-	82	212	145	-	2 370	1 438	- 243	112	- 350	228	- 10
Barbados	217	207	-	328	-	-	-	3	3	8	-	-	-	- 86
British Virgin Islands	559	1 001	204	391	631	32	26 958	5 085	- 2 375	- 1 579	21	733	1 968	1 869
Cayman Islands	-	487	3	84	- 112	130	40	757	2 544	- 1 363	743	1 188	909	444
Dominican Republic	42	- 108	0	7	39	1 264	213	93	-	-	31	-	-	-
Haiti	-	-	1	59	-	-	-	-	-	-	-	-	-	-
Jamaica	595	-	-	-	9	-	-	105	14	28	1	-	-	15
Netherlands Antilles[c]	-	-	2	19	235	276	16	-	14	- 30	- 156	52	- 158	-
Puerto Rico	862	-	587	1 037	1 214	88	1 079	- 261	- 2 454	22	77	202	120	- 9
Saint Kitts and Nevis	-	-	-	-	-	-	-	-	-	0	- 0	-	-	-
Trinidad and Tobago	-	2 236	-	-	973	16	- 600	- 2	207	- 10	-	- 15	-	- 244
Turks and Caicos Islands	-	-	-	-	-	-	-	-	-	-	-	-	-	-
US Virgin Islands	-	-	-	473	-	-	-	-	-	4	-	1 150	-	400
Oceania	234	- 742	4	8 844	23	- 67	4	275	906	174	- 4	- 35	15	78
American Samoa	-	-	-	-	-	11	-	-	-	-	-	-	- 29	86
Fiji	12	2	-	1	-	-	0	-	-	-	-	-	-	-
French Polynesia	-	-	-	-	-	-	-	-	-	1	-	-	44	-
Marshall Islands	45	-	-	-	-	-	-	-	136	0	-	- 35	-	3
Micronesia, Federated States of	-	-	-	-	-	-	-	-	-	-	-	-	-	4
Nauru	-	-	-	-	-	-	-	-	-	172	-	-	-	-
Norfolk Island	-	-	-	-	-	-	-	-	-	-	-	-	0	-
Papua New Guinea	160	- 758	0	8 843	5	- 78	-	275	1 051	-	- 4	-	-	-
Samoa	3	13	-	-	-	-	-	-	- 324	-	-	-	-	- 14
Solomon Islands	14	-	-	-	19	-	-	-	-	-	-	-	-	-
Tokelau	-	-	-	-	-	-	-	-	-	1	-	-	-	-
Tuvalu	-	-	-	-	-	-	-	-	43	-	-	-	-	-
Vanuatu	-	-	4	-	-	-	3	-	-	-	-	-	-	-
Transition economies	32 388	25 879	6 893	4 095	32 762	6 852	- 3 820	18 620	11 005	7 789	5 378	13 378	9 296	56 970
South-East Europe	1 511	587	529	65	1 367	3	16	1 031	- 9	- 174	-	51	2	-
Albania	164	3	146	-	-	-	-	-	-	-	-	-	-	-
Bosnia and Herzegovina	1 014	9	8	-	-	1	6	-	-	-	-	-	1	-
Montenegro	0	-	362	-	-	-	-	4	-	-	-	-	-	-
Serbia	280	501	10	19	1 340	2	9	1 038	- 7	- 174	-	51	1	-
Serbia and Montenegro	-	7	3	-	-	-	-	-	- 3	-	-	-	-	-
The Former Yugoslav Republic of Macedonia	53	67	-	46	27	-	-	-	-	-	-	-	-	-
Yugoslavia (former)	-	-	-	-	-	-	-	- 11	-	-	-	-	-	-
CIS	30 824	25 188	6 349	4 001	31 395	6 849	- 3 838	17 590	11 014	7 963	5 378	13 139	9 294	56 970
Armenia	423	204	-	-	26	23	-	-	-	-	-	-	0	-
Azerbaijan	-	2	-	0	-	-	-	-	519	-	-	2	748	-
Belarus	2 500	16	-	649	10	-	13	-	-	-	-	-	-	215
Kazakhstan	727	398	1 621	101	293	- 831	217	1 833	1 634	-	1 462	8 088	- 32	-
Kyrgyzstan	209	-	-	44	72	- 5	-	-	-	-	-	-	-	-
Moldova, Republic of	24	4	-	-	- 9	-	-	-	-	-	-	-	-	-
Russian Federation	25 120	18 606	4 579	2 882	29 589	7 228	- 3 901	15 497	7 869	7 957	3 875	4 943	8 302	56 158
Tajikistan	5	-	-	-	14	-	-	-	-	-	-	-	-	-
Ukraine	1 816	5 931	145	322	1 400	434	- 169	260	993	6	40	106	276	597
Uzbekistan	-	25	4	1	-	-	3	-	-	-	-	-	-	-
Georgia	53	104	14	30	-	1	2	-	-	-	- 0	188	-	-
Unspecified	-	-	-	-	-	-	-	9 761	12 645	8 170	16 586	7 158	10 894	10 541
Memorandum														
Least developed countries (LDCs)[d]	668	- 2 552	- 765	2 204	501	374	26	- 80	- 261	16	259	353	- 102	- 12
Landlocked developing countries (LLDCs)[e]	1 395	778	1 983	615	700	- 574	258	1 814	2 262	- 9	1 727	8 076	544	6
Small island developing States (SIDS)[f]	1 144	1 819	41	9 448	1 223	97	- 596	3 004	2 772	- 16	542	- 651	- 2	- 266

Source: UNCTAD FDI-TNC-GVC Information System, cross-border M&A database (www.unctad.org/fdistatistics).

[a] Net sales by the region/economy of the immediate acquired company.

[b] Net purchases by region/economy of the ultimate acquiring company.

[c] This economy dissolved on 10 October 2010.

[d] Least developed countries include Afghanistan, Angola, Bangladesh, Benin, Bhutan, Burkina Faso, Burundi, Cambodia, the Central African Republic, Chad, the Comoros, the Democratic Republic of the Congo, Djibouti, Equatorial Guinea, Eritrea, Ethiopia, the Gambia, Guinea, Guinea-Bissau, Haiti, Kiribati, the Lao People's Democratic Republic, Lesotho, Liberia, Madagascar, Malawi, Mali, Mauritania, Mozambique, Myanmar, Nepal, Niger, Rwanda, Samoa (which, however, graduated from LDC status effective 1 January 2014), São Tomé and Principe, Senegal, Sierra Leone, Solomon Islands, Somalia, South Sudan, Sudan, Timor-Leste, Togo, Tuvalu, Uganda, the United Republic of Tanzania, Vanuatu, Yemen and Zambia.

[e] Landlocked developing countries include Afghanistan, Armenia, Azerbaijan, Bhutan, the Plurinational State of Bolivia, Botswana, Burkina Faso, Burundi, the Central African Republic, Chad, Ethiopia, Kazakhstan, Kyrgyzstan, the Lao People's Democratic Republic, Lesotho, the former Yugoslav Republic of Macedonia, Malawi, Mali, the Republic of Moldova, Mongolia, Nepal, Niger, Paraguay, Rwanda, South Sudan, Swaziland, Tajikistan, Turkmenistan, Uganda, Uzbekistan, Zambia and Zimbabwe.

[f] Small island developing States include Antigua and Barbuda, the Bahamas, Barbados, Cabo Verde, the Comoros, Dominica, Fiji, Grenada, Jamaica, Kiribati, Maldives, the Marshall Islands, Mauritius, the Federated States of Micronesia, Nauru, Palau, Papua New Guinea, Saint Kitts and Nevis, Saint Lucia, Saint Vincent and the Grenadines, Samoa, São Tomé and Principe, Seychelles, Solomon Islands, Timor-Leste, Tonga, Trinidad and Tobago, Tuvalu and Vanuatu.

Note: Cross-border M&A sales and purchases are calculated on a net basis as follows: Net cross-border M&A sales in a host economy = Sales of companies in the host economy to foreign TNCs (-) Sales of foreign affiliates in the host economy; Net cross-border M&A purchases by a home economy = Purchases of companies abroad by home-based TNCs (-) Sales of foreign affiliates of home-based TNCs. The data cover only those deals that involved an acquisition of an equity stake of more than 10 per cent.

Annex table 4. Value of cross-border M&As, by sector/industry, 2007–2013

(Millions of dollars)

Sector/industry	Net sales[a]							Net purchases[b]						
	2007	2008	2009	2010	2011	2012	2013	2007	2008	2009	2010	2011	2012	2013
Total	1045 085	626 235	285 396	349 399	556 051	331 651	348 755	1045 085	626 235	285 396	349 399	556 051	331 651	348 755
Primary	93 918	89 682	52 891	67 605	149 065	51 521	67 760	120 229	47 203	28 446	46 861	93 236	3 427	27 229
Agriculture, hunting, forestry and fisheries	9 006	2 920	730	2 524	1 426	7 585	7 422	1 078	2 313	1 783	408	381	-1 423	318
Mining, quarrying and petroleum	84 913	86 761	52 161	65 081	147 639	43 936	60 338	119 152	44 890	26 663	46 453	92 855	4 850	26 911
Manufacturing	329 135	195 847	74 871	133 936	203 319	113 110	125 684	217 712	137 715	37 889	128 194	224 316	138 230	96 165
Food, beverages and tobacco	49 040	10 618	5 117	35 044	48 394	18 526	53 355	35 233	-42 860	- 467	33 629	31 541	31 748	35 790
Textiles, clothing and leather	14 977	3 840	426	668	4 199	2 191	4 545	-1 946	- 51	555	2 971	2 236	2 466	1 757
Wood and wood products	1 202	1 022	645	804	5 060	4 542	2 828	2 780	434	1 450	8 471	3 748	3 589	3 044
Publishing and printing	601	- 347	-	5	- 190	31	20	78	- 284	30	906	- 112	65	16
Coke, petroleum products and nuclear fuel	5 768	90	1 506	1 964	-1 430	-1 307	- 663	7 202	-3 356	- 844	-6 767	-2 625	-3 748	-2 003
Chemicals and chemical products	103 990	76 637	28 077	33 708	77 201	38 524	33 949	89 327	60 802	26 539	46 889	91 138	41 485	28 339
Rubber and plastic products	2 527	1 032	1	5 475	2 223	1 718	760	1 691	461	- 285	127	1 367	581	368
Non-metallic mineral products	36 913	27 103	2 247	6 549	927	1 619	5 733	17 502	23 013	- 567	5 198	1 663	755	3 609
Metals and metal products	84 012	19 915	- 966	6 710	5 687	9 662	9 490	46 492	23 018	2 746	5 171	19 449	9 820	647
Machinery and equipment	-25 337	8 505	2 180	6 412	14 251	1 291	5 296	-34 240	8 975	1 815	5 989	14 564	12 836	6 804
Electrical and electronic equipment	46 852	22 834	19 789	21 375	28 279	22 219	7 538	40 665	48 462	4 335	11 816	38 561	26 823	13 506
Motor vehicles and other transport equipment	-2 364	13 583	12 539	8 644	4 299	6 913	1 234	1 065	9 109	73	6 737	10 899	5 039	1 058
Other manufacturing	10 955	11 015	3 309	6 578	14 420	7 181	1 598	11 862	9 992	2 509	7 059	11 888	6 773	3 229
Services	622 032	340 706	157 635	147 857	203 667	167 020	155 311	707 144	441 317	219 062	174 344	238 499	189 993	225 361
Electricity, gas and water	108 003	48 128	59 062	-6 602	21 100	11 984	9 988	45 036	26 551	44 514	-14 759	6 758	3 116	7 739
Construction	16 117	4 582	11 646	10 763	3 074	2 253	3 174	7 047	-2 890	-2 561	-1 995	-1 466	2 772	4 868
Trade	33 875	29 258	3 631	7 278	15 645	12 730	-4 165	-4 590	18 851	3 203	6 029	6 415	23 228	-1 591
Accommodation and food service activities	872	6 418	995	1 937	1 494	- 411	4 537	-6 903	3 511	354	854	684	-1 847	925
Transportation and storage	32 242	14 800	5 468	10 795	16 028	10 439	5 732	18 927	7 236	3 651	7 652	8 576	9 336	3 146
Information and communication	47 371	29 122	45 076	19 278	25 174	35 172	31 317	32 645	49 854	38 843	19 313	23 228	17 417	26 975
Finance	306 249	108 472	13 862	59 270	64 279	39 512	49 292	562 415	316 903	123 704	139 648	166 436	116 121	155 996
Business services	60 455	88 745	14 675	30 661	48 321	43 723	43 819	48 944	32 923	7 760	16 878	26 353	18 854	26 642
Public administration and defense	793	4 209	1 271	1 380	2 910	3 602	4 078	-2 484	-11 118	- 594	-4 147	- 288	-1 165	-1 049
Education	807	1 225	509	881	953	213	76	42	155	51	266	347	317	-1 040
Health and social services	4 194	3 001	653	9 936	2 947	6 636	4 091	7 778	- 620	187	3 815	729	954	2 315
Arts, entertainment and recreation	4 114	1 956	525	1 565	1 404	971	1 591	262	1 116	- 47	635	526	275	406
Other service activities	6 940	793	263	715	339	196	1 780	-1 973	-1 154	- 3	155	199	615	29

Source: UNCTAD FDI-TNC-GVC Information System, cross-border M&A database (www.unctad.org/fdistatistics).

[a]   Net sales in the industry of the acquired company.

[b]   Net purchases by the industry of the acquiring company.

Note: Cross-border M&A sales and purchases are calculated on a net basis as follows: Net Cross-border M&As sales by sector/industry = Sales of companies in the industry of the acquired company to foreign TNCs (-) Sales of foreign affiliates in the industry of the acquired company; net cross-border M&A purchases by sector/industry = Purchases of companies abroad by home-based TNCs, in the industry of the acquiring company (-) Sales of foreign affiliates of home-based TNCs, in the industry of the acquiring company. The data cover only those deals that involved an acquisition of an equity stake of more than 10%.

Annex table 5. Cross-border M&A deals worth over $3 billion completed in 2013

Rank	Value ($ billion)	Acquired company	Industry of the acquired company	Host economy[a]	Acquiring company	Industry of the acquiring company	Home economy[a]	Shares acquired
1	27.0	TNK-BP Ltd	Crude petroleum and natural gas	British Virgin Islands	OAO Neftyanaya Kompaniya Rosneft	Crude petroleum and natural gas	Russian Federation	50
2	27.0	TNK-BP Ltd	Crude petroleum and natural gas	British Virgin Islands	OAO Neftyanaya Kompaniya Rosneft	Crude petroleum and natural gas	Russian Federation	50
3	21.6	Sprint Nextel Corp	Telephone communications, except radiotelephone	United States	SoftBank Corp	Radiotelephone communications	Japan	78
4	19.1	Nexen Inc	Crude petroleum and natural gas	Canada	CNOOC Canada Holding Ltd	Investors, nec	Canada	100
5	18.0	Grupo Modelo SAB de CV	Malt beverages	Mexico	Anheuser-Busch Mexico Holding S de RL de CV	Malt beverages	Mexico	44
6	9.4	Ping An Insurance(Group)Co of China Ltd	Life insurance	China	Investor Group	Investors, nec	Thailand	16
7	8.5	Elan Corp PLC	Biological products, except diagnostic substances	Ireland	Perrigo Co	Pharmaceutical preparations	United States	100
8	8.3	DE Master Blenders 1753 BV	Roasted coffee	Netherlands	Oak Leaf BV	Investment offices, nec	Netherlands	85
9	7.7	Kabel Deutschland Holding AG	Cable and other pay television services	Germany	Vodafone Vierte Verwaltungsgesellschaft mbH	Radiotelephone communications	Germany	77
10	6.9	Fraser & Neave Ltd	Bottled & canned soft drinks & carbonated waters	Singapore	TCC Assets Ltd	Investment offices, nec	British Virgin Islands	62
11	6.0	Neiman Marcus Group Inc	Department stores	United States	Investor Group	Investors, nec	Canada	100
12	5.8	Activision Blizzard Inc	Prepackaged Software	United States	Activision Blizzard Inc	Prepackaged Software	United States	38
13	5.7	Canada Safeway Ltd	Grocery stores	Canada	Sobeys Inc	Grocery stores	Canada	100
14	5.3	Bank of Ayudhya PCL	Banks	Thailand	Bank of Tokyo-Mitsubishi UFJ Ltd	Banks	Japan	72
15	4.8	MIP Tower Holdings LLC	Real estate investment trusts	United States	American Tower Corp	Real estate investment trusts	United States	100
16	4.8	Smithfield Foods Inc	Meat packing plants	United States	Shuanghui International Holdings Ltd	Meat packing plants	China	100
17	4.4	Springer Science+Business Media SA	Books: publishing, or publishing & printing	Germany	Investor Group	Investors, nec	United Kingdom	100
18	4.4	BNP Paribas Fortis SA/NV	Banks	Belgium	BNP Paribas SA	Security brokers, dealers, and flotation companies	France	25
19	4.3	Avio SpA-Aviation Business	Aircraft engines and engine parts	Italy	General Electric Co(GE)	Power, distribution, and specialty transformers	United States	100
20	4.2	Siam Makro PCL	Grocery stores	Thailand	CP ALL PCL	Grocery stores	Thailand	64
21	4.2	ENI East Africa SpA	Crude petroleum and natural gas	Mozambique	PetroChina Co Ltd	Crude petroleum and natural gas	China	29
22	4.2	Ally Financial Inc-European Operations	Personal credit institutions	United Kingdom	General Motors Financial Co Inc	Personal credit institutions	United States	100
23	4.1	Aegis Group PLC	Advertising, nec	United Kingdom	Dentsu Inc	Advertising agencies	Japan	86
24	4.1	Ally Credit Canada Ltd	Personal credit institutions	Canada	Royal Bank of Canada	Banks	Canada	100
25	4.1	ANA Aeroportos de Portugal SA	Airports and airport terminal services	Portugal	VINCI Concessions SAS	Highway and street construction	France	95
26	4.0	Gambro AB	Surgical and medical instruments and apparatus	Sweden	Baxter International Inc	Surgical and medical instruments and apparatus	United States	100
27	3.9	Sterlite Industries(India)Ltd	Primary smelting and refining of copper	India	Sesa Goa Ltd	Iron ores	India	100
28	3.7	T-Mobile USA Inc	Radiotelephone communications	United States	MetroPCS Communications Inc	Radiotelephone communications	United States	100
29	3.6	Hindustan Unilever Ltd	Soap & other detergents, except specialty cleaners	India	Unilever PLC	Food preparations, nec	United Kingdom	15
30	3.6	Focus Media Holding Ltd	Outdoor advertising services	China	Giovanna Acquisition Ltd	Investors, nec	China	100
31	3.6	Tele2 Russia Holding AB	Telephone communications, except radiotelephone	Russian Federation	VTB Group	National commercial banks	Russian Federation	100
32	3.5	Slovak Gas Holding BV	Natural gas transmission	Slovakia	Energeticky a Prumyslovy Holding as	Electric services	Czech Republic	100
33	3.3	TYSABRI	Pharmaceutical preparations	United States	Biogen Idec Inc	Biological products, except diagnostic substances	United States	50
34	3.2	Statoil ASA-Gullfaks Field	Crude petroleum and natural gas	Norway	OMV AG	Crude petroleum and natural gas	Austria	19
35	3.1	The Shaw Group Inc	Fabricated pipe and pipe fittings	United States	Chicago Bridge & Iron Co NV	Special trade contractors, nec	Netherlands	100
36	3.1	ICA AB	Grocery stores	Sweden	Hakon Invest AB	Investors, nec	Sweden	60
37	3.1	Transport et Infrastructures Gaz France SA(TIGF)	Natural gas transmission	France	Investor Group	Investors, nec	Italy	100

Source: UNCTAD FDI-TNC-GVC Information System, cross-border M&A database (www.unctad.org/fdistatistics).

[a] Immediate country.

Note: As long as the ultimate host economy is different from the ultimate home economy, M&A deals that were undertaken within the same economy are still considered cross-border M&As.

Annex table 6. Value of greenfield FDI projects, by source/destination, 2007–2013

(Millions of dollars)

Partner region/economy	World as destination							World as source						
	2007	2008	2009	2010	2011	2012	2013	2007	2008	2009	2010	2011	2012	2013
	By source							By destination						
World	880 832	1 413 540	1 008 273	860 905	902 365	613 939	672 108	880 832	1 413 540	1 008 273	860 905	902 365	613 939	672 108
Developed countries	632 655	1 027 852	734 272	625 190	636 843	413 541	458 336	310 109	425 276	318 385	298 739	297 581	224 604	215 018
Europe	414 450	599 130	445 470	384 529	355 244	231 327	256 094	222 398	317 370	200 298	168 435	176 488	136 320	125 087
European Union	374 544	548 639	412 323	352 752	327 446	214 416	229 275	216 647	307 460	194 248	161 758	172 635	133 181	121 601
Austria	14 783	22 426	10 057	9 309	8 309	4 641	5 395	3 144	3 028	1 717	2 289	4 134	1 579	1 095
Belgium	6 569	12 860	8 872	5 817	6 030	3 703	4 241	8 149	10 797	3 796	6 067	3 351	2 575	2 980
Bulgaria	81	286	30	147	121	81	217	7 695	11 231	4 780	3 680	5 300	2 756	1 906
Croatia	2 909	3 261	146	1 071	105	175	240	1 795	3 194	1 707	2 397	1 798	1 141	1 039
Cyprus	428	323	856	543	4 379	1 561	974	465	629	249	720	385	204	152
Czech Republic	5 158	4 615	1 729	2 298	2 109	2 184	1 960	7 491	5 684	4 575	7 733	4 874	2 690	3 805
Denmark	7 375	13 944	9 951	4 534	8 151	7 597	7 050	2 001	1 968	2 195	457	794	850	743
Estonia	2 654	559	188	1 088	358	259	861	840	1 481	1 260	947	883	997	788
Finland	13 189	11 071	3 628	4 351	5 891	4 795	6 751	1 269	2 415	1 208	1 692	2 153	1 691	2 461
France	55 234	89 486	66 071	52 054	49 030	27 881	30 710	19 367	24 114	11 371	9 109	10 519	7 072	9 354
Germany	73 929	98 526	73 239	72 025	69 841	50 718	48 478	16 417	30 620	19 585	17 081	18 504	12 210	10 722
Greece	1 700	4 416	1 802	1 300	1 450	1 574	763	5 096	5 278	2 090	1 123	2 377	1 553	3 092
Hungary	1 913	4 956	1 159	431	1 245	1 055	599	9 550	9 031	3 739	7 557	3 213	2 502	2 118
Ireland	7 629	9 510	14 322	5 743	4 704	5 630	4 346	4 679	8 215	4 932	4 453	6 982	5 045	4 577
Italy	22 961	41 297	29 744	23 431	23 196	21 334	21 124	11 760	12 618	10 471	11 365	5 692	4 037	3 919
Latvia	284	660	761	821	279	75	149	717	2 545	828	965	717	1 042	656
Lithuania	303	723	305	252	158	640	273	1 485	1 542	1 238	1 558	7 304	1 271	971
Luxembourg	9 097	14 103	10 879	7 085	9 418	5 802	4 315	695	431	759	731	290	270	336
Malta	68	212	773	12	566	68	46	299	395	467	300	174	308	199
Netherlands	24 566	39 940	32 555	19 651	17 697	9 441	13 731	5 840	9 438	9 459	8 469	5 650	4 075	7 119
Poland	2 252	1 790	1 241	2 238	850	1 409	855	18 776	31 977	14 693	11 566	13 024	11 891	7 960
Portugal	4 522	11 162	7 180	5 088	2 153	2 058	2 087	6 476	6 785	5 443	2 665	1 732	1 231	1 474
Romania	108	430	131	708	129	127	293	21 006	30 474	15 019	7 764	16 156	9 852	9 210
Slovakia	474	135	393	1 314	277	356	246	5 485	3 350	3 152	4 149	5 664	1 420	1 758
Slovenia	683	1 658	586	536	346	335	165	1 037	612	282	748	692	469	175
Spain	31 236	45 465	42 209	37 687	29 365	18 000	24 617	23 529	27 530	15 984	16 444	11 501	11 918	13 271
Sweden	11 875	21 448	15 508	14 895	13 906	7 152	10 385	4 372	2 930	2 827	2 364	3 160	1 354	1 027
United Kingdom	72 562	93 379	78 000	78 322	67 382	35 765	38 406	27 209	59 149	50 423	27 367	35 611	41 177	28 696
Other developed Europe	39 906	50 491	33 147	31 777	27 798	16 911	26 819	5 751	9 911	6 050	6 676	3 853	3 139	3 486
Andorra	-	14	30	145	18	114	-	-	-	20	5	-	-	1
Iceland	1 545	568	123	633	433	39	4 215	53	1 077	-	705	203	136	248
Liechtenstein	74	105	136	111	133	92	39	131	8	-	9	-	-	115
Monaco	6	15	34	48	258	-	32	71	234	43	33	123	38	17
Norway	10 792	12 058	10 588	5 433	6 634	3 325	2 999	794	3 200	2 334	2 243	830	583	1 279
San Marino	-	-	-	-	-	3	-	-	-	-	-	-	-	-
Switzerland	27 489	37 732	22 236	25 408	20 323	13 339	19 535	4 703	5 391	3 654	3 682	2 698	2 382	1 826
North America	145 789	299 570	196 675	164 915	185 207	123 651	134 222	54 485	71 110	85 957	80 779	100 002	63 504	67 277
Canada	14 748	43 513	30 928	20 023	28 507	19 146	14 187	8 630	19 763	14 084	17 789	27 256	8 447	15 098
United States	131 040	256 058	165 747	144 892	156 700	104 504	120 035	45 855	55 347	71 873	62 990	72 746	55 058	52 179
Other developed countries	72 416	129 152	92 126	75 746	96 392	58 563	68 020	33 226	36 795	32 131	49 525	21 091	24 779	22 653
Australia	14 191	31 052	18 421	12 441	14 486	10 456	8 939	22 816	22 624	19 990	41 253	12 245	16 488	10 552
Bermuda	3 937	3 440	8 108	1 573	1 198	844	1 943	15	-	1	165	6	14	4
Greenland	214	35	-	-	-	-	-	-	-	-	457	-	-	-
Israel	4 347	12 725	2 726	6 655	3 447	2 816	3 134	457	853	3 333	856	696	1 692	1 148
Japan	49 189	81 290	61 868	54 210	76 176	42 891	51 701	7 768	11 287	8 240	6 407	6 177	5 273	9 700
New Zealand	537	611	1 004	867	1 085	1 555	2 303	2 171	2 030	568	388	1 967	1 312	1 249
Developing economies	228 856	361 610	254 896	215 212	247 631	190 448	195 161	499 559	880 220	634 961	510 098	547 047	349 946	429 221
Africa	5 564	12 765	13 386	14 517	35 428	7 764	15 807	82 133	160 790	91 629	81 233	81 130	47 455	53 596
North Africa	2 639	5 207	2 396	1 095	746	2 735	1 496	49 382	63 135	41 499	24 542	11 931	15 946	10 569
Algeria	60	620	16	-	130	200	15	8 952	19 107	2 380	1 716	1 204	2 370	4 286
Egypt	1 880	3 498	1 828	990	76	2 523	1 132	12 780	13 376	20 678	12 161	6 247	10 205	3 035
Libya	-	-	19	-	-	-	-	4 061	3 004	1 689	1 858	49	98	121
Morocco	50	619	393	58	87	12	115	5 113	16 925	6 189	4 217	2 535	1 398	2 461
South Sudan	-	-	-	-	-	-	-	19	1 181	54	139	235	382	180
Sudan	42	-	-	-	432	-	-	-	1 612	2 025	2 440	58	66	55
Tunisia	609	471	140	47	21	-	235	18 458	7 931	8 484	2 010	1 602	1 426	432
Other Africa	2 925	7 558	10 990	13 422	34 682	5 029	14 311	32 751	97 655	50 130	56 692	69 199	31 509	43 028
Angola	39	78	15	494	-	362	112	8 138	11 204	5 536	1 147	305	3 022	552
Benin	-	-	-	-	-	-	-	-	9	-	14	46	17	160
Botswana	-	-	11	9	138	70	36	344	2 220	349	660	492	148	103
Burkina Faso	-	-	-	-	-	-	-	9	281	272	479	165	1	217
Burundi	-	-	-	-	-	12	11	-	19	47	25	41	19	66

/...

Annex table 6. Value of greenfield FDI projects, by source/destination, 2007–2013 (continued)
(Millions of dollars)

Partner region/economy	World as destination							World as source						
	2007	2008	2009	2010	2011	2012	2013	2007	2008	2009	2010	2011	2012	2013
	By source							By destination						
Cabo Verde	-	-	-	-	-	-	-	9	128	-	38	62	-	8
Cameroon	-	-	19	-	-	-	-	2 460	351	1 155	5 289	4 272	566	502
Central African Republic	-	-	-	-	-	-	-	361	-	-	-	-	59	-
Chad	-	-	-	-	-	-	-	-	758	402	-	135	101	150
Comoros	-	-	-	-	-	-	-	9	9	-	-	7	138	11
Congo	-	-	-	-	-	-	-	198	9	1 281	-	37	119	434
Congo, Democratic Republic of	-	161	-	7	-	-	-	1 238	3 294	43	1 238	2 242	517	556
Côte d' Ivoire	-	13	10	19	-	48	326	71	372	131	261	937	1 038	1 873
Djibouti	-	-	-	-	-	-	-	5	1 555	1 245	1 255	-	25	180
Equatorial Guinea	-	-	-	-	-	-	12	-	6	1 300	9	1 881	2	13
Eritrea	-	3	-	-	-	-	-	-	-	-	-	-	-	-
Ethiopia	-	18	12	-	-	54	70	919	762	321	290	630	441	4 510
Gabon	-	-	-	-	9	-	-	328	3 298	927	1 231	219	267	46
Gambia	-	-	-	-	-	-	-	9	31	31	405	26	200	9
Ghana	-	-	7	15	51	51	28	129	4 918	7 059	2 689	6 431	1 319	2 780
Guinea	-	-	-	-	-	-	-	-	-	61	1 411	548	33	35
Guinea-Bissau	-	-	-	-	-	-	-	361	-	19			-	-
Kenya	198	616	314	3 920	421	835	441	332	549	1 896	1 382	2 855	988	3 644
Lesotho	-	-	-	-	-	-	-	51	16	28	51	710	10	-
Liberia	-	-	-	-	-	-	-	-	2 600	821	4 591	287	53	558
Madagascar	-	-	-	-	-	-	-	3 335	1 325	365	-	140	363	182
Malawi	-	9	9	-	-	2	-	-	19	713	314	454	24	559
Mali	-	19	10	19	9	-	11	-	172	59	13	0	794	13
Mauritania	-	-	-	-	-	-	-	37	272	-	59	279	361	23
Mauritius	38	307	1 809	2 642	3 287	149	3 252	481	317	147	71	1 749	142	49
Mozambique	-	-	-	-	-	59	-	2 100	6 600	1 539	3 278	9 971	3 456	6 108
Namibia	-	23	-	-	-	344	420	473	1 907	1 519	390	832	777	1 057
Niger	-	-	-	-	-	-	-	-	3 319	-	100	277	-	350
Nigeria	190	698	659	1 048	1 046	723	3 061	3 213	27 381	7 978	8 340	4 543	4 142	5 983
Reunion	-	-	-	-	-	-	-	-	-	-	-	-	-	-
Rwanda	-	-	26	-	-	19	-	283	252	312	1 839	779	110	424
São Tomé and Principe	-	-	-	-	-	-	-	2	351	-	-	-	-	150
Senegal	-	-	-	-	10	8	389	536	1 281	548	883	69	1 238	1 260
Seychelles	-	-	-	-	-	-	-	125	130	1	121	9	43	156
Sierra Leone	-	-	-	-	-	-	-	-	73	260	230	212	119	611
Somalia	-	-	-	-	-	-	-	-	361	-	59	-	44	381
South Africa	2 393	4 841	7 820	5 146	29 469	2 082	5 833	5 247	13 533	7 695	6 819	12 430	4 777	5 643
Swaziland	-	-	-	-	-	-	-	-	23	12	-	646	7	150
Togo	49	94	142	34	214	19	122	351	146	26	-	-	411	363
Uganda	9	40	28	9	-	-	7	291	3 057	2 147	8 505	2 476	569	752
United Republic of Tanzania	9	9	57	49	27	24	138	327	2 492	623	1 077	3 806	1 137	852
Zambia	-	-	9	-	-	168	33	422	1 276	2 375	1 376	2 366	840	1 074
Zimbabwe	-	629	34	10	-	-	8	557	979	889	754	5 834	3 074	480
Asia	211 077	329 843	226 047	178 906	191 076	173 175	161 096	349 751	583 342	424 092	313 488	331 839	231 496	227 492
East and South-East Asia	130 227	154 975	122 130	123 597	115 164	110 393	106 067	243 703	321 831	251 936	202 925	205 922	147 303	146 465
East Asia	83 797	107 698	83 957	87 393	86 185	71 304	83 494	127 920	151 963	135 605	117 637	119 919	93 099	82 464
China	32 765	47 016	25 496	20 684	40 140	19 227	19 295	104 359	126 831	116 828	96 749	100 630	73 747	69 473
Hong Kong, China	17 313	15 528	17 468	8 147	13 023	11 953	49 225	4 742	7 164	9 073	8 217	7 127	7 960	5 137
Korea, Democratic People's Republic of	-	-	-	-	-	-	-	560	533	228	-	59	-	227
Korea, Republic of	21 928	33 775	29 119	30 285	20 896	30 031	9 726	9 108	11 828	4 583	3 601	7 087	6 279	4 731
Macao, China	-	2	-	-	-	-	-	4 224	909	310	282	430	2 382	257
Mongolia	-	-	-	150	-	-	-	448	330	302	1 608	183	122	595
Taiwan Province of China	11 792	11 377	11 875	28 127	12 126	10 094	5 248	4 477	4 367	4 280	7 179	4 403	2 608	2 045
South-East Asia	46 430	47 277	38 173	36 203	28 979	39 089	22 573	115 783	169 868	116 331	85 288	86 003	54 204	64 001
Brunei Darussalam	-	77	-	-	2	-	-	722	435	470	156	5 969	77	45
Cambodia	-	51	149	-	-	-	184	261	3 581	3 895	1 759	2 365	1 625	1 956
Indonesia	1 824	393	1 043	415	5 037	843	395	18 512	36 019	29 271	13 740	24 152	16 881	9 983
Lao People's Democratic Republic	-	192	-	-	-	-	-	1 371	1 151	2 118	335	980	589	458
Malaysia	26 806	13 818	14 904	21 319	4 140	18 458	2 557	8 318	23 110	13 580	15 541	13 694	6 827	5 536
Myanmar	20	-	-	-	84	-	160	378	1 434	1 889	449	712	2 029	13 444
Philippines	1 541	563	1 410	1 790	324	629	504	15 509	14 800	9 719	4 645	2 813	4 263	2 988
Singapore	13 432	21 444	12 985	8 631	13 308	16 537	12 633	24 979	13 983	12 940	16 992	20 562	9 838	8 378
Thailand	2 159	7 936	6 032	3 128	4 443	2 432	5 072	6 601	15 122	7 678	8 641	4 121	5 699	5 645
Timor-Leste	-	-	-	-	-	-	-	-	-	-	1 000	-	116	-
Viet Nam	647	2 804	1 651	920	1 643	190	1 070	39 133	60 234	34 772	22 030	10 634	6 259	15 570
South Asia	24 343	39 788	23 226	21 115	32 560	27 714	15 789	55 632	87 161	68 983	55 433	58 669	39 525	24 499
Afghanistan	-	-	-	-	8	-	15	6	269	2 978	634	305	245	320
Bangladesh	-	72	37	103	109	144	1	53	860	645	2 720	490	2 361	872

/...

Annex table 6. Value of greenfield FDI projects, by source/destination, 2007–2013 (continued)

(Millions of dollars)

Partner region/economy	World as destination							World as source						
	2007	2008	2009	2010	2011	2012	2013	2007	2008	2009	2010	2011	2012	2013
	By source							By destination						
Bhutan	-	-	-	-	-	-	-	-	-	135	83	86	39	183
India	18 136	38 039	17 338	20 250	31 589	24 891	14 740	43 445	70 207	55 156	44 491	48 921	30 947	17 741
Iran, Islamic Republic of	6 137	429	5 743	535	515	1 578	-	6 217	6 911	2 982	3 034	1 812	-	79
Maldives	-	-	-	-	-	-	-	206	462	453	2 162	1 012	329	107
Nepal	-	2	-	6	31	125	232	3	740	295	340	128	-	853
Pakistan	40	1 220	42	153	227	106	686	5 049	6 390	3 955	1 255	2 399	4 315	3 033
Sri Lanka	29	27	66	68	82	871	115	652	1 323	2 383	714	3 517	1 290	1 312
West Asia	56 507	135 081	80 691	34 195	43 352	35 069	39 240	50 417	174 350	103 173	55 130	67 248	44 668	56 527
Bahrain	8 995	15 987	14 740	1 070	912	1 145	598	820	8 050	2 036	1 997	3 931	3 535	1 154
Iraq	42	-	20	-	48	-	52	474	23 982	12 849	5 486	10 597	976	14 998
Jordan	244	627	1 650	591	52	1 037	105	1 250	11 903	2 506	2 824	3 250	1 401	10 946
Kuwait	2 936	16 108	4 585	2 850	4 502	1 331	10 833	373	2 256	987	673	494	1 051	2 183
Lebanon	596	626	639	246	301	393	153	428	1 292	1 772	1 336	531	201	104
Oman	87	84	3 110	39	165	101	479	1 794	8 954	5 608	4 255	5 043	4 970	2 641
Qatar	972	8 839	13 663	2 891	13 044	8 749	1 546	1 368	19 021	21 519	5 434	4 362	2 172	1 573
Saudi Arabia	2 089	5 795	6 105	1 441	5 027	2 389	2 746	14 630	36 718	14 860	8 139	15 766	8 393	6 430
State of Palestine	-	-	-	-	-	15	-	52	1 050	16	15	-	-	8
Syrian Arab Republic	-	326	59	-	193	0	0	1 854	4 949	3 134	2 165	1 315	10	-
Turkey	2 399	4 464	4 068	4 031	3 155	3 216	6 864	14 655	17 127	23 859	8 917	10 323	9 540	9 491
United Arab Emirates	38 147	82 175	32 053	21 034	15 954	16 684	15 844	12 372	36 218	13 067	12 870	11 623	12 053	6 821
Yemen	-	49	-	2	-	9	20	347	2 830	961	1 019	11	366	178
Latin America and the Caribbean	12 215	18 926	15 442	21 773	20 776	9 508	18 257	63 442	131 592	117 061	113 098	130 791	69 731	145 066
South America	8 539	16 196	12 040	18 602	10 520	6 715	11 864	39 422	83 232	81 409	89 861	96 732	50 071	67 334
Argentina	625	470	1 118	1 284	871	1 422	1 381	5 466	7 193	9 217	7 112	12 000	6 004	4 342
Bolivia, Plurinational State of	-	-	-	-	-	-	66	49	789	1 947	797	305	10	1 028
Brazil	4 372	11 073	7 736	10 323	4 649	3 200	6 865	17 516	40 201	40 304	43 860	56 888	26 373	29 055
Chile	2 239	855	1 758	2 564	1 578	1 106	1 566	3 093	6 360	12 888	5 874	13 814	10 233	10 212
Colombia	139	500	102	3 390	1 020	884	1 111	3 986	8 281	2 945	10 616	6 892	2 909	11 479
Ecuador	89	67	330	166	60	38	-	518	511	348	132	648	603	784
Guyana	-	-	-	-	-	-	-	10	1 000	12	160	15	302	38
Paraguay	-	-	-	-	-	-	-	607	378	83	3 873	108	287	395
Peru	315	17	108	25	380	12	391	2 974	9 859	11 831	11 956	4 074	2 184	6 340
Suriname	-	-	-	-	-	-	-	-	101	-	-	384	34	13
Uruguay	25	3	49	3	5	-	4	2 910	4 381	504	749	1 030	720	1 620
Venezuela, Bolivarian Republic of	735	3 211	840	847	1 956	53	480	2 293	4 179	1 331	4 732	574	413	2 029
Central America	2 880	1 186	2 459	2 869	9 820	2 441	5 785	21 438	41 320	31 929	20 025	25 614	17 217	68 714
Belize	-	-	-	-	5	-	-	-	-	3	5	-	241	100
Costa Rica	95	6	45	63	11	1	110	2 157	570	1 427	1 981	3 364	476	825
El Salvador	102	-	281	147	20	-	55	356	562	716	276	462	171	863
Guatemala	79	58	131	86	125	211	222	979	905	1 330	963	209	53	1 059
Honduras	61	-	-	-	-	40	378	951	1 089	126	226	551	43	549
Mexico	2 444	990	1 923	2 101	9 498	2 184	4 954	13 652	34 896	25 059	14 809	18 741	15 401	23 101
Nicaragua	54	67	-	251	-	-	31	62	185	877	280	274	135	40 602
Panama	47	65	80	220	161	5	35	3 282	3 114	2 391	1 485	2 013	697	1 616
Caribbean	795	1 544	944	302	437	353	609	2 581	7 039	3 723	3 212	8 445	2 444	9 018
Antigua and Barbuda	-	-	-	-	-	-	-	-	82	-	-	-	-	-
Aruba	-	-	-	-	-	-	-	-	64	-	6	25	70	-
Bahamas	19	18	42	-	2	7	97	18	61	5	64	333	24	15
Barbados	2	-	-	5	26	19	-	-	-	29	137	303	16	-
Cayman Islands	166	554	853	52	243	297	41	36	326	104	253	349	351	6
Cuba	-	77	-	-	21	-	0	127	2 703	1 015	1 567	465	223	195
Dominica	-	-	-	-	-	-	-	63	-	-	-	-	-	-
Dominican Republic	498	-	30	25	-	-	-	749	2 044	1 399	330	5 143	584	2 684
Grenada	-	-	-	-	-	-	-	3	-	-	5	5	30	0
Guadeloupe	-	-	-	-	-	-	-	-	267	-	-	25	-	-
Haiti	-	-	-	9	-	-	10	-	2	110	59	376	2	426
Jamaica	2	889	17	160	128	30	460	29	317	41	23	491	13	1 363
Martinique	63	-	-	13	-	-	-	35	-	6	-	-	23	-
Puerto Rico	20	6	4	36	18	-	1	713	739	716	570	752	926	2 530
Saint Kitts and Nevis	-	-	-	-	-	-	-	-	-	-	-	-	64	-
Saint Lucia	-	-	-	-	-	-	-	12	-	3	144	64	-	65
Saint Vincent and the Grenadines	-	-	-	-	-	-	-	-	-	-	-	-	-	-
Trinidad and Tobago	26	-	-	3	-	-	-	797	372	296	22	114	119	1 514
Turks and Caicos Islands	-	-	-	-	-	-	-	-	64	-	34	-	-	221
Oceania	-	76	20	16	351	-	-	4 234	4 496	2 179	2 279	3 287	1 265	3 067
Fiji	-	-	2	8	-	-	-	206	117	339	-	179	41	13
French Polynesia	-	-	10	-	-	-	-	-	-	-	108	-	-	-

/...

Annex table 6. Value of greenfield FDI projects, by source/destination, 2007–2013 (concluded)
(Millions of dollars)

Partner region/economy	World as destination							World as source						
	2007	2008	2009	2010	2011	2012	2013	2007	2008	2009	2010	2011	2012	2013
	By source							By destination						
Micronesia, Federated States of	-	-	-	-	-	-	-	-	-	-	-	-	156	-
New Caledonia	-	-	-	-	202	-	-	3 800	1 400	22	-	8	-	-
Papua New Guinea	-	73	-	8	149	-	-	228	2 438	1 786	1 944	3 050	1 068	3 054
Samoa	-	2	-	-	-	-	-	-	500	-	-	-	-	-
Solomon Islands	-	-	8	-	-	-	-	-	42	32	228	51	-	-
Transition economies	19 321	24 077	19 105	20 503	17 891	9 950	18 611	71 164	108 044	54 926	52 067	57 736	39 389	27 868
South-East Europe	31	658	326	485	202	82	220	11 399	18 167	6 192	5 241	7 464	7 568	5 851
Albania	-	-	-	105	-	-	3	4 454	3 505	124	68	525	288	57
Bosnia and Herzegovina	-	7	-	16	2	9	26	2 623	1 993	1 368	283	1 253	1 287	880
Montenegro	-	-	-	7	-	-	9	694	851	120	380	436	355	613
Serbia	31	651	314	356	150	74	84	3 131	9 196	3 816	4 040	4 295	4 459	3 721
The former Yugoslav Republic of Macedonia	-	-	12	1	49	-	99	497	2 622	763	470	956	1 179	579
CIS	19 290	23 337	18 746	20 009	17 514	9 620	18 360	58 431	87 069	44 336	45 809	48 292	31 397	20 757
Armenia	-	51	-	9	83	171	-	434	690	1 003	265	805	434	773
Azerbaijan	4 307	1 223	3 779	580	435	3 246	221	1 999	1 921	1 939	711	1 289	1 573	964
Belarus	76	1 323	391	2 091	133	91	540	487	977	1 134	1 888	1 268	787	581
Kazakhstan	109	411	706	636	383	138	221	4 251	17 844	1 949	2 536	7 816	1 191	1 370
Kyrgyzstan	-	60	30	-	-	-	-	3 362	539	50	-	358	83	49
Moldova, Republic of	-	557	-	-	0	-	3	162	163	488	301	320	118	285
Russian Federation	13 657	16 976	13 055	15 476	15 527	5 019	16 185	38 157	51 949	29 792	34 519	22 781	18 537	12 213
Tajikistan	-	82	10	-	-	-	-	327	226	570	3	1 076	669	44
Turkmenistan	-	-	-	-	-	-	-	1 051	3 974	1 433	458	1 926	8	-
Ukraine	1 142	2 656	776	1 218	954	954	1 191	7 185	7 686	4 561	4 061	3 094	3 192	4 191
Uzbekistan	-	-	-	-	-	0	-	1 016	1 101	1 418	1 068	7 560	4 806	289
Georgia	-	82	33	8	174	248	31	1 334	2 808	4 398	1 017	1 980	424	1 261
Memorandum														
Least developed countries (LDCs)[a]	168	798	502	732	923	1 005	1 528	21 220	55 740	34 229	39 853	33 647	21 923	39 043
Landlocked developing countries(LLDCs)[b]	4 425	3 290	4 675	1 429	1 137	4 005	1 033	18 840	47 069	25 449	28 026	39 438	17 931	17 211
Small island developing States (SIDS)[c]	87	1 290	1 877	2 825	3 592	205	3 809	2 187	5 325	3 132	5 957	7 429	2 298	6 506

Source: UNCTAD, based on information from the Financial Times Ltd, fDi Markets (www.fDimarkets.com).

[a] Least developed countries include: Afghanistan, Angola, Bangladesh, Benin, Bhutan, Burkina Faso, Burundi, Cambodia, the Central African Republic, Chad, the Comoros, the Democratic Republic of the Congo, Djibouti, Equatorial Guinea, Eritrea, Ethiopia, the Gambia, Guinea, Guinea-Bissau, Haiti, Kiribati, the Lao People's Democratic Republic, Lesotho, Liberia, Madagascar, Malawi, Mali, Mauritania, Mozambique, Myanmar, Nepal, Niger, Rwanda, Samoa (which, however, graduated from LDC status effective 1 January 2014), São Tomé and Principe, Senegal, Sierra Leone, Solomon Islands, Somalia, South Sudan, Sudan, Timor-Leste, Togo, Tuvalu, Uganda, the United Republic of Tanzania, Vanuatu, Yemen and Zambia.

[b] Landlocked developing countries include: Afghanistan, Armenia, Azerbaijan, Bhutan, Bolivia, Botswana, Burkina Faso, Burundi, the Central African Republic, Chad, Ethiopia, Kazakhstan, Kyrgyzstan, the Lao People's Democratic Republic, Lesotho, the former Yugoslav Republic of Macedonia, Malawi, Mali, the Republic of Moldova, Mongolia, Nepal, Niger, Paraguay, Rwanda, South Sudan, Swaziland, the Republic of Tajikistan, Turkmenistan, Uganda, Uzbekistan, Zambia and Zimbabwe.

[c] Small island developing States include: Antigua and Barbuda, the Bahamas, Barbados, Cabo Verde, the Comoros, Dominica, Fiji, Grenada, Jamaica, Kiribati, Maldives, Marshall Islands, Mauritius, the Federated States of Micronesia, Nauru, Palau, Papua New Guinea, Saint Kitts and Nevis, Saint Lucia, Saint Vincent and the Grenadines, Samoa, São Tomé and Principe, Seychelles, Solomon Islands, Timor-Leste, Tonga, Trinidad and Tobago, Tuvalu and Vanuatu.

Note: Data refer to estimated amounts of capital investment.

Annex table 7. List of IIAs at end 2013ᵃ

	BITs	Other IIAsᵇ	Total
Afghanistan	3	4	7
Albania	43	7	50
Algeria	47	8	55
Angola	8	7	15
Anguilla	-	1	1
Antigua and Barbuda	2	9	11
Argentina	58	15	73
Armenia	40	3	43
Aruba	-	1	1
Australia	22	14	36
Austria	66	61	127
Azerbaijan	46	4	50
Bahamas	1	9	10
Bahrain	29	15	44
Bangladesh	28	4	32
Barbados	10	9	19
Belarus	60	4	64
Belgiumᶜ	93	61	154
Belize	7	9	16
Benin	16	9	25
Bermuda	-	1	1
Bhutan	-	2	2
Bolivia, Plurinational State of	17	12	29
Bosnia and Herzegovina	38	5	43
Botswana	8	7	15
Brazil	14	16	30
British Virgin Islands	-	1	1
Brunei Darussalam	8	16	24
Bulgaria	68	62	130
Burkina Faso	14	9	23
Burundi	7	9	16
Cambodia	21	14	35
Cameroon	16	6	22
Canada	30	17	47
Cape Verde	9	6	15
Cayman Islands	-	1	1
Central African Republic	4	5	9
Chad	14	6	20
Chile	50	28	78
China	130	17	147
Colombia	8	20	28
Comoros	6	10	16
Congo	14	5	19
Congo, Democratic Republic of the	16	10	26
Cook Islands	-	2	2
Costa Rica	21	17	38
Côte d'Ivoire	10	10	20
Croatia	58	62	120
Cuba	58	3	61
Cyprus	27	62	89
Czech Republic	79	62	141
Denmark	55	62	117
Djibouti	9	10	19

/...

Annex table 7. List of IIAs at end 2013 (continued)

	BITs	Other IIAs[b]	Total
Dominica	2	9	11
Dominican Republic	15	4	19
Ecuador	18	8	26
Egypt	100	13	113
El Salvador	22	9	31
Equatorial Guinea	9	5	14
Eritrea	4	6	10
Estonia	27	63	90
Ethiopia	29	6	35
Fiji	-	3	3
Finland	71	62	133
France	102	62	164
Gabon	14	6	20
Gambia	16	7	23
Georgia	31	4	35
Germany	134	62	196
Ghana	26	7	33
Greece	43	62	105
Grenada	2	9	11
Guatemala	19	11	30
Guinea	20	7	27
Guinea-Bissau	2	8	10
Guyana	8	10	18
Haiti	7	9	16
Honduras	11	10	21
Hong Kong, China	16	4	20
Hungary	58	62	120
Iceland	9	30	39
India	84	12	96
Indonesia	64	14	78
Iran, Islamic Republic of	61	2	63
Iraq	7	6	13
Ireland	-	62	62
Israel	37	5	42
Italy	93	62	155
Jamaica	17	9	26
Japan	22	17	39
Jordan	53	9	62
Kazakhstan	45	7	52
Kenya	14	7	21
Kiribati	-	2	2
Korea, Democratic People's Republic of	24	-	24
Korea, Republic of	91	13	104
Kuwait	74	14	88
Kyrgyzstan	29	7	36
Lao People's Democratic Republic	24	15	39
Latvia	44	62	106
Lebanon	50	8	58
Lesotho	3	7	10
Liberia	4	7	11
Libya	35	11	46
Liechtenstein	-	1	1

/...

Annex table 7. List of IIAs at end 2013 (continued)

	BITs	Other IIAs[b]	Total
Lithuania	54	62	116
Luxembourg[c]	93	62	155
Macao, China	2	2	4
Madagascar	9	5	14
Malawi	6	9	15
Malaysia	68	21	89
Maldives	-	3	3
Mali	17	8	25
Malta	22	62	84
Mauritania	20	7	27
Mauritius	40	10	50
Mexico	29	15	44
Moldova, Republic of	39	4	43
Monaco	1	-	1
Mongolia	43	3	46
Montenegro	18	4	22
Montserrat	-	9	9
Morocco	63	9	72
Mozambique	25	7	32
Myanmar	7	14	21
Namibia	14	7	21
Nauru	-	2	2
Nepal	6	3	9
Netherlands	97	62	159
New Caledonia	-	1	1
New Zealand	5	12	17
Nicaragua	18	11	29
Niger	5	9	14
Nigeria	24	8	32
Norway	15	28	43
Oman	34	14	48
Pakistan	46	7	53
Palestinian Territory	3	7	10
Panama	24	10	34
Papua New Guinea	6	3	9
Paraguay	24	15	39
Peru	31	27	58
Philippines	37	13	50
Poland	62	62	124
Portugal	55	62	117
Qatar	49	14	63
Romania	82	62	144
Russian Federation	72	3	75
Rwanda	7	10	17
Saint Kitts and Nevis	-	9	9
Saint Lucia	2	9	11
Saint Vincent and the Grenadines	2	9	11
Samoa	-	2	2
San Marino	8	-	8
São Tomé and Principe	1	3	4
Saudi Arabia	24	14	38
Senegal	25	9	34

/...

Annex table 7. List of IIAs at end 2013 (concluded)

	BITs	Other IIAs[b]	Total
Serbia	51	4	55
Seychelles	4	9	13
Sierra Leone	3	7	10
Singapore	41	26	67
Slovakia	55	62	117
Slovenia	38	62	100
Solomon Islands	-	2	2
Somalia	2	5	7
South Africa	43	10	53
South Sudan	-	1	1
Spain	82	62	144
Sri Lanka	28	5	33
Sudan	27	10	37
Suriname	3	10	13
Swaziland	6	10	16
Sweden	69	62	131
Switzerland	119	31	150
Syrian Arab Republic	42	5	47
Taiwan Province of China	23	5	28
Tajikistan	34	7	41
Thailand	39	21	60
The former Yugoslav Republic of Macedonia	39	5	44
Timor-Leste	3	1	4
Togo	4	9	13
Tonga	1	2	3
Trinidad and Tobago	13	9	22
Tunisia	55	9	64
Turkey	89	19	108
Turkmenistan	25	6	31
Tuvalu	-	2	2
Uganda	15	8	23
Ukraine	73	5	78
United Arab Emirates	45	14	59
United Kingdom	105	62	167
United Republic of Tanzania	19	7	26
United States	46	64	110
Uruguay	30	17	47
Uzbekistan	50	5	55
Vanuatu	2	2	4
Venezuela, Bolivarian Republic of	28	4	32
Viet Nam	60	17	77
Yemen	37	6	43
Zambia	11	8	19
Zimbabwe	30	8	38

Source: UNCTAD, IIA database.

[a]   The number of BITs and "other IIAs" in this table do not add up to the total number of BITs and "other IIAs" as stated in the text, because some economies/territories have concluded agreements with entities that are not listed in this table. Because of ongoing reporting by member States and the resulting retroactive adjustments to the UNCTAD database, the data differ from those reported in *WIR13*.

[a]   These numbers include agreements concluded by economies as members of a regional integration organization.

[b]   BITs concluded the Belgo-Luxembourg Economic Union.

WORLD INVESTMENT REPORT PAST ISSUES

WIR 2013: Global Value Chains: Investment and Trade for Development

WIR 2012: Towards a New Generation of Investment Policies

WIR 2011: Non-Equity Modes of International Production and Development

WIR 2010: Investing in a Low-carbon Economy

WIR 2009: Transnational Corporations, Agricultural Production and Development

WIR 2008: Transnational Corporations and the Infrastructure Challenge

WIR 2007: Transnational Corporations, Extractive Industries and Development

WIR 2006: FDI from Developing and Transition Economies: Implications for Development

WIR 2005: Transnational Corporations and the Internationalization of R&D

WIR 2004: The Shift Towards Services

WIR 2003: FDI Policies for Development: National and International Perspectives

WIR 2002: Transnational Corporations and Export Competitiveness

WIR 2001: Promoting Linkages

WIR 2000: Cross-border Mergers and Acquisitions and Development

WIR 1999: Foreign Direct Investment and the Challenge of Development

WIR 1998: Trends and Determinants

WIR 1997: Transnational Corporations, Market Structure and Competition Policy

WIR 1996: Investment, Trade and International Policy Arrangements

WIR 1995: Transnational Corporations and Competitiveness

WIR 1994: Transnational Corporations, Employment and the Workplace

WIR 1993: Transnational Corporations and Integrated International Production

WIR 1992: Transnational Corporations as Engines of Growth

WIR 1991: The Triad in Foreign Direct Investment

All downloadable at www.unctad.org/wir

SELECTED UNCTAD PUBLICATION SERIES ON TNCs AND FDI

World Investment Report
www.unctad.org/wir

FDI Statistics
www.unctad.org/fdistatistics

World Investment Prospects Survey
www.unctad.org/wips

Global Investment Trends Monitor
www.unctad.org/diae

Investment Policy Monitor
www.unctad.org/iia

Issues in International Investment Agreements: I and II (Sequels)
www.unctad.org/iia

International Investment Policies for Development
www.unctad.org/iia

Investment Advisory Series A and B
www.unctad.org/diae

Investment Policy Reviews
www.unctad.org/ipr

Current Series on FDI and Development
www.unctad.org/diae

Transnational Corporations Journal
www.unctad.org/tnc

HOW TO OBTAIN THE PUBLICATIONS

The sales publications may be purchased from distributors of United Nations publications throughout the world. They may also be obtained by contacting:

United Nations Publications Customer Service
c/o National Book Network
15200 NBN Way
PO Box 190
Blue Ridge Summit, PA 17214
email: unpublications@nbnbooks.com

https://unp.un.org/

For further information on the work on foreign direct investment and transnational corporations, please address inquiries to:

Division on Investment and Enterprise
United Nations Conference on Trade and Development
Palais des Nations, Room E-10052
CH-1211 Geneva 10 Switzerland

Telephone: +41 22 917 4533
Fax: +41 22 917 0498
web: www.unctad.org/diae